T0220766

Communications in Computer and Information Science   **1437**

More information about this series at http://www.springer.com/series/7899

Leonid Sokolinsky · Mikhail Zymbler (Eds.)

Parallel Computational Technologies

15th International Conference, PCT 2021
Volgograd, Russia, March 30 – April 1, 2021
Revised Selected Papers

 Springer

Editors
Leonid Sokolinsky ⓘ
South Ural State University
Chelyabinsk, Russia

Mikhail Zymbler ⓘ
South Ural State University
Chelyabinsk, Russia

ISSN 1865-0929   ISSN 1865-0937 (electronic)
Communications in Computer and Information Science
ISBN 978-3-030-81690-2   ISBN 978-3-030-81691-9 (eBook)
https://doi.org/10.1007/978-3-030-81691-9

This Springer imprint is published by the registered company Springer Nature Switzerland AG
The registered company address is: Gewerbestrasse 11, 6330 Cham, Switzerland

Preface

This volume contains a selection of the papers presented at the 15th International Scientific Conference on Parallel Computational Technologies (PCT 2021). The PCT 2021 conference was supposed to be held in Volgograd, Russia, during March 30 – April 1, 2021. The Organizing Committee took the decision to hold PCT 2021 online, considering the safety and well-being of all conference participants during the COVID-19 pandemic as a priority.

The PCT series of conferences aims at providing an opportunity to discuss the future of parallel computing and to report the results achieved by leading research groups in solving both scientific and practical issues using supercomputer technologies. The scope of the PCT series of conferences includes all aspects of high-performance computing in science and technology, such as applications, hardware and software, specialized languages, and packages.

The PCT series is organized by the Supercomputing Consortium of Russian Universities and the Federal Agency for Scientific Organizations. Originating in 2007 at the South Ural State University (Chelyabinsk, Russia), the PCT series of conferences has now become one of the most prestigious Russian scientific meetings on parallel programming and high-performance computing. PCT 2021 in Volgograd continued the series after Chelyabinsk (2007), St. Petersburg (2008), Nizhny Novgorod (2009), Ufa (2010), Moscow (2011), Novosibirsk (2012), Chelyabinsk (2013), Rostov-on-Don (2014), Ekaterinburg (2015), Arkhangelsk (2016), Kazan (2017), Rostov-on-Don (2018), Kaliningrad (2019), and Perm (2020).

Each paper submitted to the conference was scrupulously evaluated by three reviewers on the basis of relevance to the conference topics, scientific and practical contribution, experimental evaluation of the results, and presentation quality. The Program Committee of PCT selected the 22 best papers to be included in this CCIS proceedings volume.

We would like to thank the Russian Foundation for Basic Research for their continued financial support of the PCT series of conferences, as well as the PCT 2021 sponsors, namely RSC Group, NVIDIA, and Hewlett Packard Enterprise.

We would like to express our gratitude to every individual who contributed to the success of PCT 2021 amid the COVID-19 outbreak. Special thanks to the Program Committee members and the external reviewers for evaluating papers submitted to the conference. Thanks also to the Organizing Committee members and all the colleagues involved in the conference organization from Volgograd State Technical University, the South Ural State University, and Moscow State University. We thank the participants of PCT 2021 for sharing their research and presenting their achievements online as well.

Finally, we thank Springer for publishing the proceedings of PCT 2021 in the *Communications in Computer and Information Science* series.

June 2021

Leonid Sokolinsky
Mikhail Zymbler

Organization

The 15th International Scientific Conference on Parallel Computational Technologies (PCT 2021) was organized by the Supercomputing Consortium of Russian Universities and the Federal Agency for Scientific Organizations, Russia.

Steering Committee

Berdyshev, V. I.	Krasovskii Institute of Mathematics and Mechanics, Russia
Ershov, Yu. L.	United Scientific Council on Mathematics and Informatics, Russia
Minkin, V. I.	South Federal University, Russia
Moiseev, E. I.	Moscow State University, Russia
Savin, G. I.	Joint Supercomputer Center, RAS, Russia
Sadovnichiy, V. A.	Moscow State University, Russia
Chetverushkin, B. N.	Keldysh Institute of Applied Mathematics, RAS, Russia
Shokin, Yu. I.	Institute of Computational Technologies, RAS, Russia

Program Committee

Sadovnichiy, V. A. (Chair)	Moscow State University, Russia
Dongarra, J. (Co-chair)	University of Tennessee, USA
Sokolinsky, L. B. (Co-chair)	South Ural State University, Russia
Voevodin, Vl. V. (Co-chair)	Moscow State University, Russia
Zymbler, M. L. (Academic Secretary)	South Ural State University, Russia
Ablameyko, S. V.	Belarusian State University, Belarus
Afanasiev, A. P.	Institute for Systems Analysis, RAS, Russia
Akimova, E. N.	Krasovskii Institute of Mathematics and Mechanics, Russia
Andrzejak, A.	Heidelberg University, Germany
Balaji, P.	Argonne National Laboratory, USA
Boldyrev, Y. Ya.	Peter the Great St. Petersburg Polytechnic University, Russia
Carretero, J.	Carlos III University of Madrid, Spain
Gazizov, R. K.	Ufa State Aviation Technical University, Russia
Gergel, V. P.	Lobachevsky State University of Nizhny Novgorod, Russia

Glinsky, B. M.	Institute of Computational Mathematics and Mathematical Geophysics, SB RAS, Russia
Goryachev, V. D.	Tver State Technical University, Russia
Il'in, V. P.	Institute of Computational Mathematics and Mathematical Geophysics, SB RAS, Russia
Kobayashi, H.	Tohoku University, Japan
Kunkel, J.	University of Hamburg, Germany
Labarta, J.	Barcelona Supercomputing Center, Spain
Lastovetsky, A.	University College Dublin, Ireland
Ludwig, T.	German Climate Computing Center, Germany
Lykosov, V. N.	Institute of Numerical Mathematics, RAS, Russia
Mallmann, D.	Jülich Supercomputing Centre, Germany
Michalewicz, M.	A*STAR Computational Resource Centre, Singapore
Malyshkin, V. E.	Institute of Computational Mathematics and Mathematical Geophysics, SB RAS, Russia
Modorsky, V. Ya.	Perm Polytechnic University, Russia
Shamakina, A. V.	High Performance Computing Center in Stuttgart, Germany
Shumyatsky, P.	University of Brasília, Brazil
Sithole, H.	Centre for High Performance Computing, South Africa
Starchenko, A. V.	Tomsk State University, Russia
Sterling, T.	Indiana University, USA
Taufer, M.	University of Delaware, USA
Turlapov, V. E.	Lobachevsky State University of Nizhny Novgorod, Russia
Wyrzykowski, R.	Czestochowa University of Technology, Poland
Yakobovskiy, M. V.	Keldysh Institute of Applied Mathematics, RAS, Russia
Yamazaki, Y.	Federal University of Pelotas, Brazil

Organizing Committee

Kuzmin, S.V. (Chair)	Volgograd State Technical University, Russia
Kidalov, N. A. (Deputy Chair)	Volgograd State Technical University, Russia
Andreev, A. E. (Secretary)	Volgograd State Technical University, Russia
Abramenko, S. A.	Volgograd State Technical University, Russia
Antonov, A. S.	Moscow State University, Russia
Avdeyuk, O. A.	Volgograd State Technical University, Russia

Antonova, A. P.	Moscow State University, Russia
Goglachev, A. I.	South Ural State University, Russia
Gorobtsov, A. S.	Volgograd State Technical University, Russia
Gurevich, L. M.	Volgograd State Technical University, Russia
Konchenkov, V. I.	Volgograd State Technical University, Russia
Kravets, A. G.	Volgograd State Technical University, Russia
Kraeva, Ya. A.	South Ural State University, Russia
Kuznetsova, A. S.	Volgograd State Technical University, Russia
Litovkin, D. V.	Volgograd State Technical University, Russia
Nikitenko, D. A.	Moscow State University, Russia
Orlova, Yu. A.	Volgograd State Technical University, Russia
Parygin, D. S.	Volgograd State Technical University, Russia
Sayapin, M. V.	Volgograd State Technical University, Russia
Shcherbakov, M. V.	Volgograd State Technical University, Russia
Sidorov, I. Yu.	Moscow State University, Russia
Sobolev, S. I.	Moscow State University, Russia
Stegachev, E. V.	Volgograd State Technical University, Russia
Styazhin, V. N.	Volgograd State Technical University, Russia
Sychev, O. A.	Volgograd State Technical University, Russia
Voevodin, Vad. V.	Moscow State University, Russia
Zavyalov, D. V.	Volgograd State Technical University, Russia
Zharikov, D. N.	Volgograd State Technical University, Russia
Zymbler, M. L.	South Ural State University, Russia

Contents

Supercomputer Simulation

High Performance Architectures, Tools and Technologies

Equivalent Transformations of Some Kinds of Computing Structures of Non-linear Recurrent Expressions for Reconfigurable Computing Systems

Ilya I. Levin⬤ and Sergei A. Dudko$^{(\boxtimes)}$

Academy for Engineering and Technology, Institute of Computer Technologies and Information Security, Southern Federal University, Taganrog, Russia
{iilevin,dudko}@sfedu.ru

Abstract. In the paper, we consider data-equivalent transformations of some kinds of non-linear computing structures, such as quadratic, fractional, and conditional ones. All computing structures contain feedbacks. If a pipeline computing structure of a task, implemented on a reconfigurable computer system, contains feedbacks, the data processing rate slows down, because it is necessary to wait for feedback results to calculate the next value. The processing rate slows down not only in the chain with feedback but in the whole computing structure. As a result, the task solution time increases. Previous fragments have to delay their data to supply them to a chain with feedback, and subsequent ones have to remain idle waiting for the feedback result data. At present, there are no software development tools for reconfigurable computer systems with automatic optimization of such computing structures. So, the user has to analyze the source code to find expressions with feedbacks and optimize them. As a result, the development time of efficient applications increases considerably. We suggest methods that reduce the data processing time interval (down to unity in the best case) for applied tasks solved on reconfigurable computer systems. Besides, the task solution time also decreases. Owing to the suggested methods, implemented in the optimizing synthesizer of circuit solutions, transformations are performed automatically. As a result, the development time for efficient applied tasks with feedbacks decreases from several days to several minutes.

Keywords: Data-equivalent transformation · Optimizing synthesizer · Reconfigurable computer system · Non-linear computing structure

1 Introduction

Currently, one of the problems that reduce the performance of reconfigurable computing systems (RCS) [1,2] based on field-programmable gate arrays (FPGAs) [3,4] is large data supply intervals in computing structures [5]. This problem arises

© Springer Nature Switzerland AG 2021
L. Sokolinsky and M. Zymbler (Eds.): PCT 2021, CCIS 1437, pp. 3–17, 2021.
https://doi.org/10.1007/978-3-030-81691-9_1

when the solved task's structure forms feedbacks due to the recursive structures of the task or the methods of organizing calculations.

The presence of recursive computing structures negatively affects the solution time of the applied task because it is necessary to wait for the output signal in the feedback before starting the next iteration of computations. For this reason, some of the computing resources remain idle while waiting for the required data. An example of a fragment of a recursive computing structure is shown in Fig. 1. Block α is recursive, so it requires data from block G and previous data generated by block α. Block F receives the output of block α and continues the necessary calculations. If block α does the calculations in S clock cycles, then this leads to block G being forced to supply its output data to the input of block α once in S clock cycles, and correspondingly, block F will receive data for processing once in S clock cycles. If $S > 1$, then this leads to an increase in both the time required to process the entire data flow and the time for solving the task.

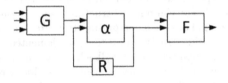

Fig. 1. Example of a feedback computing structure

In the most general case, the time required to solve a task on a conveyor computing structure for a given hardware resource can be calculated using the following formula:

$$T_R = NS\tau,$$

where T_R is the time required to solve the task with the available hardware resource R, N is the length of the data flow, S is the data supply interval, and τ is the clock cycle.

To reduce the time required to solve the task, it is necessary to reduce the value of one of the factors in this formula. It is not possible to reduce the number of processed data or the clock cycle. The only way to reduce T_R is to reduce the data supply interval.

The existing tools for the development of programs for RCS [6–8] may warn the user that feedbacks are found in the computing structure of the task but no optimization of such structures is done. The user has to analyze the source code to find expressions with feedbacks and optimize them. The task of finding feedbacks in the source code is difficult because feedback structures can be located in different parts of the source code and different related files.

This leads to a significant increase in the time for creating effective application programs on RCS since it is difficult, even for an experienced user, to find and optimize all feedbacks.

To reduce the development time for effective application programs, it is necessary to automate the procedure for optimizing feedbacks in the computing structure of the task. Optimization of feedbacks is the process of reducing the data supply interval (in the best case, to 1, i.e., $S = 1$) relative to the data supply interval of the original task.

The search and optimization of recursive structures are not processed in the source code but in its intermediate representation as a flat computing structure, thereby making it possible to find and process feedbacks faster since all nodes that form the feedback are located sequentially one after another.

The representation of the original problem in the form of an information graph ensures that the equivalent transformations will not change the final result because they are localized for changing with saving the input and output streams. For the user, the part of the information graph subjected to optimization can be represented as a black box. Changes inside this box do not affect the computing structure (context) surrounding it.

It is important to note that these transformations require additional hardware resources, and this fact limits their scope. The implementation of additional hardware nodes in a computing system can also cause an increase in the energy consumption required for its application. Therefore, in the general case, it is suggested to apply these transformations only when other parallelization methods do not help to speed up the computations and also when there are sufficient hardware resources available. We do not consider these limitations in this article. Their study is left for further research.

Transformation methods of linear computing structures with feedback were considered previously (see [9]). This article describes transformation methods of some kinds of non-linear computing structures, such as quadratic, conditional, and fractional ones.

2 Transformations of Quadratic Computing Structures

Quadratic structures arise when solving expressions similar to quadratic equations [10,11]. An example of a quadratic equation can be represented as follows:

$$y_i = y_{i-1}^2 * a_i + b_i,$$

Let us denote the operation of *multiplication* by β and the operation of *addition* by φ. The computational structure corresponding to this equation is shown in Fig. 2.

The operational nodes β and φ may represent any algebraic operations performed on any sets that form a ring with respect to these operations [12,13]. If a computing structure has feedbacks, then the data supply interval can be calculated by the following formula:

$$S = \frac{\sum L}{R}, \tag{1}$$

where L is the latency of individual operational nodes in the feedback path and R is the number of registers in the feedback. A feedback path is a sequence of nodes that form feedback.

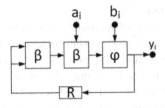

Fig. 2. Quadratic computing structure

We will assume that the latency of the operational nodes β and φ is equal to 1. In this case, the data supply interval, according to formula (1), equals 3.

To reduce the data supply interval in such structures, we use the auto-substitution method [9]. We expand the original feedback by one step (Fig. 3a). This leads to an increase in the number of hardware resources required for the implementation but, at the same time, it allows us to install an additional register in the feedback. Based on the equivalent transformations of the distributive and associative operational nodes [9], we transform the computing structure shown in Fig. 3a.

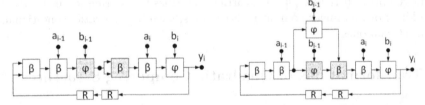

a) Transformation by expanding the feedback by one step

b) Duplicating the operational node to remove branching

Fig. 3. Equivalent transformations of a quadratic computing structure

As we see, there is an operational node in the feedback whose output signal branches into two signals (Fig. 3a). This branching does not allow to use the transformation of distributive operational nodes. It is necessary to get rid of this branching using the method of duplicating computations (Fig. 3b). The use of this method leads to the need for additional hardware resources to implement the computing structure, namely to implement the duplicated nodes. Furthermore, by applying the transformation of distributive operational nodes to the shaded nodes in Fig. 3b, we get rid of the branching. As a result of the transformation of distributive operational nodes, a new operational node appears, which requires additional hardware resources (Fig. 4). After these transformations, the data supply interval does not decrease (7/2 according to formula 1), but the number of hardware resources employed increases, so transformations must continue.

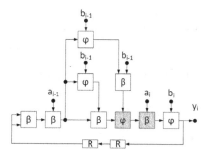

Fig. 4. Computing structure after applying equivalent transformations for distributive operational nodes and de-branching

Next, we continue to perform transformations of distributive and associative operational nodes as long as possible. The resulting computing structure is shown in Fig. 5. To simplify the computing structure, here and below, blocks that are not directly related to feedback have been replaced with compound expressions that are input arguments of operational nodes. This computational structure cannot be further transformed using distributive or associative transformations. In this case, the data supply interval (6/2) is equal to the interval of the original computing structure shown in Fig. 2.

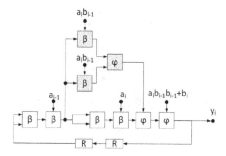

Fig. 5. Computing structure after transformations of distributive and associative nodes

Since it is impossible to reduce the data supply interval, we introduce the inverse transformation of distributive nodes for further optimizations (Fig. 6).

Input arguments k_1 and k_2 are input signals that can be represented by any expression or constant, similar to the input signals a and b. If the input data k_1 and k_2 are equal, we can use the transformation of associative nodes with a

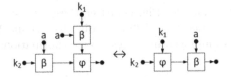

Fig. 6. Inverse transformation of distributive nodes

general input operand (Fig. 7) and continue to optimize the original computing structure.

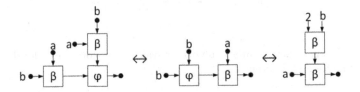

Fig. 7. Inverse transformation of distributive nodes and transformation of associative nodes with a general input operand

Using the transformations described above, we can change the computing structure shown in Fig. 5 and then apply transformations of the distributive and associative operational nodes to move some of the computations beyond the feedback and reduce the length of the feedback path (Fig. 8).

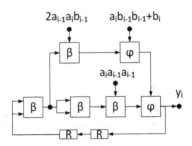

Fig. 8. Computing structure after applying a transformation of associative nodes

For the resulting computing structure, we obtain, according to formula (1), the data supply interval $S = 2$ (i.e., four nodes divided by two registers), which is 1.5 times less than the original data supply interval in the feedback ($S = 3$). To achieve a denser data flow and increase the speed of solution of the task, we can use the auto-substitution method again.

3 Transformations of Conditional Computing Structures

When solving applied tasks, the order in which operations are carried out often depends on the fulfillment of some conditions [14]. Conditional statements are used to control the order in which operations are executed. In high-level programming languages, such an operator is IF THEN ELSE or its analogs [15]. However, conditional statements can also form recursive expressions. In conditional recursive expressions, the output value of a signal depends on the fulfillment of some conditions. In circuit design, multiplexers are used to implement conditional operators [16,17]. In the general case, conditional computing structures can be represented by the following expression:

```
if (CE) then
    y[i] := z[i];
else
    y[i] := y[i-1] * b[i] + c[i];
```

The fragment of the conditional computing structure will look as portrayed in Fig. 9, where the CE signal is any condition responsible for choosing one of the computation branches. Input and output signals b_i, x_i, z_i, y_i are any expressions. Let us denote the operation of *multiplication* by β and the operation of *addition* by φ.

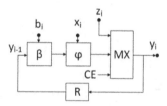

Fig. 9. Example of conditional feedback

The multiplexer is responsible for choosing one or the other branch of computation, the result of which is input into the feedback. Transformations of such a construction cannot be carried out using the auto-substitution method because the multiplexer does not possess the required distributivity and associativity properties. It is necessary to replace the multiplexer in the feedback with a set of other operational nodes. In the general case, the logical operations "OR" and "AND" on the bit representation of data can be used to replace the multiplexer [18,19]. However, these operations do not satisfy the properties of associativity and distributivity together with other operations in the feedback. Therefore, it is advisable to replace the multiplexer with the same set of operations that are already included in the feedback (Fig. 10). This transformation is based on properties from group theory [20].

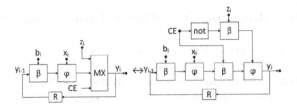

Fig. 10. Replacing the multiplexer with a set of distributive and associative operational nodes

For the correctness of this transformation, it is necessary that the set K, over which the operations β and φ are defined, form an algebraic ring [12,13].

The transformation that consists in replacing the multiplexer with a set of distributive nodes (Fig. 10) is possible because the multiplicative property of zero is defined in ring theory [20].

After replacing the multiplexer with a set of distributive operational nodes, it is necessary to use equivalent transformations of the distributive and associative operational nodes to simplify the resulting computing structure. These transformations are shown in Fig. 11, where the node $\overline{(CE)}$ is the result of performing the logic "NOT" operation on the node CE. In the first step, we apply the distributivity transformation to the shaded nodes, and then, in the second step, the associativity transformation.

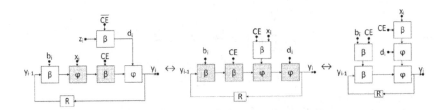

Fig. 11. Chain of transformations of distributive and associative nodes

After that, we can apply the auto-substitution transformation to the simplified computing structure to reduce the data supply interval. So, replacing the multiplexer with a set of distributive operational nodes makes it possible to transform the original computing structure, to which we can then apply methods of equivalent transformations to reduce the data supply interval.

4   Equivalent Transformations of Direct and Inverse Operational Nodes

Before proceeding to examine the next type of non-linear computing structures, it is necessary to consider a set of basic equivalent transformations over inverse operational nodes (nodes corresponding to operations inverse to operations β and φ). Let G be a set in which operations β and φ are performed. To perform the transformations considered below, the set G must be an algebraic field [13, 20]. For this, the following conditions must hold:

1. For operations β and φ, there exist neutral elements n^1 and n^0, respectively.
2. For each element x from the set G, there exists an inverse element $\overline{x}$.
3. For operations β and φ, inverse operations β^{-1} and φ^{-1} are defined in such a manner that:

$$\overline{x} = n^1\beta^{-1}x,$$
$$\overline{x} = n^0\varphi^{-1}x.$$

If all these conditions are valid, then the following equivalent transformations can be applied to the computing structure.

The equivalent transformation of replacing an inverse operational node β^{-1} with a direct operational node β (Fig. 12) is performed by inverting the input operator at one of the inputs (depending on the type of distributivity of the inverse operational node). The "1/x" block denotes the operation of taking the inverse operand.

When performing a direct operation with direct and inverse operands, the result is a neutral element, which makes it possible to exclude the operational node from the computing structure of the task. This transformation is called the *taking of the inverse node*.

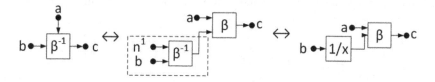

Fig. 12. Equivalent transformation of replacing the inverse operation node

If the taking of the inverse node is performed two times in a row, then the result does not change the input operand. This makes it possible to exclude the operational nodes of taking the inverse from the computing structure.

If at the output of an operational node there is an operation of taking the inverse value, then it can be transferred to all inputs of this operational node. The converse is also true: if there is an operation of taking the inverse value at each input of a node, then all these operations can be replaced by one operation of taking the inverse value at the output of a given operational node (Fig. 13).

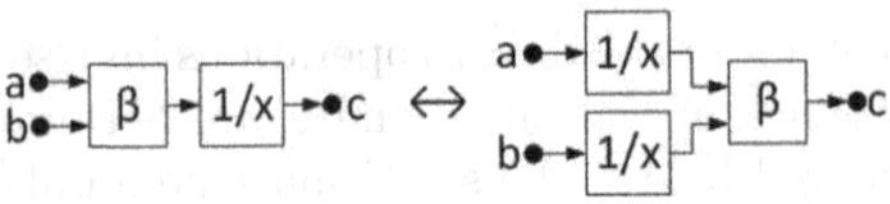

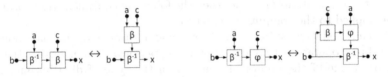

Fig. 13. Carrying the operation of getting the inverse value through the node

The transformations of both associative nodes (Fig. 14a) and distributive nodes (Fig. 14b) are also defined for direct and inverse operational nodes. In some cases, the distribution may be one-way. Then the order of the operands plays an important role as, for example, in the case of the *division* operation, which is only distributive on the right.

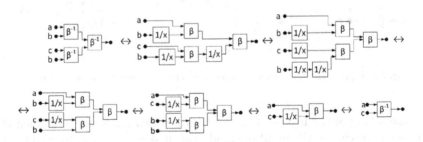

a) Transformation of associative inverse operational nodes

b) Transformation of distributive inverse operational nodes

Fig. 14. Equivalent transformations for inverse operational nodes

Furthermore, consider the equivalent transformation of a "pyramid" of inverse operations nodes with a general input operand, shown in Fig. 15.

Fig. 15. Converting a "pyramid" of inverse nodes with a general input operand

This transformation replaces the "pyramid" of inverse operational nodes with one inverse operational node by applying the transformations discussed earlier. This chain of transformations is called the transformation of a "pyramid" of inverse operational nodes with one general input operand.

The use of these equivalent transformations allows getting rid of inverse operational nodes in the type of non-linear computing structures considered below and simplifying the structure of the task.

5   Transformations of Fractional Computing Structures

Fractional computing structures are another example of non-linear computing structures. Such structures can be optimized in some cases. For clarity, consider these transformations for the operations "+", "∗", and "/", which generally correspond to the operations "φ", "β", and "β^{-1}". Consider transformations of such structures using, as in the example, the following non-linear equation:

$$y_i = \frac{y_{i-1} * a_i + b_i}{y_{i-1} * c_i + d_i}.$$

The computing structure that corresponds to this equation is shown in Fig. 16.

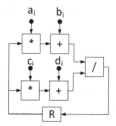

Fig. 16. Original non-linear fractional computing structure

This computing structure defines a *division* operation, which is the inverse of the multiplication operation.

We transform the original computing structure by relying on transformations of the inverse operational nodes. Assuming that the latency of each operational node is equal to 1, we obtain that the data supply interval in the feedback equals 3. Let us try to optimize this computing structure by applying the auto-substitution method to it. Let us expand the original computing structure by one step (Fig. 17a), while spending additional hardware resources and adding an additional register to the feedback. Then, we get rid of the branches by applying the method of duplication of calculations, and we obtain the computing structure shown in Fig. 17b. The data supply interval for this computing structure remains unchanged ($6/2 = 3$).

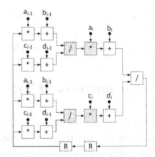

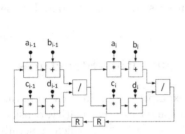

a) Expanding feedback by one step   b) Duplicating computation transformation

Fig. 17. Applying equivalent transformations for a fractional computing structure

Next, relying on transformations with direct and inverse operational nodes, we apply to the shaded nodes (Fig. 17b) the transformation of associative inverse operational nodes, and then the transformation of distributive inverse operational nodes (Fig. 18). The data supply interval for the resulting structure remains unchanged ($6/2 = 3$), but there is a significant increase in hardware costs.

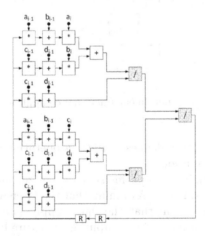

Fig. 18. Computing structure after applying equivalent transformations of associative inverse nodes and distributive inverse nodes

After that, we use the equivalent transformation of the "pyramid" of inverse operational nodes and the transformation of distributive operational nodes (Fig. 19).

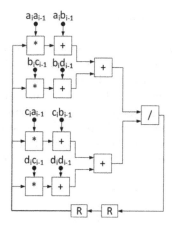

Fig. 19. Computing structure after applying equivalent transformations

The resulting computing structure has a smaller data supply interval than the original one, $S = 2$ (4/2), thus, we obtain the result of calculations in fewer cycles. To achieve a denser data flow, the auto-substitution method can be reapplied until the required data supply interval is obtained.

Additional hardware costs required for transforming non-linear computing structures include additional nodes obtained as we apply transformations of distributive operational nodes and the resource obtained by duplicating computations. In the most general case, the number of additional hardware resources required can be calculated by the formula

$$\frac{N^2 + N}{2} + \sum_{i=1}^{s}(k - 1),$$

where N is the initial number of distributive operational nodes, S is the data supply interval, k is the number of operational nodes in the initial feedback. The sum corresponds to the number of elements formed as a result of branching. At the same time, distributive transformations can also be applied to the newly formed branches. Therefore, the methods described above are advisable when other transformation methods are unsuitable and there are enough hardware resources available.

6   Conclusions

The proposed transformation methods of non-linear recursive expressions make it possible, without the user intervention, to optimize fragments of a computing structure with a large data supply interval and, at the same time, reduce the time required to solve an applied problem.

The transformations require additional hardware resources, which limits their scope. The auto-substitution method can be applied when other optimization methods have reached the critical resource limit (for example, when the FPGA channels have run out).

The developed transformations can be applied to various types of computing structures, such as quadratic, fractional, and conditional ones. A distinctive feature of the suggested methods is the possibility of applying them to the information-computing structure of the task and not to the source code.

Implementing these transformations in an optimizing synthesizer of circuitry solutions would allow all transformations to be carried out automatically without user intervention and reduce the development time of effective application programs containing feedback, from several days to several minutes.

References

1. Guzik, V.F., Kalyaev, I.A., Levin, I.I.: Reconfigurable Computer Systems/Study Guide Endorsed by I.A. Kalyaev 2016. SFedU Publishing, Rostov-on-Don (2016). 472 pp. ISBN 978-5-9275-1980-7
2. Compton, K.: Reconfigurable computing: a survey of systems and software. ACM Comput. Surv. **34**(2), 171–210 (2002). https://doi.org/10.1145/508352.508353
3. Popov, A.U.: Designing Digital Devices Using FPGAs/Study Guide. BMSTU Publishing, Moscow (2009). 80 pp
4. Krishna, G., Sahadev, R.: Fundamentals of FPGA Architecture. Advanced Engineering Technical and Scientic Publisher, chap. 2, pp. 12–30 (2017)
5. Kalyaev, A.V., Levin, I.I.: Modular-Scalable Multiprocessor Systems with Structural and Procedural Organization of Calculations. Yanus-K, Moscow (2003). 380 pp
6. Intel Quartus Prime Standard Edition User Guide 18.1. Getting Started. UG-20173 — 2018.09.24, pp. 44–47. https://www.intel.com/content/dam/www/programmable/us/en/pdfs/literature/ug/archives/ug-qps-getting-started-18-1.pdf. Accessed 01 Oct 2020
7. Xilinx Vivado Design Suite: User Guide. Synthesis. UG901 (v2017.1), pp. 7–38, 19 April 2017. https://www.xilinx.com/support/documentation/sw_manuals/xilinx2017_1/ug901-vivado-synthesis.pdf. Accessed 25 Sept 2020
8. Synopsys Identify Microsemi Edition Instrumentor User Guide, pp. 50–51, January 2018. https://www.microsemi.com/document-portal/doc_download/136672-synopsys-identify-rtl-l2016-09m-2-debugger-instrumentor-for-libero-soc-v11-8. Accessed 28 Sept 2020
9. Dudko, S.A.: Transforming method of recursive expressions in an information graph. In: XVI Annual Youth Scientific Conference South of Russia: Challenges of Time, Discoveries, Prospects: Conference Proceedings (Rostov-on-Don, 13–28 April 2020). SSC RAS Publishing, Rostov-on-Don (2020). 168 p
10. Agapova, E.G.: Computational Mathematics/Study guide endorsed by T.M. Popov. Pacific National University Publishing, Khabarovsk (2017). 92 pp
11. Lindenhovius, B., Mislove, M., Zamdzhiev, V.: Mixed linear and non-linear recursive types. Proc. ACM Program. Lang. **3** (2019). https://doi.org/10.1145/3341715. Article 111
12. Vasiliev, A.V., Mazurov, V.D.: Abstract Algebra: In 2 parts/Lecture notes. NSU Publishing, Novosibirsk (2010). Part 1, 143 pp

13. Aditya, R., Zulfikar, M.T., Manik, N.I.: Testing division rings and fields using a computer program. Procedia Comput. Sci. **59**, 540–549 (2015). https://doi.org/10.1016/j.procs.2015.07.537
14. Tugashev, A.A.: Basics of programming. Part I. ITMO University Publishing, St. Petersburg (2016). 160 pp
15. Nielsen, F.: A Concise and Practical Introduction to Programming Algorithms in Java, Undergraduate Topics in Computer Science. Springer, London (2009). https://doi.org/10.1007/978-1-84882-339-6
16. Akchurin, A.D., Usupov, K.M.: Verilog Programming/Study Guide. Kazan (2016). 90 pp
17. Nabulsi, M., Al-Husainy, M.: Using combinational circuits for control purposes. J. Comput. Sci. **5**(7), 507–510 (2009). https://doi.org/10.3844/jcssp.2009.507.510
18. Wang, X.: Estimation of number of bits in binary representation of an integer. Int. J. Res. Stud. Comput. Sci. Eng. **2**, 28–31 (2015)
19. Harris, D.M., Harris, S.L.: Digital Design and Computer Architecture, 2nd edn. DMK-Press (2018). https://doi.org/10.1016/b978-012370497-9/50007-x. 792 pp
20. Voevodin, V.V.: Linear Algebra, 2nd edn. Main edition of physical and mathematical literature, Moscow (1980)

Development and Practical Application of Methods for Detecting Similar Supercomputer Jobs

Denis Shaikhislamov[1](✉)[ID] and Vadim Voevodin[1,2][ID]

[1] Research Computing Center of Lomonosov Moscow State University,
Moscow, Russia
`vadim@parallel.ru`
[2] Moscow Center of Fundamental and Applied Mathematics, Moscow, Russia

Abstract. In the field of supercomputer technologies, the task of detecting similar applications is poorly developed, despite frequently popping up in the solution of many practically important problems. One of them is the detection of software packages and libraries used in supercomputer applications. In this paper, we address this task. It is worth noting that the task can be partially solved with the help of specialized system software. However, there are many situations when such tools are not enough. We discuss two mutually complementary approaches: the static one, involving the analysis of data obtained by parsing executable files, and the dynamic one, which relies on the analysis of monitoring data during the execution of an application. The analysis of real-life data from the Lomonosov-2 supercomputer confirms that the methods suggested in this paper ensure high accuracy and can be handy in detecting new cases of package usage that can not be identified by other available methods.

Keywords: Supercomputers · High-performance computing · Similar applications · Data analysis · Software package detection

1 Introduction

The popularity of supercomputers grows as users aim to solve more and more tasks for which the computing power of personal computers, servers, and cloud solutions has become insufficient. As the numbers of users involved and tasks to be solved increase, the variety and the number of jobs running on each supercomputer also increase. The huge number of jobs run on a supercomputer produces a lot of data, which can be used by administrators to analyze and optimize the workload and the efficiency of operation of their systems. These data can be used to detect jobs that are similar in behavior or used libraries, for instance. This allows solving other, more practically important, tasks, such as predicting the behavior or properties of a recently stated job using the available knowledge about previously executed jobs, or, as we will show in this paper, detecting software packages used in a job.

© Springer Nature Switzerland AG 2021
L. Sokolinsky and M. Zymbler (Eds.): PCT 2021, CCIS 1437, pp. 18–30, 2021.
https://doi.org/10.1007/978-3-030-81691-9_2

By *software package*, we mean a set of interconnected modules designed to solve certain problems in a selected subject area. An example of a software package is GROMACS [9], which is designed to simulate proteins, lipids, and nucleic acids in molecular dynamics. Package detection methods can be used, for example, to provide hints to users on how to increase the efficiency of use of selected packages. Also, package detection can provide system administrators with insights into which packages are more popular among users, which need to be updated, which are not relevant anymore, and so on.

The task of detecting similar applications can be solved in different ways. This paper discusses two possible detection methods: dynamic and static. Initial versions of these methods were proposed in [11], where they were optimized and adapted to solve the problem of software package detection in supercomputer jobs.

The dynamic method for the detection of similar jobs uses monitoring data on job performance during execution. These data include CPU/GPU utilization, memory/network usage intensity, and others. An example of applications similar in terms of their behavior during execution is provided in Fig. 1. We can see the change of four performance characteristics for two jobs during their execution. Note that locally the behavior may differ but the global profile of behavior is very similar.

The static method for the detection of similar jobs does not know anything about the job behavior during its execution. In the case we are considering here, the input data for the static method are the executable files of the job, namely the function names obtained from such files.

The main advantage of static methods, in general, is that they make it possible to analyze jobs right after they are submitted to the queue, while dynamic methods usually require a job to run for quite a long time (around 1 h in our case) to be able to collect sufficient information about its behavior. This, in turn, means that dynamic methods may not be applicable at all for the analysis of short jobs, whereas, for static methods, it makes no difference whether the job takes several minutes or several days to run. However, the dynamic approach has an essential advantage: its persistence. This means that monitoring data are always collected, regardless of the job properties, while static data may not be available due to specific launch features, access rights, and so forth.

The main contribution of our study is the development and software implementation of two different methods for package detection. Both the static and the dynamic methods show high-quality work; they can be used along with other methods for even better results. The methods were evaluated on the Lomonosov-2 supercomputer [13]. It should be noted that the portability of the static method is very high, while the dynamic method requires data from the monitoring system as well as normalization tuning for specific dynamic characteristics.

The paper is organized as follows. In Sect. 2, we outline our previous work on this topic and give an overview of related studies. Section 3 offers a description of the details concerning the static analysis method; here, we give the results of

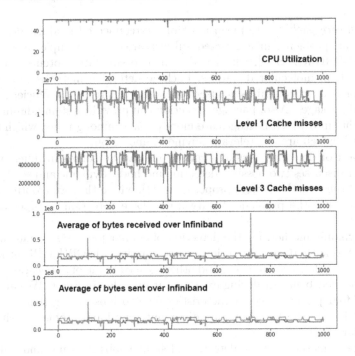

Fig. 1. An example of performance characteristics for two jobs with similar behavior

its application in practice. Section 4 deals with the dynamic analysis method. In Sect. 5, we summarize the results and outline plans for future research.

2   Background and Related Work

As stated before, the main objective of this work is the development of various methods for detecting software packages used in supercomputer jobs. To address this issue, we suggest two methods for the detection of similar applications: a static one and a dynamic one.

As far as we know, the only solution for package detection apart from ours: XALT [1]. The static approach used by this software provides a lot of relevant information by replacing the linker (ld) and launcher (mpirun) commands. It can detect which libraries are linked to the launched executable, what environmental variables are used, and other similar information.

The authors were unable to find any other works directly related to software package detection. Nevertheless, as noted earlier, methods for the detection of similar applications can be used as an alternative. There are several related works in the field of static analysis. Our static analysis method is based on [14], where the Doc2Vec model [6] is used to process the names of functions and variables found in executable files and compare them. After the comparison, the jobs are categorized into application classes, which are then employed to predict their power consumption. Even though the aim of that study differs from that of ours, the method employed for identifying classes of problems is well suited to our problem, which is why we considered it in previous work [11]. We should also note [2], wherein a method is developed to identify and categorize similar jobs, yet does this by analyzing the source code itself. The authors of that paper were able to come up with a method to tackle the task of identifying similar applications, regardless of the programming language the software is written in. Unfortunately, that method does not suit us since we do not have access to the source code of job executables.

In the field of dynamic analysis, the search for similar applications boils down to comparing time series, which in our case are dynamic characteristics (such as CPU load or amount of MPI bytes received per second). There are many methods for comparing time series, the main of them being Dynamic Time Warping (DTW from here on, [3]) with its variations [5, 10], as well as the ones based on neural networks. DTW is a method for calculating the distance between time series. Although the method is 50 years old, it is still considered one of the best for time-series comparison and is studied in most papers on this topic. The method is about matching the points of time series with each other to minimize the total distance between matched points. The main feature of DTW is that the algorithm pays attention to neither global nor local shifts along the timeline of the time series. This is exactly what is shown in Fig. 2. The graph describes the change in level-1 cache misses per second for two different jobs and how DTW can match points despite the fact that there are shifts at different phases of the execution. It is worth noting that the computational complexity of the method is quadratic, namely $O(NM)$, where N and M are the lengths of the compared time series. This fact makes it cumbersome for processing long time series in real time.

Neural networks also can be used to compare time series. In particular, the so-called Siamese Neural Networks have been remarkably useful in tackling the problem. It works in such a way that each of the compared time series is fed to the input of its own neural network, which then tries to extract only the most important information needed for the comparison of these time series. The parameters of these neural networks are shared, hence the name Siamese. The extracted information is fed to the input of the third neural network, which decides whether the time series are similar. Other kinds of neural networks can also be used to process time series. For example, a recurrent neural network is used in [8], and a convolutional one is considered in [4]. Although the results obtained with these networks are impressive, they have a major drawback (which is common to many methods that rely on neural networks): a significant number of labeled time series is needed to train the networks. Since we only have a small number of labeled time series (less than 500), we can not train the neural networks to the point where we can use them to solve the considered problem.

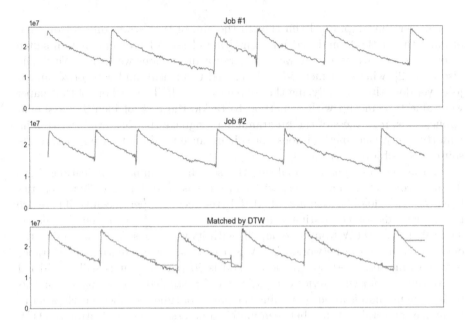

Fig. 2. Graphs of level-1 cache misses per second for two jobs and the combined graph after DTW matching

3   Static Analysis Method for Package Detection

3.1   Description of the Static Method

In previous work, we suggested a method for the detection of similar applications based on the analysis of executable files [11]. The method consists of the following:

- It extracts function and variable names from the executable file using the "nm" UNIX utility.
- It uses the Doc2Vec model, trained on function and variable names of more than 7000 executable files collected on the Lomonosov-2 supercomputer. This model converts the extracted names into a fixed-length vector.
- The obtained vectors are compared to identify the closest one in terms of cosine similarity, which is calculated as the cosine of the angle between two nonzero vectors.

To test the efficiency of the method, we asked one of the users of the Lomonosov-2 supercomputer to label his jobs according to the problems they solve. There were 52 jobs in total but we only had access to 38 executable files. Although the number of jobs was rather small, we were able to obtain a good estimate of whether the method works in general. More thorough testing was carried out on this work, as described hereunder. We compared the labeled jobs with the output of the static method using MojoFM [15], which gives an estimate of how close two labeled groups of objects are to each other. During the testing, we got a score of 0.97, which indicated an excellent quality of the identification of similar applications (in terms of the class of problems being solved).

3.2 Solving the Problem of Package Detection

In this research, we planned to configure and adapt the method described above to solve the problem of package detection. Adapting this algorithm to get insights about package usage is quite straightforward. To do this, it is necessary to create a knowledge base, which will store information about executable files for which we know exactly what software packages were used in them. This information is provided by the XALT software installed on the Lomonosov-2 supercomputer. Of course, there is a possibility that XALT provides incorrect data on the job but this is a rather uncommon situation in practice. At the moment, the database collected on the Lomonosov-2 supercomputer contains information about 20 packages, including unique examples of executable files for each one. For very frequently used packages, the number of such examples is quite large (more than 50); for rarely used ones, the number of examples may be less than 10. However, the database will certainly grow over time. After the job is launched, it can be compared with jobs from the database. As a result of this comparison, we get an estimate of how close the current job is to the reference examples. The closest reference jobs were selected using a threshold empirically determined according to user-labeled jobs, among which it was clear when the jobs stopped being similar. If several packages are found among the closest jobs, we assume that all these packages are used in the new job being analyzed.

To evaluate the efficiency and accuracy of this method, we conducted large-scale testing on the Lomonosov-2 supercomputer. More than 3600 jobs were processed from early October to mid-November 2020, and more than 2600 jobs using packages were detected. We compared the results with data from XALT, which yielded an accuracy value of 0.85. It is worth noting that we manually looked over the cases wherein our method detected a package while XALT did not. The opposite case was considered a misclassification since the probability that XALT incorrectly detects a package is rather small. After a manual examination, we found more than 200 jobs wherein our method showed the presence of packages not detected otherwise, and we manually confirmed that those packages were indeed present in the selected jobs. Those 200 jobs used ~15 different packages and were launched by ~40 different users.

To increase the accuracy of our method, it is necessary to pay more attention to the cases where it could not detect any packages, even if the packages were actually used in those jobs (there were about 350 jobs of this kind). There may be several reasons for that. Firstly, there are cases when our method cannot extract information from the executable file, e.g., if the user restricts access to his files or changes them before the analysis was performed (for example, he recompiles his application). Secondly, this can happen when new function names appear in executable files. Doc2Vec cannot consider function names that did not occur during its training, and consequently, it discards them. This means that, in the case of new names, we do not use all the available information to make a decision, and this can lead to errors. This problem is solved by periodically retraining the model with the addition of new executable files to the training set. Thirdly, if either there is no record about a package in our database or the program was compiled differently, then the content of the executable file may differ greatly from the examples known to the Doc2Vec classifier.

This problem is solved by regularly updating the database with new jobs. In particular, adding new records to the knowledge base has already greatly improved the performance of our method. In the last week of November, about 300 jobs were launched for which the packet extraction accuracy increased to 0.9. Throughout the week, more than 10 cases were identified in which our method detected packages while XALT could not.

The quality of the method is clearly demonstrated in Fig. 3, where the distribution of unique executable files is pictured based on Doc2vec output and built by t-SNE [7], an algorithm used to embed high-dimensional vectors in low-dimensional space, where similar objects are modeled by nearby points. Labels for the points are provided by the XALT-based package detection system that is used on the Lomonosov-2 supercomputer. We can clearly see that there are many green points, which represent jobs with no detected packages. Although the points in the center are distributed rather chaotically, we can clearly distinguish several large clusters. Group 1 (Cabaret package, delimited by the red circle on the left) contains only one labeled job. Despite the obvious similarity, XALT could not assign this package to other jobs. On the contrary, our static method handled correctly this task and labeled the jobs accordingly. The same can be said of the LAMMPS (light green) and GROMACS (dark blue) packages.

The graph also demonstrates that this method can be used to identify new packages or libraries previously unknown to the system. For example, after analyzing the function names used in the executable files of jobs from group 2, we found that they resort to the XAMG library, used to solve a system of linear equations with multiple right-hand sides.

Sometimes, however, manually going through function names is not enough to determine which library is used. This refers to group 3, in which our method can detect two clusters but it is still necessary to contact the users to clarify which packages were exactly used in these jobs.

To notify supercomputer administrators about the results provided by the static method, we send them an e-mail message containing a summary report on the detected cases. The report is generated daily. The contents of the letter can be seen in Fig. 4. Each row corresponds to a job. The rows are colored if our method's output differs from that of XALT, namely if our method detected packages and XALT did not, the color is green; if the opposite occurs, the color is red. Otherwise, no color is used. Note that the report makes it easy to find the cases when one or another method of package detection was triggered. It is also worth noting that the report helps to easily identify instances of misclassification by the static method and promptly take measures to overcome these shortcomings.

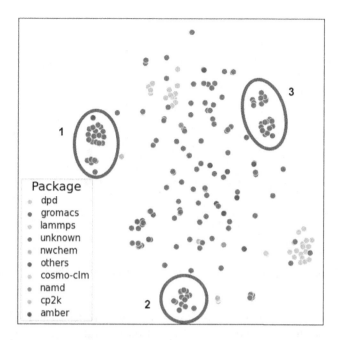

Fig. 3. The distribution of unique executables, built using t-SNE. Highlighted clusters: 1—Cabaret, 2—XAMG, 3—unknown.

4   Dynamic Analysis Method for Package Detection

4.1   Description of the Dynamic Method

The second approach for package detection resorts to a method for the identification of similar applications based on data about the job behavior during its execution, that is, dynamic characteristics provided by the supercomputer monitoring system (on the Lomonosov-2, we use the DiMMon monitoring system [12]). However, given the high quality of the static analysis method, one may ask why we should try another, more computationally complex method.

The main problem encountered by the static method is the aforementioned impossibility to analyze jobs for some reasons, such as insufficient access rights, inability to extract the names of used functions, and modifications of the executable file before the analysis starts. The issue associated with the lack of rights can be resolved. On the other hand, the modification of the executable file makes it basically impossible to analyze it since the file used to launch the job is no longer available. All these scenarios are quite frequent (more than 15% of the analyzed jobs). Therefore, we can rely only on monitoring data available for all launched jobs.

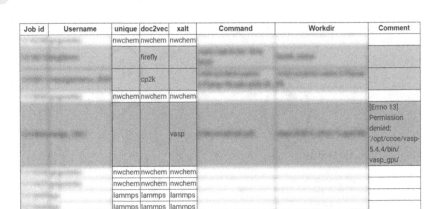

Fig. 4. A sample report with cases of package detection by the static method

Our method for the detection of similar applications uses the DTW method to calculate the distance between jobs based on the values of dynamic characteristics. Detailed information is given in our previous paper [11]. Here, we only briefly describe the algorithm:

- When the job is finished, the dynamic characteristics are retrieved from the monitoring system database. This method is currently employed only for analyzing completed jobs (due to its high complexity). In the future, after its optimization, it will be possible to use it to analyze running jobs as well.
- Data normalization is applied. Basically, we are talking here about standardization, but values of some characteristics (such as the intensity of memory use) are not normally distributed, which is why we take the logarithm and only then standardize them.
- DTW is used to calculate the distance between a new job and previously completed jobs. This makes it possible to find the closest job by behavior.

It is worth paying special attention to the stage of data normalization. DTW uses the Euclidean distance, which heavily depends on how the individual dynamic characteristics are normalized. For some characteristics, such as CPU/GPU utilization, the maximum possible value is understandable and reachable, making normalization easy. However, in the case of cache misses, this is far from trivial. We know the theoretical maximum of these values, but it would be incorrect to use them for normalization since most jobs do not even come close to them. To address this issue, we manually marked more than 300 pairs of similar and dissimilar jobs. Later on, we used them to select the normalization parameters for some dynamic characteristics. The parameter selection process is iterative. In the course of this work, we tried different variants of normalization and attempted to find which characteristics are more important for similar-behavior detection. For example, we found out that such characteristics as GPU utilization, load average, and frequency of memory read and write operations heavily affect the detection of similarity, while such characteristics as the number of packets sent over the InfiniBand network make almost no contribution and, sometimes, even degrade the quality of detection of similar jobs.

4.2   Solving the Problem of Package Detection

We can use the algorithm described above to solve the package detection problem, in a very similar manner to how it was done in Sect. 3. A new job we want to analyze is compared with already completed jobs from the previous period (one to two months in our case) to identify the closest jobs in behavior. It is difficult to increase the period due to the computational complexity of the method. Throughout the experiments, however, we found that jobs launched one to two months earlier are enough in the considered situation. If we detect packages used in the closest jobs, then we can assume that those packages are also used in the new job.

To test the efficiency of this method, we analyzed all jobs executed during a week in October. Users often launch a lot of similar jobs with minor parameter tweaks; the behavior profiles of such jobs are very close to each other. If we consider only a few jobs from such groups, we significantly reduce the total number of jobs. This does not worsen the resulting test sample in any way since the probability that the output results yielded by the dynamic method for jobs within the same group differ is rather small. We manually reviewed more than 350 jobs in total. In this case, this was done mainly to confirm that the dynamic method correctly detected similar jobs. From all these jobs, we picked out 120 with fairly unique behavior (i.e., their behavior noticeably differed from that of any other selected job). This was done to obtain a representative sample in which no behavior profiles overshadow others in terms of quantity, which could have severely affected the resulting accuracy. The package detection accuracy for these 120 jobs was 0.9. It should be noted that, apart from these 120 jobs, the method detected other 25 jobs with packages that no other method could find (including XALT and the previously described static analysis method).

We understand that 120 jobs are not enough for quality assessment. For this reason, we decided to conduct a larger-scale test without overall manual verification (since it is almost impossible to perform a complete manual verification of thousands of cases). We selected all jobs launched in October and November 2020. The test was carried out as follows. After obtaining the dynamic characteristics of a job, we compared it with other jobs from the same period. Then we applied the method and obtained an estimate of the current job's similarity to other jobs. With the help of the manually selected empiric threshold, we could find which jobs were the closest (the threshold was previously determined using manually labeled jobs). If we, among the closest jobs, detected at least a job with a package that was previously detected by any other detection system, then we considered that the new job also contained that package. It should be noted that the threshold, in this case, does certainly differ from the threshold in the static method since different entities of jobs are now compared.

In total, more than 3300 jobs were tested. The method showed an accuracy value of ~0.85. The test results are given in Table 1. We manually reviewed all the jobs in which the methods disagreed. It should be noted that, in most cases, it is difficult to determine manually whether the packages were actually used by only looking into the data of the monitoring system and the job scheduler; however, there are still cases that are obvious to administrators. We found that the dynamic method correctly identified package usage at least in 112 jobs (3 different packages were used), while other methods could not detect anything. The rest of the cases required more detailed analysis and, possibly, contacting users to clarify which packages were used in their jobs.

Table 1. Results of the comparison of the dynamic method against other methods of package detection (XALT + static method)

		Dynamic method for package detection	
		Package detected	No package detected
Other package detection methods	Package detected	1783 (1779 are the same)	250
	No package detected	358	903

According to the test results, the method shows high-quality work and can already be used in daily practice. As noted earlier, at first, we are going to use the method for post-mortem analysis of completed jobs only. After further optimization of the DTW method, it will be possible to run the analysis process more frequently and, therefore, apply it to running jobs as well. During the testing, it will be necessary to pay special attention to cases where only the dynamic method correctly detects package usage.

5   Conclusions and Future Work

In this paper, we suggested two approaches to solving the problem of software package detection (such as GROMACS, NAMD, and others) in supercomputer jobs. We regard this problem as highly important. Indeed, it can be used not only to obtain new statistics on the usage of a supercomputer or provide administrators with new insights into the needs of users but also as part of a recommendation system. For example, if we know the properties of a package (scalability, intensity of GPU/CPU/memory usage), we can give users hints on how to use the package more efficiently.

The first approach is based on static analysis. It showed an accuracy value of 0.9 on the test set. Throughout the testing, it correctly detected more than 10%

of new jobs with packages compared to other methods. We also showed that it can detect known packages and, what is more, help discover new unknown packages, such as, for example, XAMG in our case. The static method is already used on the Lomonosov-2 supercomputer on a regular basis. It sends a daily summary report of found cases to administrators.

The second approach is based on dynamic analysis. It also showed good accuracy on the test set: 0.85. When considering jobs with unique behavior, this method revealed up to 20% of new jobs with packages that were detected by neither existing methods nor the static method considered within this research. This gives us grounds to assert that the combined use of both methods allows detecting packages even more accurately in practice.

The dynamic method currently processes only completed jobs. We plan to adapt it to handle running jobs in real time. We also intend to explore other problems in which our methods for detection of similar applications could help, such as the prediction of job properties or execution time, and the development of a recommendation system to assist users in working with software packages more efficiently.

Acknowledgements. The research was supported by the Russian Foundation for Basic Research (grant No. 20-07-00864). The study was carried out using the shared HPC research facilities at Lomonosov Moscow State University.

References

1. Agrawal, K., Fahey, M., Mclay, R., et al.: User environment tracking and problem detection with XALT, pp. 32–40 (2014). https://doi.org/10.1109/HUST.2014.6
2. Altarawy, D., Shahin, H., Mohammed, A., Meng, N.: Lascad: language-agnostic software categorization and similar application detection. J. Syst. Softw. **142**, 21–34 (2018). https://doi.org/10.1016/j.jss.2018.04.018. http://www.sciencedirect.com/science/article/pii/S0164121218300682
3. Berndt, D.J., Clifford, J.: Using dynamic time warping to find patterns in time series. In: Proceedings of the 3rd International Conference on Knowledge Discovery and Data Mining, AAAIWS 1994, pp. 359–370. AAAI Press (1994)
4. Hou, L., Jin, X., Zhao, Z.: Time series similarity measure via siamese convolutional neural network. In: 2019 12th International Congress on Image and Signal Processing, BioMedical Engineering and Informatics (CISP-BMEI), pp. 1–6 (2019). https://doi.org/10.1109/CISP-BMEI48845.2019.8966048
5. Keogh, E., Pazzani, M.: Derivative dynamic time warping. In: First SIAM International Conference on Data Mining, vol. 1 (2002). https://doi.org/10.1137/1.9781611972719.1
6. Le, Q.V., Mikolov, T.: Distributed representations of sentences and documents. CoRR abs/1405.4053 (2014)
7. van der Maaten, L., Hinton, G.: Viualizing data using t-SNE. J. Machine Learn. Res. **9**, 2579–2605 (2008)
8. Pei, W., Tax, D.M.J., van der Maaten, L.: Modeling time series similarity with siamese recurrent networks. CoRR abs/1603.04713 (2016)

9. Pronk, S., Pll, S., Schulz, R., et al.: GROMACS 4.5: a high-throughput and highly parallel open source molecular simulation toolkit. Bioinformatics **29**(7), 845–854 (2013). https://doi.org/10.1093/bioinformatics/btt055

10. Salvador, S., Chan, P.: Toward accurate dynamic time warping in linear time and space. Intell. Data Anal. **11**(5), 561–580 (2007)

11. Shaikhislamov, D., Voevodin, V.: Solving the problem of detecting similar supercomputer applications using machine learning methods. In: Sokolinsky, L., Zymbler, M. (eds.) PCT 2020. CCIS, vol. 1263, pp. 46–57. Springer, Cham (2020). https://doi.org/10.1007/978-3-030-55326-5_4

12. Stefanov, K., Voevodin, V., Zhumatiy, S., et al.: Dynamically reconfigurable distributed modular monitoring system for supercomputers (DiMMon). Procedia Comput. Sci. **66**, 625–634 (2015). https://doi.org/10.1016/j.procs.2015.11.071

13. Voevodin, V.V., Antonov, A.S., Nikitenko, D.A., et al.: Supercomputer Lomonosov-2: large scale, deep monitoring and fine analytics for the user community. Supercomput. Front. Innov. **6**(2), 4–11 (2019). https://doi.org/10.14529/jsfi190201

14. Yamamoto, K., Tsujita, Y., Uno, A.: Classifying jobs and predicting applications in HPC systems. In: Yokota, R., Weiland, M., Keyes, D., Trinitis, C. (eds.) ISC High Performance 2018. LNCS, vol. 10876, pp. 81–99. Springer, Cham (2018). https://doi.org/10.1007/978-3-319-92040-5_5

15. Wen, Z., Tzerpos, V.: An effectiveness measure for software clustering algorithms. In: Proceedings. 12th IEEE International Workshop on Program Comprehension, pp. 194–203 (2004). https://doi.org/10.1109/WPC.2004.1311061

Detecting Changes in Communication Properties of Parallel Programs by InfiniBand Traffic Analysis

Daria Domracheva$^{(\boxtimes)}$ and Konstantin Stefanov

M. V. Lomonosov Moscow State University, Moscow, Russia

Abstract. Modern computational systems and parallel applications quite often are highly complicated. As a result, their interaction becomes difficult to analyze. There is a wide variety of profiling tools that can help in finding bottlenecks and inefficient parts in programs running on high-performance clusters. However, those tools involve additional overheads. This might be partially avoided by introducing methods of analysis that work on the network layer. In this article, we describe the development of a new tool for exploring visually and analyzing the behavior of different MPI parallel programs. The tool is based on an existing method of collecting traffic data from the InfiniBand network on the Lomonosov supercomputer. The comprehensive implementation includes constructing communication matrices of MPI processes and displaying various parts of the application timeline through these matrices, plotting communicational graphs and message distribution graphs built on several parameters of InfiniBand packets. The obtained visual representation of traffic of parallel applications may enable the analysis of such applications without inspecting the code directly, as demonstrated by examining a few NPB tests.

Keywords: MPI · InfiniBand traffic · Packet analysis · Communication properties

1 Introduction

Today supercomputer systems are based on large numbers of computing nodes and modern multiprocessor architectures. Computer networking communication standards are actively evolving to ensure a high level of performance from applications in such systems. One of the most remarkable representatives is the InfiniBand standard.

At present, the development of parallel applications widely relies on the Message Passing Interface (MPI), which allows creating parallel versions of various computational algorithms.

The contribution of the paper can be described as follows. Firstly, we outline an approach to analyzing and finding changes in the behavior of programs that use MPI operations. The analysis is based on the traffic of the programs in the

© Springer Nature Switzerland AG 2021
L. Sokolinsky and M. Zymbler (Eds.): PCT 2021, CCIS 1437, pp. 31–44, 2021.
https://doi.org/10.1007/978-3-030-81691-9_3

InfiniBand network. Secondly, we develop several methods of visualization of InfiniBand traffic for the analysis of the communication properties of parallel programs.

This paper is organized as follows. Section 2 gives an overview of related studies. In Sect. 3, we describe the basic concepts and structure of InfiniBand and MPI. In Sect. 4, we give a brief account of the method used for collecting the traffic. The approach to extracting and analyzing data from collected packets is explained in Sect. 5. This approach determines the composition of the communication profile of an application and how it can assist in the search for behavior changes. Section 6 gives a more detailed analysis of various MPI functions and presents a few more comprehensive tests. In Sect. 7, we put forward our conclusions and indicate future directions of research.

2 Related Work

At present, administrators of supercomputer centers and developers of parallel applications use several tools to analyze different components of high-performance systems. There are tools specifically created for analyzing the operation of InfiniBand switches (Nagios [1], Ganglia [2], Mellanox Fabric IT[1], INAM [3]). There are also profiling applications to analyze the behavior of MPI programs (HPCToolkit [4], TAU [5], PMPI [6]).

If we specifically speak of the interaction of MPI applications and the InfiniBand network, then we should mention the INAM2 tool [7], which uses the MPI Tools Information Interface (MPI_T) [8] for internal analysis of applications. The INAM2 tool enables the analysis of both the software and network components of the application. The method described in this paper can work in real-time and provides the data through a Java-based web server.

3 Basics of InfiniBand Internals and Analysis Difficulties of MPI over InfiniBand

InfiniBand technology is a high-speed interconnect designed to link the modules of high-performance computing systems. Such a network has a high bandwidth and a low latency. Structurally, the InfiniBand network is divided into subnets, each of which has its own subnet manager. Here are some basic concepts related to InfiniBand which we will be referring to in the course of this study:

- LID (Local Identifier): a unique identifier used for intra-subnet addressing assigned to each element.
- PMTU (Path Maximum Transmission Unit): the maximum supported length of a packet sent between given nodes, not including a part of the header length (up to and including transport header); can be up to 4096 bytes.

---

[1] Mellanox Technologies, Mellanox Integrated Switch Management Solution: http://www.mellanox.com/products/management-software/fabricit.

The structure of transmitted packets should be considered to extract correctly the necessary information from the headers when analyzing traffic. The general organization of the header of a packet sent within the network is shown in Table 1 [9].

We use the information from Local Routing Header and Base Transport Header, in particular source and destination LIDs, packet length, and its OpCode.

Table 1. The structure of the packet header. The solid outline indicates the mandatory parts of the header.

Local Routing Header	Global Routing Header	Base Transport Header	Extended Transport Header(s)	Immediate Data	Message Payload	Invariant CRC	Variant CRC

To separate MPI packets from the rest of those transmitted by the network at the time of code execution, we use the OpCode field from the Base Transport Header along with the notion of identifiers of the nodes on which the programs are run. These data are gathered at the stage of setting up the environment for the program execution.

Each OpCode corresponds to a specific operation performed by the Infini-Band network. It was found that MPI packets may have the OpCodes shown in Table 2 [9].

Table 2. OpCodes of MPI packets

OpCode	Packet type	OpCode	Packet type
0	SEND First	6	RDMA WRITE First
1	SEND Middle	7	RDMA WRITE Middle
2	SEND Last	8	RDMA WRITE Last
3	SEND Last with Immediate	10	RDMA WRITE Only
4	Send Only	12	RDMA READ Request
5	SEND Only with Immediate	14	RDMA READ Response

Since the analysis of InfiniBand traffic is not done at the application layer, it is essential to know the structure of the MPI packet. However, this is not a documented interface point. Therefore, it was necessary to use auxiliary means to get some idea of the approximate location of data in the header. In particular, it was possible to find out the position of the sender's rank, the message tag in point-to-point operations, and, most likely, the communicator's identifier (however, this assumption has yet to be verified) in the packet by using Wireshark[2].

---

[2] Wireshark: https://www.wireshark.org/.

4 InfiniBand Traffic Collection

For gathering the packets from the supercomputer, we use the method described in [10]. In essence, this method provides a set of scripts that are used to submit a program to the supercomputer queue and collect all the packets sent within the specified nodes in a single file. This file is then filtered, the packets of the submitted program can be extracted from it, and the correspondence between LIDs and MPI ranks is found. It makes it possible to perform further analysis of data from headers of packets. The method had to be slightly adjusted in the course of the research due to the presence of a few minor inaccuracies.

5 The Proposed Approach

5.1 Architecture Overview

The following scheme of operation of the analysis tool is suggested:

1. Primary data collection on a supercomputer, to files in .pcap format.
2. Cleaning up the trace from duplicate packets and assembling it into a single .pcap file, which will be used for further analysis.
3. Initial decomposition of packet headers in the trace using a C++ program. Simultaneously, the ranks of processes are determined at this step. Next, the program generates an output file that contains the number of processes and lines describing the properties of each packet: time of sending, source and destination ranks, length, and OpCode of the packet.
   This file is the main source of data for further analysis as it contains the simplest data representation format that can be used by other programs. Moreover, these data are sufficient for most aspects of the analysis.
4. The resulting file is analyzed using a set of programs in the Python language. There are two modes of viewing the data:
   (a) using the graphical interface provided by the Python Tkinter library, which at the moment is rather used for simple tests;
   (b) using the Python Dash library[3], which allows running a web server based on Flask, Plotly.js, and React, making it possible to interactively visualize data online.

5.2 Analysis Features

The approach we propose enables the analysis of programs that are executed on a supercomputer equipped with an InfiniBand network and use the OpenMPI implementation [11]. The analysis is performed in several directions:

- Building a general communication profile of the program (a modification of the method from previous work [10], described in Sect. 4 of this article).

---

[3] Python Dash library: https://dash.plotly.com/.

- Construction of communication matrices at any separate time interval from the program's timeline. This feature makes it possible to analyze three types of communication matrices:
  1. matrices where each element represents the number of bytes sent between processes;
  2. matrices containing the number of transmitted packets;
  3. matrices containing the average size of the transmitted packet.

  Thus, for example, in certain situations, there are lots of auxiliary transfers of small packets. Therefore, the average packet length is small.
- Analysis of the resulting matrices to track down the moments when the program's behavior changes, that is, detect such points in time at which the nature of the interaction between processes changes in the program. This can be a change in the type of operations used or a transition from an auxiliary transfer to a direct data transfer.
- Construction of communication graphs, in an attempt to change and possibly make the visualization of transfers more understandable. Directed graphs are used.
- Building a graph of the number of messages sent throughout the program.
- Tracking down cases of splitting large MPI packets into smaller ones.
- Building the distribution of packages by OpCode types.
- Plotting a histogram of packet length distribution.

Unfortunately, the analysis capabilities are limited by the existing features of MPI. In particular, this is the lack of information about the content of the message header, which was mentioned in Sect. 3. Consequently, for instance, there is no way to accurately determine at least the type of operation at the moment, let alone the specific function used. This makes it necessary to establish the types of transfers indirectly, based on other data, which can be the communication profiles of the program at certain time intervals.

Also, the method currently used to process a trace involves establishing a one-to-one correspondence between a network node and a process running on it. This means that a program can only be run in a certain manner, with only one process per node, which imposes new limitations.

5.3 Communication Matrices

Usually, a communication matrix represents the amount of data sent between processes during the execution of a given program. Our tool offers a way of visualizing communication matrices for specific time steps of the application.

The analyzing program receives a step measured in seconds, a file generated during the initial analysis containing data on packets, and the type of the output matrix. Next, for each time slice equal to a given step, a communication matrix of transfers is compiled, depending on the specified type (the total amount of data sent, the total number of packets sent, the average amount of data sent for the current step). It should be noted that the web interface visualization method does not include "empty" time slices without any message sent if such are present in the program. We can observe the change in the communication matrices over time in Fig. 1.

Matrix

	0	1	2	3	4	5	6	7	8
0	0	71788	21268	65670	0	59552	21268	19136	0
1	21268	0	71268	59552	63716	0	0	21268	19136
2	71788	21268	0	0	59552	59552	19136	0	21268
3	19136	19136	0	0	71788	21268	65870	0	67760
4	0	19136	21788	21268	0	71788	61542	60683	0
5	21788	0	19136	71788	21268	0	0	67760	65870
6	65870	0	65670	21268	19136	0	0	59552	19136
7	65670	65670	0	0	21268	19136	19136	0	59552
8	0	71788	65670	19136	0	21268	59552	19136	0

Accumulative matrix

	0	1	2	3	4	5	6	7	8
0	0	387954	124590	380714	350	374690	124128	122050	412
1	124870	0	387558	375664	278768	808	78	124128	122074
2	386910	124870	0	100	375252	374596	123064	78	124128
3	121996	122652	100	0	387542	124190	386832	808	382898
4	78	121996	122652	124838	0	386948	376748	386832	496
5	122042	528	121996	386910	124260	0	550	383460	386832
6	386832	46	381418	124128	122058	550	0	386964	124784
7	380776	388832	46	528	124128	122652	124276	0	387542
8	100	386894	386832	122042	528	124128	387504	124854	0

Fig. 1. Example of communication matrices of a time slice

5.4 Communication Graphs

For this method of visualizing transfers, it is convenient to use directed graphs with nodes associated with processes. Indeed, each edge in such a graph is assigned a direction, and the edges (v_1, v_2) and (v_2, v_1) for some two vertices v_1 and v_2 are distinguishable, thereby demonstrating transfers between any two processes.

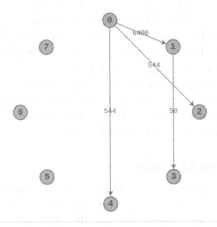

Fig. 2. Example of communication graph of a time slice

The first step when creating a graph is to determine the required number of vertices, that is, the number of processes working within the analyzed program. This number is passed as input. Then, similar to the construction of the matrices, the existing packets are divided into time intervals with a given step, and for each time interval, a transfer graph is built, wherein it is possible to choose to view both the total number of bytes sent and the number of packets sent. By default, the vertices of the graph in the web interface are arranged along a circle, as shown in Fig. 2, but their position can be changed interactively.

5.5 Time Step

We considered various programs during this research, including small ones intended for the analysis of distinct functions and large tests. It was necessary to find out the optimal time step for the programs. However, it turned out that this is a rather individual parameter, which depends on many variables, for example, on the program's execution time, the number of messages, and so on.

Thus, the choice of this parameter is, most likely, carried out empirically (however, the existence of a more rigorous justification for the choice of a certain time step is not ruled out). Therefore, within the interactive visualization, we added the option to manually change the time step to one that displays more clearly the stages of the program.

5.6 Analysis of the Communication Matrices

It is necessary to compare and analyze the matrices in adjacent time slices to find changes in the behavior of the program. One of the possible comparison methods is the computation of the norm of the difference of adjacent matrices.

It was decided to turn to existing libraries that enable software calculation of matrix norms. For example, the NumPy.linalg [12] library supports four different norms:

- matrix norm, induced by the 1-norm for vectors: $\|A\|_1 = \max_{1 \leq j \leq n} \sum_{i=1}^{m} |a_{ij}|$;
- spectral norm: $\|A\|_2 = \sigma_{\max}(A)$;
- Schatten norm $(p = 1)$: $\|A\|_p = \left(\sum_{i=1}^{\min(m,n)} \sigma_i^p(A)\right)^{1/p}$;
- Frobenius norm: $\|A\|_F = \left(\sum_{i=1}^{m} \sum_{j=1}^{n} |a_{ij}|^2\right)^{1/2}$.

The norms may differ in the range of values. Therefore, the normalized values are taken into consideration for each of the four listed norms.

5.7 Detecting Behavior Changes

The choice of points for the supposed changes in the behavior of the program is based on the analysis of the graphs for the norms of the communication matrices in adjacent time slices. It makes sense to conduct large tests to identify which matrix norm is the most suitable for the analysis since large tests are more informative and time-consuming and, as a rule, have several inherently different segments of work.

It was noted that, in general, the norms in each test behave similarly. In an independent analysis not involving the software, we can distinguish various peaks of the norms, segments of growth, decrease, and plateau (when the norm changes very little or does not change at all).

An attempt was made to find points of change in the program behavior in automatic mode. For this, it was necessary to decide which change of the norm was to be considered significant.

Let n_i and n_{i+1} be neighboring values of the norms. A total of N points are considered. If $\frac{|n_{i+1}-n_i|}{N\cdot\text{step}} > 1$, where step is the time step, then the point corresponding to the value n_i is chosen as the point of behavior change. That is, we selected the points where the slope (the tangent of the inclination angle) of the straight line going from this point to the next was greater than N. The proposed method works as expected in most situations, except for the case when the chosen time step is too small, which results in marking more points as behavior changes. This can be explained by the fact that a small time step can make separate MPI functions calls and the corresponding transfers more distinguishable, which results in communication matrices more diverse in terms of their norms.

6   Experiments

6.1   Individual MPI Operations

First of all, we give an analysis of individual MPI operations and their combinations to demonstrate our tool features.

Point-to-Point Operations. Let us consider the point-to-point operations, namely the non-blocking MPI_Isend() and MPI_Irecv() operations. A simple test for these functions would be a program with one MPI communicator and ring communication topology. The processes send each other arrays of length 2^{11} containing variables of type double. The total running time of the program is about 0.01 s.

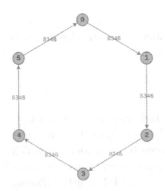

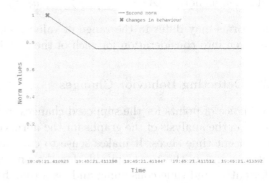

Fig. 3. Communication graph for the program with ring topology for six processes

Fig. 4. Graph of the spectral norm of the program with ring topology for six processes. The time step is 0.001 s.

The communication profile of the test program does not include any short auxiliary messages, which are sometimes sent before the actual message with data. The communication graph is shown in Fig. 3.

The graph of the spectral norm in Fig. 4 shows only one point of behavior change at the beginning of execution, then the norm experiences a slight drop and stays the same until the very end. This may be attributed to the fact that the program has a rather homogeneous behavior.

It can also be noted that each MPI message here is divided into five packets with different OpCodes (SEND First, SEND Middle, SEND Last with Immediate), as the length of a message is larger than the PMTU. The analysis of other point-to-point operations (MPI_Send(), MPI_Recv(), MPI_Sendrecv()) with similar configurations shows that SEND Only (with Immediate) and SEND Last OpCodes can be used as well.

Collective Operations. Collective operations may use the auxiliary messages more intensively, as, for example, the following analysis of a program with MPI_Bcast() call shows.

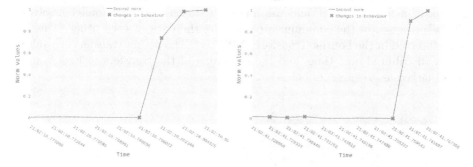

Fig. 5. The graph of the spectral norm of MPI_Bcast() for seven processes. The time step is 0.001 s.

Fig. 6. The graph of the spectral norm of the program with ring topology and MPI_Bcast() combination for seven processes. The time step is 0.001 s.

The test program has the data transferred from the process with rank 0, in the form of arrays of length 2^{10} containing variables of type double. At first, processes exchange short messages 46 bytes long; after that, the actual arrays of variables are sent. This is obvious from Fig. 5, where the spectral norm experiences a steep increase at the moment the auxiliary transfers stop.

If we consider a program that has both point-to-point operations and the MPI_Bcast() call, then we see in Fig. 6 that the proposed method marks both types of communication on the graph of the norm as behavior changes, though it still experiences the aforementioned issue of the small time step.

The MPI_Allgather() operation has a distinct picture of various packet length and OpCodes use; it includes both small auxiliary packets and larger ones that

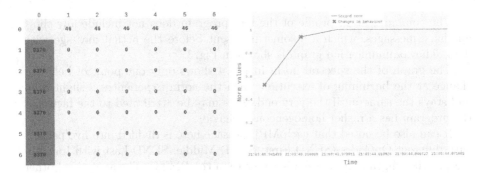

Fig. 7. The communication profile of MPI_Gather()

Fig. 8. The graph of the spectral norm of MPI_Gather() for seven processes. The time step is 0.005 s.

contain the data. If we compare a single MPI_Allgather() call to a combination of point-to-point operations with MPI_Allgather(), then we can see that this collective operation can be identified by the use of RDMA READ operations.

MPI_Gather() and MPI_Alltoall() both have unique communication profiles, as shown in Figs. 7 and 9, and use auxiliary packets. MPI_Alltoall() involves all the processes of the communicator sending the data to each other. This is later observed in the Fourier Transform NPB test. The packet transfers are quite evenly distributed over time, and the beginning of the transfers in Figs. 8 and 10 is marked as a change in behavior.

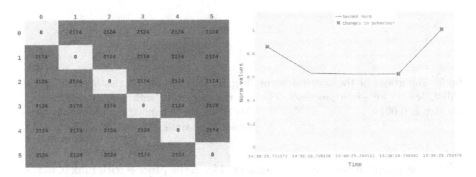

Fig. 9. The communication profile of MPI_Alltoall()

Fig. 10. The graph of the spectral norm of the combination of MPI_Alltoall() and MPI_Allreduce() for six processes. The time step is 0.003 s.

If we take a closer look at MPI_Reduce() and MPI_Allreduce(), we notice that these operations do not use auxiliary packets and their OpCodes are the same as in the case of point-to-point operations. However, we can still observe certain characteristics of their communication profiles.

6.2   NPB Tests

The BT, LU, and FT tests from the NAS Parallel Benchmarks (NPB) set [13] were taken as the large programs to be analyzed.

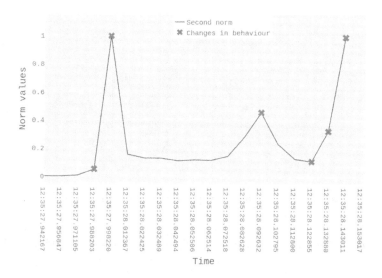

Fig. 11. The graph of the spectral norm for the BT test

Block Tri-Diagonal Solver. The following configurations were launched: class S (suitable for small quick tests) and nine processes.

At the start of the program, messages with data are sent from the root process to other processes in the group using the MPI_Bcast() function. Then, point-to-point operations are performed. At the end of the program, the MPI_Reduce() function is invoked. This can be seen from the graph in Fig. 11. The peaks of the norm for collective operations and the segment during which the transfer takes place using the functions MPI_Isend() and MPI_Irecv() are visible due to the uniformity of the transfers, while the rate changes little.

Lower-Upper Gauss–Seidel Solver. The following configurations were launched: class S and eight processes.

In the LU test, the MPI_Bcast() function is also used at the beginning of the program, while in the middle, mainly point-to-point transfers take place. In the end, the computed data are collected by the MPI_Allreduce() function. Thus, in the graph in Fig. 12, we observe something similar to what we see in the graph in Fig. 11.

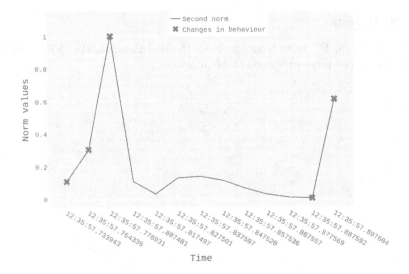

Fig. 12. The graph of the spectral norm for the LU test

Fourier Transform. The following configurations were launched: class S and nine processes.

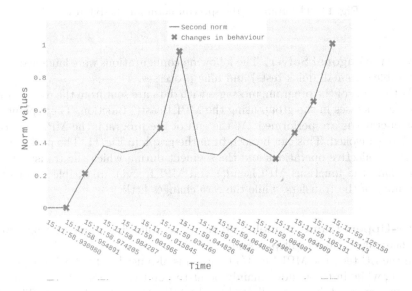

Fig. 13. The graph of the spectral norm for the FT test

At the initial stage of the program, the MPI_Bcast() function is used; then, MPI_Alltoall() is invoked. The peak of the norm can be observed in the middle of the program execution since all communicator processes are involved in the MPI_Alltoall() operation. In this test, only collective operations are used for data transfer. Therefore, the graph in Fig. 13 does not have such low values of the norm as the graphs in Figs. 11 and 12.

7 Conclusions and Future Work

In this paper, we outlined an approach to analyzing changes in the behavior of programs that use MPI operations. The analysis is based on the traffic of the programs in the InfiniBand network. By extracting data from the headers of packets, we were able to create visualizations of various programs, explore their runtime, and find patterns of some MPI functions. We showed that the tool we developed can help in detecting situations when a given program uses small auxiliary packets, switches from collective operations to point-to-point operations and vice versa, or intensively uses certain collective operations. This can potentially assist in evaluating performance issues resulting from the specific behavior of a program or assessing the overall program structure at the network level.

The web interface provides a way of visualizing different aspects of an application, thereby making it possible to have a closer look at how the application uses the MPI functionality and interacts with the network.

In the future, we plan to overcome the current limitation of one MPI process per node and adapt our tools to newer InfiniBand hardware, which uses an incompatible way of collecting traffic dumps.

References

1. Nagios. http://www.nagios.org/
2. Massie, M.L., Chun, B.N., Culler, D.E.: The ganglia distributed monitoring system: design, implementation, and experience. Parallel Comput. **30**(7), 817–840 (2004). https://doi.org/10.1016/j.parco.2004.04.001
3. Dandapanthula, N., et al.: INAM - a scalable InfiniBand network analysis and monitoring tool. In: Alexander, M., et al. (eds.) Euro-Par 2011. LNCS, vol. 7156, pp. 166–177. Springer, Heidelberg (2012). https://doi.org/10.1007/978-3-642-29740-3_20
4. Adhianto, L., Fagan, M., Krentel, M., Marin, G., Mellor-Crummey, J., Tallent, N.R.: HPCToolkit: performance measurement and analysis for supercomputers with node-level parallelism. In: Workshop on Node Level Parallelism for Large Scale Supercomputers, in Conjuction with Supercomputing 2008 (2008)
5. Malony, A.D., Shende, S.: Performance technology for complex parallel and distributed systems. In: Kotsis, G., Kacsuk, P. (eds.) Distributed and Parallel Systems. SECS, vol. 567, pp. 37–46. Springer, Boston (2000). https://doi.org/10.1007/978-1-4615-4489-0_5

6. Karrels, E., Lusk, E.: Performance analysis of MPI programs. In: Proceedings of the Workshop on Environments and Tools for Parallel Scientific Computing, pp. 195–200 (1994)
7. Subramoni, H., et al.: INAM2: InfiniBand Network Analysis and Monitoring with MPI (2016). https://doi.org/10.1007/978-3-319-41321-1_16
8. Message Passing Interface Forum. MPI: A Message-Passing Interface Standard Version 3.0, section 14.3 (2012)
9. Infiniband Architecture Specification, Volume 1, Release 1.1 (2002)
10. Gradskov, A., Stefanov, K.: InfiniBand traffic analysis for building application communication profile. In: Russian Supercomputing Days: Proceedings of the International Conference, pp. 768–775 (2017). (in Russian)
11. Gabriel, E., et al.: Open MPI: goals, concept, and design of a next generation MPI implementation. In: Proceedings, 11th European PVM/MPI Users' Group Meeting, pp. 97–104 (2004). https://doi.org/10.1007/978-3-540-30218-6_19
12. Travis, E.: Oliphant: A Guide to NumPy. Trelgol Publishing, Austin (2006)
13. Bailey, D.H.: The NAS Parallel Benchmarks. United States (2009). https://doi.org/10.2172/983318

Transformation of Graphs with Associative Operations in Terms of the Set@l Programming Language

Ilya Levin[1] , Alexey Dordopulo[2] , Ivan Pisarenko[2(✉)] ,
and Andrey Melnikov[3]

[1] Academy for Engineering and Technology, Institute of Computer Technologies
and Information Security, Southern Federal University, Taganrog, Russia
`iilevin@sfedu.ru`
[2] Supercomputers and Neurocomputers Research Center, Taganrog, Russia
`{dordopulo,pisarenko}@superevm.ru`
[3] "InformInvestGroup" CJSC, Moscow, Russia
`ak@iigroup.ru`

Abstract. Usually, an information graph with associative operations
has a sequential ("head/tail") or a parallel ("half-splitting") topology
with an invariable quantity of operational vertices. If the computational
resources are insufficient for the implementation of all vertices, the reduction transformations of graphs with basic structures do not allow for the
creation of an efficient resource-independent program for reconfigurable
computer systems. In this paper, we suggest transforming the topology of
a graph with associative operations into a combined variant with sequential and parallel fragments of calculations. The resultant combined topology depends on the computational resources of a reconfigurable computer
system, and such transformation provides the improvement of specific
performance for the reduced computing structure. We develop an algorithm for the conversion of the initial sequential graph into either several
combined topologies or the limit case of the "half-splitting" topology
while bearing in mind the available hardware resources. This technique
is described using the Set@l programming language.

Keywords: Associative operations · Resource-independent
programming · Reconfigurable computer systems · Performance
reduction · Set@l · "Head/tail" and "half-splitting" attributes

1 Introduction

Associativity is a fundamental property of binary operations. It determines the
independence of the calculation result from the order of the operation [1,2]. Typical graphs based on associative operations perform addition and multiplication
(they are associative if certain conditions are met), conjunction and disjunction
of array elements, search for maximum and minimum, and others. There are

© Springer Nature Switzerland AG 2021
L. Sokolinsky and M. Zymbler (Eds.): PCT 2021, CCIS 1437, pp. 45–58, 2021.
https://doi.org/10.1007/978-3-030-81691-9_4

two basic variants for the topology of such graphs having the same number of vertices: sequential (linear structure) and parallel (pyramidal or cascade structure) [3–5]. In fact, besides the two aforementioned cases, multiple combined topologies exist, and they are composed of alternating parallel and sequential fragments of calculations [6].

Performance reduction methods are used [7] to scale parallel calculations for the solution of applied problems on computer systems with reconfigurable architecture [8–11]. Reduction transformations of associative information graphs with sequential and parallel topologies do not enable the creation of an efficient resource-independent parallel program: a graph with the pyramidal structure is characterized by irregular inter-iteration linking, and the sequential embodiment has the largest latency, which leads to a significant increase in the duty cycle of data after reduction. Since all operations in the considered graphs are associative, it is possible to modify the topology for the sake of usability of reduction transformations. The transformation of a graph into a *cadr* is only possible when it has an isomorphic structure, so it is necessary to use one of the alternative combined topologies that contain isomorphic subgraphs. Here, a *cadr* is a set of hardware-implemented operations [12]. For a given number of computational resources, it is possible to synthesize an informationally equivalent graph containing hardware-implemented isomorphic subgraphs with a maximum degree of parallelism of associative operations. Traditional programming methods for reconfigurable and hybrid computer systems [13] do not allow changing the information graph of an applied problem depending on available computing resources, and each topology can be described only in the form of a separate subprogram.

In [14–16], we outlined Set@l (Set Aspect-Oriented Language), a language of architecture-independent parallel programming, which is based on the paradigm of aspect-oriented programming (AOP) and the set-theoretical representation of the program's source code. By describing the basic principles of construction of associative graphs using a special processing method featured in Set@l, it is possible to synthesize many variants of topologies and switch between them through the change in types and partitions of basic sets. Thus, the graph can be reduced for a given number of hardware resources available in a reconfigurable computer system without the modification of the program's source code.

The rest of the paper is organized as follows. Section 1 describes the resource-independent implementation of information graphs with associative operations. In Sect. 2, we suggest an algorithm of graph transformation according to available hardware resources for further performance reduction. In Sect. 3, we use the Set@l programming language for the specification of the basic sequential and parallel topologies and represent the principle of graph alternation. Section 4 demonstrates the structure of a resource-independent Set@l program that performs the aforementioned technique. In the Conclusions, we summarize the main points of the study and indicate possible directions for further research.

2   Transformation of Graphs with Associative Operations for Efficient Performance Reduction

Information graphs, which consist of two-place associative operations f with one output (for example, operations of addition, multiplication, conjunction or disjunction, search for maximum or minimum), can be constructed according to two basic principles [3–5]. Examples of standard topologies for such graphs with two-input operational vertices are shown in Fig. 1. The "head/tail" principle (Fig. 1a) assumes a sequential execution of the associative operation f on the elements a_i from the input set A. At each iteration of calculations, the operation f is performed on one of the input data elements a_i ("head") [17] and the intermediate element s_j, which is the result of processing the rest of the data ("tail") [17]. The exception is the iteration in which two elements of input data, a_1 and a_2, are processed at once. At the output of each operation, either the intermediate (s_j) or the final (Res) calculation result is generated.

Another principle, the "half-splitting" or "halving" (Fig. 1b), implies the parallel execution of associative operations f and is based on the well-known "divide and conquer" approach, which is widely used in programming [18]. If we consider the graph from the output to its input vertices, then the set of input data $A = \{a_1, a_2, \ldots, a_8\}$ (in the first iteration) or all subsets (in other iterations) are divided in each iteration into two subsets A_1 and A_2 containing the same number of processed elements. The intermediate results s_i and s_{i+1} of processing A_1 and A_2 are the inputs of the operation f in the current iteration. The partition in the "half-splitting" graph continues while each subset of the original set A contains more than two elements.

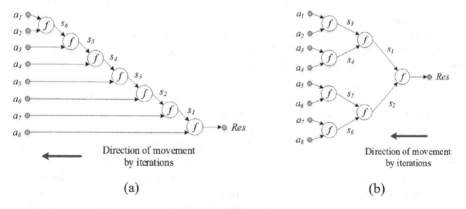

Fig. 1. Topologies of graphs with two-place associative operations f based on the "head/tail" (a) and "half-splitting" (b) principles

The graph topologies shown in Fig. 1 contain the same number of operational vertices but have different latencies of computational structures: $\tau = n - 1$ for the "head/tail" variant (Fig. 1a) and $\tau = \log_2 n$ for the "half-splitting" topology (Fig. 1b), where n is the cardinality of the input data set A.

If the hardware resources available in the reconfigurable computer system are sufficient for the implementation of all operational vertices in the information graph with associative operations, then the topology with the lowest latency i.e. "half-splitting" is used (see case $R/R_0 = n-1$ in Fig. 2, where R is the number of available computational resources and R_0 is the number of resources required for one operational vertex f). In case of a lack of hardware resources, it is reasonable to scale the calculations using performance reduction methods [11]. However, the description of reduction transformations for the "half-splitting" topology is quite cumbersome and inconvenient due to irregular interconnections between iterations and also to the fact that the decomposition is dependent on the problem dimension. The associative property of basic operations makes it possible to modify the graph topology according to the "head/tail" principle, which provides a regular interconnecting structure suitable for an efficient reduction.

On the other hand, if it is impossible to place all operational vertices of the graph, the structural and procedural implementation of the "head/tail" topology is reduced to one vertex with feedback (see case $R/R_0 = 1$ in Fig. 2) [12], which ensures high specific performance only in the case of a minimal number R_0 of computing resources available. If the configuration of hardware resources is in the range from $R/R_0 = 2$ to $(n - 2)$, it is reasonable to choose one of the combined topology versions, which contains sequential and parallel fragments of calculations [6] and has increased specific performance. Previously, combined topologies were not considered since most of them do not have a regular and isomorphic structure, and it is problematic to scale calculations and reduce the performance automatically. Thus, a resource-independent description of a graph with associative operations should take into account not only the two limit cases of "head/tail" and "half-splitting" processing but also various combined structures and transition rules for efficient performance reduction in different computer system configurations.

The topology of the information graph with associative operations is modified to reduce the performance of calculations with a given number of hardware resources available in a reconfigurable computer system. Since the transformation of a graph into a *cadr* is possible only when it has an isomorphic structure [12], the first component is formed by the isomorphic subgraphs DIV2 (see Fig. 2), which are built using the "half-splitting" principle and contain the maximum number of hardware-implemented operational vertices. The second component is the "head/tail" H/T block (see Fig. 2), which is necessary for processing intermediate data and for the calculation of the final result.

If the duty factor of data in feedback equals one cycle, the H/T unit is reduced to one operational vertex [6]. Therefore, the hardware-implemented computing structure (see Fig. 2) includes one basic subgraph G_i and one vertex ν_i that corresponds to the reduced H/T block. If the computational resources are

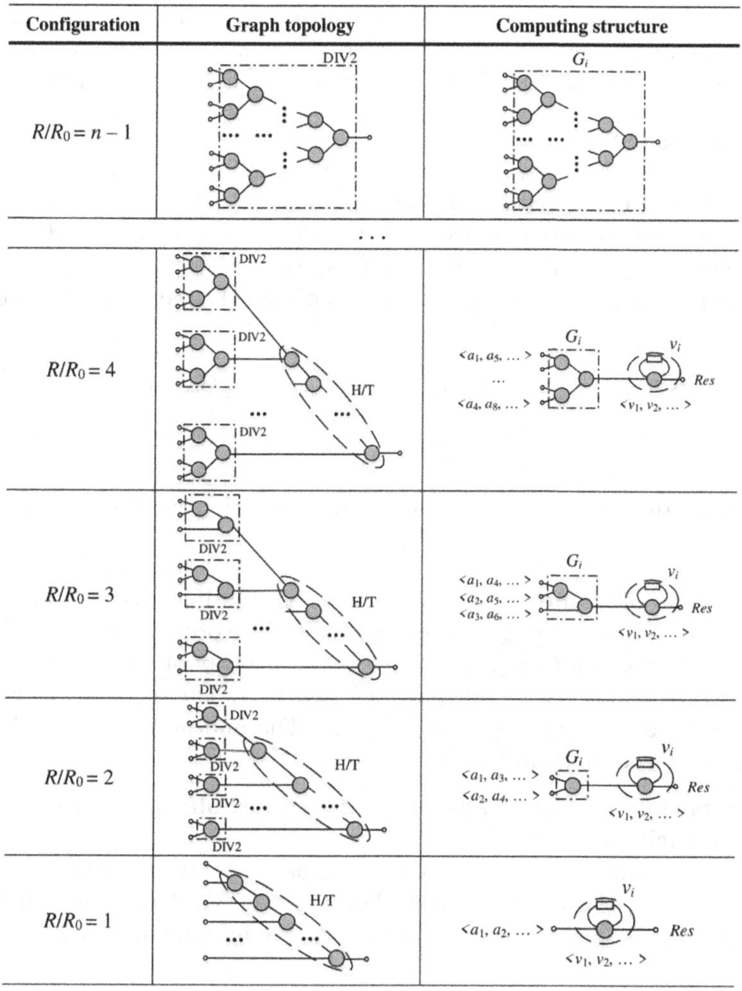

Configuration	Graph topology	Computing structure
$R/R_0 = n - 1$		
. . .		
$R/R_0 = 4$		
$R/R_0 = 3$		
$R/R_0 = 2$		
$R/R_0 = 1$		

Fig. 2. Topologies of information graphs with associative operations and corresponding computing structures for different numbers R of hardware resources available in a reconfigurable supercomputer

enough to handle only one operational vertex ($R/R_0 = 1$ in Fig. 2), the combined topology is converted into the classical "head/tail" one: subgraphs DIV2 are not implemented, and the only operational vertex in the whole computational structure corresponds to the H/T block of dimension $(n - 1)$. In the other limit case, when the hardware resources in the computer system are enough to place all the vertices of the information graph (case $R/R_0 = (n-1)$ in Fig. 2), the combined topology is turned into the standard "half-splitting" topology: the single subgraph DIV2 includes every operational vertex.

It is possible to convert the initial "head/tail" graph into the combined (see Fig. 2) or "half-splitting" structure considering the hardware resources available in the computer system. To achieve this, we use the following algorithm:

1. **Preparatory stage:**
   Divide all operational vertices of the original graph into r groups of k vertices each, where r is the reduction coefficient and $k = \lfloor R/R_0 \rfloor - 1$. Leave one vertex between neighboring groups for the processing of intermediate data, as shown in Fig. 3. If the last group is fewer than k vertices, then add several operational vertices and complement it to obtain the required dimension.

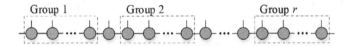

Fig. 3. The partition of operational vertices of the initial "head/tail" graph into groups

2. **Generation of isomorphic subgraphs with "half-splitting" topology:**
   Select pairs of neighboring vertices and change the order of the operations in each pair, according to Fig. 4a. Convert the topology of each group of operational vertices into the "half-splitting" structure. The sequence of transformations for one group is shown in Fig. 4b. The information graph obtained after this step is given in Fig. 4c.

3. **Combination of the "half-splitting" subgraphs using the "head/tail" principle:**
   Change the order of the operations for all pairs "individual vertex–group of vertices" using the rearrangement shown in Fig. 5a. After the transformation, obtain the final topology of the associative information graph, shown in Fig. 5b.

The topological modification of the information graph with associative operations yields the informationally independent isomorphic subgraphs $G_1, G_2, \ldots, G_r$ (see Fig. 5b). In the case of the structural and procedural implementation, they are transformed into the sub-*cadr* [19] G_i (Fig. 5c). In the *cadr*, data tuples are supplied to the sub-*cadr* inputs. The block G_{r+1}, which includes the informationally dependent operational vertices $\nu_1, \nu_2, \ldots, \nu_{r-1}$, is converted into the single vertex ν_i with feedback.

It is worth noting that another version of combined topology for information graphs with associative operations is of interest for the efficient implementation of structural and procedural calculations (see Fig. 5d). If the latency of the operational vertex f exceeds one cycle, H/T sequential processing units are converted into independent devices with accumulation, and these devices are combined according to the "embedded pipeline" scheme [19]. This approach will be thoroughly discussed in ensuing papers.

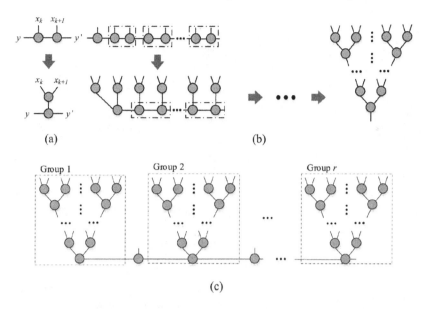

Fig. 4. Transformation of two neighboring operational vertices (a), the sequence of transformations in the group of vertices (b), and the topology of the associative information graph (c) obtained after the conversion of all groups in the original graph using the "half-splitting" principle

3 Description of "Head/Tail" and "Half-Splitting" Attributes in the Set@l Programming Language

Traditional parallel programming methods tend to operate with information graphs with fixed structures. Therefore, their application for the description of topological transformations under the proposed algorithm (see Fig. 3, 4 and 5) is quite cumbersome and inefficient. In terms of classical programming languages, the code of a resource-independent program that implements the aforementioned graph conversions consists of multiple subprograms connected by conditional operators. Each subprogram specifies only one variant of topology. In contrast to the multiprocedural paradigm, the capabilities of the Set@l architecture-independent programming language allow describing the principles of graph construction in the form of special processing method attributes assigned to the basic set of data A. In this case, the program's source code describes not individual implementations but the whole set of possible graph topologies for a given dimension of the computational problem. Aspects select a specific topology taking into consideration the values of the computer system's configuration parameters. To modify the structure of the information graph, it is enough to edit the type and partition of the basic set A, while the source code of the program remains mostly unchanged.

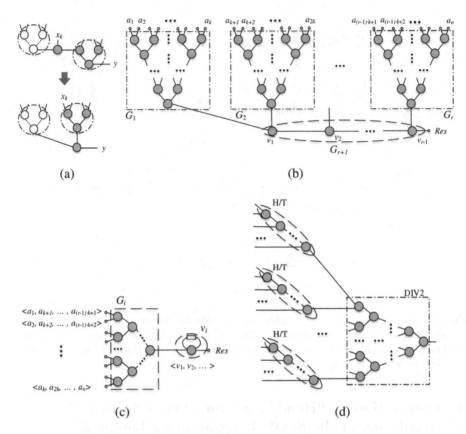

Fig. 5. Transformation of the pair "individual vertex–group of vertices" (a), the final topology of an information graph with associative operations (b), the corresponding computing structure (c), and the combined topology with isomorphic subgraphs based on the "head/tail" principle (d)

Let us consider the description of the "head/tail" and "half-splitting" principles for the standard topologies of information graphs with associative operations (see Fig. 1) in the Set@l programming language. The code of additional features introduced with the use of the `attribute` syntax construct [20] is given in Fig. 6. The attribute of the basic associative operation `f` is specified in a generalized form: a certain operation type `Op` is declared in another module of the parallel program and can take different values (e.g., "+" or "*"). The `operand` directive describes the types of objects to which an attribute can be assigned.

Figure 7 demonstrates the description of the "head/tail" principle (H/T) in the Set@l programming language. Here, we rely on it to construct the sequential information graph shown in Fig. 1a. The attribute of serial operations `Lf` is declared recursively (`Rec`) using the previously mentioned basic binary operation `f` (see code in Fig. 6) and defines the relationship between the set of processed data `A` and the result of calculations `Res`. The graph is built from

```attribute [f(a,b,c)|type(f)=Op]:```
  ```operand(element(a,b,c),attribute(Op));```
  ```c=f(a,b);```
```end(Op2);```
	```attribute Head(A):```
	  ```operand(set(A),element(Head(A)));```
	  ```Head(A)=A(1);```
	```end(Head);```

```attribute Tail(A):```
  ```operand(set(A),set(Tail(A)));```
  ```Tail(A)=dif(A,A(1));```
```end(Tail);```
	```attribute d2(A,A1,A2):```
	  ```operand(set(A,A1,A2));```
	  ```n=card(A);```
	  ```A1=(A(k)|k<=n/2);```
	  ```A2=dif(A,A1);```
	```end(d2);```

Fig. 6. The attribute of an abstract binary operation (**f**), that of the allocation of "head" (**Head**) and "tail" (**Tail**) in a set, and that of the partition of a set into two subsets with the same cardinality (**d2**), in the Set@l programming language

the output vertex to the inputs. At each iteration, the sequential set of operations **Lf** on the elements of the set **A** can be represented as the combination of sequential operations **Lf** on the "tail" of set **A** and the separate vertex **f**. The "head" of set **A** and the intermediate result **s** of the **Tail(A)** sequential processing are the inputs of the selected vertex, and its output **Res** is the final or intermediate result of calculations (see line 5 in Fig. 7). The syntax construct **break[<condition>:<operation>]** (line 4 in Fig. 7) establishes the termination condition of the recursion and describes the operation that completes the construction of the graph structure. If the condition is met, the last operator **Lf** is converted into a special vertex, whose inputs are supplied with the two remaining elements of the set **A**.

```
(1)   attribute [Lf(A,Res)|Lf=Rec(f),type(A)='H/T']:
(2)      operand(set(A),element(Res));
(3)      element(s);
(4)      Lf(A,Res)=break[card(Tail(A))=1: f(Head(Tail(A)),Head(A),Res)],
(5)               union[Lf(Tail(A),s),f(s,Head(A),Res)];
(6)   end(Lf);
```

Fig. 7. The code of the **Lf** attribute in the Set@l programming language. It implements the "head/tail" principle (**H/T**) for constructing the information graph with associative operations **f**.

Using the same method of recursive description, it is possible to define the parallel "half-splitting" principle of graph construction (DIV2, graph in Fig. 1b) in the Set@l programming language. Figure 8 shows the code, in which the information graph is described from the output vertex to the input. At each iteration, the attribute **d2** divides the original set **A** into two subsets **A1** and **A2** with the same number of elements (line 3 in Fig. 8). In this case, the pyramid of operations **Pf** on the elements of **A** can be represented as the combination of parallel operations **Pf** on elements of the subset **A1**, parallel operations **Pf** on elements of the subset **A2**, and a separate vertex **f** (line 6 in Fig. 8). The intermediate

```
(1)    attribute [Pf(A,Res)|Pf=Rec(f),type(A)='DIV2')]:
(2)        operand(set(A),element(Res));
(3)        d2(A,A1,A2);
(4)        element(s1,s2);
(5)        Pf(A,Res)=break[card(A1)=1 and card(A2)=1: f(Head(A1),Head(A2),Res)],
(6)                  union[Pf(A1,s1),Pf(A2,s2),f(s1,s2,Res)];
(7)    end(Pf);
```

Fig. 8. The code of the Pf attribute in the Set@l programming language. It implements the "half-splitting" principle (DIV2) for the description of parallel information graphs with associative operations f.

results s1 and s2 of performing pyramid operations Pf on subsets of the set A are the inputs of this vertex f, and its output Res is the final or intermediate result of calculations. The recursion completes if the condition shown in line 5 of Fig. 8 is met. The parallelization of calculations is achieved by doubling the number of recursion branches at each step of the transformation.

Thus, the architecture-independent Set@l programming language allows describing the basic principles for the construction of graphs with single-output associative operations in the form of the special processing method attributes H/T and DIV2, which are assigned to the set of input data A. In contrast to previously proposed parallelism types par, seq, pipe, conc, and imp [15,16], which specify methods for parallelizing calculations, these attributes determine the general structure of an information graph and modify it according to the architecture and configuration of a parallel computer system. If the "head/tail" and "half-splitting" principles are described once, it is possible to obtain various topologies without changes in the program's source code. Some examples of code fragments using H/T and DIV2 processing types to synthesize different information graphs are given in Fig. 9.

Line of adders:	Pyramid of adders:
G=Gf(A,Res);	G=Gf(A,Res);
Gf=(Rec(f),type(A)='H/T');	Gf=(Rec(f),type(A)='DIV2');
type(f)='+';	type(f)='+';
Line of multipliers:	Pyramid for maximum search:
G=Gf(A,Res);	G=Gf(A,Res);
Gf=(Rec(f),type(A)='H/T');	Gf=(Rec(f),type(A)='DIV2');
type(f)='*';	type(f)='max';

Fig. 9. Code fragments that employ the "head/tail" (H/T) and "half-splitting" (DIV2) attributes of set processing to describe different information graphs based on associative single-output operations

The structure of the information graph G (see program code in Fig. 9) is determined by the relation Gf between the processed set A and the result of calculations Res. As far as the user is concerned, it is enough to change only the type of the set A to obtain an information graph with a completely different interconnection structure, while the generalized descriptions of the "head/tail" and "half-splitting" attributes remain unchanged. The type of the basic associative operation f defines the functionality of operational vertices in the synthesized information graph.

4   Development of Resource-Independent Programs in the Set@l Language

Using the processing method attributes H/T and DIV2 (see the code in Figs. 7 and 8), it is possible to describe the topological transformation of an information graph with associative operations taking into account the number of available computing resources (Fig. 2) as a change in the typing and partitioning of the processed data set A. In general, the set A must have the following form, which ensures that isomorphic subgraphs are yielded, as well as the minimum latency of the computational structure, and the convenience of further reduction transformations:

$$A = \mathbf{H/T}[subA_1, subA_2, \ldots, subA_r]; \tag{1}$$

$$subA_p = \mathbf{DIV2}\{a_b, a_{b+1}, \ldots, a_c\}, \tag{2}$$

where $subA_p$ is the p-th subset (type DIV2) of the set A (type H/T); r is the coefficient of performance reduction, while b and c are the bounds of the range of indices of elements of the set A belonging to the subset $subA_p$. If $r = 1$, then formulas (1) and (2) describe the "half-splitting" topology: a single subset $subA_1$ contains all elements $a_1, \ldots, a_n$. If $r = n - 1$, then the set A consists of n subsets with one element each, which corresponds to the "head/tail" topology.

The graph_modification attribute, which converts the initial set of processed data Array into the resulting set A with a parameterized structure defined by formulas (1) and (2), is described according to the same principle as reduction transformations of sorting networks in [14]. The snippet of code shown in Fig. 10 selects the topology of an information graph with associative operations in conformity with the number R of computational resources available in the reconfigurable computer system, the dimension of the processed array n, and the number RO of hardware resources used by the operational vertex. The approach we suggest makes it possible to synthesize the most suitable topology for further reduction transformations for a given number of computational resources. In limit cases, the combined topology transforms into either the basic "head/tail" or the "half-splitting" variant. At the same time, the minimal latency of the computational structure is ensured by both the structural and the structural-procedural implementations of calculations.

```
Q=floor(R/R0); // quantity of vertices that can be realized on
              // available computational resource R;
r=ceil(n/Q);                 // calculation of reduction coefficient;
graph_modification(Array,A,r); // partition and typing of set A;
```

Fig. 10. Program code in Set@l that modifies the topology of an information graph with associative operations in conformity with the number of available computational resources

The translator of the programming language Set@l processes the set A (see formulas (1) and (2)) and synthesizes the set G that describes the topology of an information graph with associative operations in the following set-theoretical form:

$$G = \overrightarrow{\{} \{subG_1, subG_2, \ldots, subG_r\}, \nu_1, \nu_2, \ldots, \nu_{r-1} \overrightarrow{\}}, \tag{3}$$

where $\overrightarrow{\{} \overrightarrow{\}}$ denotes the parallel-dependent parallelism type (conc in terms of Set@l [9,10]); { } is the notation of the parallel-independent processing type (par parallelism type [9,10]); $subG_i$ is the i-th subgraph built using the "half-splitting" principle (DIV2 in Fig. 2); ν_i is the i-th operational vertex included in the unit for processing intermediate results, which is based on the "head/tail" principle (H/T in Fig. 2). A further performance reduction is carried out using the special aspect **reduction**, which converts set (3)) into the following partitioned set:

$$G = \langle subG_1, \overrightarrow{\{} subG_2, \nu_1 \overrightarrow{\}}, \overrightarrow{\{} subG_3, \nu_2 \overrightarrow{\}}, \ldots, \overrightarrow{\{} subG_r, \nu_{r-1} \overrightarrow{\}} \rangle. \tag{4}$$

The elements of the original set G are rearranged in such a manner that the hardware-implemented computational structure contains a subgraph with the "half-splitting" topology and an additional vertex that corresponds to the sequential unit H/T for processing intermediate results (see Fig. 2). The final structure occupies the entire number R of computing resources available and has minimal latency.

5   Conclusions

Thus, the standard topologies of information graphs with associative operations are efficient only in the limit cases of minimal and maximal computational resources available in a reconfigurable computer system. In other cases, it is reasonable to modify the topology of the graph according to the algorithm we suggested in the paper and convert it into a form suitable for performance reduction. However, traditional parallel programming methods treat information graphs as fixed structures, and their application to the description of topological transformations in conformity with the configuration parameters of the computer system is quite cumbersome and inefficient. To solve this problem, we propose the architecture-independent programming language Set@l. Under Set@l, all possible topologies of graphs with associative operations can be represented in the form of two processing method attributes assigned to the set of source data and its subsets. We have developed a resource-independent parallel program in Set@l that includes the aspects of topology modification and performance reduction.

Acknowledgements. The reported study was funded by the Russian Foundation for Basic Research (project No. 20-07-00545).

References

1. Knuth, D.E.: The Art of Computer Programming. Volume 4A: Combinatorial Algorithms. Addison-Wesley Professional, Boston (2011)
2. Novikov, F.: Discrete Mathematics. 3rd edn. Piter, Saint Petersburg (2019). (in Russian)
3. Karepova, E.D.: The Fundamentals of Multithread and Parallel Programming. Siberian Federal University Publishing, Krasnoyarsk (2016).(in Russian)
4. The problem of array element summation (in Russian). https://parallel.ru/fpga/Summ2
5. Starchenko, A.V., Bercun, V.N.: Methods of Parallel Computing. Tomsk University Publishing, Tomsk (2013). (in Russian)
6. Efimov, S.S.: Review of parallelizing methods for algorithms aimed at solution of certain problems of computational discrete mathematics. Math. Struct. Model. **17**, 72–93 (2007). (in Russian)
7. Levin, I.I., Dordopulo, A.I.: On the problem of automatic development of parallel applications for reconfigurable computer systems. Comput. Technol. **25**(1), 66–81 (2020). https://doi.org/10.25743/ICT.2020.25.1.005. (in Russian)
8. Kalyaev, I.A., Levin, I.I., Semernikov, E.A., SHmojlov, V.I.: Evolution domestic of multichip reconfigurable computer systems: from air to liquid cooling. In: SPIIRAS Proceedings, vol. 1, pp. 5–31 (2017). (in Russian). https://doi.org/10.15622/sp.50.1
9. Mittal, S., Vetter, J.: A survey of CPU-GPU heterogeneous computing techniques. ACM Comput. Surv. **47**(4), 69 (2015). https://doi.org/10.1145/2788396
10. Waidyasooriya, H.M., Hariyama, M., Uchiyama, K.: Design of FPGA-Based Computing Systems with OpenCL. Springer, Cham (2018). https://doi.org/10.1007/978-3-319-68161-0
11. Tessier, R., Pocek, K., DeHon, A.: Reconfigurable computing architectures. Proc. IEEE **103**(3), 332–354 (2015). https://doi.org/10.1109/JPROC.2014.2386883
12. Kalyaev, A.V., Levin, I.I.: Modular-Expandable Multiprocessor Systems with Structural and Procedural Organization of Calculations. YAnus-K, Moscow (2003)
13. Levin, I.I., et al.: Tools for programming of reconfigurable and hybrid computer systems based on FPGAs. In: XIII International Conference "Parallel computational technologies" (PCT 2019), short papers and poster descriptions, pp. 299–312 (2019). (in Russian)
14. Pisarenko, I.V., Alekseev, K.N., Melnikov, A.K.: Resource-independent representation of sorting networks in Set@l programming language. Herald Comput. Inf. Technol. **11**, 53–60 (2019). https://doi.org/10.14489/vkit.2019.11. (in Russian)
15. Levin, I.I., Dordopulo, A.I., Pisarenko, I.V., Melnikov, A.K.: Aspect-Oriented Set@l language for architecture-independent programming of high-performance computer systems. In: Voevodin, V., Sobolev, S. (eds.) RuSCDays 2019. CCIS, vol. 1129, pp. 517–528. Springer, Cham (2019). https://doi.org/10.1007/978-3-030-36592-9_42

16. Levin, I.I., Dordopulo, A.I., Pisarenko, I.V., Melnikov, A.K.: Architecture-independent Set@l programming language for computer systems. Herald Comput. Inf. Technol. **3**, 48–56 (2019). https://doi.org/10.14489/vkit.2019.03. (in Russian)
17. Knuth, D.E.: The Art of Computer Programming. Volume 1: Fundamental Algorithms. 3rd edn. Addison-Wesley Professional, Boston (1997)
18. Dasgupta, S., Papadimitriu, H., Vazirani, U.: Algorithms. MCNMO, Moscow (2014). (in Russian)
19. Kovalenko, A.G., Levin, I.I., Melnikov, A.K.: Automatization of parallel-pipeline program development for reconfigurable computer systems. Herald Comput. Inf. Technol. **5**, 50–56 (2013)
20. Levin, I.I., Dordopulo, A.I., Pisarenko, I.V., Melnikov, A.K.: Objects of alternative set theory in Set@l programming language. In: Malyshkin, V. (ed.) PaCT 2019. LNCS, vol. 11657, pp. 18–31. Springer, Cham (2019). https://doi.org/10.1007/978-3-030-25636-4_3

Parallel Numerical Algorithms

GPU-Accelerated Fuzzy Inference Based on Fuzzy Truth Values

Sergey V. Kulabukhov[✉] and Vasily G. Sinuk

Belgorod State Technological University named after V. G. Shukhov,
46 Kostyukova Street, Belgorod 308012, Russia

Abstract. The paper deals with the computational complexity of fuzzy inference in the case of multiple fuzzy inputs and/or rules. We consider an inference method based on the fuzzy truth values and its parallel implementation employing the CUDA technology. The main problem of the method consists of multiple independent reductions of discrete fuzzy sets through an associative binary operation of high computational complexity. This fact raises the problem of barrier synchronization among specific ranges of blocks. The article describes the design of a parallel inference algorithm and considers the capabilities of CUDA technology, which might be suitable for the implementation of the algorithm. The article also provides profiling results.

Keywords: Fuzzy inference · Fuzzy truth value · GPGPU

1 Introduction

Fuzzy inference systems are gaining popularity. They are used in many fields of practical interest. As a matter of fact, they are more consistent with the nature of human thinking than systems of traditional formal logic since they can be used for building models that reflect various aspects of uncertainty in a more adequate manner [6]. Those models are defined via fuzzy rule bases. Fuzzy inference systems have applications in such fields as control of technical systems, speech and image recognition, and diverse expert systems.

The theoretical basis of fuzzy inference was settled by Zadeh in [11]. Other solutions to the problem were proposed after that. According to [11], the computational complexity of the inference for an individual rule exponentially depends on the number of fuzzy inputs. This fact makes Zadeh's inference method inapplicable in its original form in the case of multiple fuzzy inputs because the inference cannot be performed in a reasonable amount of time. In many applications, input data contain either nonnumerical (linguistic) assessments [2,8] or input signals that are received with noise [9,10].

The reported study was partially funded by the RFBR under research project No. 20-07-00030.

L. Sokolinsky and M. Zymbler (Eds.): PCT 2021, CCIS 1437, pp. 61–75, 2021.
https://doi.org/10.1007/978-3-030-81691-9_5

A significant advantage of fuzzy inference based on fuzzy truth values is the single space of truthfulness for all premises. This is achieved by transforming the relationship between fact and premise into a so-called fuzzy truth value. Bringing all the relationships between different facts and premises into a single fuzzy space of truthfulness simplifies the computation of the compound truthfulness function and reduces its complexity to a linear dependency on the number of inputs. Therefore, this approach is devoid of the problems of multidimensional analysis. It does not seem, however, to be possible to implement this inference method in an analytical form due to the complicated transformations involved. Because of this, membership functions are replaced with arrays of samples.

We considered CUDA-based learning of a neuro-fuzzy system based on fuzzy truth values in previous work (see [5]). In that research, we used an evolution strategy (μ, λ). Similar to other evolutionary algorithms [10], it involves computing the fitness function for each individual (i.e., a vector of parameters) of the offspring population. The fitness function used in the research relies on the computation of the inference result for each element of the training set. This raises the problem of performing numerous inferences, possibly simultaneous, that represent independent tasks. Thus, these tasks are distributed over the grid as one inference per block. Processed samples during inference operations are distributed among the threads of blocks. Another fact that makes the GPU-based implementation reasonable is the small amounts of input and output data.

In this paper, we consider a situation when it is necessary to efficiently perform a single inference at a time. Even though block-level parallelism is still suitable, using a single block limits the utilization of the GPU to only one streaming multiprocessor. A way to split a single inference into a set of relatively independent tasks is suggested in [7], where the network of fuzzy inference operations and the flow of their arguments and results are depicted. These operations can be executed in individual blocks. However, it raises the problem of barrier synchronization among blocks. The paper is dedicated to the solution to these problems.

The paper is structured as follows. In Sect. 2, we give define the fuzzy inference method based on fuzzy truth values. Section 3 is devoted to the implementation of the provided algorithms with computations spread within a single CUDA block. In Sect. 4, we consider the problem of distributing the computations all over the CUDA grid. Finally, in the Conclusions, we summarize the study and point out directions for further research.

2   Fuzzy Inference Based on Fuzzy Truth Values

The problem that is to be solved by using a fuzzy inference system is formulated as follows. Consider a system with n inputs $\boldsymbol{x} = [x_1, \ldots, x_n]$ and a single output y. The relationship between inputs and the output is defined using N fuzzy rules expressed as

$$R_k: \text{If } x_1 \text{ is } A_{1k} \text{ and } \ldots \text{ and } x_n \text{ is } A_{nk}, \text{ then } y \text{ is } B_k, \quad k = \overline{1, N}, \quad (1)$$

where $x \in X = X_1 \times X_2 \times \cdots \times X_n$, $y \in Y$, and $A_k = A_{1k} \times A_{2k} \times \cdots \times A_{nk} \subseteq\subseteq X$ and $B_k \subseteq Y$ are fuzzy sets.

According to the classification proposed in [11], the specific feature of logical-type systems is that the rules expressed in (1) are formalized via a fuzzy implication as $(n+1)$-ary fuzzy relations $R_k \subseteq X_1 \times \cdots \times X_n \times Y$, namely

$$R_k = A_{1k} \times \cdots \times A_{nk} \times Y \rightarrow X_1 \times \cdots \times X_n \times B_k, \quad k = \overline{1, N},$$

where "$\rightarrow$" denotes a fuzzy implication expressing a causal relationship between the antecedent "x_1 is A_{1k} and ... and x_n is A_{nk}" and the consequent "y is B_k". The task is to determine the inference result $B'_k \subseteq Y$ for a system given in the form expressed in (1), provided that the inputs are given as $A' = A'_1 \times \cdots \times A'_n \subseteq\subseteq X$ or "x_1 is A'_1 and ... and x_n is A'_n".

The generalized *fuzzy modus ponens* rule

$$B'_k = A' \circ R_k, \quad k = \overline{1, N},$$

where "$\circ$" is the composition of fuzzy sets, has a computational complexity of order $O(|X| \cdot |Y|) = O(|X_1| \cdot |X_2| \cdot \ldots \cdot |X_n| \cdot |Y|)$. For the membership functions, it is equivalent to the following:

$$\mu_{B'_k}(y) = \sup_{x \in X} \{\mu_{A'}(x) \; \mathrm{T} \; I(\mu_{A_k}(x), \mu_{B_k}(y))\}, \quad k = \overline{1, N}, \tag{2}$$

where T is a t-norm and I is a fuzzy implication.

The specific feature of the considered approach to fuzzy inference is that the inference is made within a single truth space for all premises, which is achieved by transforming the relationships between premise and fact into so-called fuzzy truth values. By using the truth modification rule (see [1]), we can write

$$\mu_{A'}(x) = \tau_{A|A'}(\mu_A(x)),$$

where $\tau_{A|A'}(\cdot)$ is the fuzzy truth value of the fuzzy set A relative to A', which represents the compatibility $CP(A, A')$ of the term A with respect to A' [3,12]:

$$\tau_{A|A'}(t) = \mu_{CP(A,A')}(t) = \sup_{\substack{\mu_A(x)=t \\ x \in X}} \{\mu_{A'}(x)\}, \quad t \in [0, 1]. \tag{3}$$

Denote $t = \mu_A(x)$. Then,

$$\mu_{A'}(x) = \tau_{A|A'}(\mu_A(x)) = \tau_{A|A'}(t). \tag{4}$$

Thus, for single-input systems, (2) takes the form of:

$$\mu_{B'_k}(y) = \sup_{t \in [0,1]} \{\tau_{A|A'}(t) \; \mathrm{T} \; I(t, \mu_{B_k}(y))\}, \quad k = \overline{1, N},$$

In systems with n inputs $(n > 1)$, the reduction of fuzzy truth values $\tau_{A_i|A'}$ is done for all inputs $i = \overline{1, n}$. For rules of the form (1), the fuzzy truth value of the antecedent A_k with respect to the inputs A' is defined as

$$\tau_{A_k|A'}(t) = \mathop{\mathrm{T}}_{i=\overline{1,n}} \tau_{A_{ki}|A'_i}(t), \quad t \in [0, 1], \tag{5}$$

where $\mathbf{T}$ is an n-ary t-norm extended by the extension principle (see [10]). In particular, if $n = 2$, then

$$\tau_{A_k|A'}(t) = \sup_{\substack{t_1 \mathbf{T} t_2 = t \\ (t_1, t_2) \in [0;1]^2}} \{\tau_{A_{k1}|A'_1}(t_1) \ \mathbf{T} \ \tau_{A_{k2}|A'_2}(t_2)\}. \tag{6}$$

The computational complexity of the latter expression is of order $O(|N_s|^2)$, where N_s is the number of samples used for the membership functions of the fuzzy truth values.

With this in mind, the inference of the output value B'_k based on the fuzzy truth values, for systems with n inputs, can be written in the form

$$\mu_{B'_k}(y) = \sup_{t \in [0,1]} \{\tau_{A_k|A'}(t) \ \mathbf{T} \ I(t, \mu_{B_k}(y))\}, \quad k = \overline{1, N}. \tag{7}$$

The computational complexity of (7) is of order $O(|t| \cdot |Y|)$.

The fuzzy set B' (the output of the system as a whole) is obtained by accumulation, and in a logical approach, it is defined as an intersection operation (see [10]):

$$B' = \bigcap_{j=\overline{1,N}} B'_j. \tag{8}$$

Accordingly, the membership function B' is defined through the minimum operation:

$$\mu_{B'}(y) = \min_{j=\overline{1,N}} \{\mu_{B'_j}(y)\}. \tag{9}$$

The center-of-gravity defuzzification method is used in the fuzzy inference to define the crisp output $\overline{y}$ of the system:

$$\overline{y} = \frac{\sum_{k=1}^{N} \overline{y}_k \cdot \mu_{B'}(\overline{y}_k)}{\sum_{k=1}^{N} \mu_{B'}(\overline{y}_k)}, \tag{10}$$

where $\overline{y}_k$, $k \in \overline{1, N}$, are points for which the following is true:

$$\mu_{B_k}(\overline{y}_k) = \sup_{y \in Y} \{\mu_{B_k}(y)\} = 1.$$

Moreover, if the rules have different significance, which can be formalized by assigning each of them a number $w_k \in [0; 1]$, $k = \overline{1, N}$, i.e., a weight, then it can be used in (10) as a coefficient for $\mu_{B'}(\overline{y}_k)$. In view of this, we can use (9) and (10) to transform (7) into

$$\overline{y} = \frac{\sum_{k=1}^{N} \overline{y}_k \cdot w_k \cdot \min_{j=\overline{1,N}} \left\{ \sup_{t \in [0,1]} \left\{ \tau_{A_k|A'}(t) \ \mathbf{T} \ I\big(t, \mu_{B_j}(\overline{y}_k)\big) \right\} \right\}}{\sum_{k=1}^{N} w_k \cdot \min_{j=\overline{1,N}} \left\{ \sup_{t \in [0,1]} \left\{ \tau_{A_k|A'}(t) \ \mathbf{T} \ I\big(t, \mu_{B_j}(\overline{y}_k)\big) \right\} \right\}}. \tag{11}$$

3   Implementation of Individual Operations of Fuzzy Inference

In this section, we consider the implementation of operations of fuzzy inference. Each running instance of the operation utilizes a single CUDA block.

3.1   Overview of the Inference Process

The inference process is the task that the learning process described in [5] consists of. The problem of the current research has much in common with [5]; the main difference is that only one pair "fuzzy system–input values" is processed. Other differences include the removal of the main kernel function and the creation of three new kernel functions which call the __device__ functions responsible for different operations of the inference. Another difference stems from the redesign of the defuzzification method, which is now performed according to (11) rather than [4]. As a result, the accumulation and computation of the inference results of individual rules now take place in the same kernel as the defuzzification.

The input data consists of the numbers of inputs n, rules N, and samples N_s; the membership functions of input values A_i', $i \in \overline{1,n}$; the terms of linguistic variables A_{ki}, B_k, $i \in \overline{1,n}$, $k \in \overline{1,N}$, encoded by their type and parameters; and the weights of rules w_k, $k \in \overline{1,N}$. The output data are the inference result $\overline{y}$. Most of the input data are copied to the device before the inference, using cudaMemcpy, whereas the remaining part is transferred via the parameters of the kernels. As previously mentioned, this fuzzy inference method leads to the discretization of the membership functions into arrays of samples. Those samples are distributed over the threads and then processed. The implementation of individual fuzzy inference operations will be described below in this section.

3.2   Global Memory Usage

Since all of the allocated global memory stores data of types int and float, hereinafter, we take four bytes as the unit of memory. The exact size of the required memory depends on n, N, N_s, and the size ξ used to store an encoded membership function (which equals 3 in the current implementation). The memory is split by purpose into five parts, as shown in Fig. 1.

The first and second parts store the results of the execution of intermediate commands, i.e., kernels other than defuzzification; these results are arrays of samples of membership functions. The first part stores the samples of fuzzy truth values $\tau_{A_{ki}|A_i'}$, $i \in \overline{1,n}$, $k \in \overline{1,N}$, and consists of $N \cdot n$ arrays of N_s floats each. The second part contains $N \cdot (n-1)$ arrays to store the reduced fuzzy truth values. The third part is designed to contain a single float, namely the output data $\overline{y}$ of the system. The fourth and fifth parts are used to pass the input data. The fourth part stores the membership functions of terms of input linguistic variables A_{ki}, $i \in \overline{1,n}$, $k \in \overline{1,N}$, and actual input values A_i', $i \in \overline{1,n}$. The fifth part consists of tuples $\langle B_k, w_k \rangle$, $k \in \overline{1,N}$, a part of the input data for the defuzzification kernel.

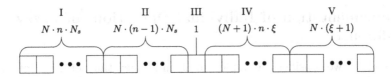

$$\begin{array}{ccccc}\text{I} & \text{II} & \text{III} & \text{IV} & \text{V} \\ N \cdot n \cdot N_s & N \cdot (n-1) \cdot N_s & 1 & (N+1) \cdot n \cdot \xi & N \cdot (\xi + 1)\end{array}$$

Fig. 1. Data distribution across the allocated memory

3.3   Computing Fuzzy Truth Values

This operation is analytically defined by (3). Its arguments are the membership functions of the term $\mu_A(x)$ and the fact $\mu_{A'}(x)$; the result is the fuzzy truth value $\tau_{A|A'}(t)$ of the term with respect to the fact. In the discrete case, we calculate sample values of the function $\tau_{A|A'}(t)$. Since this function is defined in the numerical range $[0; 1]$, we split it into N_s samples and define the value of each sample as follows:

$$\tau_{A|A'}(t_i) = \sup_{\substack{\mu_A(x) \in [t_i; t_{i+1}] \\ x \in X}} \{\mu_{A'}(x)\}, \quad t_i = \frac{i}{N_s}, \quad i = \overline{0, N_s - 1}, \quad (12)$$

whence, taking into account (4), it follows that

$$\tau_{A|A'}(t_i) = \sup_{t \in [t_i; t_{i+1}]} \{\tau_{A|A'}(t)\}. \quad (13)$$

The procedure for computing $\tau_{A|A'}(t_i)$ for each t_i has a computational complexity of order $O(N_s)$. It is divided into three subroutines. Flowcharts of two of them at the level of individual threads are shown in Fig. 2. The main subroutine of the operation is $ftv(dst, A, A', N_s)$, which fills an array of N_s elements at dst with values as specified by (12). It is also a function that is invoked within the first kernel. Membership functions $\mu_A(x)$ and $\mu_{A'}(x)$ are expressed as numerical sequences padded to the length of ξ, in which the first number is an integer that defines the type of the function, and the rest are `float`s that define function's parameters. The destination address dst points to an array in the first part of the allocated memory.

The computation of individual samples of $\tau_{A|A'}(t_i)$ is distributed among all threads of the block. Hereafter, x and h denote the thread index `threadIdx.x` and the number of threads in the block `blockDim.x` respectively. In ftv, a loop is executed for $i = \overline{0, N_s - 1}$, each thread performs every h-th iteration starting with the x-th. Since the value of the i-th sample equals the upper boundary of the fuzzy truth value in the range $[t_i; t_{i+1}]$ (see (13)), the ends of this range are calculated in the loop body and stored in variables t_1 and t_2. Then, the function $ftv_1(A, A', t_1, t_2)$ is invoked, and it returns the value of (12) for the given range $[t_1; t_2]$, which is then assigned to the i-th element of the array at dst.

Depending on both the type of the membership function $\mu_A(x)$ and the values of its parameters, ftv_1 determines all numerical ranges $\hat{X} = [x_{\min}; x_{\max}]$ such that $\forall x \in \hat{X} \Rightarrow \mu_A(x) \in [t_1; t_2]$. The function ftv_1 features algorithms

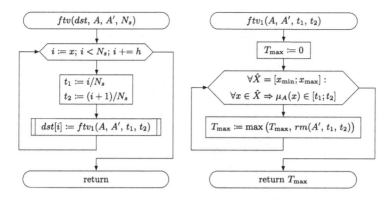

Fig. 2. Flowcharts of fuzzy truth value computation

to determine these ranges for all supported types of membership functions. For example, the ranges for a Gaussian membership function with center m and standard deviation σ are

$$\left[m - \sigma\sqrt{-\ln t_1}; m - \sigma\sqrt{-\ln t_2} \right], \left[m + \sigma\sqrt{-\ln t_2}; m + \sigma\sqrt{-\ln t_1} \right].$$

For each of these ranges, ftv_1 invokes the function $rm(\mu_{A'}(x), x_{\min}, x_{\max})$, which returns the maximum membership degree of the fact within this range. Then, ftv_1 returns the maximum of the values returned by rm.

The flowchart of rm is not shown in the figure since it contains only the formulas that express the maximum value within a given range $[x_{\min}; x_{\max}]$ for all supported types of membership functions. In the aforementioned case of a Gaussian function, this value is given as

$$\sup_{x \in [x_{\min}; x_{\max}]} \{\mu_{A'}(x)\} = \begin{cases} 1, & \text{if } x_{\min} \le m \le x_{\max}, \\ \exp((x_{\max} - m)^2/\sigma^2), & \text{if } x_{\max} < m, \\ \exp((x_{\min} - m)^2/\sigma^2), & \text{if } x_{\min} > m. \end{cases}$$

3.4   Reducing Fuzzy Truth Values

If a rule contains more than one subcondition (i.e., involves multiple inputs), then the fuzzy truth value of the entire antecedent A_k with respect to the inputs A' is computed according to (5). This formula contains an n-ary t-norm extended by the extension principle. In the case $n = 2$, it is defined as (6). If $n > 2$, then $\mathbf{T}$ can be applied as an associative binary operator to the result of the reduction of the previous $(n - 1)$ arguments and the n-th argument. However, this operator is also commutative.

The algorithm for computing the result of this operation is depicted in Fig. 3. Its computational complexity is $O(N_s^2)$. The operation is implemented for $n = 2$; the reduction for larger values of n is done by multiple invocations of the reduction, which takes place within the second kernel. The arguments A, B, and the result dst are fuzzy truth values in a discrete form (arrays of samples). Therefore, t_1 and t_2 take on values in the discrete set $\{i/N_s\}_{i=\overline{0,N_s-1}}$.

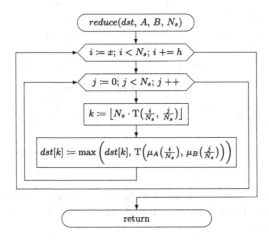

Fig. 3. Flowchart for the reduction of fuzzy truth values

The enumeration of all values of t_1 and t_2 is implemented by a double loop for the variables i and j, respectively. The iterations of the external loop for the variable i are distributed among all threads of the block in the same manner as in the case of ftv (see Fig. 2). The internal loop for j is entirely executed by a single thread. The values of i and j correspond to $t_1 = i/N_s$ and $t_2 = j/N_s$, respectively. Then, $t = t_1 \, \mathrm{T} \, t_2$ is computed. The index of the result sample corresponding to t is $k = \lfloor t * N_s \rfloor$. Let us denote by $\hat{\tau}_t$ the argument of the supremum in (6), i.e., $\hat{\tau}_t = \tau_{A_{k1}|A_1'}(t_1) \, \mathrm{T} \, \tau_{A_{k2}|A_2'}(t_2)$, which is calculated as $\mathrm{T(A[i], B[j])}$, where T is the implementation of the t-norm. If $\hat{\tau}_t$ is greater than the current value of $dst[k]$, then $dst[k]$ is assigned the value of $\hat{\tau}_t$.

The index k is calculated using the t-norm. In the implemented distribution of iterations for i and j, the threads may process the elements of the destination array with the same index. If multiple threads read the value of $dst[k]$ and, afterward, conditionally update it, then data races may occur. However, distributing the iterations in such a way that no pair of threads obtain similar values of k depends on the t-norm and is computationally inefficient since threads will get different numbers of payloads. Data races can be eliminated by using the atomic maximum operation provided by the CUDA framework, which can be invoked by calling the function `atomicMax`. This function accepts `address` and the value `val` as arguments. If the value at `address` is less than `val`, then `val` is written to `address`. Since the function accepts only integer numbers, $\lfloor \hat{\tau}_t * \mathrm{INT\_MAX} \rfloor$ is passed instead of $\hat{\tau}_t$. Given that $\hat{\tau}_t \in [0;1]$, no overflow can occur.

During the execution of the algorithm, the integer representation of the resulting array is located in the shared memory. This memory is used since it has a shorter access time than global memory. When the execution is completed, the result is transferred to the global memory at *dst*, with each element converted into a floating-point number and divided by INT_MAX. This process is also iterative and involves all threads of the block in the same way as in previous cases.

3.5   Defuzzification

This operation is performed as per (11). In addition to the defuzzification itself, this operation incorporates the accumulation and computation of the inference result of individual rules. It is designed to be invoked once in the third kernel. The arguments of this operation include the reduced fuzzy truth value of each rule's antecedent $\tau_{A_k|A'}(t)$, the membership function of the consequent of each rule B_k, and the weight of each rule w_k, $k = \overline{1, N}$. The reduced fuzzy truth values are placed into the global memory by the previous operation and are ordered and adjacent; the address of the first one is passed via the parameters of the kernel. The process is depicted in Fig. 4.

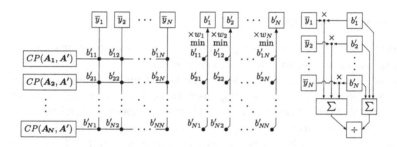

Fig. 4. Data flow in the defuzzification process

As it can be seen in the figure, the operation is divided into three stages, which are separated by invocations of __syncthreads and use the shared memory to transfer the results between them. Throughout the operation, let us consider the used piece of shared memory as float $[N^2 + N]$. In the first stage, the inference results $\mu_{B'_j}(\overline{y}_k)$ of all rules $j = \overline{1, N}$ in all points $k = \overline{1, N}$ are computed according to (7). The computation of each value (denoted by b'_{jk}) has a complexity of order $O(N_s)$; therefore, the overall complexity of the stage is $O(N^2 \cdot N_s)$. To evenly distribute the computing of N^2 values over h threads, a loop of N^2 distributed iterations (as mentioned above) is executed for a variable l, in which the index j is determined as (l div N) and the index k equals (l mod N). The maximum of the expression under the supremum operator in (7) is computed inside an internal loop, which iterates over the samples of the reduced fuzzy truth value of the j-th rule's antecedent. For the i-th sample, the value of t is assumed to be (i/N_s). The result is placed into the l-th element of the float array in the shared memory.

The second stage is the accumulation of previously computed values b'_{jk} with equal index k, which is done according to (8). The computational complexity of this stage is of order $O(N^2)$. The x-th thread computes the minimum of $\{b'_{jk}\}$ for each $k \in \{x+i\cdot h \mid i \in \mathbb{Z}\} \cap [0; N-1]$ and stores the result in the (N^2+k)-th element of the float array in the shared memory. It is also multiplied by the k-th rule's weight w_k before being stored, as shown in the figure. This value is denoted by b'_k.

The last stage is the defuzzification itself, which is the computation of (10), where $\mu_{B'_j}(\overline{y}_k)$ is replaced with b'_k. The computational complexity is $O(N)$, thus, it is performed by a single thread. The result is written to the third part of the allocated global memory, and its address is passed via kernel parameters.

4   Multi-block Implementation

In this section, we consider the manners of distributing the computations over multiple CUDA blocks and, therefore, streaming the multiprocessors to reduce the overall computation time.

4.1   General Remarks

The fuzzy system constructed for profiling has $n = 64$ fuzzy inputs and $N = 64$ rules. For the inference, we use $N_s = 12288$ samples.

For historical reasons, the names of the kernel functions are somewhat different from those of the corresponding operations. The kernel that is responsible for the computation of fuzzy truth values is named `transformationKernel`, the reduction kernel is named `aggregationKernel` or `aggregationRoundKernel`, and the defuzzification kernel is named `alternativeKernel`. These names are used in the screenshots of NVIDIA Visual Profiler.

4.2   Recursive Parallel Reduction and CUDA Streams

The reduction of n values with an associative binary operator may be recursively split into parallel subtasks as depicted in Fig. 5. The main idea of the algorithm is that if the processed expression consists of a single value, then return it, otherwise split the expression into two, process them in parallel, and then return the reduced results. The algorithm requires the barrier synchronization to be performed before calling *reduce* since both threads must return the result. Assuming that any reduction of two values consumes a constant time T, it follows that waiting for the synchronization is the shortest when the expression is split into parts of equal length. If there are at least $n/2$ parallel processors, the overall computation time is expected to be $T \cdot \lceil \log_2(n) \rceil$, against $T \cdot (n-1)$ in the serial case.

As follows from the above, the reductions have to be computed by multiple CUDA blocks. Since the barrier synchronization among blocks can only be performed for the whole grid, the most obvious approach is to use multiple

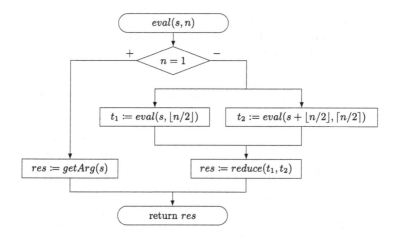

Fig. 5. Flowchart of the algorithm of recursive parallel reduction

grids, that is, multiple invocations of the kernel. However, if the kernel performs a single reduction, it utilizes a single block. We use CUDA streams to be able to run multiple kernels simultaneously. It is done implicitly by passing the `--default-stream=per-thread` flag to the NVIDIA CUDA Compiler, so every thread of the process is assigned its own CUDA stream. Since the algorithm fits the fork–join model, OpenMP is used as well in the following way:

```
void performInference() {
    #pragma omp parallel num_threads(nRules)
    reduceRecursive(omp_get_thread_num(), 0, nInputs);

    defuzzify();
}

void reduceRecursive(int k, int s, int n) {
    if (n == 1) return computeTruthValue(getArg(k, s, n), k, s);

    #pragma omp parallel num_threads(2)
    {
        int i = omp_get_thread_num();
        reduceRecursive(k, i ? s + n/2 : s, i ? n - n/2 : n/2);
    }

    reduce(getArg(k, s, n), getArg(k, s, n/2), getArg(k, s + n/2, n - n/2));
}
```

The `getArg(int k, int s, int n)` function returns the address of the corresponding array of samples where the input fuzzy truth values are or where the result must be stored. Each invocation of `reduce(float *dst, float *A, float *B)` launches `aggregationKernel` to reduce two fuzzy truth values, and every call to `computeTruthValue(float *dst, int rule, int input)` invokes the `transformationKernel` to compute $\tau_{A_{ks}|A'_s}$.

The profiling results of the implementation of this algorithm are given in Fig. 6. Keeping in mind that every kernel invocation can utilize only one streaming multiprocessor, it is clear from the timeline that about one-third of the computation time is spent in very low concurrency. The major problem seems to be caused by `transformationKernel` since it has much lower computational complexity than the reduction and occupies quite a large part of the time.

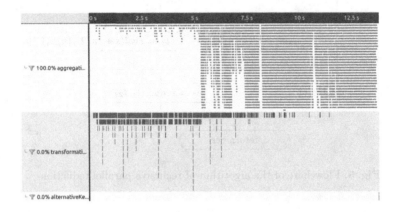

Fig. 6. Execution timeline of the recursive parallel reduction

An improvement can be achieved by, firstly, redesigning `transformation Kernel` in a manner that makes it compute all fuzzy truth values at once and, then, launching it on a grid of $n \cdot N$ blocks before making any reductions. Such improvement was done and profiled as well. The results are given in Fig. 7. The overall computation time changed from 13.79 to 9.36 s. However, the gaps in the timeline are still present, which means that the computation time may be further improved.

Fig. 7. Execution timeline of the algorithm of reduction-only recursive parallel reduction

4.3   Breadth-First Reduction

The algorithm from the previous subsection performs the reductions for a single rule in such a manner that they can be represented as a binary tree. The leaves of this tree represent the fuzzy truth values computed by `transformationKernel`, whereas all the other nodes represent individual reduction operations, and the value computed in the tree's root is the reduced fuzzy truth value for the corresponding rule. The algorithm performs a depth-first traversal. Let us consider breadth-first traversal in the reverse order, that is, from the leaves to the root. At any given level of the tree, all its nodes may be processed concurrently since they are roots of independent subtrees. This procedure is depicted in Fig. 8. It is assumed that the number of inputs is a power of two. Otherwise, it may be padded to the next power of two by adding dummy inputs that do not affect the reduction operations when processed.

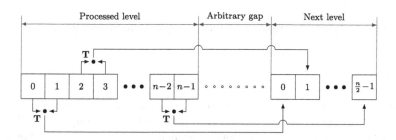

Fig. 8. Reduction of a tree level for a single rule

The values of each pair of nodes at the processed level produce a value of a node at the next level. If the size of the level is odd, then the remaining value is passed through. The profiling results for the implementation of this algorithm are provided in Fig. 9. The overall computation time is 6.76 s.

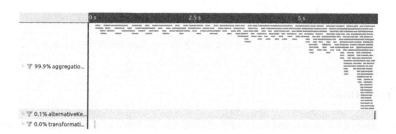

Fig. 9. Execution timeline of the per-rule breadth-first reduction algorithm

The reduction is performed by `aggregationRoundKernel`, which is executed in parallel for each rule (using OpenMP) on a grid of $(n/2)$ blocks at the first time, $(n/4)$ at the second, and so on, down to 1. The number of kernel invocations can be further reduced by processing a given level of all rules in a single call of the kernel. The process is graphically represented in Fig. 10. A correspondingly modified implementation was also profiled; the timeline is shown in Fig. 11. The

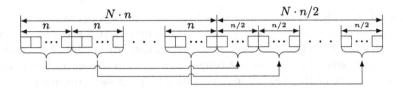

Fig. 10. Reduction of a tree level for all rules at once

Fig. 11. Execution timeline of the breadth-first reduction algorithm

inference took 6.9 s, which is greater than in the previous case. A possible reason is that some multiprocessors become idle by the end of the kernel execution. In the previous case, that effect is reduced by simultaneous execution of kernels.

We also employed grid synchronization through CUDA Cooperative Groups. In this implementation, the reduction kernel is launched once, iterating over the level size and synchronizing by means of `grid_group::sync()` at the end of the loop body. The profiling results of the implementation are depicted in Fig. 12. The computation time for this implementation reached 8.55 s. This is likely to be caused by restrictions on device launch parameters imposed by limitations of the cooperative kernel launch.

Fig. 12. Using `grid_group::sync()` in the last implementation

5   Conclusions

In this paper, we considered several methods of efficient implementation of fuzzy inference based on fuzzy truth values. In contrast with the problem considered in [5], where multiple independent tasks are distributed among CUDA blocks, the inference represents a single task which aggregates the results of all intermediate computations to produce a single result. A specific feature of this task is the reduction operation, which has a much greater computational complexity than the rest of the inference process. Each instance of the reduction operation is performed by an individual block.

To maximize the number of reduction operations that can run concurrently, the entire process of reduction of fuzzy truth values for a single rule was organized as a traversal of a binary tree. This tree has a height equal to $\lceil \log_2(n) \rceil$, and so is the minimal number of required barrier synchronizations. In the case of multiple rules, they are processed independently. We considered depth-first and reverse breadth-first traversals. The first approach requires the reduction operation kernel to be invoked for each tree node, thus making $N \cdot (n - 1)$ invocations. This results in significant overhead. Breadth-first traversal requires only $\lceil \log_2(n) \rceil$ kernel invocations, and it turns out to have the smallest computation time among the considered implementations.

During the research, CUDA Streams and Cooperative Groups were considered. We used CUDA Streams together with OpenMP technology to enable the kernels to run concurrently. Cooperative Groups were used to replace the multiple kernel invocations for barrier synchronization purposes, but this imposes restrictions on device launch parameters and makes the overall performance worse in the current implementation.

References

1. Borisov, A., Alekseev, A., Krumberg, O., Fedorov, I.: Decision making models based on linguistic variable. Zinatne, Riga (1982). (in Russian)
2. Borisov, V., Kruglov, V., Fedulov, A.: Fuzzy models and networks. Hot Line - Telecom, Moscow (2007). (in Russian)
3. Dubois, D., Prade, H.: Possibility theory. Applications to the representation of knowledge in informatics. Radio and Communication, Moscow (1990). (in Russian)
4. Programmable Controllers - Part 7: Fuzzy control programming. Standard, International Electrotechnical Commission, Geneva, Switzerland (2000)
5. Kulabukhov, S.V., Sinuk, V.G.: GPU-accelerated learning of neuro-fuzzy system based on fuzzy truth value. In: Sokolinsky, L., Zymbler, M. (eds.) PCT 2019. CCIS, vol. 1063, pp. 152–167. Springer, Cham (2019). https://doi.org/10.1007/978-3-030-28163-2_11
6. Leonenkov, A.: Fuzzy modeling in MATLAB and FuzzyTech environment. BHV - Petersburg, Saint Petersburg (2003). (in Russian)
7. Mikhelev, V.V., Sinyuk, V.G.: Methods of inference for logical-type systems based on the fuzzy degree of truth. J. Comput. Syst. Sci. Int. **57**(3), 463–470 (2018). https://doi.org/10.1134/S1064230718030073
8. Rothstein, A., Shtovba, S.: Identification of nonlinear dependence by fuzzy training set. Cybern. Syst. Anal. (2), 17–24 (2006). (in Russian)
9. Rutkowska, D., Pilinsky, M., Rutkowsky, L.: Neural networks, genetic algorithms and fuzzy systems. Hot Line - Telecom, Moscow (2004). (in Russian)
10. Rutkowsky, L.: Methods and techniques of computational intelligence. Hot Line - Telecom, Moscow (2010). (in Russian)
11. Zadeh, L.: Outline of a new approach to the analysis of complex systems and decision processes. IEEE Trans. Syst. Man Cybern. **3**(1), 28–44 (1973)
12. Zadeh, L.: PRUF - a meaning representation language for natural language. Int. J. Man-Mach. Stud. **10**, 395–460 (1978)

Deflation of Periodic Orbits in Large-Scale Systems: Algorithm and Parallel Implementation

N. M. Evstigneev[(✉)][iD]

Federal Research Center "Computer Science and Control"
of the Russian Academy of Sciences, Moscow, Russia

Abstract. We consider a nonlinear autonomous large-scale dynamical system with a parameter. Such systems usually stem from the discretization of initial boundary value problems for nonlinear partial differential equations. We are interested in finding all periodic orbits of such a system for a particular value of the parameter. We employ the deflation method together with the Poincaré section method to solve the problem. The deflation operator is constructed in the hyperplane used for the Poincaré return map and is iterated by the Newton–Raphson method. Two approaches are used for parallelization: the solution of the dynamical system, which is symmetrically parallel, and the deflation process, which is parallel and relies on the master-slave approach. The master controls the process of deflation and exchanges information between slaves. We show that the process can be successfully applied to the discrete system obtained from the Galerkin projection of the Navier–Stokes equations.

Keywords: Deflation of periodic orbits · Periodic orbits in large-scale systems · Poincaré section · Parallel deflation · CUDA

1 Introduction

We consider a nonlinear autonomous dynamical system in the form of a System of Ordinary Differential Equations (ODEs):

$$\mathbf{u}_t = F(\mathbf{u}, \lambda), \tag{1}$$

where $\mathbf{u} \in \mathbb{R}^n$, $(\ )_t$ is a time derivative, λ is a parameter, and F is a nonlinear operator. Such systems often emerge after a spatial semidiscrete form of partial differential equations (PDEs) is considered. It is assumed that the operator F includes some form of dissipation. A periodic orbit of the system with a period

The study was supported by the Russian Foundation for Basic Research (grants No. 18-29-10008mk and No. 20-07-00066).

$T > 0$ is a nonconstant solution satisfying the condition $\mathbf{u}(t) = \mathbf{u}(t + T)$ for the minimum possible value of the period. An image of the periodicity interval $[0, T)$ in the phase space $\mathbb{R}^n$ is called a periodic orbit or a limit cycle.

The problem of detecting and stabilizing periodic orbits of (1) is a common task in the analysis of middle- and large-scale systems [16] originating from different research fields, including, but not limited to, robotics [27], network analysis [4,17], physics [1,5,14,24], mechanics [3,6,7,12,15], and others. This allows one to trace the dynamics of the systems more closely by considering the values of periods, the stability of cycles, and the regions of periodic orbits in the parameter space. One of the new significant applications to research in turbulence is the analysis of unstable periodic solutions embedded in the turbulent flow [3,12,15]. In this case, it is essential to find as many distinct unstable periodic orbits as possible in the system (1).

In large-scale dynamical systems, it is usual that a fixed value of the parameter λ has many periodic orbits. If this is the case then one needs a method that distinguishes periodic orbits. The method should converge to a new periodic solution every time the algorithm is executed. This gives rise to the deflation method [8,9], which purges already obtained periodic solutions out of the basin of attraction. The only deflation method used for finding periodic solutions known to the authors is given in [10], where it is applied to the Hénon map and the Duffing oscillator, hence limited to $n = 2$ in (1).

The present research suggests an efficient parallel method for finding distinct periodic orbits in large-scale dynamical systems using deflation for a fixed value of λ. First, we briefly describe the methods used to detect and find periodic orbits in large-scale systems. Then, we provide an overview of the parallel methodology applied to these methods.

Detection and Stabilization of Periodic Orbits. Several methods can be used to detect and stabilize periodic orbits. The shooting method considered in [18] uses an extended system to find both a state on the limit cycle $\mathbf{u}(0)$ and the period T of the limit cycle. Newton's method is applied to the residual vector $\mathbf{r} = \mathbf{u}(0) - \mathbf{u}(T)$ in an attempt to minimize it. The augmented system is obtained by updating the residual vector with the perturbation $(\delta\mathbf{u}, \delta T)^{\intercal}$. This results in iterations of the updated system, whose size is $n + 1$ (rank one update). This approach is the easiest to implement, but presents some issues with convergence properties in the case of unstable periodic solutions in large-scale systems [18] (e.g., those coming from the Navier–Stokes equations) and requires preconditioning techniques.

Another approach is related to the formulation of the problem in the space of 2π-periodic functions. One introduces the unknown frequency parameter $\omega = 2\pi/T$, thereby recasting the problem in a nondimensional form by the substitution $\theta = \omega t$ in (1). The resulting system is then expressed as $\omega\mathbf{u}_{\theta} = F(\mathbf{u}, \lambda)$ and $\mathbf{u}(\theta) = \mathbf{u}(\theta + 2\pi)$. The unknown ω is expressed using the Rayleigh quotient in the form $\omega = (\mathbf{u}_{\theta}, F(\mathbf{u}))/(\mathbf{u}_{\theta}, \mathbf{u}_{\theta})$, where $(\cdot, \cdot)$ is an inner product in $\mathbb{R}^n$. The resulting nonlinear system can be solved using Newton's method. The temporal discretization of problem (1) is spectral in this approach.

This method is very efficient for small- and middle-sized problems; it possesses high spectral accuracy and yields both stable and unstable limit cycles. However, the linear system that is solved at each Newton update becomes ill-conditioned as the problem size increases and requires complex preconditioning.

Another method is the Newton-GMRES-hookstep algorithm, which is a generalization of the simple shooting algorithm. It exploits the symmetries of system (1). It was first published in [26] and used in [3,12] to find unstable limit cycles in the Navier–Stokes system. The basic idea is to add infinitesimal generators of transformations, modified by continuous and discrete parameters, to the shooting algorithm. A close alternative to this method is the variational periodic detection method, described in [2]. However, it has worse convergence properties than the Newton-GMRES-hookstep method.

Finally, the Poincaré shooting method is frequently used (see [6,16,22,29]). It is based on Newton iterations in the Poincaré map that acts on the state vector. Thus, the Newton's method system is of size $n - 1$ in this case. This method is satisfactory in terms of the convergence for the stabilization of unstable periodic orbits and uses Krylov-subspace methods to solve the linear system in each Newton iteration. If the dimension of the unstable manifold is not large compared to that of the stable one, then the linear system solved in each Newton iteration is diagonalizable, and its eigenvalues have a peculiar structure. This linear operator is a monodromy (*Greek* for "a single run around") operator [28] shifted by 1. In this case, most of the eigenvalues (which correspond to the stable manifold) are clustered around the point $(1, 0)$ of the complex plane. Besides, most of the spectrum is separated from the origin (this will be discussed later in this paper). Such an eigenvalue structure ensures good convergence properties for the GMRES method (see [19, Corollary 6.33, p. 217]). Additionally, the period T and the monodromy matrix eigenvalues (used to estimate the linear stability of the limit cycle and the dimension of the unstable manifold) come as a byproduct of the method and require no additional computational work. However, the setup of the method is more difficult than in the case of the standard shooting method. It requires information about the approximate location of the periodic orbit in $\mathbb{R}^n$ to place the correct hyperplane, which must be transversal to the trajectory.

Application of Parallel Computing. There are two levels of parallelism that can be applied. All the above-mentioned methods of stabilization of periodic orbits can be executed in parallel, which means that there is no additional cost due to parallel execution to find a periodic orbit if the original system (1) is already implemented in the parallel algorithm. A more difficult situation arises when the method used to find the cycle is parallelized. A parallel multiple Poincaré shooting method is suggested in [21], where N transversal hyperplanes are applied along the possible cycle trajectory, and each section of the trajectory is stabilized by a separate parallel thread. This requires the use of the invariant-subspace preconditioning method [13] since the clustering of the shifted monodromy matrix eigenvalues is no longer optimal as far as the GMRES convergence properties are concerned. Another successful example of the multiple Poincaré shooting method is given in [29], where it is applied to a thermoacoustic system of size $n = \mathcal{O}(10^3)$ with subspace preconditioning.

A limited number of programs exist to detect and stabilize periodic orbits for large-scale systems. We can mention PDECONT, which can be applied to middle-sized systems, and a new package for bifurcation analysis written in the Julia programming language [25], which can be used for large-scale systems (its capabilities will be tested in the future). These software packages do not offer any options for the deflation of periodic orbits.

The aim of the present study is the application of the deflation method. For this reason, we must consider specific difficulties associated with the parallel implementation. We consider here the Poincaré shooting method since it is more suitable for large-scale dynamical systems, owing to its good convergence properties. The issue of the initial guess (the hookstep) is not discussed here. The following problems must be solved: reformulation of the Poincaré shooting method for the parallel computational architecture; formulation of the deflation method of large-scale periodic problems (such a formulation must include preconditioning); implementation of the Poincaré shooting method and the deflation method in a parallel framework that can be parallelized with respect to both the problem size n and the parallel execution of the deflation process.

The paper is laid out as follows. First, we describe the Poincaré shooting method. Then, we consider a certain modification of the method that allows including the deflation operator and the subspace preconditioning method. The parallel implementation is discussed in the next section, which is followed by the demonstration of the parallel performance results. In the final section, we summarize the contents of the paper and give the conclusions drawn.

2 Poincaré Shooting Method and Preconditioning

Poincaré Shooting Method. The stabilization of periodic solutions in the Poincaré shooting method is achieved by applying the Newton–Raphson method on the return map. Let Π be a hyperplane transversal to the solution trajectory $\gamma \subset \mathbb{M}$, and let $\mathbb{M}$ denote a phase space of (1). Then the Poincaré map is defined as follows:

$$\mathcal{P} \colon \mathcal{V} \subset \Pi \to \Pi. \tag{2}$$

The hyperplane Π can be constructed arbitrarily but must be transversal to the phase trajectory. One of the methods to achieve this consists in finding and fixing a solution component $u_* = u_k(t)$, where $k = \arg\max\limits_{0 \leq j < n} |(u_j)_\tau|$. Once the hyperplane is set, the trajectory γ is traced from the initial point $\mathbf{u}(0) \in \mathcal{V}$ on the hyperplane, where $\mathbf{u}$ is a solution of (1), and the component k of $\mathbf{u}(0)$ is equal to u_*. The normal vector to the hyperplane Π is defined as $\mathbf{n} = (0, \ldots, 1, \ldots, 0)^{\mathsf{T}}$, where 1 is at position k. This setup of the hyperplane differs from the canonical approach (see [22,29]).

The tracing of the trajectory γ is done using an appropriate time-stepping method that can be applied to the solution of the initial value problem for (1) with initial conditions $\mathbf{u}(0) \in \mathcal{V}$. The image of the mapping $\mathcal{P}$ is the closure of all intersections of Π by the trajectory in an appropriate direction, that is, $\gamma \cap \Pi = \{\mathbf{u}(T)\} \subset \Pi, T > 0, (\mathbf{n}, \mathbf{u}_t(T)) > 0$. The intersection can be constructed in different ways. In this paper, the intersection is constructed using the bisection algorithm, which modifies the length of the last time-step interval dt_* in such a manner that $|u_k(t + dt_*) - u_*| < \varepsilon$. The error ε of the bisection is set to be close to the machine precision. Thus, we obtain the period $T = t + dt_*$ of the limit cycle. The vector of the trajectory at the intersection point $\mathbf{u}(T)$ with the plane is defined as $\mathbf{m} = F(\mathbf{u}(T), \lambda) / \|F(\mathbf{u}(T), \lambda)\|$.

The projection operator $\mathrm{P} \colon \Pi \to \mathbb{R}^{n-1}$ is expressed as

$$\mathrm{Pu} := \mathbf{x} = (u_0, u_1, \ldots, u_{k-1}, u_{k+1}, \ldots, u_{n-1})^{\mathsf{T}} \in \mathbb{R}^{n-1}, \tag{3}$$

and the interpolation operator $\mathrm{R} \colon \mathbb{R}^{n-1} \to \Pi$ is given as

$$\mathrm{Rx} = (u_0, u_1, \ldots, u_{k-1}, u_*, u_{k+1}, \ldots, u_{n-1})^{\mathsf{T}} \in \mathbb{R}^n. \tag{4}$$

Then, the fixed point of the Poincaré mapping in the $(n-1)$-dimensional space is expressed as

$$\mathcal{R}(\mathbf{x}) - \mathbf{x} = \mathbf{0}, \tag{5}$$

where the operator $\mathcal{R}$ is formally defined as the composition of operators $\mathcal{R} := \mathrm{P} \circ \mathcal{P} \circ \mathrm{R}$. The Newton–Raphson method is used to minimize the residual vector $\mathbf{r} = \mathcal{R}(\mathbf{x}) - \mathbf{x} = \mathbf{u}(T) - \mathbf{u}(0)$ by introducing the correction $\delta \mathbf{x}$ from $\mathcal{R}(\mathbf{x} + \delta \mathbf{x}) - (\mathbf{x} + \delta \mathbf{x}) = \mathbf{0}$. By means of the first-order expansion near the point $\mathbf{x}$, we obtain the following linear system, which must be solved to find the correction:

$$(\mathrm{E} - \mathrm{M}) \delta \mathbf{x} = \mathcal{R}(\mathbf{x}) - \mathbf{x}, \tag{6}$$

where E is the identity matrix, and $\mathrm{M} := \partial \mathcal{R}(\mathbf{x}) / \partial \mathbf{x}$ is called the monodromy matrix. The correction is applied to the solution by Newton's method iterations until $\|\mathbf{r}\| \leq \varepsilon_1$, where ε_1 is the predefined tolerance. The differentiation of the composite operator $\mathcal{R}$ results in different projection and interpolation operators, which operate with the vector of perturbations on the hyperplane. The interpolation operator changes u_* to 0 in (4), and the projection is changed by the oblique projection along the vector $\mathbf{m} \colon \mathrm{P}^{\mathrm{obl}} \mathbf{u} = \mathrm{P}(\mathbf{u} - (\mathbf{u}, \mathbf{n})\mathbf{m}/m_k)$.

For a dynamical system with large n, one cannot form the matrix M explicitly. It is usually available as a matrix-vector product via the integration of the vector $\delta \mathbf{x}$ along the trajectory γ as

$$(\mathrm{M}\,\delta \mathbf{x}) := \mathrm{P}^{\mathrm{obl}} e^{\int_0^T \mathrm{J}(\mathbf{y}(t))\,dt}\,\delta \mathbf{y}(0), \tag{7}$$

where $\delta \mathbf{y}(0) = \mathrm{R}\,\delta \mathbf{x}$, and $\mathbf{y}(0) = \mathrm{Rx}$. Here, $\mathrm{J}(\mathbf{u}) := \partial F(\mathbf{u}) / \partial \mathbf{u}$ is the Jacobi matrix of the original system (1). The integration is performed using the same time-stepping method appropriate for (1). The result of the integration in (7) can be included in the Krylov-type subspace linear solver, which only requires the matrix-vector application $\delta \mathbf{x} - (\mathrm{M}\,\delta \mathbf{x})$. A single iteration of the linear solver requires time integration along the trajectory γ, hence it is desirable to reduce the number of iterations.

Preconditioning. It is known [28] that the eigenvalues of the monodromy matrix M for stable limit cycles are clustered around the origin of the complex plane, and only a small number of eigenvalues are located farther from the origin but inside the unit circle. The eigenvalue corresponding to the direction $\mathbf{u}_t(0)$ is excluded from the matrix thanks to the projection operator onto the $(n-1)$-dimensional space. The eigenvalues of the matrix $\mathtt{A} := \mathtt{E} - \mathtt{M}$ are the eigenvalues of M shifted by 1, that is, for its spectrum, we have $\mathrm{sp}(\mathtt{A}) = 1 - \mathrm{sp}(\mathtt{M})$. The resulting matrix is diagonalizable, i.e., $\mathtt{A} = \mathtt{X}\Lambda\mathtt{X}^{-1}$. In this case, the spectrum $\mathrm{sp}(\mathtt{A})$ is located in a circle $B_r(1,0)$ of radius $r < 1$; therefore, the origin of the complex plane is excluded from the circle $B_r(1,0)$. We can use the Corollary 6.33 [19, p. 217] and show that the reduction rate of the residual of the GMRES method after q iterations satisfies the estimate

$$\frac{\|\mathbf{r}_q\|}{\|\mathbf{r}_0\|} \leq \left(\frac{r}{1 + \sqrt{1-r}}\right)^q k_2(\mathtt{X}),$$

where $k_2(\mathtt{X})$ is the condition number of the matrix X. The matrix A is close to the identity matrix for stable limit cycles [28]; thus, $k_2(\mathtt{X}) = \mathcal{O}(1)$. In this case, it only takes a few GMRES iterations to obtain a substantial reduction of the residual without a preconditioner. For example, if $r = 0.8$, then the residual reduction for $q = 10$ is about $1 \cdot 10^{-3}$.

If we try to stabilize an unstable limit cycle, then the convergence of the linear system can degrade. In this case, we can apply the invariant-subspace preconditioning method [13, 29]. It is convenient to move all spread eigenvalues (corresponding to the unstable manifold of the limit cycle) closer to the point $(1,0)$ of the complex plane. The unstable part of the spectrum lies outside the circle $B_1(1,0)$ and can be efficiently captured by the Arnoldi process in the Implicitly Restarted Arnoldi method (IRAm), which is tuned to find eigenvalues with a large module (see [20]). Let the size of the reprojected invariant subspace be fixed and equal to l. Then, the partial Schur decomposition of the matrix A is expressed as $\mathtt{AU} = \mathtt{US}$, where U is a matrix of size $(n-1) \times l$ constructed with orthonormal column vectors, and S is an upper triangular matrix of size $l \times l$. The application of the IRAm yields the decomposition $\mathtt{AV} = \mathtt{VH}$, where V is a matrix of size $(n-1) \times l$ constructed with Krylov orthonormal vectors, and H is an upper Hessenberg matrix (see [20, p. 166]). Then, the matrix S is obtained through a QR iteration: $\mathtt{HQ} = \mathtt{QS}$ and $\mathtt{U} = \mathtt{VQ}$. Note that QR iterations used to produce the preconditioning matrix (by a series of Givens rotations) are computationally stable (see [13]).

If the Arnoldi process does not break down, then the matrix S is not singular, and the inverse $\mathtt{A}^{-1}\mathtt{U} = \mathtt{US}^{-1}$ exists. The preconditioner is defined in such a manner that it has l eigenvalues close to the l largest eigenvalues of the matrix A in the invariant subspace and unit eigenvalues in all directions orthogonal to the invariant subspace. Such a preconditioner is explicitly defined as

$$\mathtt{G} = \mathtt{USU}^\mathsf{T} + \left(\mathtt{E} - \mathtt{UU}^\mathsf{T}\right). \tag{8}$$

The inverse of (8) maps all eigenvalues in the invariant l-dimensional subspace to $(1, 0)$ and can be explicitly derived as

$$G^{-1} = US^{-1}U^\mathsf{T} + (E - UU^\mathsf{T}). \tag{9}$$

The application of (9) is efficient in the form of the right preconditioner since $AUS^{-1}U^\mathsf{T} = USS^{-1}U^\mathsf{T}$. Then, the composition AG^{-1} can be explicitly written as

$$AG^{-1} = UU^\mathsf{T} + A(E - UU^\mathsf{T}). \tag{10}$$

The application of the right preconditioner to the system $Ax = b$ is done in two steps. First, the system is expressed as $AG^{-1}Gx = b$, or $AG^{-1}y = b$. After the preconditioned system converges, the original solution is found as $x = G^{-1}y$. The residual of the preconditioned system is the same as that of the original one. The application of the matrix-preconditioner composition (10) can be done in a matrix-free fashion (without the explicit definition of the matrix A) as long as matrices U and S are explicitly available. Nevertheless, the application of the preconditioner is worth it only if the cost of its expression and application is lower than the convergence speed of the unpreconditioned system. In practical terms, we usually execute one or two iterations of the IRAm and, after that, use this information to express the preconditioner with $l \leq 20$.

3   Deflation

Preliminary Operations. Let us assume that we have found a periodic orbit. This means that, up to the desired tolerance, we have found a fixed point of (5) for the particular hyperplane Π corresponding to some u_{k_1} (denoted with Π_{k_1}). It is impractical to store the periodic orbit as the converged trajectory γ as this would require too much memory. Instead, the periodic orbit can be defined by the tuple $\langle u, k_1, T \rangle$, which contains the interpolated solution fixed point, the coordinate number, and the cycle period. Information on the time-stepping method and desired tolerance settings are also added to the tuple in the practical implementation. The trajectory γ of the periodic orbit can be restored from this tuple by executing the time-stepping process once again. If the parameters of the time-stepping method are not changed, then the periodic orbit is restored to the desired tolerance. In practice, one usually executes the same Poincaré shooting with Newton's method applied to the initial guess and the hyperplane data taken from the tuple. This ensures the geometric convergence of the iterative process since the initial guess is very close to the solutions even for unstable cycles or after a change in time-stepping parameters. We shall denote such a periodic trajectory restored from the tuple k_1 with γ_{k_1}.

Once some converged periodic orbits are stored, one wants to use this information to avoid the convergence of the Poincaré shooting method to the already obtained solutions. To do so, one needs to find possible intersections of the known periodic orbits with the new section, that is, find $\gamma_l \cap \Pi_{k_*}$, where k_* is the coordinate of the new section. This is done by executing the bisection algorithm while obtaining the γ_l periodic trajectory for all l. The resulting intersection point of the known periodic orbit with the new hyperplane is denoted with $\mathcal{I}(j, k_*)$, where j is the tuple number and $j = 1, \ldots, N$, with N being the number of stored tuples. If a new intersection point is found, it can be projected as $\mathtt{PI}(j, k_*)$ using the new hyperplane. Thus, this process yields solutions for the fixed-point problem (5) for the same j-th periodic orbit but relative to the new section, defined by k_*.

Deflation Operator. Following [8], we can define the deflation operator relative to the new section coordinate k_*, namely

$$M\left(\mathbf{x}, k_*\right) := \frac{1}{N} \left(\sum_{j=1}^{N} \|\mathbf{x} - \mathtt{PI}(j, k_*)\|_2^{-p} + \sigma \right) \mathsf{E}, \tag{11}$$

where σ and p are parameters. In the current paper, $\sigma = 1$ and $p = 2$. The constructed deflation operator (11) is applied to the original system (5) in the same way as in [8]:

$$M\left(\mathbf{x}, k_*\right)\left(\mathcal{R}(\mathbf{x}) - \mathbf{x}\right) = \mathbf{0}. \tag{12}$$

The inclusion of the correction $\mathbf{x} + \delta\mathbf{x}$ results in the system

$$M\left(\mathbf{x} + \delta\mathbf{x}, k_*\right)\left(\mathcal{R}(\mathbf{x} + \delta\mathbf{x}) - \mathbf{x} - \delta\mathbf{x}\right) = \mathbf{0}. \tag{13}$$

The first order expansion near the point $\mathbf{x}$ yields a linear system for the unknown correction, similar to (6):

$$(M\mathsf{A} + \mathbf{f}\mathbf{v}^\mathsf{T})\,\delta\mathbf{x} = -M\mathbf{f}, \tag{14}$$

where $M := M(\mathbf{x}, k_*)$, $\mathbf{f} = \mathcal{R}(\mathbf{x}) - \mathbf{x}$, and $\mathbf{f}\mathbf{v}^\mathsf{T}$ is the Jacobian matrix $(\partial M(\mathbf{x})/\partial\mathbf{x})$ of the deflation operator with

$$\mathbf{v}(\mathbf{x})^\mathsf{T} = -\frac{p}{N} \sum_{j=1}^{N} \frac{1}{\|\mathbf{x} - \mathtt{PI}(j, k_*)\|_2^{p+2}} \left(\mathbf{x} - \mathtt{PI}(j, k_*)\right)^\mathsf{T}$$

(see [8] for the corresponding derivation). System (14) is solved in each iteration of Newton's method to correct the solution as $\mathbf{x} \leftarrow \mathbf{x} + \delta\mathbf{x}$ until $\|\mathbf{f}\| \leq \varepsilon_1$.

The solution of the linear system (14) can be carried out in a matrix-free manner since the deflation operator M is a number multiplied by the identity matrix, and the whole system is a rank-one update. The last component in the augmented matrix is expressed as $\mathbf{f}(\mathbf{v}^\mathsf{T}\delta\mathbf{x})$. A more complicated situation arises when one wants to apply preconditioning. The same invariant subspace preconditioner (9) can be used. However, the spread of eigenvalues is no longer optimal for the IRAm to converge fast due to the rank-one updated system. Alternatively, we apply the same trick we did in [8] with the Sherman–Morrison formula [23]. In this case, the inverse (9) is computed for the undeflated matrix A using the same Arnoldi process and incomplete Schur decomposition.

Once the inverse preconditioner (G^{-1}) is computed, we apply the Sherman–Morrison formula as follows:

$$\mathsf{K}^{-1} := (M\mathsf{G} + \mathbf{f}\mathbf{v}^\mathsf{T})^{-1} = \mathsf{G}^{-1}M^{-1} - \frac{\mathsf{G}^{-1}M^{-1}\mathbf{f}\mathbf{v}^\mathsf{T}\mathsf{G}^{-1}M^{-1}}{1 + \mathbf{v}^\mathsf{T}\mathsf{G}^{-1}M^{-1}\mathbf{f}}, \tag{15}$$

which is the preconditioner of the matrix $M\mathsf{A} + \mathbf{f}\mathbf{v}^\mathsf{T}$. Note that if $\mathsf{A}\mathsf{G}^{-1} = \mathsf{E}$, then $(M\mathsf{A} + \mathbf{f}\mathbf{v}^\mathsf{T})\mathsf{K}^{-1} = \mathsf{E}$. The right preconditioned system (14) is expressed as

$$- (M\mathsf{A} + \mathbf{f}\mathbf{v}^\mathsf{T})\,\mathsf{K}^{-1}\underbrace{(\mathsf{K}\,\delta\mathbf{x})}_{\delta\mathbf{y}} = -M\mathbf{f}. \tag{16}$$

The application of (15) in (16) is accomplished in a matrix-free manner as follows: $\mathbf{z} = \mathsf{G}^{-1}M^{-1}\mathbf{f}$, $\delta\mathbf{z} = \mathsf{G}^{-1}M^{-1}\delta\mathbf{y}$, hence $\mathsf{K}^{-1}\delta\mathbf{y} = \delta\mathbf{z} - (\mathbf{z}(\mathbf{v}^\mathsf{T}\delta\mathbf{z}))/(1 + \mathbf{v}^\mathsf{T}\mathbf{z})$. Then, the preconditioned vector is applied to the original system. After the iterations converge to the desired residual reduction, the resulting vector $\delta\mathbf{x}$ is restored by applying the inverse preconditioner (15) to the result. The resulting deflated system (12) possesses the same properties as the deflated system used in [8,9] to find distinct stationary solutions. This means that if a solution is found during the Newton–Raphson iterations, then it is a new solution that has not been included in the deflation operator yet. Then, a new tuple is formed and is included in the deflation operator.

4   The Parallelization

As mentioned in the introduction, parallelization can be carried out in two ways. The first option is just a parallel execution of the time-stepping method for the original system (1). Then, the whole algorithm is symmetric with respect to the underlying parallelism and has negligible cost compared to the simple execution of the parallel time-stepping method. The second option is to use the multiple Poincaré shooting method, as described in [29]. However, this approach requires the usage of the preconditioner even for stable periodic orbits, and that is what we want to avoid. The third option is related to deflation, i.e., we can execute the deflation process in parallel. This accelerates the search for new periodic orbits and allows avoiding the convergence to already obtained ones. The implementation of this third option is discussed here.

Let N_p be the total number of MPI processes spawned. Each group of Q_p processes is executed to solve the system (14) or (16) in parallel. The groups take the form of M_p sets of jobs and one control process, and hence $N_p = Q_p M_p + 1$. The master-slave paradigm is used for M_p block slave processes and one master process (see Fig. 1).

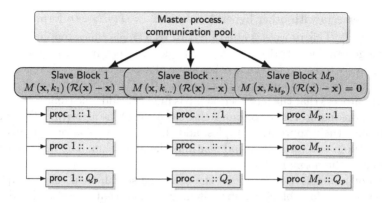

Fig. 1. Parallel architecture scheme using master process-slave blocks. Processes are grouped into M_p blocks, and each block contains Q_p processes to solve the main problem.

An additional abstraction layer was added to the MPI interface forming a block link and an abstract communication pool. This block link allows building processes into separate blocks. Inside each block, the numbering of the processes is unique, which makes it possible to execute the code as a standalone application that uses Q_p MPI processes; each block link is addressed as $block\_number :: process\_number$ in Fig. 1. The communication pool (as a single master process) implements the data exchange and synchronization (implemented via the MPI C functions MPI_Comm_group and MPI_Comm_split, and virtual topology functions) between the M_p blocks, each containing Q_p processes, by mapping data from the j-th block to the l-th block as $(j :: q) \rightarrow (l :: q), \forall q \in [1, \ldots, Q_p]$. The master process only sends controlling data to block links, while the exchange of bulky data is performed in a block-to-block manner. A current limitation is that all blocks contain the same number of processes. This abstraction layer is implemented in C++ and uses CUDA-aware MPI.

Each slave block has its problem (all of the same size n) to solve, with section coordinate k_j (not necessarily unique), which it uses to find a fixed point of the return map in parallel with Q_p processes. The deflation process is organized via the master process. In the normal state, the master process awaits the convergence or the termination flags. The termination flag is sent either by the user or by each slave block process as soon as all deflation attempts finish. The master process awaits the confirmation of the termination flag from all slave blocks before terminating the job or terminates everything if the user signals the flag.

Once the slave block j converges, it sends the convergence flag to the master process, and the slave block waits for the reply. As soon as the master process receives the convergence flag from the slave block j, it requests a pair of hyperplane coordinates from all other slave blocks (pair of variables $\langle k_l, u_l \rangle$). Once all pairs are received, the master process sends all pairs to the slave block j and waits for it to send an "all done" signal. The slave block j restores the periodic orbit and finds its intersects with other hyperplanes, as $\mathbf{u}_l = \mathcal{I}(j, k_l)$, to form the tuples $\{\langle \mathbf{u}_l, k_l, T \rangle\}_{l=1}^{M_p}$. This process is almost as fast as a single time-stepping loop over the converged periodic trajectory γ. The tuples are sent from the slave block j asynchronously to each one of the other slave blocks as soon as it is ready. If the intersection is null, then an empty flag is sent. After that, the slave block j signals the master process that the intersection job is finished, adds the tuple $<\mathbf{u}_j, k_j, T>$ to its deflation operator, and continues the execution of the algorithm. Other slave blocks receive their appropriate tuples, add them to the deflation operator (if a nonempty tuple was returned), and continue the algorithm. The master process is returned to the normal state.

If two or more slave blocks send the converge signal, then they are queued according to the slave block number. It may happen that a new deflated tuple is sent to the slave block just before it converges to the same solution. Then, a singular-matrix signal may arise. To avoid that, a nearly converged slave block verifies the value of M in (11) before applying the tuple to the deflator. If $M > 10.0$, then the algorithm in this slave block is restarted and the tuple is added to the deflator.

The implementation of this parallel paradigm allows one to use a heterogeneous computational architecture efficiently. The slave blocks can be organized over different computational models (e.g., some slave blocks can use GPUs or Xeon Phi co-processors, while other slave blocks can use CPUs). Block data exchange is only necessary when a periodic orbit is found and the deflation operator is updated. The code for the parallel deflation process is written in C++ and CUDA C++ for the solution of large-scale problems on GPUs. The call from the deflated Poincaré shooting algorithm to lower-level Newton–Krylov methods is performed in an abstract way using template classes.

5   Results

First, we present the results of the test problem that was used to perform benchmark verifications and examine the parallel efficiency. Next, the parallel efficiency was measured under different approaches with symmetric parallelism against deflation parallelism. All problems were tested on the following hardware: Intel Xeon E5-2697V2 Ivy Bridge with up to six K40 Nvidia GPUs installed in a chassis.

Test Problem. The problem of detection and stabilization of unstable periodic orbits in a 2D Kolmogorov flow served as a test problem. The particular choice of parameters gives rise to the following problem: the domain is the torus $\Omega :=$ $[0; 2\pi] \times [0; 2\pi]$, i.e., all functions are periodic on the domain boundary. The velocity vector function $\mathbf{U}$ and the pressure scalar function $\mathbf{P}$ obey the Navier–Stokes system of equations, namely

$$\partial \mathbf{U}/\partial t + (\mathbf{U} \cdot \nabla)\,\mathbf{U} = -\nabla P + R^{-1}\,\triangle \mathbf{U} + (\sin{(4y)}\,; 0)^{\mathsf{T}}, \tag{17}$$
$$\nabla \cdot \mathbf{U} = 0,$$

where R is the Reynolds number, which is used as a parameter λ in (1). We use the Galerkin projection method with complex exponential basis functions to derive the dynamical system from (17) in the form of (1), explicitly given as

$$\overbrace{\mathbf{u}_t = -\mathbb{P}[\mathbb{N}(\mathbf{u})] + R^{-1}\mathbb{D}\mathbf{u} + \mathbf{f}}^{F(\mathbf{u},R)}, \tag{18}$$
$$\mathbf{u}(0) = \mathbf{u}_0 \text{ s.t. } \nabla \cdot \mathbf{u}_0 = 0,$$

where $\mathbf{u}$ is a time-dependent discrete vector representing velocity vector function, $\mathbb{D}$ is the Laplace operator (a diagonal matrix), $\mathbf{f}$ is the external divergence-free forcing vector, $\mathbb{N}$ is a nonlinear operator (2/3 de-aliasing pseudo-spectral scheme), and $\mathbb{P}$ is the projection operator onto the space of divergence-free vector functions, formally defined as $\mathbb{P} := \mathrm{id} - \nabla \triangle^{-1}\nabla\cdot$. Thus, the pressure is eliminated from the system (18).

To perform the time-stepping of (18), we used the explicit exponential third-order Runge–Kutta scheme [11, Table 1, p. 172] with automatic selection of the time step, where the diffusion operator $\mathbb{D}$ is treated analytically. The setup of the problem is similar to the one considered in [3]. To drive the dynamical system into the possible basins of attraction, problem (18) was executed for 10^6 time steps, starting from the random divergence-free vector $\mathbf{u}_0$. Then, we recorded another 10^5 time steps and selected the coordinates of the hyperplanes according to the description given in Sect. 2. In the test, we set $R = 40$ in (18) intending to benchmark the results against a detailed analysis performed in [3] for the same Reynolds number. To minimize the number of periodic orbits, we removed the translation invariance of the system (18) by considering pure imaginary basis functions.

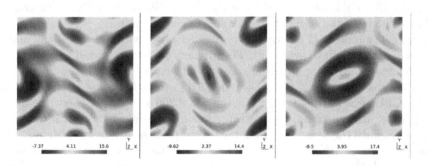

Fig. 2. Visualization of different periodic orbits using curl isosurfaces (the positive value corresponds to a CCW rotation), $T = \{5.380, 2.830, 2.917\}$ (from left to right)

The three obtained solutions are portrayed in Fig. 2. The solutions are identical to the ones obtained in [3, Table 2]. To test the performance of the deflation method, we computed a preconditioner (15) using 10 basis vectors in the orthogonal subspace. The convergence results both with and without preconditioning are shown in Fig. 3.

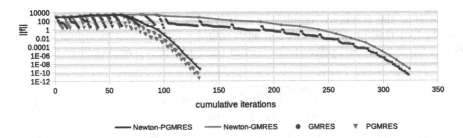

Fig. 3. Convergence of a periodic orbit for $R = 80$ using the deflated Newton–Raphson method and the GMRES method both with and without the subspace preconditioner

We can note better convergence of the GMRES method when using the subspace preconditioner given (15). However, the wall time of convergence was improved only by a factor of 1.5 due to the high cost of computation of the subspace preconditioner.

Parallel Efficiency. We compared two implementations, namely symmetric and deflation parallelism, assuming Q_p fixed, i.e., Q_p processes were used to solve the problem in the symmetric variant. The acceleration is expected to be linear and equal to M_p for perfect deflation parallelism. We tested multithreaded-CPU and multiple-GPU implementations. This was possible thanks to the abstract manner the code was implemented, that is, it was only necessary to switch the memory manager, as well as the matrix and vector operation classes from the CPU to the GPU implementation, and vice versa. We made use of the Fast Fourier Transform (FFT) library, which is used to solve (18) through the abstraction layer using either the CUFFT library for GPUs or the FFTW library for CPUs. The graphs in Fig. 4 illustrate the results for several values of Q_p and M_p.

For each number Q_p of symmetric parallel processors, we found the maximum number of periodic orbits (6). The problem size was adjusted in such a way that the underlying computational core was efficiently loaded. The problem size for GPUs was 1024×1024 for $Q_p = 1$ and 2048×2048 for $Q_p = 2$. The problem size for CPUs was 64×64 for $Q_p = 2$ and 256×256 for $Q_p = 4$. Next, the deflation parallel implementation was executed using M_p slave blocks with the same value of Q_p until the same maximum number of periodic orbits was obtained. We defined the acceleration as the ratio of the wall times needed to solve the same problem with the symmetric and the deflation parallel implementations. Some results showed superlinear acceleration due to the larger hyperplane parametrization space in the deflation parallel implementation. The test was repeated for different random initial conditions to yield statistically significant data for the deflation parallel implementation.

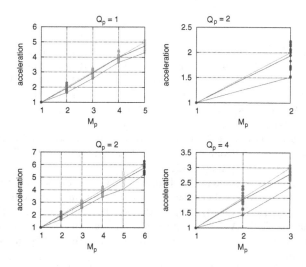

Fig. 4. Parallel acceleration of both the symmetric and the deflation implementations on multiple GPUs (top) and CPU threads (bottom). The circles represent data corresponding to the solution of an independent problem with randomized initial conditions. Five GPUs and twelve CPU threads were used. Magenta, green, and light blue lines correspond to the mean, the worst, and the reference linear accelerations, respectively. (Color figure online)

6   Conclusions

We presented a new variant of the parallel deflation method for finding periodic orbits. It is based on the Poincaré shooting method [22] and uses deflation operators [8,9] for large-scale systems. We introduced a new deflation operator that extensively uses the idea of the Poincaré return map to construct a set of deflated solutions in the fixed-point problem of the return map. Furthermore, we included the invariant subspace preconditioner in the deflator, thereby accelerating the convergence of the deflated linear system in each Newton iteration, while finding new unstable periodic solutions with nontrivial unstable manifolds.

We developed a new parallel implementation of the method, which relies on the master-slave parallel paradigm to carry out the deflation process in parallel. The measurements of the acceleration confirmed that the suggested parallel method can efficiently accelerate the problem solution, having almost linear mean acceleration. The particular acceleration depends on the problem and selected initial data used for the stabilization of periodic orbits.

The developed software will be incorporated into the deflated pseudo arc-length continuation method to perform research in the field of turbulence.

References

1. Aoki, K.: Stable and unstable periodic orbits in the one-dimensional lattice φ 4theory. Phys. Rev. E **94**(4) (2016). https://doi.org/10.1103/physreve.94.042209
2. Boghosian, B.M., Fazendeiro, L.M., Lätt, J., Tang, H., Coveney, P.V.: New variational principles for locating periodic orbits of differential equations. Philos. Trans. Roy. Soc. A Math. Phys. Eng. Sci. **369**(1944), 2211–2218 (2011). https://doi.org/10.1098/rsta.2011.0066
3. Chandler, G.J., Kerswell, R.R.: Invariant recurrent solutions embedded in a turbulent two-dimensional Kolmogorov flow. J. Fluid Mech. **722**, 554–595 (2013). https://doi.org/10.1017/jfm.2013.122
4. Choe, C.U., Jang, H., Flunkert, V., Dahms, T., Hövel, P., Schll, E.: Stabilization of periodic orbits near a subcritical Hopf bifurcation in delay-coupled networks. Dyn. Syst. **28**(1), 15–33 (2013). https://doi.org/10.1080/14689367.2012.730500
5. Dutt, P., Sharma, R.K.: Analysis of periodic and quasi-periodic orbits in the Earth-Moon system. J. Guidance Control Dyn. **33**(3), 1010–1017 (2010). https://doi.org/10.2514/1.46400
6. Evstigneev, N., Magnitskii, N., Ryabkov, O.: Numerical bifurcation analysis in 3D Kolmogorov flow problem. J. Appl. Nonlinear Dyn. **8**(4), 595–619 (2019). https://doi.org/10.5890/jand.2019.12.007
7. Evstigneev, N., Magnitskii, N., Sidorov, S.: Nonlinear dynamics of laminar-turbulent transition in three dimensional Rayleigh-Benard convection. Commun. Nonlinear Sci. Numer. Simul. **15**(10), 2851–2859 (2010). https://doi.org/10.1016/j.cnsns.2009.10.022
8. Evstigneev, N.M.: On the convergence acceleration and parallel implementation of continuation in disconnected Bifurcation diagrams for large-scale problems. In: Sokolinsky, L., Zymbler, M. (eds.) PCT 2019. CCIS, vol. 1063, pp. 122–138. Springer, Cham (2019). https://doi.org/10.1007/978-3-030-28163-2_9
9. Farrell, P.E., Birkisson, Á., Funke, S.W.: Deflation techniques for finding distinct solutions of nonlinear partial differential equations. SIAM J. Sci. Comput. **37**(4), A2026–A2045 (2015). https://doi.org/10.1137/140984798
10. Kalantonis, V., Perdios, E., Perdiou, A., Ragos, O., Vrahatis, M.: Deflation techniques for the determination of periodic solutions of a certain period. Astrophys. Space Sci. **288**(4), 591–599 (2003). https://doi.org/10.1023/b:astr.0000005101.83773.0e
11. Luan, V.T., Ostermann, A.: Explicit exponential Runge-Kutta methods of high order for parabolic problems. J. Comput. Appl. Math. **256**, 168–179 (2014). https://doi.org/10.1016/j.cam.2013.07.027
12. Lucas, D., Kerswell, R.: Sustaining processes from recurrent flows in body-forced turbulence. J. Fluid Mech. **817** (2017). https://doi.org/10.1017/jfm.2017.97
13. Lust, K., Roose, D.: An adaptive Newton-Picard algorithm with subspace iteration for computing periodic solutions. SIAM J. Sci. Comput. **19**(4), 1188–1209 (1998). https://doi.org/10.1137/s1064827594277673
14. Miino, Y., Ito, D., Asahara, H., Kousaka, T., Ueta, T.: A general method to stabilize unstable periodic orbits for switched dynamical systems with a periodically moving threshold. Int. J. Circ. Theory Appl. **46**(12), 2380–2393 (2018). https://doi.org/10.1002/cta.2573
15. Mishra, P.K., Herault, J., Fauve, S., Verma, M.K.: Dynamics of reversals and condensates in two-dimensional Kolmogorov flows. Phys. Rev. E **91**(5) (2015). https://doi.org/10.1103/physreve.91.053005

16. Net, M., Sánchez, J.: Continuation of bifurcations of periodic orbits for large-scale systems. SIAM J. Appl. Dyn. Syst. **14**(2), 674–698 (2015). https://doi.org/10.1137/140981010
17. Rodríguez-Méndez, V., Ser-Giacomi, E., Hernández-García, E.: Clustering coefficient and periodic orbits in flow networks. Chaos Interdisc. J. Nonlinear Sci. **27**(3), 035803 (2017). https://doi.org/10.1063/1.4971787
18. Roose, D., Lust, K., Champneys, A., Spence, A.: A Newton-Picard shooting method for computing periodic solutions of large-scale dynamical systems. Chaos, Solitons Fractals **5**(10), 1913–1925 (1995). https://doi.org/10.1016/0960-0779(95)90873-q
19. Saad, Y.: Iterative Methods for Sparse Linear Systems. Society for Industrial and Applied Mathematics (2003). https://doi.org/10.1137/1.9780898718003
20. Saad, Y.: Numerical Methods for Large Eigenvalue Problems. Society for Industrial and Applied Mathematics (2011). https://doi.org/10.1137/1.9781611970739
21. Sánchez, J., Net, M.: On the multiple shooting continuation of periodic orbits by Newton-Krylov methods. Int. J. Bifurcat. Chaos **20**(01), 43–61 (2010). https://doi.org/10.1142/s0218127410025399
22. Sánchez, J., Net, M., Garcia-Archilla, B., Simó, C.: Newton-Krylov continuation of periodic orbits for Navier-Stokes flows. J. Comput. Phys. **201**(1), 13–33 (2004). https://doi.org/10.1016/j.jcp.2004.04.018
23. Sherman, J., Morrison, W.J.: Adjustment of an inverse matrix corresponding to a change in one element of a given matrix. Ann. Math. Stat. **21**(1), 124–127 (1950). https://doi.org/10.1214/aoms/1177729893
24. Socolar, J.E.S., Sukow, D.W., Gauthier, D.J.: Stabilizing unstable periodic orbits in fast dynamical systems. Phys. Rev. E **50**(4), 3245–3248 (1994). https://doi.org/10.1103/physreve.50.3245
25. Veltz, R.: BifurcationKit.jl (2020). https://hal.archives-ouvertes.fr/hal-02902346
26. Viswanath, D.: Recurrent motions within plane Couette turbulence. J. Fluid Mech. **580**, 339–358 (2007). https://doi.org/10.1017/s0022112007005459
27. Wang, H., Zhang, H., Wang, Z., Chen, Q.: Finite-time stabilization of periodic orbits for under-actuated biped walking with hybrid zero dynamics. Commun. Nonlinear Sci. Numer. Simul. **80**, 104949 (2020). https://doi.org/10.1016/j.cnsns.2019.104949
28. Wang, X., Hale, J.K.: On monodromy matrix computation. Comput. Methods Appl. Mech. Eng. **190**(18–19), 2263–2275 (2001). https://doi.org/10.1016/s0045-7825(00)00243-7
29. Waugh, I., Illingworth, S., Juniper, M.: Matrix-free continuation of limit cycles for bifurcation analysis of large thermoacoustic systems. J. Comput. Phys. **240**, 225–247 (2013). https://doi.org/10.1016/j.jcp.2012.12.034

Parallel Computations for Solving Multicriteria Mixed-Integer Optimization Problems

Victor Gergel[✉] and Evgeniy Kozinov

Lobachevsky State University of Nizhny Novgorod, Nizhny Novgorod, Russia
gergel@unn.ru, evgeny.kozinov@itmm.unn.ru

Abstract. The paper discusses a new approach to solving computation-ally time-consuming multicriteria optimization problems in which some variable parameters can only take on discrete values. Under the proposed approach, the solution of mixed-integer optimization problems is reduced to solving a family of optimization problems where only continuous parameters are used. All problems of the family are solved simultaneously in time-shared mode, where the optimization problem for the next global search iteration is selected adaptively, taking into account the search information obtained in the course of the calculations. The suggested algorithms enable parallel computing on high-performance computing systems. The computational experiments confirm that the proposed approach can significantly reduce the computation volume and time required for solving complex multicriteria mixed-integer optimization problems.

Keywords: Multicriteria optimization · Mixed-integer optimization problems · Methods of criteria scalarization · Global optimization · Search information · Parallel computing · Computational experiment

1 Introduction

Multicriteria optimization (MCO) problems arise whenever optimal decisions need to be made during the development of complex technical devices and systems. The scale of demand for MCO problems determines the high intensity of research in this area (see, for example, the monographs [6, 8, 26–28] and reviews of scientific and practical results in this area [19, 22, 25, 42]).

Usually, the solution to an MCO problem is a set of efficient (non-dominated) decisions which cannot be improved under some criteria without deteriorating the efficiency under some other criteria. The definition of the whole set of efficient decisions (the Pareto set) may, on the one hand, require a large amount of computation and, on the other, may be redundant as the analysis of a large number of efficient decisions may require a significant effort from the person who makes the decision (the decision maker, DM). Thus, it may be practically

ⓒ Springer Nature Switzerland AG 2021
L. Sokolinsky and M. Zymbler (Eds.): PCT 2021, CCIS 1437, pp. 92–107, 2021.
https://doi.org/10.1007/978-3-030-81691-9_7

justified to find only a relatively small set of efficient decisions that can be formed according to the optimality requirements defined by the DM.

By restricting the set of efficient decisions to be computed, one can achieve a noticeable reduction in the number of computations required. However, efficiency criteria may be complex, *multiextremal*, and calculating the values of these criteria can prove *computationally demanding*. Besides, some variables may only take on discrete values. In such cases, MCO problems involve a **significant computational complexity**, which can only be overcome by using high-performance supercomputer systems.

Many different approaches have been proposed for solving MCO problems (see, for example, [4,6,25,41]. Most commonly, various methods based on the reduction of the vector criterion to a particular scalar function are used [8,9]. The number of works concerned with multicriteria mixed-integer problems is however more limited; in most cases, the issues of discrete parameter analysis are considered in connection with scalar optimization problems (see, for example, reviews [3,5]). The widely used deterministic methods for solving problems of this class are usually based on either the Branch-and-Bound [2] or the Branch-and-Reduce approaches [40]. Several meta-heuristic and genetic algorithms are also known and are based, in one way or another, on the random search concept [7,31].

This paper presents the results of a study concerned with the development of highly effective parallel methods of multicriteria optimization making use of all the search information obtained throughout computations [13,16,17]. A new contribution to this research field is the development of an approach for solving MCO problems in which some of the varied parameters can only take on discrete values. The suggested approach reduces the solution of mixed-integer optimization problems to a family of optimization problems where only continuous parameters are used. All problems of the family are solved simultaneously in time-shared mode, where the selection of the optimization problem for the next iteration of the global search is performed adaptively, taking into account the search information obtained in the course of computations. The developed algorithms enable efficient parallel computing on high-performance computing systems.

The rest of the paper is structured as follows. In Sect. 2, we statement of multicriteria optimization problems, present a minimax scheme for scalarization of the vector efficiency criterion, and introduce the concept of multistage solution for multicriteria optimization problems. In Sect. 3, we describe the proposed approach based on the reduction of mixed-integer optimization problems to the solution of a family of optimization problems using only continuous parameters. In that section, we also describe a dimensionality reduction scheme by which multidimensional optimization problems can be reduced to one-dimensional global search problems. Section 4 presents a parallel algorithm for solving multicriteria mixed-integer optimization problems under of the proposed approach. Section 5 contains the results of numerical experiments that confirm that the approach we propose is promising. In the Conclusions section, we discuss the results obtained and outline possible directions for future research.

2   Problems of Multicriteria Mixed-Integer Optimization

The problem of multicriteria mixed-integer optimization (MCOmix) can be expressed as follows

$$f(y, u) \rightarrow \min, \ y \in D, \ u \in U, \tag{1}$$

where $f(y, u) = (f_1(y, u), f_2(y, u), \ldots, f_s(y, u))$ is the vector criterion of efficiency, in which the varied parameters belong to two different types:

- continuous parameters $y = (y_1, y_2, \ldots, y_n)$, whose domain of possible values is represented by an N-dimensional hyperparallelepiped,

$$D = \{y \in R^n : a_i \leq y_i \leq b_i, 1 \leq i \leq n\}, \tag{2}$$

  for specified vectors a and b;
- discrete parameters $u = (u_1, u_2, \ldots, u_m)$, each of which can only take on a fixed (discrete) set of values,

$$U = U_1 \times U_2 \times \cdots \times U_m = \{w_k = \langle w_{1k}, w_{2k}, \ldots, w_{mk} \rangle : 1 \leq k \leq l\}, \ w_{ik} \in U_i, \tag{3}$$

  where $U_i = \{v_{i1}, v_{i2}, \ldots, v_{il_i}\}, 1 \leq i \leq m$, is a set of $l_i > 0$ admissible discrete values for the parameter u_i, i.e., the set U of all possible discrete parameter values contains

$$l = \prod_{i=1}^{m} l_i \tag{4}$$

different elements (tuples $w_k, 1 \leq k \leq l$). Without loss of generality, we assume below that the criteria $f_i(y, u), 1 \leq i \leq s$, are non-negative, and their reduction corresponds to an increase in the efficiency of the decisions selected.

In the most difficult case, the criteria $f_i(y, u), 1 \leq i \leq s$, may be multiextremal, and the procedures for calculating their values can be computationally time-consuming. We also assume that the criteria $f_i(y, u), 1 \leq i \leq s$, meet the Lipschitz condition

$$|f_i(y_1, u_1) - f_i(y_2, u_2)| \leq L_i \|(y_1, u_1) - (y_2, u_2)\|, 1 \leq i \leq s, \tag{5}$$

where L_i is the Lipschitz constant for the criterion $f_i(y, u), 1 \leq i \leq s$, and $\| * \|$ denotes the Euclidean norm in R^N.

Efficiency criteria in an MCO problem are usually controversial, and there may not exist parameters $(y^*, u^*) \in D \times U$ with values simultaneously optimal for all criteria. In such situations, it is a common practice in MCO problems to search for efficient (non-dominated) decisions, for which an improvement in the values of some criteria leads to a deterioration of the efficiency indicators for other criteria. Obtaining the whole set of efficient decisions (the Pareto set) can require a lot of computation and, for this reason, a different approach is often used, namely search only for a relatively small set of efficient decisions defined according to the decision maker's requirements.

A commonly used approach to obtaining efficient decisions is to transform the vector criterion into some combined scalar efficiency function[1]

$$\min F(\alpha, y, u), \ y \in D, \ u \in U, \tag{6}$$

where F is an objective function generated by scalarization of the criteria f_i, $1 \leq i \leq s$, α is the vector of parameters of the criteria convolution applied, while D and U are the domains of possible parameter values from (2)–(3). By virtue of (5), the function $F(\alpha, y, u)$ also satisfies the Lipschitz condition with some constant L, that is,

$$|F(\alpha, y_1, u_1) - F(\alpha, y_2, u_2)| \leq L\|(y_1, u_1) - (y_2, u_2)\|. \tag{7}$$

To construct a combined scalar efficiency function $F(\alpha, y, u)$ from (6), one of the most frequently used scalarization methods is to use a minimax criteria convolution [8,28]:

$$F(\lambda, y, u) = \max\left(\lambda_i f_i(y, u), 1 \leq i \leq s\right),$$
$$\lambda = (\lambda_1, \lambda_2, \ldots, \lambda_s) \in \Lambda \subset R^s : \sum_{i=1}^{s} \lambda_i = 1, \lambda_i \geq 0, \ 1 \leq i \leq s. \tag{8}$$

It should be noted that, due to the possible changes in the requirements for optimality in the process of calculation, it may be necessary to change the parameters of the convolution λ from (8). Such variations yield a set of scalar global optimization problems (6)

$$\mathbb{F}_T = \{F(\alpha_t, y, u) : 1 \leq t \leq T\}, \tag{9}$$

which is necessary for solving the MCOmix problem. This set of problems can be formed sequentially during the calculations; the problems of the set can be solved strictly sequentially or simultaneously in time-shared mode. Furthermore, the problems of the set $\mathbb{F}_T$ can be solved in parallel using high-performance computing systems. The possibility of forming the set $\mathbb{F}_T$ determines *a new approach to the multistage solution of multicriteria optimization* (MMCO) problems (see, for instance, [18]).

3   The Approach: Unrolling Mixed-Integer Optimization Problems and Dimensionality Reduction

The solution of multicriteria optimization problems becomes considerably more complicated in the presence of discrete parameters: in many cases, it is necessary to calculate the criterion values for all possible values of the discrete parameters. The proposed approach to improving the efficiency of the solution of MCOmix problems is based on two basic ideas: unrolling mixed-integer optimization problems [14] and dimensionality reduction [37,39].

---

[1] It should be noted that this approach ensures that a wide range of already existing global optimization methods can be used to solve MCO problems.

3.1 Simultaneous Solution of Mixed-Integer Optimization Problems

To solve the global optimization problem (6), a two-stage nested optimization scheme can be used:

$$F(\alpha, y^*, u^*) = \min F(\alpha, y, u) = \min_{y \in D} \min_{u \in U} F(\alpha, y, u)$$
$$= \min_{y \in D} \big(F(\alpha, y, w_1), F(\alpha, y, w_2), \ldots, F(\alpha, y, w_l)\big), \qquad (10)$$
$$w_i \in U, \ 1 \le i \le l.$$

In computational scheme (10), the values of the function $F(\alpha, y, u)$ for any value of continuous parameters $y \in D$ are computed for all possible values of the discrete parameters $u \in U$. However, the smallest value of the function $F(\alpha, y, u)$ is achieved only with one specific value of the discrete parameters u^*, so the computation of the values of the function $F(\alpha, y, u)$ for other values of the discrete parameters is redundant. For example, consider the problem

$$\min\{u^2(\sin(x) + \sin(10x/3)) : x \in [2.7, 7.5], \ u \in \{1, 2\}\}, \qquad (11)$$

which has one continuous and one discrete parameter. The plots of the function $F(\alpha, y, u)$ for different values of the discrete parameter have the form shown in Fig. 1 and, as we can see, there is no need to compute the value of the function $F(\alpha, y, u)$ for $u = 1$.

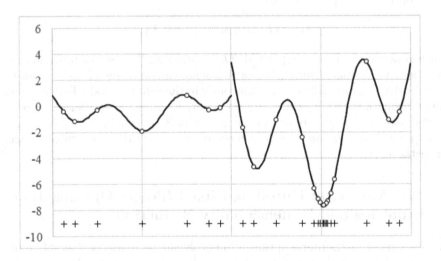

Fig. 1. The function $F(\alpha, y, u)$ from problem (11) plotted for different values of the discrete parameter (on the left, $u = 1$; on the right, $u = 2$)

It is possible to increase the efficiency and, accordingly, to reduce the computational complexity when solving the problem (6), by excluding (or, at least, by reducing) the computation of the function $F(\alpha, y, u)$ for discrete parameters

$u \neq u^*$. In some rare situations, we may know a priori information about the values of discrete parameters that do not allow the function $F(\alpha, y, u)$ to reach a minimum value. In most cases, that information can be obtained only in the process of computations based on the calculated search information.

Assume that

$$\Omega_k = \{y^i, u^i, z^i = F(\alpha, y^i, u^i) : 1 \leq i \leq k\} \tag{12}$$

is the search information obtained in the process of calculation after $k > 1$ global search iterations. Then, the procedure for adaptive estimation of the discrete parameter value at which the function $F(\alpha, y, u)$ is expected to reach the minimum value can be determined using the decision rule

$$\theta = \Theta(\Omega_k), \ 1 \leq \theta \leq l, \tag{13}$$

which determines the most promising value of the discrete parameter $u \in U$ at each step of the global search.

With the decision rule Θ from (13), the general computational scheme for solving the problem can be presented as follows.

Rule 1. Apply the decision rule Θ from (13) to the available search information Ω_k from (12) and determine the value of the discrete parameter $u = w_\theta$, $w_\theta \in U$.
Rule 2. Determine the point $y \in D$ of the global search iteration that needs to be performed with a fixed value of the discrete parameter $u = w_\theta$, $w_\theta \in U$.
Rule 3. Check the stopping condition of the computation. If the required accuracy of the global search is not achieved, it is necessary to supplement the search information Ω_k from (12) with the results of the current iteration and continue the computation starting from Rule 1.

The above computational scheme will be presented in more detail after the description of the global search algorithm.

3.2 Dimensionality Reduction of Mixed-Integer Optimization Problems

Note that the computational complexity of the solution of global optimization problems increases exponentially as the dimensionality grows. The problem of growth of the computational complexity was even called the "dimensionality curse". In particular, when applying the computational scheme discussed in Subsect. 3.1, it is necessary to accumulate and analyze the multidimensional search information Ω_k from (12). This computational complexity can be significantly reduced by reducing the optimization problems to be solved, through the use of *Peano curves* or *evolvents* $y(x)$ that unambiguously and continuously map the segment $[0, 1]$ onto an n-dimensional hypercube D (see, for example, [37,39]).

As a result, the multidimensional global optimization problem in (6) is reduced to a one-dimensional problem, namely

$$\min_{y \in D, u \in U} F(\alpha, y, u) = \min_{x \in [0,1]} \left(F(\alpha, y(x), w_1), F(\alpha, y(x), w_2), \ldots, F(\alpha, y(x), w_l) \right)$$

$$(14)$$

We should also note that one-dimensional functions $F(\alpha, y(x), u)$ resulting from the reduction satisfy a uniform Hölder condition,

$$|F(\alpha, y(x_1), u_1) - F(\alpha, y(x_2), u_2)| \leq H|x_1 - x_2|^{1/n}, \qquad (15)$$

where the constant H is determined by the relation $H = 2L\sqrt{N+3}$, L is the Lipschitz constant from (7), and n is the dimensionality of the MCOmix problem from (1).

As a result of the dimensionality reduction, the search information Ω_k from (12) obtained by computation can be expressed as

$$A_k = \{(x_i, u_i, z_i, f_i = f(y(x_i), u_i) : 1 \leq i \leq k\}, \qquad (16)$$

where x_i, u_i, $1 \leq i \leq k$, are the points of the global search iterations, and z_i, f_i, $1 \leq i \leq k$, are the values of the scalar criterion $F(\alpha, y(x), u)$ and criteria the $f_i(y)$, $1 \leq i \leq s$, computed at the points x_i, u_i, $1 \leq i \leq k$. Note that the data in the set A_k are arranged in ascending order[2] of the points x_i, $1 \leq i \leq k$, that is,

$$x_1 < x_2 < \cdots < x_k, \qquad (17)$$

for more efficient execution of global search algorithms.

Dimensionality reduction makes it possible to combine (concatenate) the one-dimensional functions $F(\alpha, y(x), w_i)$, $1 \leq i \leq l$, from (14) into a single one-dimensional function $\Phi(\alpha, y(x))$ defined over the segment $[0, l]$ (see Fig. 1),

$$\Phi(\alpha, y(x)) = \begin{cases} F(\alpha, y(x), w_1), & x \in [0, 1], \\ F(\alpha, y(x), w_2), & x \in (1, 2], \\ \cdots\cdots\cdots\cdots\cdots\cdots\cdots \\ F(\alpha, y(x), w_l), & x \in (l-1, l], \end{cases} \qquad (18)$$

where l, as expressed in (4), is the number of different variants of the values of discrete parameters $u \in U$. The mapping of the extended segment $[0, l]$ onto the domain D of continuous parameter values from (2) can be determined as

$$Y(x) = y(x - E(x)), \ x \in [0, l] \qquad (19)$$

where $E(x)$ denotes the integral part of the number x. Note that the function $\Phi(\alpha, y(x))$ is discontinuous at the points x_i, $1 \leq i \leq l-1$. Below, we consider the values of the function $\Phi(\alpha, y(x))$ at these points undefined and will not use them in computations.

_____

[2] The order is indicated by the subscript.

4 Parallel Computation for Solving Mixed-Integer Optimization Problems

In the general case, the problem of minimizing the function $F(\lambda, y, u)$ from (8) is one of the global optimization problems. The solution to such problems involves the construction of grids covering the search domain D (see, for example, [11, 24, 29, 30, 37, 39, 43, 44]).

The proposed approach relies on the algorithm of global mixed-integer search (AGMIS) to minimize the function $F(\lambda, y, u)$. This algorithm expands the possibilities of multiextremal optimization methods developed within the framework of the information-statistical theory of global search [13, 14, 16–18, 20, 23, 32–36, 38] to minimize the reduced one-dimensional function $\Phi(\alpha, y(x))$ from (18).

The AGMIS general computational scheme can be described as follows (see also [17]).

At the initial iteration of AGMIS, the value of the minimized function is calculated at some arbitrary point of the interval $(0, l)$ (below, the computation of the function value is called a *trial*). Next, assume that k, $k > 1$, global search iterations have already been performed. The selection of the trial point $(k + 1)$ for the next iteration is done according to the following rules.

Rule 1. For each interval (x_{i-1}, x_i), $1 < i \le k$, compute the value $R(i)$, (below, we refer to it as the *interval characteristic*).

Rule 2. Determine the interval (x_{t-1}, x_t) that the maximum characteristic

$$R(t) = \max\{R(i) : 1 < i \le k\}. \tag{20}$$

corresponds to.

Rule 3. Perform a new trial at x^{k+1} in the interval (x_{t-1}, x_t) with maximum characteristic

$$x^{k+1} \in (x_{t-1}, x_t). \tag{21}$$

(the values of the discrete parameters $u \in U$ are given as specified in (18)).

The stopping condition under which the trials are stopped is determined as

$$(x_t - x_{t-1})^{1/n} \le \varepsilon, \tag{22}$$

where t is taken from (20), n is the dimensionality of the problem being solved (see (1)), and $\varepsilon > 0$ is the specified accuracy of the problem solution. If the stopping condition is not satisfied, the number of iterations k is increased by one, and a new global search iteration is executed.

To explain the computation scheme under consideration, note the following. The calculated characteristics $R(i)$, $1 < i \le k$, can be interpreted as some measure of the importance of the intervals in terms of the presence of the global minimum point. The interval selection scheme for the next trial becomes obvious: the point x^{k+1} of each subsequent trial from (21) is chosen in the interval with the maximum value of the interval characteristic (i.e., in the interval where the global minimum is most likely to be located).

It should also be noted that the AGMIS computational scheme, considered above, refines the general scheme of global search for mixed-integer optimization problems from Subsect. 3.1. Thus, the choice of the function $F(\alpha, y(x), w_i)$, $1 \leq i \leq l$, for the next iteration is provided by the procedure of finding the interval with the maximum characteristic.

A full description of multiextremal optimization algorithms and conditions for their convergence developed within the framework of the information-statistical theory of global search are given in [39]. Thus, with a proper numerical estimation of the Hölder constants H from (15), the AGMIS algorithm converges to all available points of the global minimum of the minimized function $F(\lambda, y, u)$.

Figure 1 depicts the use of AGMIS for the problem (11) under the proposed approach. In this example, the function value $F(\lambda, y, u)$ is calculated only seven times for the discrete-parameter value $u = 1$, and seventeen times for the value $u = 2$, that is, the global search iteration is performed mainly for the value of the discrete parameter, which makes it possible to achieve the smallest value of the function $F(\lambda, y, u)$.

Now, let us return to the initial problem statement (1) and remember that for solving the MCOmix problem it may be necessary to solve the set of problems $\mathbb{F}_T$ from (9). One more key property of the proposed approach becomes apparent when solving this set of problems by the AGMIS algorithm: the results of all previous computations of criteria values can be reused to calculate the values of the next optimization problem $F(\alpha, y(x), u)$ from (6), which is to be solved with new values of α' from (8), without having to repeat any time-consuming calculation of criteria values, that is,

$$z_i' = F(\alpha', y(x_i), u), \ 1 \leq i \leq k. \tag{23}$$

Thus, all search information A_k from (16), recalculated according to (23), can be reused to continue the solution of the next problem $F(\alpha, y(x), u)$. This reuse of search information can significantly reduce the number of computations performed for each subsequent problem of the set $\mathbb{F}_T$ from (9), which may require only a relatively small number of global search iterations. This has been confirmed in our computational experiments (see Sect. 5).

The AGMIS algorithm supplemented with the ability to reuse search information in MCOmix problems will be further referred to as the Algorithm for Multicriteria Mixed-Integer Search (AMMIS).

The final stage in improving the efficiency of solving MCOmix problems in the proposed approach is to organize parallel computing on parallel high-performance systems. Unfortunately, attempts to develop parallel variants of AGMIS and AMMIS algorithms using existing parallelization methods have not succeeded. For example, data parallelization (splitting the computation domain between available computing elements) results in only one processor processing the subdomain of the search domain containing the sought global optimal solution of the problem, while other processors perform redundant calculations. A new approach to parallelizing calculations for solving global optimization problems is proposed in [38,39]: the parallelism of calculations is ensured by organizing simultaneous computation of values of the minimized function $F(\alpha, y, u)$

from (8) at several different points of the search domain D. This approach makes it possible to parallelize the most time-consuming part of the global search process and, due to its general nature, it can be applied to almost any global search method for a wide variety of global optimization problems.

Applying this approach and taking into account the interpretation of the characteristics $R(i)$, $1 < i \leq k$, of search intervals (x_{i-1}, x_i), $1 < i \leq k$, from (20) as a measure of the interval importance in terms of containing the global minimum point, we can obtain a parallel version of the AGMIS algorithm with the following generalization of rules (20)–(21) (see [21, 38]):

Rule 2'. Arrange the characteristics of intervals in descending order,

$$R(t_1) \geq R(t_2) \geq \cdots \geq R(t_{k-2}) \geq R(t_{k-1}), \tag{24}$$

and select p intervals with numbers t_j, $1 \leq j \leq p$, having maximum values of their characteristics (p is the number of processors (cores) used for parallel computations).

Rule 3'. Perform new trials (calculate the values of the minimized function $F(\alpha, y(x), u)$) at the points x^{k+j}, $1 \leq j \leq p$, located in the intervals with the maximum characteristics from (24).

Stopping condition (22) for the algorithm must be checked for all the intervals in which the next trials are performed,

$$(x_{t_j} - x_{t_j-1})^{1/n} \leq \varepsilon, \ 1 \leq j \leq p. \tag{25}$$

As in the cases considered before, if the stopping condition is not fulfilled, the number of iterations k is increased by p, and a new global search iteration is executed.

This parallel variant of the AGMIS algorithm will be further referred to as the Parallel Algorithm for Global Mixed-Integer Search (PAGMIS), and the parallel variant of the AMMIS algorithm, as PAMMIS.

To assess the efficiency of the parallel algorithms, we conducted a large series of computational experiments, in which it was confirmed that the suggested approach can significantly reduce the number of computations and the time required to solve complex multicriteria mixed-integer optimization problems (see Sect. 5).

5   Results of Numerical Experiments

The numerical experiments were performed on the supercomputers Lobachevsky (University of Nizhni Novgorod), Lomonosov (Moscow State University), MVS-10P (Joint Supercomputer Center of RAS), and Endeavor. Each computational node was equipped with two processors Intel Xeon Platinum 8260L 2.4 GHz (i.e., a total of 48 CPU cores on each node) and 256 GB of RAM. The executable program code was built with the software package Intel Parallel Studio XE 2019. For the numerical experiments, we used the Globalizer system [15].

The multiextremal optimization algorithms used under the suggested approach have demonstrated their effectiveness in numerical experiments and have been widely used to solve practical global search problems (see, for example, [14,16–18]). Below, we present the results of previous numerical experiments obtained that prove the effectiveness of this approach [17]. The following bi-criteria test problem, proposed in [10], was solved in the experiments:

$$f_1(y) = (y_1 - 1)y_2^2 + 1, \; f_2(y) = y_2, \; 0 \le y_1, y_2 \le 1. \tag{26}$$

The solution of the MCO problem consisted of the construction of a numerical approximation of the Pareto set. To assess the quality of the approximation, the completeness and uniformity of the Pareto set coverage were compared using the following two indicators [10,45]:

- The hypervolume index (HV). This indicator evaluates the approximation of the Pareto set in terms of completeness (a higher value corresponds to a more complete coverage of the Pareto domain).
- The distribution uniformity index (DU). This indicator evaluates the uniformity of the Pareto domain coverage (a lower value corresponds to a more uniform coverage of the Pareto domain).

Five multicriteria optimization algorithms were compared in this experiment: the Monte-Carlo (MC) method [10], the genetic algorithm SEMO from the PISA library [10], the non-uniform coverage (NUC) method [10], the bi-objective Lipschitz optimization (BLO) method [45], and the AMMIS method, developed by the authors under the proposed approach.

Fifty global optimization problems were solved with AMMIS for different values of the convolution coefficients $\lambda \in \Lambda$ from (8), with accuracy $\varepsilon = 0.05$ and reliability parameter $r = 3.0$ from (22). The results of the experiments are given in Table 1.

Table 1. Comparison of the efficiency of multicriteria optimization algorithms

Solution method	MC	SEMO	NUC	BLO	AMMIS
Number of iterations of the method	500	500	515	498	**370**
Number of points found in the Pareto domain	67	104	29	68	**100**
HV index		0.300	0.312	0.306	0.308	**0.316**
DU index		1.277	1.116	0.210	0.175	**0.101**

The experiments confirmed that AMMIS has a noticeable advantage over the multicriteria optimization methods considered here, even when solving relatively simple MCO problems.

The results of the computational experiments with 100 MCOmix problems of the set $\mathbb{F}_T$ from (9) are given below. Each problem in the set $\mathbb{F}_T$ contained two criteria. Each criterion was defined through functions obtained by the GKLS generator [12], with some of the parameters being discrete [1]. To generate the MCOmix problems, we considered four continuous parameters y from (2) and five discrete parameters u from (3), with only two values for each of them (i.e., $n = 4$, $m = 5$, $l = 32$).

Fifty uniformly distributed values of the convolution coefficients $\lambda \in \Lambda$ from (8) were used to solve each MCOmix problem. To estimate the values of the HV and DU efficiency indicators, we calculated an approximation of the Pareto domain for each MCOmix problem, using a uniform grid in the search domain $D \times U$ from (2)–(3). The following parameter values were used for PAMMIS: accuracy $\varepsilon = 0.05$ from (25) and reliability $r = 5.6$ (the r parameter is used in PAMMIS to construct estimates of the Hölder constant H in (15)).

Table 2 contains the results of the numerical experiments, averaged by the number of MCOmix problems solved. The first column shows the number of cores used. The second column contains information on the average number of trials (computations of criteria values) performed during the global search. The third column shows the resulting speedup (reduction in the number of trials) when using parallel computations. The last two columns show the values of the HV and DU indicators.

Table 2. Efficiency of PAMMIS in the solution of MCOmix problems

Cores	Iterations	Speedup	DU	HV
Pareto domain estimate obtained by exhaustive search				
48	1706667	–	20.6	29784.9
Pareto domain estimate obtained using the PAMMIS method				
1	86261.6	1.0	13.8	30212.3
6	15406.2	5.6	14.4	30317.6
12	6726.1	12.8	16.2	30248.3
18	5972.7	14.4	14.3	30551.1
24	3657.4	23.6	13.9	30092.3
30	3162.3	27.3	14.9	30443.9
36	2888.7	29.9	14.6	30528.7
42	2028.8	42.5	15.6	30046.1
48	1767.6	48.8	15.3	30255.5

The results of the experiments demonstrate that PAMMIS is scalable as the speedup of parallel computations increases almost linearly with the number of computing cores used. The obtained values of the HV and DU indicators indicate that the Pareto set estimate obtained by the PAMMIS method is calculated with greater accuracy and requires a significantly smaller number of trials compared to the results obtained by using uniform grids in the search domain $D \times U$.

6   Conclusions

In this paper, we proposed a new approach to solving computationally intensive optimization problems, where some varied parameters can only take on discrete values (MCOmix). It is assumed that the efficiency criteria may be multiextremal, and the computation of criterion values may involve a large number of calculations. Due to the high computational complexity of this class of problems, parallel solution methods that rely on the efficient use of high-performance computing systems need to be developed.

Under the proposed approach, the solution of mixed-integer optimization problems is reduced to solving a family of global search optimization problems that use only continuous parameters. All problems of the family are solved simultaneously in time-shared mode, where the optimization problem for the next global search iteration is selected adaptively taking into account the search information obtained in the course of the calculations. The results of numerical experiments prove that this approach can significantly reduce the computational intensity when solving MCOmix problems.

Finally, it should be noted that the approach we propose is quite promising and requires further research. First of all, it is necessary to perform numerical experiments involving multicriteria mixed-integer optimization problems with a greater number of efficiency criteria and higher dimensionality. It is also necessary to assess the possibility of implementing parallel computations on high-performance systems with distributed memory.

Acknowledgements. The work was supported by the Ministry of Science and Higher Education of the Russian Federation (project no. 0729-2020-0055) and by the Research and Education Mathematical Center (project no. 075-02-2020-1483/1).

References

1. Barkalov, K., Lebedev, I.: Parallel global optimization for non-convex mixed-integer problems. In: Voevodin, V., Sobolev, S. (eds.) RuSCDays 2019. CCIS, vol. 1129, pp. 98–109. Springer, Cham (2019). https://doi.org/10.1007/978-3-030-36592-9_9
2. Belotti, P., Lee, J., Liberti, L., Margot, F., Wächter, A.: Branching and bounds tightening techniques for non-convex MINLP. Optim. Methods Softw. **24**(4–5), 597–634 (2009). https://doi.org/10.1080/10556780903087124
3. Boukouvala, F., Misener, R., Floudas, C.: Global optimization advances in mixed-integer nonlinear programming, MINLP, and constrained derivative-free optimization, CDFO. Eur. J. Oper. Res. **252**(3), 701–727 (2016). https://doi.org/10.1016/j.ejor.2015.12.01
4. Branke, J., Deb, K., Miettinen, K., Slowinski, R.: Multiobjective Optimization: Interactive and Evolutionary Approaches, vol. 5252. Springer, Berlin (2008). https://doi.org/10.1007/978-3-540-88908-3

5. Burer, S., Letchford, A.: Non-convex mixed-integer nonlinear programming: a survey. Surv. Oper. Res. Manag. Sci. **17**, 97–106 (2012). https://doi.org/10.1016/j.sorms.2012.08.001

6. Collette, Y., Siarry, P.: Multiobjective Optimization: Principles and Case Studies (Decision Engineering). Springer, Heidelberg (2011). https://doi.org/10.1007/978-3-662-08883-8

7. Deep, K., Singh, K., Kansal, M., Mohan, C.: A real coded genetic algorithm for solving integer and mixed integer optimization problems. Appl. Math. Comput. **212**(2), 505–518 (2009). https://doi.org/10.1016/j.amc.2009.02.044

8. Ehrgott, M.: Multicriteria Optimization. Springer, Heidelberg (2005). https://doi.org/10.1007/3-540-27659-9

9. Eichfelder, G.: Scalarizations for adaptively solving multi-objective optimization problems. Comput. Optim. Appl. **44**, 249–273 (2009). https://doi.org/10.1007/s10589-007-9155-4

10. Evtushenko, Y., Posypkin, M.: Method of non-uniform coverages to solve the multicriteria optimization problems with guaranteed accuracy. Autom. Remote. Control. **75**(6), 1025–1040 (2014). https://doi.org/10.1134/S0005117914060046

11. Floudas, C., Pardalos, M.: Recent Advances in Global Optimization. Princeton University Press, Princeton (2016)

12. Gaviano, M., Kvasov, D., Lera, D., Sergeyev, Y.: Software for generation of classes of test functions with known local and global minima for global optimization. ACM Trans. Math. Softw. **29**(4), 469–480 (2003)

13. Gergel, V.: A unified approach to use of coprocessors of various types for solving global optimization problems. In: 2nd International Conference on Mathematics and Computers in Sciences and in Industry, pp. 13–18 (2015). https://doi.org/10.1109/MCSI.2015.18

14. Gergel, V., Barkalov, K., Lebedev, I.: A global optimization algorithm for non-convex mixed-integer problems. In: Battiti, R., Brunato, M., Kotsireas, I., Pardalos, P.M. (eds.) LION 12 2018. LNCS, vol. 11353, pp. 78–81. Springer, Cham (2019). https://doi.org/10.1007/978-3-030-05348-2_7

15. Gergel, V., Barkalov, K., Sysoyev, A.: A novel supercomputer software system for solving time-consuming global optimization problems. Numer. Algebra Control Optim. **8**(1), 47–62 (2018)

16. Gergel, V., Kozinov, E.: Accelerating parallel multicriterial optimization methods based on intensive using of search information. Procedia Comput. Sci. **108**, 1463–1472 (2017). https://doi.org/10.1016/j.procs.2017.05.051

17. Gergel, V., Kozinov, E.: Efficient multicriterial optimization based on intensive reuse of search information. J. Glob. Optim. **71**(1), 73–90 (2018). https://doi.org/10.1007/s10898-018-0624-3

18. Gergel, V., Kozinov, E.: Multilevel parallel computations for solving multistage multicriteria optimization problems. In: Krzhizhanovskaya, V.V., et al. (eds.) ICCS 2020. LNCS, vol. 12137, pp. 17–30. Springer, Cham (2020). https://doi.org/10.1007/978-3-030-50371-0_2

19. Greco, S., Ehrgott, M., Figueira, J.: Multiple Criteria Decision Analysis: State of the Art Surveys. Springer, New York (2016). https://doi.org/10.1007/978-1-4939-3094-4

20. Grishagin, V., Israfilov, R., Sergeyev, Y.: Comparative efficiency of dimensionality reduction schemes in global optimization. In: AIP Conference Proceedings, vol. 1776, p. 060011 (2016). https://doi.org/10.1063/1.4965345

21. Grishagin, V., Sergeyev, Y., Strongin, R.: Parallel characteristical algorithms for solving problems of global optimization. J. Glob. Optim. **10**, 185–206 (1997). https://doi.org/10.1023/A:1008242328176
22. Hillermeier, C., Jahn, J.: Multiobjective optimization: survey of methods and industrial applications. Surv. Math. Ind. **11**, 1–42 (2005)
23. Lera, D., Sergeyev, Y.: Lipschitz and Hölder global optimization using space-filling curves. Appl. Numer. Math. **60**(1–2), 115–129 (2010). https://doi.org/10.1016/j.apnum.2009.10.004
24. Locatelli, M., Schoen, F.: Global Optimization: Theory, Algorithms, and Applications. SIAM, Philadelphia (2013)
25. Marler, R., Arora, J.: Survey of multi-objective optimization methods for engineering. Struct. Multidisc. Optim. **26**, 369–395 (2004). https://doi.org/10.1007/s00158-003-0368-6
26. Marler, R., Arora, J.: Multi-objective optimization: concepts and methods for engineering (2009)
27. Miettinen, K.: Nonlinear Multiobjective Optimization. Springer, Boston (1998). https://doi.org/10.1007/978-1-4615-5563-6
28. Pardalos, P., Žilinskas, A., Žilinskas, J.: Non-Convex Multi-Objective Optimization, vol. 123. Springer, Cham (2017). https://doi.org/10.1007/978-3-319-61007-8
29. Paulavičius, R., Žilinskas, J.: Simplicial Global Optimization. Springer, New York (2014). https://doi.org/10.1007/978-1-4614-9093-7
30. Pintér, J.: Global Optimization in Action (Continuous and Lipschitz Optimization: Algorithms, Implementations and Applications). Kluwer Academic Publishers, Dordrecht (1996)
31. Schlüter, M., Egea, J., Banga, J.: Extended ant colony optimization for non-convex mixed integer nonlinear programming. Comput. Oper. Res. **36**(7), 2217–2229 (2009). https://doi.org/10.1016/j.cor.2008.08.015
32. Sergeyev, Y.: An information global optimization algorithm with local tuning. SIAM J. Optim. **5**(4), 858–870 (1995). https://doi.org/10.1137/0805041
33. Sergeyev, Y., Famularo, D., Pugliese, P.: Index branch-and-bound algorithm for global optimization with multiextremal constraints. J. Glob. Optim. **21**(3), 317–341 (2001). https://doi.org/10.1023/A:1012391611462
34. Sergeyev, Y., Grishagin, V.: Parallel asynchronous global search and the nested optimization scheme. J. Comput. Anal. Appl. **3**(2), 123–145 (2001). https://doi.org/10.1023/A:1010185125012
35. Sergeyev, Y., Kvasov, D.: A deterministic global optimization using smooth diagonal auxiliary functions. Commun. Nonlinear Sci. Numer. Simul. **21**(1–3), 99–111 (2015). https://doi.org/10.1016/j.cnsns.2014.08.026
36. Sergeyev, Y., Nasso, M., Mukhametzhanov, M., Kvasov, D.: Novel local tuning techniques for speeding up one-dimensional algorithms in expensive global optimization using Lipschitz derivatives. J. Comput. Appl. Math. **383** (2021). https://doi.org/10.1016/j.cam.2020.113134
37. Sergeyev, Y., Strongin, R., Lera, D.: Introduction to Global Optimization Exploiting Space-Filling Curves. Springer, New York (2013). https://doi.org/10.1007/978-1-4614-8042-6
38. Strongin, R., Sergeyev, Y.: Global multidimensional optimization on parallel computer. Parallel Comput. **18**(11), 1259–1273 (1992). https://doi.org/10.1016/0167-8191(92)90069-J

39. Strongin, R., Sergeyev, Y.: Global Optimization with Non-Convex Constraints. Sequential and Parallel Algorithms. Kluwer Academic Publishers, Dordrecht (2000). 2nd edn. (2013), 3rd edn. (2014)
40. Vigerske, S., Gleixner, A.: SCIP: global optimization of mixed-integer nonlinear programs in a branch-and-cut framework. Optim. Methods Softw. **33**(3), 563–593 (2018). https://doi.org/10.1080/10556788.2017.1335312
41. Voutchkov, I., Keane, A.: Multi-objective optimization using surrogates. In: Tenne, Y., Goh, C.K. (eds.) Computational Intelligence in Optimization. ALO, vol. 7, pp. 155–175. Springer, Heidelberg (2010). https://doi.org/10.1007/978-3-642-12775-5_7
42. Zavadskas, E., Turskis, Z., Kildiene, S.: State of art surveys of overviews on MCDM/MADM methods. Technol. Econ. Dev. Econ. **20**, 165–179 (2014). https://doi.org/10.3846/20294913.2014.892037
43. Zhigljavsky, A.: Theory of Global Random Search. Kluwer Academic Publishers, Dordrecht (1991)
44. Zhigljavsky, A., Žilinskas, A.: Stochastic Global Optimization, vol. 9. Springer, Berlin (2008). https://doi.org/10.1007/978-0-387-74740-8
45. Žilinskas, A., Žilinskas, J.: Adaptation of a one-step worst-case optimal univariate algorithm of bi-objective Lipschitz optimization to multidimensional problems. Commun. Nonlinear Sci. Numer. Simul. **21**(1–3), 89–98 (2015). https://doi.org/10.1016/j.cnsns.2014.08.025

Parallel Intelligent Computing
in Algebraic Problems

Valery Il'in[✉]

Institute of Computational Mathematics and Mathematical Geophysics SB RAS,
Novosibirsk State University, Novosibirsk, Russia
ilin@sscc.ru

Abstract. We consider the issues associated with the creation of an
intelligent computing environment for the high-performance solution of a
wide class of large algebraic problems, which makes up the most resource-
intensive stage of mathematical modeling. The first area of research is
devoted to automating the construction of parallel algorithms and their
mapping onto supercomputer architecture by investigating the problem
of classification and identification of matrix statements and selecting
algorithms for specific situations relying on optimization methods. The
second aspect is related to the creation of intelligent interfaces, both
for internal inter-module interactions and for end-users from various
professional backgrounds. The rich functionality of the high-tech software under discussion requires an advanced system content to manage
machine experiments. The scale of this development puts on the agenda
the creation of an integrated tool environment or ecosystem, as well as
the concept of a mathematical knowledge base.

Keywords: Algebraic problems · Large sparse matrices ·
Classification and identification of statements · Selection of optimal
parallel algorithms · Intelligent computing environment

1 Introduction

The advent of the 4th Industrial Revolution, with post-petaFLOPS computers and the expected arrival of exaFLOPS computing systems (10^{18} arithmetic
operations per second and approximately the same number of bytes of memory),
makes mathematical modeling of real-world processes and phenomena, along
with theoretical and experimental research, the main tool to grasp fundamental and applied knowledge. Large-scale computations are associated with the
high-performance solution of interdisciplinary direct and inverse initial-boundary
value problems with large data, described by multidimensional, non-stationary,
and nonlinear differential and/or integral systems of equations.

Despite all the functional complexity and variety of such problems, after
their discretization and approximation, computational algorithms boil down to
linear algebra problems: matrix-vector operations, solution of systems of linear algebraic equations (SLAEs) and matrix equations, search for eigenvalues

L. Sokolinsky and M. Zymbler (Eds.): PCT 2021, CCIS 1437, pp. 108–117, 2021.
https://doi.org/10.1007/978-3-030-81691-9_8

and eigenvectors of matrices. These are the bottleneck of machine experiments and account for more than 80% of supercomputer time because the number of computing resources required at this stage of mathematical modeling increases nonlinearly with the number of degrees of freedom, i.e., the total number of unknowns. The most popular and relevant problems are associated with the solution of ultra-high-order SLAEs (10^8 to 10^{11}), in which computations with standard double precision are no longer possible. We are interested in ill-conditioned algebraic systems derived from multiscale initial-boundary value problems with complex domain geometry and contrasting material properties, approximated on unstructured meshes by finite difference, finite volume, finite element methods, and discontinuous Galerkin algorithms of various orders of accuracy [1]. From a technological point of view, it is important that the generated matrices are stored in sparse-compressed formats, which dramatically reduces the amount of memory required but significantly complicates the access to the values of matrix entries.

Depending on the applications, matrices can be real or complex, symmetric or non-symmetric, Hermitian or non-Hermitian, positive-definite or indefinite, singular or non-singular, consistent or inconsistent. A separate class of systems consists of SLAEs with stochastic initial data and problems with interval arithmetic, where each real value is given not by a number but by the interval in which it is located. Of great importance are the structural properties of matrices, inheriting, in a sense, the features of the original continuous problems (elasticity, hydrogasdynamics, electrophysics, and others). Examples of typical block SLAEs are saddle-type systems. A significant variety of algebraic systems can be generated even within a specific subject area by various methods for scaling or reordering the unknowns.

In such a "zoo" of problems, one can imagine how many methods for solving them exist and are constantly updated. The main modern approaches are based on preconditioned methods in Krylov subspaces that have diverse variational, orthogonal, and projectional properties. There are many books (see, for example [2–5]) and huge numbers of journal papers and specialized conference proceedings devoted to these issues.

To date, there is a large amount of software designed to deal with problems and methods of computational algebra. An overview can be found in [6]; a systematization of implemented methods is given in [7]. There are advanced libraries of algorithms as well as numerous new-generation and consistent data structures. However, the current trends have placed on the agenda the creation of a new generation of open integrated computing environments (ICE) [8], focused on a long life cycle and wide demand from the community, including developers of algorithms and programs and end-users with various professional backgrounds.

The suggested ICE concept is based on forming an intelligent software tool environment (an ecosystem) focused, on the one hand, on a qualitative increase in the productivity of software developers and, on the other, on the creation of flexible user interfaces that would conceal the "inner mechanism" of high-tech algorithms and technologies by designing calculation modules in the form of "black" or "gray" boxes.

The key point here is an active knowledge base that contains information about the tasks to be solved, the algorithms and technologies used, and all the necessary software and accompanying documentation (including external software products, as provided by ICE technologies). It should be noted that the description of the statement of algebraic problems, their computational models, and implemented methods may contain not only technical data but also "intellectual" information, i.e., some qualitative characteristics. The AlgoWiki project [9], created under J. Dongarra's and V. Voevodin's guidance, can serve as a prototype of such a development that implements the information part based on Wikipedia technologies.

A significant part of the efforts to intellectualize algebraic solutions should address the technological problem of embedding the computational stage into the general scheme of mathematical modeling [10] and focus on the automated parallelization of algorithms and their mapping onto supercomputer architecture taking into consideration the evolution of computer platforms [11].

One of the main tasks of artificial intelligence is the creation of self-learning computing and information systems. It should be emphasized that this problem, both algorithmically and technologically, must be solved as an inverse problem of conditional optimization by forming an objective functional that must be minimized under several specified constraints [12]. The final solution is obtained by successive approximations based on the purposeful solution of a set of direct problems and the comparison of the results of the computational model with external data.

This study is structured as follows. In Sect. 2, we give a brief classification of the problems to be solved using SLAEs as an example and interpreting this information as an introduction to the content of the algebraic knowledge base. Section 3 deals with classes of algorithms in terms of their applicability to the corresponding kinds of problems. Section 4 considers the issues of intellectualization of technological solutions, including scalable parallelization. In the Conclusions, we discuss the problem motivation and topics for further research.

2   The Problem of Classification of Algebraic Tasks

The problems of finding eigenvalues and/or eigenvectors, and solutions to SLAEs or matrix equations (for example, of Lyapunov or Sylvester types) are mainly determined by the type of matrices involved. It is these aspects that we focus on, meaning primarily linear algebraic systems with sparse matrices. In some sense, within this subject area, we are speaking about the systematization and analysis of mathematical models.

Task classification means creating a hierarchical structure that includes not only the relationships between different classes of problems but also their quantitative and qualitative characteristics. The primary objective of such procedure is related to the recognition problem: for a certain task to be solved, it is necessary to identify it, i.e., determine whether it belongs to a set with known properties, and then, use this information to select the most appropriate algorithm.

Matrices can be systematized according to the following characteristics: structural, spectral, hereditary, and representative. All these properties require an explanation; they are loosely related and understood in a generalized sense. Structural specifications include dimensions and distributions of nonzero matrix entries (portraits), their block shapes (band, saddle type, and others). An important tool for the analysis and transformation is the matrix graph, especially, in the case of large sparse SLAEs arising from approximations of multidimensional boundary value problems with a complex configuration of the computational domain on unstructured grids, where graph theory is also an effective research tool. Structural specifications include as well the properties of symmetry, skew symmetry, monotonicity, projectivity, orthogonality, and other qualitative features that are important when constructing numerical methods.

Spectral characteristics can be quantitative or qualitative, scalar (e.g., eigenvalues, singular values), or vectorial ones. Some relevant properties within this category are the following: positive definiteness and indefiniteness, singularity and nonsingularity, consistency and inconsistency of SLAEs, characteristics of the matrix kernel and/or its image, norms, and condition numbers, which determine the stability quality of algorithms.

By hereditary properties, we mean those related to the origin of the considered matrices and systems of equations, which must be taken into account when constructing methods for their solution. On the one hand, it is determined by the types of initial tasks considered (for instance, electrophysics, hydrogasdynamics, elastic plasticity, heat and mass transfer, and so on). On the other hand, it depends on the methods of discretization and approximations used on various grids (finite difference methods, finite volume, finite element, discontinuous Galerkin algorithms of several orders of accuracy, and others). Of special importance are interdisciplinary tasks, including inverse ones, which constitute the quintessence of problems of predictive modeling of processes and phenomena with real big data.

Concerning the representative or informational characteristics of algebraic problems, we will refer to the methods and formats for their assignment in programs or computer devices, which directly determines the performance of the executable code. Matrix-vector computations can be carried out with simple or double precision in real or complex arithmetic, which significantly affects the implementation time of algorithms. There are programming solutions that are quite expensive in terms of arithmetic operations performed with quadruple and higher accuracy, and therefore it is reasonable to employ them with instances of extremely unstable numerical methods. The ideal solution would be to use the dynamic length of the machine word, based on an a priori or a posteriori stability analysis of all stages of algorithm execution. Special problems are to be solved in the case of systems of extreme size when the big-data factor turns from quantitative to qualitative, and the source information can be stochastic, incomplete, and even contradictory. Existing methods and software systems based on

interval analysis are of considerable interest (see [13] and the extensive literature therein). Such methods can perform not only computations with ensured
accuracy but also some provable statements.

Another problem with large sparse SLAEs is the cost-effective storage of
nonzero matrix entries, which certainly reduces the amount of memory used but,
at the same time, significantly complicates and slows down the access to numbers. There exists a worldwide collection containing typical compressed-sparse
representations along with their corresponding converters, but the problem of
large matrix data remains open.

3   Optimization of the Selection of Algorithms

First, we define an optimal algorithm for solving a given class of problems with
the required accuracy on a certain computer system as the one that gives the
desired result in a minimum estimated time. A few comments should be made
regarding this interpretation, which is, to a certain extent, pragmatic. For the
optimization of the objective functional, the elapsed real time (wall-clock time)
required for the solution is regarded as the criterion of optimality but not the
number of computing resources or anything similar for that matter, since the
size of the required memory or the total number of arithmetic operations, for
example, may indirectly affect the duration of computation. This criterion can
be understood as both experimentally measured computer time and its theoretical estimate. The optimality of the algorithm is determined for a fixed set of
problems and/or a specified level of accuracy of the result since another algorithm may be the best when these conditions change. Obviously, binding to a
specific computer (or a class of multiprocessor computing systems, MPS) is also
mandatory: of two methods compared, one can be faster on a dual-core personal
computer and the other one can be faster on a 1000-core cluster. Finally, the
comparison is not actually made for mathematical formulas but their software
implementation or a model.

Various types of preconditioning matrices are constructed from the principles
of projection, incomplete factorization, splitting, segregation, algebraic domain
decomposition, multigrid algorithms, and so forth. The iterative processes themselves are formed by constructing efficient spectral methods of Chebyshev acceleration or conjugate directions in Krylov subspaces for Hermitian SLAEs. Otherwise, biorthogonal algorithms are used, and also methods of semi-conjugate
directions or generalized minimal residuals, which have optimal variational properties but are based on resource-intensive long vector recursions. For all these
approaches, accelerating techniques such as deflation, augmentation, coarse grid
correction, low-rank matrix approximation, et cetera, are actively used (see
[14–20] and the literature therein). It should also be noted that combinatorial methods for solving grid SLAEs based on graph transformations have been
actively developed in recent decades [21].

Besides efforts put forth to improve the mathematical efficiency of iterative
processes, there is another technological trend that is actively being developed to

increase the productivity of software implementations of algorithms, and automate their construction and mapping on MPS architecture. It largely relies on scalable parallelization by means of hybrid programming: forming processes with message transfer between cluster nodes with distributed memory (MPI), multithread computations on shared memory (OPEN MP), vectorization (AVX), graphics accelerators (GPGPU), and special programmable calculators (FPGA). One of the basic tasks in code optimization consists of improving big-data structures and minimizing communication operations, which are not only the slowest but the most energy-intensive as well.

The functional part of the ICE must have a redundant and multiversion composition of algorithms to ensure the choice of an optimal method for solving a task in a specific operating environment or, moreover, the development of recommendations and hints to the user. This will help in solving the conventional problem of incompatibility between conflicting qualities as universality and efficiency. This approach entails the need to create a testing automation system with collections of matrix problems and accumulated statistical data based on the results of comparative numerical experiments, which, in particular, will allow us to assess the accuracy of the results to be obtained. In some sense, we mean an automated in-depth study of the class of problems to be solved and the algorithms used, as well as a process of making decisions on the appropriate use of an implemented system. In fact, this creates an intellectual structure capable of self-learning, as in life, by the trial and error method and based on the accumulation of experimental information and its analysis by conditional optimization methods, which, to some extent, corresponds to developing conditioned reflexes in living beings.

4   Intelligent Mathematical Technologies

At first glance, all the three words in the title of this section are in clear contradiction with each other. Indeed, how can one still add intelligence to higher mathematics? What is the connection of mathematics with technical issues? However, we know that "the devil is in the details", and if we want to introduce basic research into practical matters, we must necessarily solve serious technological problems. Moreover, since their implementation is a high-tech specialized software that can only be understood by a math-computer scientist, another intellectual task arises: it is necessary to create a friendly interface for a wide range of end-users from various professional backgrounds. For an ideal software tool environment, i.e., an ecosystem, the following technical requirements can be formulated:

- Flexible expansion of the set of problems that are to be solved and algorithms used, adaptation to the evolution of computer architectures and network technologies, cross-platform software, and multilinguality. It is assumed that the content of the ICE, being rich and functional, should ensure for a problem the choice of a modern method that would show high performance on this multiprocessor computing system.

- Effective reuse of external software products representing, in general, a huge intellectual potential. In particular, the search for an optimal algorithm for a specific problem can be carried out not only in one's "own" library but also on the Internet.
- Coordinated participation of various groups of developers and users in a project, with various forms of interaction of interested representatives of the computing community.

These conditions are aimed at providing a long and successful life cycle for the project. This implies the creation of a highly developed system content that actually supports the algebraic knowledge base determining the form and content of the ICE.

Providing high intelligence requires serious technological support, namely automation tools for analytical formula transformations and set-theoretical operations, optimization methods for the choice of algorithms, automated construction of parallel processes, tools for geometric and functional modeling based on the CAD and/or CAE systems and geared toward the analysis of computation results and decision-making, multiversion reconfiguration of computing modules, automation systems for testing and verifying library programs on representative collections of specific tasks, "factories" of natural and artificial languages for human-machine and internal inter-module interfaces, and so on. It should be mentioned that these computational and information tools are more or less present in various projects. The main challenge is to integrate them into one ecosystem in a manner that would be convenient for mass use.

The fundamental problem of automated parallelization of algorithms or synthesis of parallel programs is one of particular importance. Despite the long history of this issue (just remember the international project High-Performance Fortran, which was closed notwithstanding the huge resources invested in it), there is no such industrial project now. Research into this direction is underway (see, for example [22, 23], and the literature cited therein), but so far the creation of a highly scalable code on a heterogeneous supercomputer is purely experimental, and its success is evaluated only by the experience gained and the programmer's mathematical intuition.

In recent decades, one of the actively developing areas of artificial intelligence is associated with neural network topics related to the problem of deep learning (see [24] and the literature cited therein). Here, the ideal goal is to represent with the help of supercomputer technologies those real processes implemented in the neurons of the human brain. Their number, according to available estimates, is of the order of one hundred billion. In a few years, an exaFLOPS-level supercomputer will probably have about one billion computing cores, i.e., the figures are fairly comparable. However, the principles of mental and emotional activity of our brain are still a mystery. Why do not computers possess creative gifts, even though they are far superior in arithmetic abilities to humans? Obviously, just because we still have, at best, only vague ideas about the laws of mental activity, which are still miles away from any mathematical model. Under these circumstances, it is only possible to speak or write about artificial neural-network approaches in computer-aided computations but without making claims of biological analogy. For example, in a multidimensional system of grid equations, it is convenient to interpret a single grid node with adjacent neighbors or a vertex of the corresponding graph with incident edges as a neuron, but it should be clearly understood that this is just a fashionable term, without any scientific background. As for the mathematical foundations of network problems, they consist of the methods and fundamental provisions of graph theory.

The key point of artificial intelligence is machine learning [25], which is directly related to the issues of planning a computational experiment and making decisions based on the results of mathematical modeling. A typical illustration here is the problem of assimilation of large volumes of data obtained from field observations (meteorological, seismic, space, et cetera). In this case, we are speaking about bringing the applied mathematical formulation and the available experimental measurements into some kind of mutual correspondence for carrying out the predictive modeling based on this. A classical example in algebra is the solution of a degenerate inconsistent SLAE in which the right-hand side vector must be orthogonalized to a previously unknown matrix kernel. The objective of computer training could be finding an appropriate model of the object or process being studied and providing the necessary (but not redundant) accuracy of computations, and optimizing algorithms to reduce the amount of machine time consumed (for example, hours instead of days). Planning a computational experiment is a serious scientific and practical task. A typical situation when using grid SLAEs is the empiric choice of the problem dimension (say, 10^6, 10^8, or 10^{10}) that would guarantee a sufficient resolution and, at the same time, would meet resource requirements. In general, theoretical and technological problems of intellectualization are the prerogative of mathematical logic and semantic modeling created by ontological and cognitive principles, as well as active knowledge bases [26–28].

5   Conclusions

The intellectualization of computations is becoming one of the main problems of supercomputer modeling, including, at its most resource-intensive stage, the solution of large-dimensional algebraic systems. Artificial intelligence tools focus on three basic goals. The first is to increase dramatically the productivity of mathematical and software developers by automating the construction and optimization of algorithms and their mapping onto supercomputer architecture. To a certain extent, we are speaking here of overcoming the current global programming crisis, which manifests itself in the huge gap between the code implementation speed and the rate of growth of the computing power of MPSs. The second goal, a mission, so to speak, is the creation of a "factory" of natural and artificial languages for building effective interfaces, both internal and external, intended for end-users from various professional backgrounds; this would ensure a wide demand for the created modeling tools. The third goal is, in fact, a direction of intellectualization: the optimization of planning and managing machine experiments, that is, the direct process whereby we grasp new fundamental and applied knowledge. Here, in some sense, mathematical modeling represents the main approach to assimilation and interpretation of field measurements. The classification and the identification of a set of problems along with the choice of the appropriate algorithms for specific situations rely on optimization methods. The broad functionality of the new generation of computing and information technologies requires the development of the content of intelligent systems. The scale of the problems under consideration puts on the agenda the development of an integrated tool environment corresponding to the concept of a mathematical knowledge base built upon the principles of machine learning and big-data handling.

Acknowledgements. The work was supported by the Russian Foundation for Basic Research (grant No. 18-01-00295).

References

1. Il'in V.: Mathematical Modeling. Part I. Continuous and Discrete Models. SBRAS, Novosibirsk (2017)
2. Axelsson, O.: Iterative Solution Methods, Cambridge University, Press, Cambridge (1994). https://doi.org/10.1017/CBO9780511624100
3. Saad, Y.: Iterative Methods for Sparse Linear Systems, 2nd edn., SIAM (2003). https://doi.org/10.1137/1.9780898718003
4. Il'in, V.: Finite Element Methods and Technologies, ICM&MG SBRAS, Novosibirsk (2007). (in Russian)
5. Olshanskii M.A., Tyrtyshnikov E.E.: Iterative Methods for Linear Systems Theory and Applications, SIAM, Philadelphia (2014). https://doi.org/10.1137/1.9781611973464
6. Dongarra, J.: List of Freely Available Software for Linear Algebra on the web (2006). http://netlib.org/utk/people/JackDongarra/la-sw.html
7. Barret, R., et al.: Templates for the Solution of Linear Systems. Building Blocks for Iterative Methods, SIAM, Philadelphia, PA (1994). https://doi.org/0.1137/1.9781611971538.bm
8. Il'in, V.: On an integrated computational environment for numerical algebra. In: Sokolinsky, L., Zymbler, M. (eds.) PCT 2019. CCIS, vol. 1063, pp. 91–106. Springer, Cham (2019). https://doi.org/10.1007/978-3-030-28163-2_7
9. Algowiki: https://algowiki-project.org/ru
10. Il'in, V.: Artificial intelligence problems in mathematical modeling. In: Voevodin, V., Sobolev, S. (eds.) RuSCDays 2019. CCIS, vol. 1129, pp. 505–516. Springer, Cham (2019). https://doi.org/10.1007/978-3-030-36592-9_41
11. Il'in, V.: Problems of parallel solution of large systems of linear algebraic equations. J. Math. Sci. **216**(6), 795–804 (2016). https://doi.org/10.1007/s10958-016-2945-4
12. Il'in, V.: The integrated computational environment for optimization of complex systems. In: 2019 Proceedings of the 15th International Asian School-Seminar "Optimization Problems of Complex Systems" (OPCS 2019), pp. 65–67 (2019).https://doi.org/10.1109/opcs.2019.8880155
13. Shary, S.P.: On full rank interval matrices. Num. Anal. Appl. **7**(3), 241–254 (2014). https://doi.org/10.1134/s1995423914030069

14. Il'in, V.: Projection methods in Krylov subspaces. J. Math. Sci. **240**(6), 772–782 (2019). https://doi.org/10.1007/s10958-019-04395-7
15. Il'in, V.: Two-Level Least squares methods in Krylov subspaces. J. Math. Sci. **232**(6), 892–901 (2019) . https://doi.org/10.1007/s10958-018-3916-8
16. Il'in, V.: High-performance computation of initial boundary value problems. In: Sokolinsky, L., Zymbler, M. (eds.) PCT 2018. CCIS, vol. 910, pp. 186–199. Springer, Cham (2018). https://doi.org/10.1007/978-3-319-99673-8_14
17. Il'in V.: Multi-preconditioned domain decomposition methods in the Krylov subspaces. In: Dimov, I., Farago, I., Vulkov, L. (eds.) Numerical Analysis and Its Applications (NAA 2016). LNCS, vol. 10187. Springer, Cham (2016). https://doi.org/10.1007/978-3-319-57099-0_9
18. Il'in, V.: Biconjugate Direction Methods in Krylov Subspaces. J. Appl. Ind. Math. **4**(1), 61–78 (2010). https://doi.org/10.1134/s1990478910010102
19. ll'in, V.: Methods of semiconjugate directions. Russian J. Numer. Anal. Math. Model. **23**(4), 369–387 (2008). https://doi.org/10.1515/rjnamm.2008.022
20. Gurieva, Y.L., Il'in, V.P., Petukhov, A.V.: On multigrid methods for solving two-dimensional boundary-value problems. J. Math. Sci. **240**(6), 13–28 (2020) . https://doi.org/10.1007/s10958-020-04926-7
21. Spielman, D.A., Teng, S.M., Nearly-linear-time algorithms for preconditioning and solving symmetric diagonal dominant linear systems. SIAM J. Matrix Anal. Appl. **35**, 835–885 (2014). https://doi.org/10.1137/090771430
22. Aleeva, V.: Designing a parallel programs on the base of the conception of Q-determinant. In: Voevodin, V., Sobolev, S. (eds.) RuSCDays 2018. CCIS, vol. 965, pp. 565–577. Springer, Cham (2019). https://doi.org/10.1007/978-3-030-05807-4_48
23. Akhmed-Zaki, D., Lebedev, D., Malyshkin, V., Perepelkin, V.: Automated construction of high performance distributed programs in LuNA system. In: Malyshkin, V. (ed.) PaCT 2019. LNCS, vol. 11657, pp. 3–9. Springer, Cham (2019). https://doi.org/10.1007/978-3-030-25636-4_1
24. LeCun, Y., Bengio, Y., Hinton, G.: Deep learning. Nature **521**, 436–444 (2015) . https://doi.org/10.1038/nature14539
25. Weinan, E.: Machine learning and computational mathematics. Commun. Comput. Phys. **28**(5), 1639–1670 (2020). https://doi.org/10.4208/cicp.oa-2020-0185
26. Borgest, N.M.: Key Terms the ontology of designing : review. Anal. Gen. Ontol. Des. **3**(9), 9–31 (2013)
27. Goncharov, S.S., Sviridenko, D.I.: Logical language of description of polynomial computing. Dokl. Math. **99**(2), 1–4 (2019). https://doi.org/10.1134/s1064562419020030
28. Zagorulko, Y.A., Borovikova, O.I.: An approach for realization of the content patterns in implementation of the scientific domains. Syst. Inform. **12**, 27–39 (2018). (in Russian)

CUDA Implementation of an Algorithm for Batch Mode Detection of Collisions

D. L. Golitsyn[1], A. V. Korzun[1], and O. I. Ryabkov[2](✉)

[1] Abagy Robotic Systems, Houston, USA
{dgolitsyn,akorzun}@abagy.com
[2] Federal Research Center "Computer Science and Control"
of Russian Academy of Sciences, Moscow, Russia

Abstract. The collision detection problem arises in many different areas, such as games, computer graphics, physics simulations, robot control systems, and others. There exist many different setups of this problem. We consider a setup associated with a special case of the collision detection problem that may arise during the process of optimization of robot control. The number of geometries of rigid bodies in this setup is relatively small (of the order of tens or hundreds), but the number of configurations (i.e., bodies in different positions) can be substantial (of the order of thousands or tens of thousands). In some cases, these configurations (scenes) may be pregenerated together, while in other cases, new scenes can appear only after the collision detection in previous ones. Several scene sources may participate simultaneously. There are well-known flexible implementations of algorithms for collision detection (for instance, Flexible Collision Library, FCL) designed for many-core CPUs. However, efficient GPU implementations (at least for the described setup) are still missing. In this paper, we outline a GPU implementation and compare it with the FCL. We measure the acceleration of our implementation against a single-threaded CPU version (which is the FCL in our case) under different regimes. In some cases, the acceleration reaches a value of the order of 60 to 70.

Keywords: CUDA · Collision detection · FCL · Robot control systems · GPGPU

1 Introduction

The collision detection problem has different setups in several applications. For example, games and physics simulation software may require the consideration of the problem in a highly detailed environment with constantly changing geometry. However, scenes arise in this case one by one according to the simulation process. The detection of self-collisions may be necessary under some setups (e.g., soft-body dynamics simulation). In different situations, the expected result may be a specific collision point. Finally, there are setups of the collision detection problem

© Springer Nature Switzerland AG 2021
L. Sokolinsky and M. Zymbler (Eds.): PCT 2021, CCIS 1437, pp. 118–133, 2021.
https://doi.org/10.1007/978-3-030-81691-9_9

with continuous time in which it is required to determine the exact time at which a collision occurs.

Here, we focus the study on the problem of collision detection. There are many different approaches to this problem, including such methods as Bounding-Volume Hierarchies (BVH), Spatial Subdivision (SS), Image-Space Techniques (IST), Stochastic Methods (SM), Distance Fields (DF), and Continuous Collision Detection (CCD).

The BVH methods are based on a tree data structure that is computed by partitioning object primitives. The tree leaves hold references to the associated object primitives, while the internal nodes contain references to the child nodes. Each node contains a bounding volume (BV) that encompasses primitives or child nodes with the smallest primitive shape. This includes spheres [11], oriented bounding boxes (OBB) [8], boxtrees [22], convex hulls [5], and so on. The collision test of two objects is performed from top to down on the BVH, and the pairs of tree nodes are recursively tested for overlapping. If overlapping is found in the leaves of the BVH, then the enclosed primitives are tested for intersection. If only one node is a leaf and the other is an internal node, then the leaf node is tested with each of the children of the internal node. If both nodes are internal, then the node with smaller BV is tested against the children of the other node. This process is recursive. The BVH methods are the most efficient of the methods for the detection of rigid-body collisions, provided that the tree can be precomputed before running the simulation. If not, then such methods need fine-tuning in terms of updating. These methods were implemented on the computational architecture of central processing units (CPUs) [12,19] and graphics processing units (GPUs) [3,13]. CPU-based approaches tend to rely heavily on communication between processors, which is not suited for current GPU-like architectures. GPUs can accelerate these methods only under the assumption that the CPU–GPU memory operations are minimized or optimized. More details are given in the next section.

The SS methods are usually applied to moving and deforming objects. The SS method partitions primitives in the world space, whereas the BVH method does the same in the object space. The space $\Omega \subset \mathbb{R}^3$ is divided into convex regions called cells. Each cell possesses a list of object primitives that are contained (fully or partially) in the cell. After all the objects are discretized into cells, the collision tests are executed in each cell that contains more than one primitive. Such partitioning of Ω greatly decreases the number of collision tests to be executed. The spatial structure is updated for moving and deforming objectives. The data structure is needed to represent the mapping between the list of objects and Ω. Different implementations approach the problem differently, which includes uniform 3D grids (molecular dynamics) [15], octrees [1], BSP trees [7,16], and KD-trees [20]. Even a perfect multidimensional hash function was applied [14] to pack sparse primitive data into a table with efficient random access.

The IST method is based on object projection to accelerate collision queries. It is usually done by rendering object primitives into the frame buffer. Such data structure is formed by the discrete representation and, thus, the collision is not exact. The accuracy of the collision detection is determined by the discretization error, so the accuracy is balanced to the acceleration at need. No preprocessing is required for this method. Many such methods are applied to problems of computer graphics. The methods are efficient on GPUs [10] but their drawback of discretization error reduced their area of application.

The SM method is based on the selection of random pairs of elements from objects as input to the exact intersection test. This drastically reduces the computational complexity and time but results in an inexact collision. It is usually combined with other collision detection methods to use different heuristics to accelerate the collision detection process (see [2]). These methods, however, are not suitable for the solution of problems where exact collision detection is required.

The DF methods depend on the estimation of the distance functional (signed or unsigned) between objects. The representation of a closed surface by distance applies no restrictions on the topology. The evaluation of the geometric information that is necessary for the collision detection is fast and independent of the geometric complexity. One usually applies a uniform (or adaptive) grid that stores distance values. However, this approach requires a rather large amount of memory. BSP trees can also be used [9] if the distance field is approximated by a piecewise linear approximation [21]; the required memory can thus be reduced. On the other hand, the BSP tree construction is computationally expensive.

The CCD methods are continuous in terms of the requirements placed on the explicit trajectory simulation and are more physical. These methods track trajectories of primitives and check the intersection of trajectories [18]. However, these methods are not well suited for massive parallel execution and do not apply to deformable bodies.

It is desirable to carry out the parallel implementation of the collision problem on GPUs to reduce the power consumption and the cost of computations. As we can see, few methods are suitable for GPU implementations. At the same time, there are good and reliable libraries for multi-core CPU architectures, such as the FCL, which we use as a benchmark [17].

Among the existing GPU implementations, we can highlight some early endeavors, such as the gProximity library [13] and the Bullet library OpenCL, creates as an acceleration attempt [4]. NVidia's PhysX library is a rather mature CUDA engine for rigid bodies that includes a collision detection solver (see https://developer.nvidia.com/gameworks-physx-overview). However, all these GPU implementations involve problems different from the ones considered in this paper. They all place an emphasis on very large scenes (scenes with large numbers of objects and large numbers of triangles), whilst our implementation deals with relatively small scenes but processes them in a so-called Batch Mode (see Subsect. 2.2 for details).

In this paper, we suggest a new method based on the BVH, implemented on CUDA C++. We chose from the BVH and the IST methods, but accuracy requirements demanded the use of the BVH method. The main features of the method are the storage of the prebuilt OBB tree on the GPU and the implementation of a manager interface that allows one to use CUDA streams for the acceleration of substantial computations.

The structure of the paper is as follows. First, we give a formulation of the problem, including the relevant terminology and the features of the method operation modes. Then, we describe in detail the implementation of the method. The next section contains the results obtained during extensive testing. The paper finishes with the conclusions.

2   Problem Formulation

2.1   Terminology

There is no universally accepted terminology in the field of collision problems. Let us introduce the following terms to make the understanding of the paper easier.

- *Mesh.* A set of triangles. A mesh represents a certain geometry.
- *Object.* Each of the individual entities available to a collision request. Each object is associated with one and only one mesh. In a given scene, each object can have its specific position. Several objects can be associated with one mesh.
- *Manager.* A special interface (actually a C++ class instance) that receives all requests from the user (such as collision requests and mesh add/remove requests). The manager has its internal state (for example, currently "registered" meshes and objects that can participate in the subsequent collision requests).
- *Set of manager objects.* The set of all objects that can theoretically participate in one collision request at the current moment. Note that the set of manager objects can be changed during the Manager lifetime through the addition and deletion of objects.
- *Set of request objects.* The set of objects that actually participate in a given collision request.
- *Set of active objects.* A subset of the set of request objects that have to be checked for collisions with all other request objects (including other active objects).
- *Allowed pairs.* The set of pairs of request objects that are "allowed" to have collisions and, therefore, do not need to be checked for collisions at all.
- *Allowed objects.* A subset of request objects that are "allowed" to have collisions with any other objects.
- *Collision request.* It consists of its set of objects, the set of pairs of objects that must be checked for collisions (it consists of the set of active objects, allowed pairs, and allowed objects), and the set of scenes that must be checked for collisions.
- *Scene.* The positions of the objects of the set of request objects. The logic unit of a request. The results (when there is a collision in the scene, and the set of pairs of colliding objects) returned for a given request are grouped separately for each scene of this request.

This study has been motivated by the problem of optimization of robot control. Due to the specific features of the problem, we may only consider the collision detection for the moment, that is, we need to output neither the specific points of intersection nor the distance for objects without intersection. Thus, for any given scene, the result consists of both a flag (the flag value indicates whether any collision has been detected in the scene) and a list of colliding objects.

We also actively exploit the fact that the objects and meshes participating in a request remain almost unchanged during the execution of the algorithm applied to the original problem. More details regarding the original control problem are given below.

2.2   Request Sources and Batch Mode Discussion

Once some basic concepts and terminology have been outlined, we can discuss some details of the problem setup specific to the CUDA implementation. The number of collision requests and their size can affect the performance in different ways, depending on the computational architecture. This influence is low for low-parallelism architectures (as multi-core CPUs) and may become substantial for high-parallelism architectures (as NVidia GPUs). GPU-based algorithm implementations can achieve a high degree of efficiency only for relatively large problems, unlike CPU-based implementations. This effect can be demonstrated for rather different computational problems (see [6], for example). The root of this difference lies primarily in the parallelization approach adopted on GPUs. First, GPUs usually have more parallel cores (arithmetic logic units) (see specifications, for example, at https://www.nvidia.com/en-us/geforce/products/10series/titan-x-pascal/). Second, GPU vectorization usually differs from that of CPU. Long vector registers (warps) are used on GPUs to perform several parallel tasks (threads) at once. A more traditional approach is used on CPUs, where vectorization is performed in a per-task fashion (for example, to perform 3D geometric transformations faster). So the problem formulation for GPUs often needs to be recast from the corresponding formulation for CPUs to achieve a decent level of acceleration. This often leads to difficulties when embedding a GPU-accelerated code into existing solutions. The most common difference is a requirement to recast a series of small tasks into groups of these tasks. This is called *batch mode*. Even though original tasks are completely independent, only their simultaneous execution can sufficiently load a GPU. However, the batch mode may be difficult to use inside the original high-level problem (the one that produces these tasks).

In our case, the original problem is a process of optimization of robot control. It performs some sample-based optimization, which requires checking a certain optimized trajectory for any possible collision with obstacles. The set of objects that participate in the search is constant for the most part, but their relative positions are different. These positions constitute a scene. It is a single logical unit of collision requests (see the Terminology section above). Here, we face a problem with the batch mode because the scenes may appear sequentially in small groups (tens of scenes, for example) which are not sufficient to load a

GPU. Moreover, these scenes may arise only after the previous ones have been checked according to the original optimization problem algorithm. Hence, the first condition for our GPU implementation: it must utilize as much parallelism as possible even for relatively small batches.

Such batch sizes are not sufficient for good performance. However, there is another possible source of parallelism that could theoretically improve the situation. The original optimization process may work in parallel (for example, using several CPU threads) to investigate several branches of optimization solutions independently. These CPU threads may produce scenes that can be processed on a GPU simultaneously. Here, we can draw up the second condition for our GPU implementation (and also for the GPU problem setup): it must utilize the different sources of scenes as effectively as possible. Small requests must not substantially slow down the whole computation. Theoretically, these scenes (from different sources) must be combined into one batch request. On the other hand, a minimum delay must occur during this packaging process. For example, assume that the collision process is idle and a small request is passed to it. Then, the process must execute this request immediately to avoid any possible latency, even though the request may not be big enough to load a GPU and achieve efficient parallel execution.

3   The CUDA Implementation

Our approach is based on the OBB BVH algorithm, as mentioned in the Introduction. First of all, we must note that our study is entirely dedicated to the collision check part of the algorithm, that is, we do not deal with the construction of BVH on a GPU. We use instead the CPU library (Proximity Query Package (PQP), library version 1.3) to prebuild BVH and load them into a GPU. This approach is justified by the specific character of the original control problem (see a brief explanation above in Sect. 2): the sets of objects and meshes that participate in collision requests remain almost unchanged during the execution of the original algorithm. Moreover, the required time for collision checks in a CPU implementation largely exceeds the time needed for the construction of BVH.

The collision detection algorithm is not discussed here as it is rather standard (one can refer to the brief description above or the referenced literature). In our CUDA implementation, we borrowed some ideas from the gProximity library (see [13]). The main difficulty in the CUDA implementation of the BVH algorithm is its recursive nature. Although dynamic parallelism is present in modern NVidia graphics cards, it is not particularly effective, and the "manual" approach is still preferable [10]. The straightforward implementation of the recursive algorithm on GPU resorts to the creation of some stack-like structure (although in [13] it is called a queue instead; one may note, however, that this structure is neither the one nor the other in the parallel approach). A single element of this structure (which we will call a *queue*, as in [13]) is a pair of bounding boxes (BB) that must be checked (this element is called a *work item*). The unit workpiece associated with the work item performs the collision check of these BBs and if there is no collision, then the work is finished. Nonetheless, two more work items are spawned and must be stored in a queue if the collision is detected. The problem of the collision detection of a single pair of objects (not in batch mode) is considered in [13]. The implementation giving there consists of two repeating stages. At the first stage, each CUDA kernel block that is involved in the solution obtains its part of the work queue. It deals with it separately. The elements of the queue are processed by the threads of the block in parallel. The threads create their own local queue, which is stored in the GPU shared memory. The work continues until the local queue is either empty or too large to be kept inside the shared memory. In the latter case, it is unloaded into the global memory. Note that a rebalancing procedure is required because the sizes of the parts of the new queue are different for different blocks. The procedure is performed in the second stage. Then, the cycle is repeated until the global queue is empty. Our initial approach was to use gProximity in the solution and check all pairs of objects for collisions one by one. However, this approach was abandoned since the GPU implementation was much slower than the CPU one. According to the profiling, most of the time (nearly 80%) was used by the balancing kernels.

Our solution also deals with a queue of work items similar to the ones in gProximity. In Fig. 1, we see the overall implementation scheme of the algorithm. The first difference from the algorithm mentioned above is that we reject the balancing procedure and the approach oriented to kernel blocks. Instead, all work items in the queue are processed uniformly by one kernel (kerBatchTreeTraverse in Fig. 1). Each thread works with one work item. The result is either an empty local queue or a local queue of two new work items. The thread saves the results of its work in a special aligned buffer ("loc_queues"). Then, the prefix sum algorithm is invoked (we used CUDA UnBound (CUB) library) to compute the positions of the newly created work items in the new global queue. After that, a special kernel (kerCopyLocQueuesToQueue) is invoked to reorganize the work items from the aligned buffer ("loc_queues") into a new queue. Then, the process is repeated. The second significant difference from the gProximity library is the batch mode. We wanted to reduce the number of CUDA kernel invocations as much as possible (each kernel invocation has its overhead) and enlarge the size of these kernels instead (larger kernels are more efficient). We take all work items from all pairs of objects, scenes and requests. These items are combined into one uniform queue. This required larger work items but all preliminary tests showed that this approach would be efficient.

Our implementation features a server-style architecture to fulfill all requirements listed in Subsect. 2.2 and use the GPU capabilities. A constantly working conveyor process is used along with the preallocated GPU buffers. This approach allows the implementation to accept new collision requests while still working on previous ones. The chosen architecture makes it possible to minimize the damage caused to the performance by small requests, which often are not well fitted for the GPU architecture, while maintaining, at the same time, an acceptable level of performance for large requests.

The solution scheme consists of four main parts:

- *Preparation and management of meshes.* It is implemented in the Meshes-Manager class. It includes all tasks of construction of BVH (using the PQP library on CPUs), their conversion into GPU format, and loading to GPU memory. Mesh addition requests are processed asynchronously and can be performed at the same time as other requests coming to the Manager. A separate CPU thread (called the Mesh Thread) and the corresponding CUDA stream (called the Mesh Stream) are dedicated to the mesh addition task.
- *Initial processing of requests (interface).* It is implemented in the Manager class. All requests are invoked in one distinct thread called the Main Thread. The corresponding CUDA stream is called the Main Stream. For some requests (collision, mesh addition), only the initialization part is performed inside the Main Thread and the Main Stream. Other requests (mesh removal, objects addition/removal) are completely processed by them.
- *Main processing sequence of collisions.* It is implemented in the Collision-Processor class. It includes the main collision conveyor and is performed in a separate thread called the Collision Processing Thread and in the corresponding CUDA stream (Collision Processing Stream).
- *Finalization of collision requests.* It is implemented in CollisionFinalizer class. It includes copying the results from the collision conveyor, their final preparation, and returning them to the user. All these tasks are executed in a separate thread (Collision Finalization Thread) and the corresponding CUDA stream (Collision Finalization Stream).

All requests including objects and meshes manipulation as well as actual collision requests are invoked as Manager class methods in the Main Thread. Mesh manipulation requests (add/remove) are passed to the MeshesManager

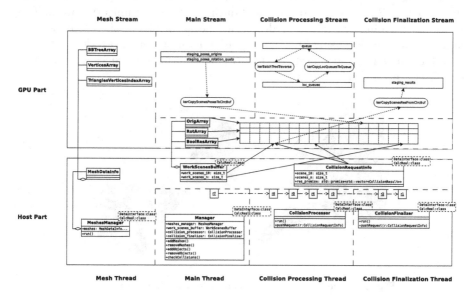

Fig. 1. Implementation design scheme

class, whereas object requests (add/remove) are passed to the ObjectsManager. All these requests are carried out synchronously in the Main Thread, except for mesh addition, which is passed to the MeshesManager queue. All collision requests are initially preprocessed directly in the Main Thread inside the Manger class. The preprocessing stage includes copying scene information from a CPU into a special staging buffer and then into a special circular buffer of scenes and corresponding results (WorkScenesBuffer). Then, the request is passed into the CollisionProcessor, which spawns the initial work items for newly added scenes and pairs of objects, and subsequently adds them into the current working queue. Note that the queue can be nonempty at this point. This is the case if the CollisionProcessor has already been working on some previous requests. Next, the CollisionProcessor proceeds with its infinite cycle of kerBatchTree-Traverse/kerCopyLocQueuesToQueue kernels (which is actually the core of the algorithm; see above). Special logic is used to detect finished requests. It includes a special cutoff: when the first intersection of the two objects is found, we stop the search for this pair and remove all corresponding work items. When the request processing is finished, it is passed into the CollisionFinalizer, which copies the collision results from the WorkScenesBuffer into a separate unstaging buffer, and then back to the CPU that forms the request result.

4   The Test Setup

A real set of objects and requests was used as the basis for the testing process. The objects and requests were obtained by sampling from the solution of a real-world optimization problem. The set of meshes consists of 17 objects totaling 10 874 triangles. The individual mesh size in the set varies from 12 triangles to 2558 triangles. The initial set of requests includes 100 000 scenes, which contain these objects. Scenes were pregenerated during the test optimization work. The benchmark timings for collision detection checks involving these scenes were measured beforehand using FCL. The collision requests for the acceleration tests were formed as random subsets of the pregenerated pool of scenes. Examples of the objects are given in Fig. 2.

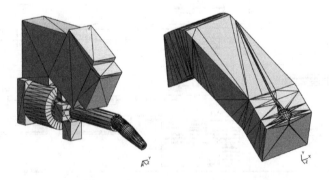

Fig. 2. Some examples of objects from the collision test set

The performance tests are organized as follows. All requests are grouped into *tests*. Each test contains several collision requests (representing requests from different CPU sources; see Sect. 2 for a justification) alongside alternating object addition requests. Object removal requests are not inserted into the tests because they are less dangerous from a performance viewpoint. Besides, the structure and logic of the tests with object removal requests would be much more complicated otherwise. The sets of request objects include some basic set of objects, which is unchanged during the whole testing process, and a randomly chosen subset of newly added objects which imitate a real queue of requests. A single test is a basic unit of time measurement. After the test, its results were compared with the reference results obtained with the FCL. All extra objects that were added during the test were removed to restore the initial Manger state. Tests were grouped into timing blocks. Inside a particular timing block, all tests have the same set of statistical parameters. These parameters include the exact number of collision and object addition requests, the mean number of scenes participating in one request, and the dispersion of its distribution. The number of requests per test is fixed and is not sampled randomly, whereas the number of scenes is sampled using the normal distribution with the above-mentioned parameters. Timing blocks are used to get statistically reliable acceleration results through the repetition of the test with the same statistical parameters.

The ultimate goal of our implementation is to achieve maximum acceleration for any values of the listed parameters. Of course, this is almost impossible due to the reasons mentioned in Subsect. 2.2 taking into account a relatively simple set of objects. However, we have to remove performance dependency at least for some of these parameters. A reasonable performance must be achieved for tests with a small number of scenes. The following sets of values for the discussed parameters were tested:

- *Number of collision requests*: {1, 2, 3, 4}. Corresponds to the possible number of CPU threads performing an optimization task.
- *Number of object addition requests*: {0, 4}. The first case corresponds to collision requests only. The second case simulates the worst possible situation when the number of object addition requests is the same (or larger) than the number of collision requests.
- *Mean value of the number of scenes participating in a request*: {10, 100, 200, 500, 1000, 2000, 5000, 10 000}.
- *Dispersion of the number of scenes participating in a request*: {0.0, 0.2, 0.5} * ⟨mean value of the number of scenes in the request⟩. The dispersion is established as a quantity relative to the chosen mean value. Simply speaking, these values correspond to the following three cases: constant request length, moderately variable request length, and highly variable request length.

Each test was repeated 20 times inside its timing block, as mentioned above. We tested the problem on two GPU devices. The first device was a GTX TITAN X NVIDIA card with 12 GB RAM, 11 TFLOPS peak single precision, 3072 CUDA Cores, and compute capability 5.2. Below, the first device will be referred to as Device 0. The second one was a GTX TITAN Black NVIDIA card with 6 GB RAM, 5.1 TFLOPS peak single precision, 2880 CUDA Cores, and compute capability 3.5. It will be referred to as Device 1. The reference results were obtained using an Intel Xeon E5-2697V2 Ivy Bridge with 12 cores.

5   Acceleration Results

In this section, we discuss the GPU acceleration dependency on different block parameters, such as the number of collision requests per test and the average number of scenes in a single request. The parameters are divided into two groups. The first contains *primary* parameters, on which the acceleration depends heavily. The second group contains *secondary* parameters, from which the performance of our implementation is almost independent. Below, we discuss these two groups in reverse order.

5.1   Secondary Parameters Dependency

After the analysis of the results, we ranked the following parameters as secondary: the number of object addition requests and the dispersion of the number of scenes per request. In this subsection, we demonstrate that our implementation is stable under variations of these parameters. First, consider the number of object addition requests. Figure 3 shows a comparison of the acceleration for the two considered values of this parameter (namely, 0 and 4). The comparison is given for almost all considered cases. The first row of plots corresponds to Device 0, the second to Device 1. The columns correspond to different values of relative dispersion. Two extreme values (1 and 4) of the "number of collision requests" parameter are given on each plot. One can see that the object addition requests do not affect the performance in almost all cases. An insignificant degradation of the acceleration is observed for 4 collision requests per test. In one specific case (1 collision request per test, Device 0, maximum dispersion), one can suspect the reverse effect when timings for tests with object addition requests seem to be better. However, we attribute this artifact to the insufficient sampling number (statistical artifacts).

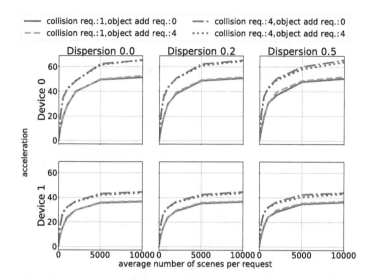

Fig. 3. Acceleration results for different devices, dispersion, collision requests, and numbers of object addition requests. The variants of the latter parameter are represented on the same plots to demonstrate their closeness.

The same data are displayed in Fig. 4 in transposed form. Here, the acceleration curves are regrouped in such a manner that the ones for different values of the relative dispersion are plotted together for better comparison. Any variations for the case of 1 collision request per test have to be considered as statistical artifacts since there is no other possible explanation for that. The most significant variation in the case of 4 collision requests can be seen on the upper right plot. One can notice a degradation of the acceleration from 62 or 63-fold to approximately 60-fold. We consider this level of degradation acceptable.

5.2 Primary Parameters Dependency

The acceleration dependency on primary parameters is discussed in this subsection. These parameters are the number of collision requests and the average number of scenes participating in one request according to our timings. For a clearer representation, on the following plots, we averaged the acceleration values over

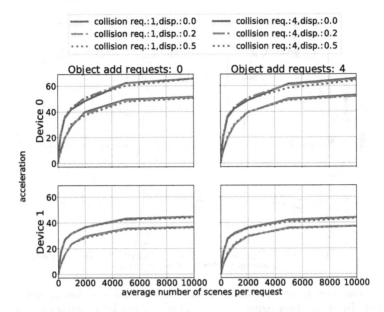

Fig. 4. Acceleration results for different devices, dispersion, collision requests, and numbers of object addition requests. The variants of the dispersion parameter are represented on the same plots to demonstrate their closeness.

all secondary parameters Fig. 5 shows how the acceleration depends on these two parameters for both tested GPUs. As one can expect, the acceleration is higher when more collision requests are invoked. It drastically drops for low numbers of scenes in a request. For both devices, a critical degradation happens approximately at the level of 1000 scenes when the acceleration becomes lower than 20-fold. The saturation happens at the level of 5000 scenes. However, we can see that full saturation was not achieved for Device 0 in the considered ranges of parameters. The maximum acceleration is approximately 65 for Device 0 and 45 for Device 1.

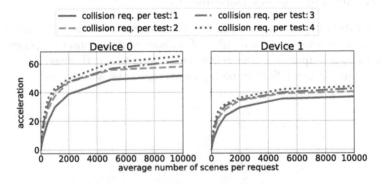

Fig. 5. Acceleration dependency on the average number of scenes per collision request. The acceleration has been averaged over the secondary parameters.

The results for the average number of scenes in one request in Fig. 5 may be interesting from the point of view of the user of the algorithm. A more synthetic parameter is considered now: the average number of scenes in one *test*. This parameter is simply the product of the average number of scenes in one *request* by the number of collision requests in one *test*. We can consider the average number of scenes in one *test* as the parameter instead of the number of scenes in one *request*, in which case the number of collision requests can be reclassified as *secondary*. Simply speaking, if the requests come in groups from different sources, only the total length of these requests, but not their number, substantially affects the performance. This assertion is only true to a certain extent but it can be considered as an advantage of our implementation. Consider Figs. 6 and 7. They both represent the acceleration as a function of the average number of scenes in one *test* for both devices and different numbers of requests. The latter parameter in Fig. 6 (small scale plot) seems to be irrelevant. Variations can be ascribed totally to statistical perturbations, as in some previously considered cases. This is particularly true for so-called "inverted" slow-downs. However, if we refer to Fig. 7 (large scale plot), we can see that some loss of efficiency occurs in small ranges of requests when the number of scenes per test is lower than 1000. Another conclusion can be drawn from Fig. 7: the performance is nearly the same for both devices in the range of small requests. This should come as no surprise because small requests can not exploit the higher level of parallelism inherent to more advanced graphics cards.

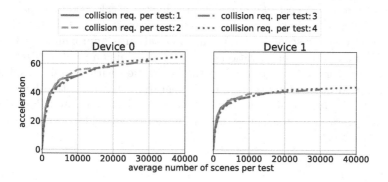

Fig. 6. Acceleration dependency on the average number of scenes per test. The acceleration has been averaged over the secondary parameters.

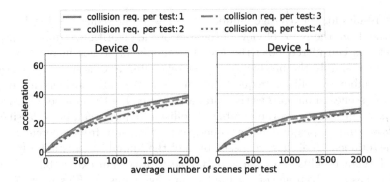

Fig. 7. Acceleration dependency on the average number of scenes per test. The acceleration has been averaged over the secondary parameters. A close-up of the range of small numbers of scenes

6   Conclusions

We considered a CUDA implementation of an algorithm for batch mode detection of collisions. It is oriented toward the optimization of robot control. It makes it possible to obtain a seamless association of collision requests coming from different sources to achieve maximum performance. The implementation demonstrates stability with respect to both the number of incoming requests and the dispersion in their size. It allows for runtime changes in the set of objects at almost no cost. The maximum achieved acceleration compared to a single-threaded FCL implementation is about 60 to 70-fold. The wall time for execution of a single scene with our implementation is approximately 3 ms for the maximum obtained acceleration on scenes containing a total of 10 000 triangles. Further work will be devoted to the integration with actual optimization algorithms and possible multi-GPU implementation. The algorithm for the construction of BB trees can be switched from a relatively outdated PQP library to the FCL library. A broad phase algorithm can be added for scenes with large numbers of objects.

References

1. Bandi, S., Thalmann, D.: An adaptive spatial subdivision of the object space for fast collision detection of animated rigid bodies. Comput. Graph. Forum (1995). https://doi.org/10.1111/j.1467-8659.1995.cgf143-0259.x
2. Baraff, D., Witkin, A., Kass, M.: Untangling cloth. In: ACM SIGGRAPH 2003 Papers (SIGGRAPH 2003), pp. 862–870. Association for Computing Machinery, New York, NY, USA (2003). https://doi.org/10.1145/1201775.882357
3. Cai, P., Cai, Y., Chandrasekaran, I., Zheng, J.: Collision Detection Using Axis Aligned Bounding Boxes, pp. 1–14. Simulation, Serious Games and Their Applications (2013)
4. Coumans, E.: Bullet: a case study in optimizing physics middleware for the GPU. In: NVIDIAs GPU Technology Conference (2009). https://doi.org/10.14529

5. Ehmann, S.A., Lin, M.C.: Accurate and fast proximity queries between polyhedra using convex surface decomposition. Comput. Graph. Forum (2001). https://doi.org/10.1111/1467-8659.00543

6. Evstigneev, N.M., Ryabkov, O.I., Tsatsorin, E.A.: On the inversion of multiple matrices on GPU in batched mode. Supercomputing Front. Innov. **5**(2) (2018). https://doi.org/10.14529/jsfi180203

7. Fan, W., Wang, B., Paul, J.C., Sun, J.: An octree-based proxy for collision detection in large-scale particle systems. Sci. China Inf. Sci. **56**(1), 1–10 (2012)

8. Gottschalk, S., Lin, M.C., Manocha, D.: OBBTree. In: Proceedings of the 23rd Annual Conference on Computer Graphics and Interactive Techniques (SIG-GRAPH 1996). ACM Press (1996). https://doi.org/10.1145/237170.237244

9. He, T., Kaufman, A.: Collision detection for volumetric objects. In: Proceedings. Visualization 1997 (Cat. No. 97CB36155). IEEE (1997). https://doi.org/10.1109/visual.1997.663851

10. Hermann, A., Drews, F., Bauer, J., Klemm, S., Roennau, A., Dillmann, R.: Unified GPU voxel collision detection for mobile manipulation planning. In: 2014 IEEE/RSJ International Conference on Intelligent Robots and Systems. IEEE (2014). https://doi.org/10.1109/iros.2014.6943148

11. Hubbard, P.M.: Approximating polyhedra with spheres for time-critical collision detection. ACM Trans. Graph. **15**(3), 179–210 (1996)

12. Kim, D., Heo, J.P., Huh, J., Kim, J., eui Yoon, S.: HPCCD: Hybrid parallel continuous collision detection using CPUs and GPUs. Comput. Graph. Forum **28**(7), 1791–1800 (2009). https://doi.org/10.1111/j.1467-8659.2009.01556.x

13. Lauterbach, C., Mo, Q., Manocha, D.: gProximity: Hierarchical GPU-based operations for collision and distance queries. Comput. Graph. Forum **29**(2), 419–428 (2010)

14. Lefebvre, S., Hoppe, H.: Perfect spatial hashing. In: ACM SIGGRAPH 2006 Papers (SIGGRAPH 2006), p. 579588. Association for Computing Machinery, New York, NY, USA (2006). https://doi.org/10.1145/1179352.1141926

15. Levinthal, C.: Molecular model-building by computer. Sci. Am. **214**(6), 42–52 (1966)

16. Melax, S.: Dynamic plane shifting BSP traversal. In: Proceedings of the Graphics Interface 2000 Conference, May 15–17, 2000, Montr'eal, Qu'ebec, Canada, pp. 213–220 (2000). http://graphicsinterface.org/wp-content/uploads/gi2000-28.pdf

17. Pan, J., Chitta, S., Manocha, D.: FCL: a general purpose library for collision and proximity queries. In: 2012 IEEE International Conference on Robotics and Automation. IEEE (2012). https://doi.org/10.1109/icra.2012.6225337

18. Redon, S., Kim, Y., Lin, M., Manocha, D., Templeman, J.: Interactive and continuous collision detection for avatars in virtual environments. In: IEEE Virtual Reality 2004. IEEE (2004). https://doi.org/10.1109/vr.2004.1310064

19. Tang, M., Manocha, D., Tong, R.: MCCD: multi-core collision detection between deformable models using front-based decomposition. Graph. Models **72**(2), 7–23 (2010)

20. Teller, S.J., Séquin, C.H.: Visibility preprocessing for interactive walkthroughs. ACM SIGGRAPH Comput. Graph. **25**(4), 61–70 (1991)

21. Wu, J., Kobbelt, L.: Piecewise linear approximation of signed distance fields. In: VMV (2003)

22. Zachmann, G.: Minimal hierarchical collision detection. In: Proceedings of the ACM Symposium on Virtual Reality Software and Technology (VRST 2002), pp. 121128. Association for Computing Machinery, New York, NY, USA (2002). https://doi.org/10.1145/585740.585761

Functionally Arranged Data for Algorithms with Space-Time Wavefront

Anastasia Perepelkina[(✉)][ID] and Vadim D. Levchenko[ID]

Keldysh Institute of Applied Mathematics, Moscow, Russia
mogmi@narod.ru, lev@keldysh.ru

Abstract. Algorithms with space-time tiling increase the performance of numerical simulations by increasing data reuse and arithmetic intensity; they also improve parallel scaling by making process synchronization less frequent. The theory of Locally Recursive non-Locally Asynchronous (LRnLA) algorithms provides the performance model with account for data localization at all levels of the memory hierarchy. However, effective implementation is difficult since modern optimizing compilers do not support the required traversal methods and data structures by default. The data exchange is typically implemented by writing the updated values to the main data array. Here, we suggest a new data structure that contains the partially updated state of the simulation domain. Data is arranged within this structure for coalesced access and seamless exchange between subtasks. We demonstrate the preliminary results of its superiority over previously used methods by localizing the processed data in the L2 GPU cache for the Lattice Boltzmann Method (LBM) simulation so that the performance is not limited by the GDDR throughput but is determined by the L2 cache access rate. If we estimate the ideal stepwise code performance to be memory-bound with a read/write ratio equal to 1 and assume it is localized in the GPU memory and performs at 100% of the theoretical memory bandwidth, then the results of our benchmarks exceed that peak by a factor of the order of 1.2.

Keywords: LRnLA algorithms · Temporal blocking · Loop skewing · Parallel algorithms · Data structure

1 Introduction

Stencil schemes on rectangular meshes are incredibly common in numerical simulations of physics, especially in wave phenomena and fluid dynamics. The codes of the simulations, however, often suffer from low-performance efficiency. A well-recognized problem is the locality wall, which is demonstrated by classifying the stencil codes as memory-bound problems in the Roofline model [15]. Additionally, it seems hard for developers to unify the approach to hybrid parallelism and storage hierarchy on modern and complex computer systems.

The graph traversal for such problems is commonly implemented with nested loops. The problem of optimization of a loop traversal arose in the earliest days

© Springer Nature Switzerland AG 2021
L. Sokolinsky and M. Zymbler (Eds.): PCT 2021, CCIS 1437, pp. 134–148, 2021.
https://doi.org/10.1007/978-3-030-81691-9_10

of computer programming, and the wavefront was introduced as an alternative for basic loop interchanging in performance optimization. The first mention of a wavefront is found in [8]. In an example for loops in two dimensions, which may be used for a one-dimensional space and a time iteration, correspondingly ($1D1T$), the wavefront is defined as a set of computations such that all computations that lie right next to a wavefront can be computed simultaneously. In [16], the idea of wavefronts was restated for automatic generation in compilers, and the term *loop skewing* was introduced.

In applications to physical phenomena, loop skewing transforms into time skewing [17]. In 3D simulations, the issue of the memory wall is the most relevant. However, despite the seemingly promising potential at the time, the wavefront idea did not evolve to be common enough in present-day practical stencil codes. Nevertheless, several prominent codes use wavefronts to achieve high performance [1,13,14,18].

While it clearly provides higher performance than traditional loops, the possible reason the wavefront is not a commonly used method is the difficulty of a multidimensional formulation that would retain the advantages of the base idea. One way to apply wavefronts is to skew the loops only in one spatial and one temporal axis. Then, one 'point' in the original wavefront formulation is an update operation of a 2D y–z plane. In this case, a wavefront is only useful if the cache size is large enough to contain the plane [12]. Three-dimensional formulations of time skewing in which the tile in the wavefront base fits into a higher memory level are provided with several complicated shapes [1,7].

This issue is solved in the theory of LRnLA (Locally Recursive non-Locally Asynchronous) algorithms [4]. The ConeTorre LRnLA algorithm in $dD1T$ is described as a direct product of $1D1T$ wavefronts. The DiamondTorre LRnLA algorithm is also of a wavefront type and provides better localization for cross-shaped stencils. The clarity of the algorithm traversal formulations has been proven by implementation of many non-trivial numerical schemes (Finite Difference Time Domain [20], Levander scheme for elastic seismic equations with TFSF source and PML boundary [19], Runge–Kutta discrete Galerkin [2], Particle-in-cell [11]) on systems with heterogeneous parallelism.

Another problem of multidimensional time skewing that was negligible in early $1D1T$ loops is the search for a data layout that satisfies the principles of data access locality, aligned for vectorization and coalesced for parallel access. Note that this important problem was never addressed in the time skewing techniques in the field of automatic compiler optimizations. Thus, loop optimization would never exceed the limits imposed with a prescribed data layout.

The problem of complicated data access was present in many LRnLA codes as well. It appears in such problems as index computation in data storage arrays during the $dD1T$ skewed traversal, insufficient coalescence in data read or write operations.

In this paper, we report the solution to the data storage problem in wavefront-type LRnLA algorithms.

This solution is not enough for other types of temporal blocking, such as diamond or trapezoidal tilings, and ConeTur LRnLA algorithms. However, the wavefront algorithms comprise an important class of graph traversals that, among other advantages, enable a computational window in stencil simulations. This is especially relevant for the use of GPU accelerators with the CPU RAM as the main data storage site, possibly descending to the SSD storage.

This solution was first reported in [10], where it was used to eliminate the performance loss of the GPU accelerator while reading the simulation data from the CPU RAM. Here, we describe for the first time how it can be used with all types of temporal blocking of wavefront type. Moreover, we provide the implementation specifications for the exchange in GPU shared memory and GPU global memory and give a detailed parameter study of the introduced data structure.

In Sect. 2, we outline the basic theory of LRnLA algorithms (Sect. 2.1) and, specifically, the ConeTorre algorithm (Sect. 2.2). The central idea of the paper is introduced in Sect. 2.3. We describe the sample implementation in Sect. 3 and report the performance study results in Sect. 4. In the Conclusions, we evaluate the implications of the idea introduced in the paper.

2   Methods

2.1   LRnLA Algorithms

Let us consider a dependency graph in the $dD1T$ (d dimensions and time) coordinate space. A point at (x, y, z, t) denotes the operation of obtaining the field value corresponding to this coordinate. The points are linked by arrows which signify data dependencies. An LRnLA algorithm is recursively defined as a polytope in that space with a rule of subdivision into constituent shapes [4]. The possible polytope shapes are constructed in three steps: (1) choose a convex shape on two planes $t = \text{const}$; (2) plot the areas of influence and dependency of the points in these shapes; (3) the intersection of those areas is the shape that defines the LRnLA algorithm. The task of updating all mesh values up to time N_T is a task that is represented by a box covering the whole dependency graph. In a traditional stepwise algorithm, it is decomposed into flat boxes (subtasks) that cover all points with the same t coordinate. They may be further decomposed into subtasks for parallel execution. The recursive subdivision terminates at an update of a mesh node.

The projection of the dependency graph to the dD coordinate space is a data space, and the projection of a polytope is a good representation of the data that has to be saved at its execution. In the stencil codes, the data that has to be loaded is in a close neighborhood of that projection.

2.2   ConeTorre

The ConeTorre LRnLA algorithm [6] is a manner of implementing the wavefront idea in any number of dimensions in a unified way. It is constructed as the intersection of the dependency and influence areas of two hypercubes as a slanted prism (see Fig. 1). The construction is possible in any number of dimensions and may be split with the help of the coordinate axes. For the sake of clarity, the illustrations in the current paper represent the $2D1T$ space, but the code implementation is done in the $3D1T$ space.

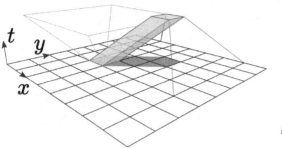 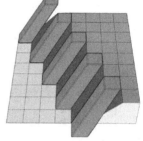

a) ConeTorre as the intersection of the influence and dependence regions of two cubes on the synchronization planes and its projection onto the data (pink), which is stored in tiles of cells

b) Wavefront of asynchronous ConeTorre. On the orange tiles, $t = N_T$ steps. On the red slopes, $0 < t < N_T$

Fig. 1. The ConeTorre LRnLA algorithm

The ConeTorre of height N_T is subdivided by planes $t = $ const into ConeTorres of height L_f. If the ConeTorres are executed by parallel threads, the synchronization takes place on these planes. The smaller shapes are subdivided into flat layers and then into unit scheme updates.

2.3 Data Exchange Between Tasks

Let us consider a cubic simulation domain. Figure 1 shows a projection of a ConeTorre onto the data space. In a basic computation, the cube at $t = 0$ is loaded to the GPU register (or any higher memory level in the target computer system) and updated according to the scheme. Then, the cells to the left of the cube are saved to the main memory storage, and the cells to the right of the cube are loaded from it. The data exchange area has the shape of a *gnomon* of the cube. After this, the computation in the ConeTorre may proceed a time step further.

In the main memory storage, the data is organized in an AoS (array of structure) fashion. An array element contains the data that is updated in a unit scheme update. The array consists of tiles for data access locality; the extreme case of this is a Z-curve array. This is a natural manner of data storage, convenient for data initialization and output for visualization, or other diagnostics.

However, the shape of the portion of the data array that is accessed in a ConeTorre (see Fig. 1) does not conform with such a pattern. There usually exists an overhead for integer operations in array index computation [6]. When the computed data is saved, an elongated hexagon should be looped over in the data structure, which is conformal to squares. Then, the hexagon is traversed again when it is read by the next ConeTorre.

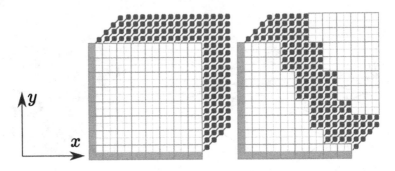

Fig. 2. Data structures in a $2D1T$ projection. The tile contains groups of $2 \times 2 \times 2$ cells. Each cell in the cube gnomon (green) corresponds to a FArSh line (red). The FArSh holds the data on the wavefront while the computation is in progress (Color figure online)

Here, we suggest a new data container optimal for data exchange between tasks in wavefront-type algorithms. The goal is to write the data in one subtask in the same manner as it is read in the next subtask that requires the data.

The input of a ConeTorre is the data for the operations on its lower base cube and its d lower slope sides. The output is the upper cube and the upper slopes. The cube is read from the base data storage `Tile`.

The data on the slopes is to be stored in a novel structure, named FArSh (Functionally Arranged Shadow). Let us consider a point (x_0, y_0, z_0, t_0) from the gnomon of the base cube. The line of points $(x_0 + i, y_0 + i, z_0 + i, t_0 + i)$, $i = 0, \ldots, N_T - 1$, is an element of FArSh. It is written in the order of increasing i in the ConeTorre below it and read in that order by the ConeTorre above it. Thus, data between ConeTorres with common faces can be exchanged by such lines of cells.

After the ConeTorre that reads a FArSh line is executed, the data in that line is no longer required. The upper face of the ConeTorre outputs new data, which replaces the data in that FArSh line.

The data in FArSh is only required at the places where the data is exchanged between subtasks. Thus, the number of lines required in the simulation is the number of cells in the gnomon of the simulation area.

Initially, the whole FArSh contains data outside the domain (see Fig. 2). As soon as the ConeTorres are executed in the correct order, the position of the starting points of the lines is shifted. Thus, FArSh moves during the simulation process to cover the actual space-time wavefront of the algorithm.

When the data is updated up to the synchronization instant, it is stored in Tile. At all other times, it is in FArSh. Thus, FArSh is not at all suitable for diagnostics and result output. The visualization of such data does not give any practical information on the simulated system state. It exists only for information transfer in the algorithm.

To summarize, the ConeTorre reads the data in the base cube from the BaseTile and the data on the slopes from FArSh. After the execution, it writes data in the upper cube to the base Tile and on its upper slopes to FArSh, replacing the previously stored data.

3   Implementation Example

3.1   Lattice Boltzmann Method

The case under study here is the implementation of the Lattice Boltzmann Method (LBM), a stencil scheme for computational fluid dynamics [3]. The Discrete Distribution Function (DDF) values f_q are stored on a rectangular mesh. They are updated according to the following expressions. For each mesh node $\mathbf{x}_i$, for each time instant t^k, we have

$$f_q(\mathbf{x}_i, t^k) = \Omega(f_1^*(\mathbf{x}_i, t^k), \ldots, f_Q^*(\mathbf{x}_i, t^k)), \tag{1}$$

$$f_q^*(\mathbf{x}_i + \mathbf{c}_q, t^k + 1) = f_q(\mathbf{x}, t^k), \quad q = 1, \ldots, Q. \tag{2}$$

Here, Ω is a collision operator, which is considered here in a common BGK form. The fluid density ρ and the velocity $\mathbf{u}$ are expressed as $\rho = \sum_q f_q$, $\rho\mathbf{u} = \sum_q \mathbf{c}_q f_q$. The equilibrium DDFs are assumed to be second-order polynomials in the components of $\mathbf{u}$.

We use the compact update scheme [5] so that only one array copy is stored. For an update of a group of 2^d cells, all DDFs from these cells are loaded, updated in a full LBM step, and stored in place, without using any neighboring cell data. Thus, the read/write ratio is always exactly 1. In odd time steps, the groups are shifted by one cell in d directions. For more explanation, see the Appendix.

3.2   CUDA GPU Implementation

Data Structure. The main data storage in the GPU global memory is the Tile array, which contains the DDF data. It may also contain other parameters, such as the indexes of the nearby boundaries.

A unit operation of the current code is an update of a cell group. Thus, an element of the Tile data structure is a group. For the purpose of both data access locality and coalesced access, the DDF data in the group is sorted, firstly, by the q index and, then, by the cell index in the group:

```
struct Group { float fi[Nq+1][8]; }
```

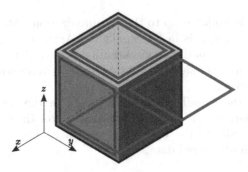

Fig. 3. FArSh indexing. The cube gnomon is projected onto a hexagon (red). Its faces are diamonds (blue) split into triangles and reorganized into diamonds with the same orientation (green). The indexing is in the 2D plane of green diamonds (Color figure online)

This way of grouping the DDF data is convenient for AVX vectorization. In the present case, it is enough to fill the L2 cache line of the GPU (32 B).

The groups are stored in a Z-curve array, filling a 3D cube with $N = 2^r$ cells on each side. Thus, the data layout is AoSoA.

For the cell index in `Tile`, an index I^{in} of dr bytes is enough. The higher bits give the group position in the array, the lower bits give the cell position within a group. In practice, 16-bit short or 32-bit integers are used. Several `Tile` structures may be used to fill the simulation area if it is not cubic. They contain data on global synchronization planes that are N_T time steps apart.

FArSh Indexing. FArSh is stored in the GPU global memory as an array of lines of cells (not groups).

An index in FArSh corresponds to each cell at (x, y, z), $0 \leq x, y, z < N$. It is found by projecting the cell in the $(-1, -1, -1)$ direction onto the left faces of the cube to the point

$$(x - x_{\min}, y - x_{\min}, z - x_{\min}); \quad x_{\min} = \min(x, y, z). \tag{3}$$

The number of such points is the size of the inner gnomon of the cube, that is, the total area of its three left faces:

$$N^d - (N - 1)^d = dN^{d-1} - O(N^{d-2}). \tag{4}$$

This is the number of required FArSh lines. It may be indexed with an integer $0 \leq I^{FArSh} < dN^{d-1}$. For the purpose of data locality, we suggest the Z-order indexation for each cube face.

A 3D cube projection to a plane with normal direction $(1, 1, 1)$ is a regular hexagon, and each cube face is projected onto a diamond (Fig. 3). The diamonds are split along the shortest diagonal, and from the obtained triangles, three equally oriented diamonds are constructed. Let us assume that the indexes i_1 and i_2 run on the sides of the diamonds:

$$i_1 = N + x - z, \quad i_2 = N + y - z, \quad 0 \leq i_1, i_2 < 2N. \tag{5}$$

```
 1          load base cube from Tile to the registers
 2          for (int it=0; it<NT; it+=Lf) {
 3            load a Lf portion of the global FArSh to the shared FArSh
 4            for(int itf=0; itf<Lf; itf++) {
 5              collision
 6              compact streaming (de-compact)
 7              shared FArSh exchange
 8              compact streaming (compact)
 9              }
10            load a Lf portion of the shared FArSh to the global FArSh
11            }
12          save data from the registers to the Tile
```

Fig. 4. The ConeTorre kernel. See Appendix for the details of the compact streaming.

Then, the FArSh index retrieval becomes low cost: instead of a conditional search for the cube face and a position on it, the index is expressed through the quotient and the remainder of the division of i_1 and i_2 by N:

$$I^{\mathrm{FArSh}} = ([i_1, N] + [i_2, N])\, N^2 + \mathrm{zip}_2(\{i_1, N\}, \{i_2, N\}), \qquad (6)$$

where $\mathrm{zip}_d()$ is an operation to obtain a Z-curve index from a d-dimensional index. The index gives a FArSh line, which contains the data of $N_T \gg 1$ cells. These cells are accessed sequentially in a ConeTorre. On the k-th tier, $0 \le k \le N_T$, the k-th cells of all FArSh lines indexed by the cells at the ConeTorre base cube are accessed synchronously. For spatial and temporal locality of such access pattern, the change in the I^{FArSh} should result in fewer shifts in memory than the change in the k index. Thus, in the current implementation, the indexes are split into pairs $I1 = [I^{\mathrm{FArSh}}, N^2], I2 = \{I^{\mathrm{FArSh}}, N^2\}$ and $k1 = [k, L_f], k2 = \{k, L_f\}$, and their order is `FArShArr[I1][k1][I2][k2]`.

ConeTorre. ConeTorre is implemented as a kernel launched on a block of $8 \times 8 \times 8$ CUDA threads (see Fig. 4). It starts by loading the cells in its base from the `Tile` in the memory to the thread registers, one cell per CUDA thread. A CUDA thread sequentially updates cells at $(x_0 + i, y_0 + i, z_0 + i)$ for $i = 0, \ldots, N_T - 1$.

The eight CUDA threads that process one cell group constitute an elementary scheme update and are always in one warp. Thus, the exchanges required for the elementary update are implemented with warp-shuffle operations.

Another kind of nonlocal thread operation is to 'move' to a cell shifted by $(+1, +1, +1)$ from the current position. There are three possibilities: (1) an exchange inside a warp ($4 \times 2 \times 2$ cells), (2) an exchange between warps, and (3) an exchange with data from the global memory. These exchanges, apart from the warp-shuffle for the first one, are implemented through the FArSh concept as well.

A FArSh for the $8 \times 8 \times 8$ cube of cells is initialized in the shared memory. The length of lines in the shared FArSh is L_f, which is necessarily a divisor of the line length N_T in the global FArSh. The shared FArSh is loaded from the global memory each L_f time steps (see Fig. 4, line 3). At each time step, the FArSh exchange (line 7) is similar to a ConeTorre progression, but inside the ConeTorre base and in one time step. The warp in the rightmost corner takes the shared FArSh data and writes its own in their place. After this, three more warps do the same asynchronously. This progression is synchronized by executing a proper number of __syncthreads() operations in each CUDA thread. Finally, after L_f time steps, the shared FArSh is saved to the appropriate place in the global FArSh.

3.3   TorreFold

Several ConeTorres start within a grid of CUDA blocks. Asynchronous computation positions can be found not only on the ConeTorre wavefront (see Fig. 1) but also in the portions of size L_f of the ConeTorre.

The TorreFold LRnLA algorithm is used [9]. The synchronization is implemented with an array of semaphores. There are N_{CT}^3 semaphores organized in a 3D array, where N_{CT}^3 is the number of ConeTorres required to update the whole domain. Thus, each ConeTorre is assigned an integer number equal to the number of time steps executed in a ConeTorre. Before executing the next portion of L_f time steps, a ConeTorre that had performed nL_f time steps waits until the three (in the 3D case) ConeTorres below it increment their semaphore to $(n + 1)L_f$.

Here, the number of ConeTorres executed at once is determined by the number of SMs. The order of execution is the Z-curve, so the bases of N_{bl} ConeTorres that start at the same time loosely tile a cube. This results in a shape in $3D1T$ space featuring high locality. The data exchanged between ConeTorres through FArSh in global memory may in fact never reach it. The exchange operations are likely to be performed through the L2 cache until the next portion of N_{bl} ConeTorres is started.

CPU RAM Communication. The GPU device memory is often comparatively small. When it is not enough, the simulation data can be localized in the next hierarchy level, i.e., in the CPU RAM. The BaseTile data structure is initialized in the CPU RAM. It is a 3D array of Tiles. The GPU device loads Tiles one by one, executes them with a TorreFold and sends the resulting Tile back. At the same time, FArSh is always stored in the GPU. In this case, the size of FArSh is determined by the gnomon of the BaseTile. Thus, it serves the purpose of transmitting the required data to the next TorreFold from the one that was computed before.

Under this kind of data exchange, it is possible to perform computations with GPU performance when the data is stored in the CPU RAM, and the overhead for data exchange can be made lower than 5% [10].

This is implemented with CUDA streams. A stream loads a Tile from the BaseTile to the GPU, performs a TorreFold and saves the Tile back into its place. Several streams are executed at once, and the synchronization is performed through CUDA events.

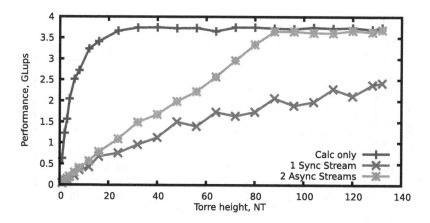

Fig. 5. Performance vs ConeTorre height N_T, D3Q19, $L_f = 2$

4   Results

The implementation was tested on a desktop workstation equipped with NVidia RTX2070 GPU and AMD Ryzen Threadripper 2920X CPU. The parameters vary in the following ranges: $1 \leq N_T \leq 360$, $1 \leq Lf \leq 14$, $1 \leq N_{bl} \leq 72$, $N = 512$, $N_{CT} = 4$, $Q = 7, 15, 19, 27$. The BaseTile data size varies from 3.5 to 13.5 GB. The FArSh data size is about 7.5 GB. The performance of the D3Q19 LBM is measured in billions of lattice node updates per second, GLups.

A simulation unit consists of N_T updates of a cube lattice area of size N^3. For each parameter set, the simulation unit is executed several times until the time threshold (30 s) is reached. The minimum time of these runs is used to evaluate the performance corresponding to the chosen parameters. The whole performance test took about a day of machine time in total.

Figure 5 shows the performance increase versus ConeTorre height N_T. The pure GPU performance (the 'Calc only' line) saturates rather fast. If the data exchange with the GPU is performed in one stream, the performance deteriorates. However, when only two asynchronous CUDA streams are used for host-device data exchange, the pure GPU performance is restored.

The size of FArSh in the shared memory decreases linearly with L_f. While it is small enough that two instances of the array can fit in the shared memory, two CUDA blocks per SM may be launched. Thus, the results for $L_f = 2$ and $L_f = 4$ in Fig. 6 are qualitatively different since twice more CUDA blocks may be used when $L_f = 2$ for higher occupancy.

In Fig. 6, we see the graph of the performance against the number N_{bl} of CUDA blocks executed simultaneously. As we can see, the graph shows an almost linear strong scaling. The two lines differ from each other in the indexing order, whether the FArSh iterator is split into L_f parts (see Sect. 3.2) or not. The performance increase shows that index splitting is a significant optimization. The benchmark demonstrates that the L_f parameter itself does not influence the

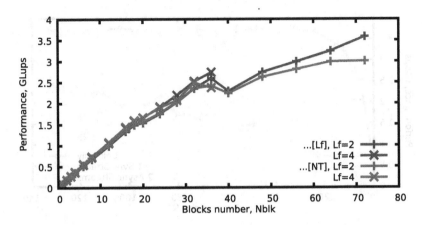

Fig. 6. Performance scaling versus the number of CUDA blocks, D3Q19, $N_T = 128$

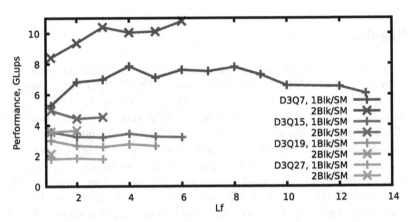

Fig. 7. Performance versus L_f parameter

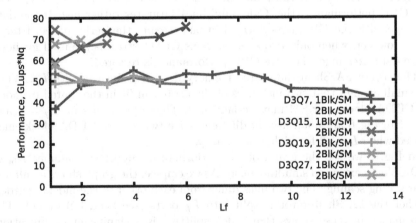

Fig. 8. Performance versus L_f parameter

performance directly (see Fig. 7); the increase in L_f gives a significant increase in performance only for the D3Q7 scheme. The higher L_f is, the better coalescing is provided and the fewer synchronization operations in the TorreFold are required. On the other hand, L_f determines the amount of shared memory required for the execution. The possibility of data exchange localization in the L2 cache depends on L_f as well.

At the same time, L_f indirectly controls the amount of cached data during the execution of the synchronized ConeTorre group. Each ConeTorre reads and writes data to the global memory in portions of L_f cells long. The number of such areas in the ConeTorre group is limited by the number of blocks that are run simultaneously. When L_f is small enough, all exchanges may be cached. This is demonstrated by the downturn in the scaling curve for $N_{bl} \sim 30$ in Fig. 6. It appears that, as N_{bl} increases, the data does not fit in the L2 cache anymore.

The increase in maximum performance as the occupancy increases is also evident in Fig. 7. We also explored the dependency on the amount of required data by trying out LBM stencils with different numbers of discrete speeds. By multiplying the result by N_Q (see Fig. 8), we confirmed that the performance is in inverse proportion to the cell data size.

5   Conclusions

All things considered, we can recommend FArSh as a panacea for the majority of problems associated with the implementation of LRnLA algorithms. Moreover, it may also prove convenient in other loop-skewing and wavefront approaches.

Just as the tile-based data structure is natural and convenient and provides high localization for spatial loops, which are still relevant for visualization, FArSh offers the same advantages for wavefront-type traversals.

The current theoretical ideal for high-performance algorithms is to use the highest memory level to localize the computation, smaller levels of the memory hierarchy for data exchange between processes, and the memory level with the largest storage capacity for storage. At the same time, the data movement across the system should be seamless and concealed under the calculation itself.

With FArSh, we get more control over the data exchange and reach as close to this goal as never before. At several levels of the algorithm hierarchy, the parallel processes update the values from larger storage, while they exchange data through faster storage. That is, the simulation data is in the CPU RAM but the data needed for exchange between subtasks in the GPU never leaves the GPU memory. The ConeTorres on a GPU work with the data in the GPU global memory but the data exchange is localized in the L2 cache. The CUDA threads exchange data with warp-shuffles where possible and through the shared memory otherwise.

We developed the first GPU-based implementation of the FArSh concept for an LBM code. The indexing scheme for a 2D projection of a 3D cube gnomon has been developed in such a manner that the index computation does not require conditional operations. If we estimate the ideal stepwise (without a temporal wavefront) code performance to be memory-bound with a read/write ratio equal to 1 and assume it is localized in the GPU memory and performs at 100% of the theoretical memory bandwidth, then the results of our benchmarks exceed that peak by a factor of the order of 1.2.

However, there are still possibilities for optimization, which we plan to implement in future works. Other types of LRnLA algorithms that may benefit from the introduction of FArSh are DiamondTorre and DiamondCandy. All these, when projected onto $1D1T$, display a space-time wavefront.

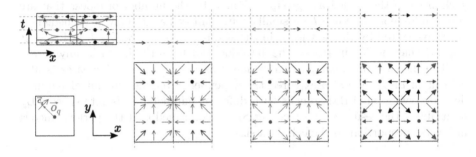

Fig. 9. The compact scheme. Three time layers are shown for $1D1T$ and three 2D slices for $2D1T$. The definition of the $\mathbf{o}_q$ vector is shown at the left bottom

```
__device__ const int3 ci3[] = {{-1, 0, 0,}, ... };
...

Cell ct; // temporary cell in the CUDA thread register
// in the ConeTorre loop:

 ct.collision(dtau);

 for (int iq=0; iq < Nq; iq++) { // compact
    if (ci3[iq].x > 0) ct.fi[iq] = __shfl_xor_sync(0xFFFFFFFF, ct.fi[iq], 1);
    if (ci3[iq].y > 0) ct.fi[iq] = __shfl_xor_sync(0xFFFFFFFF, ct.fi[iq], 2);
    if (ci3[iq].z > 0) ct.fi[iq] = __shfl_xor_sync(0xFFFFFFFF, ct.fi[iq], 4);
 }

 .... //FArSh exchange and cell ct shift

 for (int iq=0; iq < Nq; iq++) { //de-compact
    if (ci3[iq].x < 0) ct.fi[iq] = __shfl_xor_sync(0xFFFFFFFF, ct.fi[iq], 1);
    if (ci3[iq].y < 0) ct.fi[iq] = __shfl_xor_sync(0xFFFFFFFF, ct.fi[iq], 2);
    if (ci3[iq].z < 0) ct.fi[iq] = __shfl_xor_sync(0xFFFFFFFF, ct.fi[iq], 4);
 }
```

Fig. 10. The ConeTorre kernel

Appendix

In the compact scheme for LBM [5] (see Fig. 9) in a group of $2 \times 2 \times 2$ cells, the f_q value for the collision in a cell is taken from the cell with the other x_α if the projection of $\mathbf{o}_q$ on the α axis is negative. Otherwise, the value is taken from the cell with the same x_α as the collision cell. After the collision in the cell, f_q is written to the cell with different x_α only if the projection of $\mathbf{o}_q$ on the α axis is positive. The collision in $\mathbf{x}_i$ is mirrored in the α direction if $x_{i\alpha} = 1$. The connection between $\mathbf{o}$ and $\mathbf{c}_q$ is defined in the collision state, namely $o_{q\alpha} = c_{q\alpha}$ if $x_{i\alpha} = 0$, and $o_{q\alpha} = -c_{q\alpha}$ otherwise. With f_q mirroring, the code is especially simple, without the need to find the q index correspondence between DDF values (see Fig. 10). Thus, the three steps of the compact streaming scheme for LBM (see Fig. 9) are:

1. de-compact (put into the collision state);
2. collision;
3. compact (put into the compacted state).

In the present paper, they are restated in the order (2)-(3)-(1) (see Fig. 10), so that the values are stored in tiles in the pre-collision state, and each cell contains its own DDFs. However, the DDFs in cells with an odd coordinate are still mirrored in the direction of that coordinate.

References

1. Akbudak, K., Ltaief, H., Etienne, V., Abdelkhalak, R., Tonellot, T., Keyes, D.: Asynchronous computations for solving the acoustic wave propagation equation. Int. J. High Perf. Comput. Appl. 1094342020923027 (2020)
2. Korneev, B., Levchenko, V.: Detailed numerical simulation of shock-body interaction in 3D multicomponent flow using the RKDG numerical method and "DiamondTorre" GPU algorithm of implementation. J. Phys. Conf. Ser. **681**, 012046 (2016)
3. Krüger, T., Kusumaatmaja, H., Kuzmin, A., Shardt, O., Silva, G., Viggen, E.M.: The Lattice Boltzmann Method. Springer, Cham (2017). https://doi.org/10.1007/978-3-319-44649-3
4. Levchenko, V., Perepelkina, A.: Locally recursive non-locally asynchronous algorithms for stencil computation. Lobachevskii J. Math. **39**(4), 552–561 (2018). https://doi.org/10.1134/S1995080218040108
5. Perepelkina, A., Levchenko, V., Zakirov, A.: New compact streaming in LBM with ConeFold LRnLA algorithms. In: Voevodin, V., Sobolev, S. (eds.) RuSCDays 2020. CCIS, vol. 1331, pp. 50–62. Springer, Cham (2020). https://doi.org/10.1007/978-3-030-64616-5_5
6. Levchenko, V., Zakirov, A., Perepelkina, A.: GPU implementation of ConeTorre algorithm for fluid dynamics simulation. In: Malyshkin, V. (ed.) PaCT 2019. LNCS, vol. 11657, pp. 199–213. Springer, Cham (2019). https://doi.org/10.1007/978-3-030-25636-4_16
7. Malas, T.M., Hager, G., Ltaief, H., Keyes, D.E.: Multidimensional intratile parallelization for memory-starved stencil computations. ACM Trans. Parallel Comput. (TOPC) **4**(3), 1–32 (2017)

8. Muraoka, Y.: Parallelism exposure and exploitation in programs. Ph.D. thesis, USA (1971). AAI7121189
9. Perepelkina, A., Levchenko, V.: Synchronous and asynchronous parallelism in the LRnLA algorithms. In: Sokolinsky, L., Zymbler, M. (eds.) PCT 2020. CCIS, vol. 1263, pp. 146–161. Springer, Cham (2020). https://doi.org/10.1007/978-3-030-55326-5_11
10. Perepelkina, A., Levchenko, V., Zakirov, A.: Extending the problem data size for GPU simulation beyond the GPU memory storage with LRnLA algorithms. J. Phys. Conf. Ser. **1740**, 012,054 (2021). https://doi.org/10.1088/1742-6596/1740/1/012054
11. Perepelkina, A.Y., Goryachev, I.A., Levchenko, V.D.: CFHall code validation with 3D3V Weibel instability simulation. J. Phys. Conf. Ser. **441**, 012,014 (2013). https://doi.org/10.1088/1742-6596/441/1/012014
12. Strzodka, R., Shaheen, M., Pajak, D., Seidel, H.P.: Cache accurate time skewing in iterative stencil computations. In: 2011 International Conference on Parallel Processing, pp. 571–581. IEEE (2011)
13. Vardhan, M., Gounley, J., Hegele, L., Draeger, E.W., Randles, A.: Moment representation in the lattice Boltzmann method on massively parallel hardware. In: Proceedings of the International Conference for High Performance Computing, Networking, Storage and Analysis, pp. 1–21 (2019)
14. Wellein, G., Hager, G., Zeiser, T., Wittmann, M., Fehske, H.: Efficient temporal blocking for stencil computations by multicore-aware wavefront parallelization. In: 2009 33rd Annual IEEE International Computer Software and Applications Conference, vol. 1, pp. 579–586. IEEE (2009)
15. Williams, S., Waterman, A., Patterson, D.: Roofline: an insightful visual performance model for multicore architectures. Commun. ACM **52**(4), 65–76 (2009)
16. Wolfe, M.: Loops skewing: the wavefront method revisited. Int. J. Parallel Prog. **15**(4), 279–293 (1986)
17. Wonnacott, D.: Time skewing for parallel computers. In: Carter, L., Ferrante, J. (eds.) LCPC 1999. LNCS, vol. 1863, pp. 477–480. Springer, Heidelberg (2000). https://doi.org/10.1007/3-540-44905-1_35
18. Yount, C., Duran, A.: Effective use of large high-bandwidth memory caches in HPC stencil computation via temporal wave-front tiling. In: 2016 7th International Workshop on Performance Modeling, Benchmarking and Simulation of High Performance Computer Systems (PMBS), pp. 65–75. IEEE, Salt Lake (2016). https://doi.org/10.1109/PMBS.2016.012. http://ieeexplore.ieee.org/document/7836415/
19. Zakirov, A., Levchenko, V., Ivanov, A., Perepelkina, A., Levchenko, T., Rok, V.: High-performance 3D modeling of a full-wave seismic field for seismic survey tasks. Geoinformatika **3**, 34–45 (2017)
20. Zakirov, A., Levchenko, V., Perepelkina, A., Zempo, Y.: High performance FDTD algorithm for GPGPU supercomputers. J. Phys. Conf. Ser. **759**, 012100 (2016). https://doi.org/10.1088/1742-6596/759/1/012100

Exploring the Limits of Problem-Specific Adaptations of SAT Solvers in SAT-Based Cryptanalysis

Stepan Kochemazov[✉][iD]

Matrosov Institute for System Dynamics and Control Theory SB RAS,
Lermontov Street 134, Irkutsk 664033, Russia
kochemazov@icc.ru

Abstract. SAT-based cryptanalysis implies using algorithms for solving the Boolean Satisfiability (SAT) problem to perform cryptographic attacks. It is a flourishing research field. Tackling individual subproblems constructed in the course of the so-called guess-and-determine attacks is the most straightforward way SAT solvers are used in cryptography. If the expected runtime of an attack is of the order of millions of hours, then it makes sense to try to squeeze any extra bit of performance out of the main algorithm. In this paper, our goal is to figure out possible ways to do exactly that with SAT solvers, going beyond simple parameter tuning. In particular, we consider tasks related to cryptanalysis of several modern keystream generators, analyze and prepare several modifications of state-of-the-art SAT solvers to tackling them, tune their parameters, and evaluate the speedup.

Keywords: SAT · CDCL · Cryptanalysis · Heuristics · Bivium · Grain

1 Introduction

The Boolean satisfiability problem (SAT) [4] is among the most well-known tasks in Computer Science. Despite being NP-complete, there are numerous practical applications in which the SAT approach is employed to tackle problems from diverse fields, such as bioinformatics, planning, combinatorics, and others. The algorithms for solving SAT are usually referred to as SAT solvers. They have seen a dramatic performance increase in the last 25 years thanks to the invention of the Conflict-Driven Clause Learning (CDCL) concept [16]. The annual SAT competitions[1] are held to motivate SAT solver development and evaluate the state-of-the-art algorithms over a wide range of benchmarks.

---

[1] http://www.satcompetition.org/.

The research was prepared with partial support from the Russian Foundation for Basic Research (grant No. 19-07-00746) and the Council for Grants of the President of the Russian Federation (stipend No. SP-2017.2019.5).

© Springer Nature Switzerland AG 2021
L. Sokolinsky and M. Zymbler (Eds.): PCT 2021, CCIS 1437, pp. 149–163, 2021.
https://doi.org/10.1007/978-3-030-81691-9_11

One of the particular areas in which SAT has many applications is cryptanalysis. Indeed, it is possible to represent the majority of cryptanalysis problems (or their parts) in the SAT form and use contemporary SAT solvers to study their properties. There exist several software systems designed specifically to reduce cryptanalysis instances to SAT, such as `Transalg` [20] and `Cryptol` [9]. A straightforward way of using SAT in cryptanalysis is to mount guess-and-determine attacks: split an original cryptanalysis instance into a (usually large) number of subproblems and then allocate each of them to a SAT solver. Even if it is not feasible to solve all the subproblems constructed in such a manner, it is possible to apply the Monte-Carlo method to estimate the cryptographic resistance of a considered cryptographic construction (see, for instance, [8, 21, 22]).

SAT-based guess-and-determine attacks consist of several parts. The first is the reduction of the original cryptanalysis instance to SAT. The second, and arguably the most important part, is the decomposition of the original cryptanalysis instance into a family of subproblems. The third is the SAT solver, which is employed to solve the constructed subproblems. The vast majority of research papers on the topic largely focus on the second part, that is, to find the best splitting of the problem into subproblems so that they can be realistically solved and the resulting attack runtime estimate is minimal. The issue of encodings and the choice of a solver usually fade into the background. In the present research, we do the opposite: for a fixed method of decomposing a problem into subproblems, we strive to find the best combination of SAT encoding, SAT solver, and the solver parameters that work better than the default option.

The structure of the paper is as follows. In Sect. 2, we briefly touch on the basics of SAT solving and SAT-based cryptanalysis. In Sect. 3, we describe our approach to adapting SAT solvers to specific instances using the Bivium cryptanalysis problem as a running example. In Sects. 4 and 5, we employ the obtained results to improve the current best-known estimates of SAT-based cryptanalysis of Bivium and Grain_v1. Then we discuss the related works and draw some conclusions.

2   Preliminaries

The Boolean satisfiability problem (SAT) consists in determining whether a given Boolean formula is satisfiable. Without loss of generality, it is sufficient to consider only Boolean formulas in conjunctive normal form (CNF). A CNF over the set of Boolean variables $X = \{x_1, x_2, \ldots, x_n\}$ is a logical conjunction of clauses. A clause is a disjunction of literals. A literal is either a variable (positive literal) or its negation (negative literal). If there exists a set of variable values that satisfy a given CNF (make it evaluate into *True*), then the CNF is said to be *satisfiable*, and the set is referred to as a *satisfying assignment*. If there are no satisfying assignments, then the formula is said to be *unsatisfiable*.

2.1   On CDCL SAT Solvers

The majority of effective SAT solvers today are based on the Conflict-Driven Clause Learning concept [16]. Given a Boolean formula in CNF, the solvers use the depth-first search with backtracking, that is, they "guess" the values of Boolean variables and propagate this information via the Unit Propagation mechanism, allowing to derive the values of other variables. If the sequence of currently guessed variable values is inconsistent with the formula, the Unit Propagation results in a so-called *conflict* by simultaneously deriving a positive and negative literal for the same variable. Upon each conflict, a special procedure is used to analyze it, extract the information about the conflict to a learned clause, add this clause to the current formula, and revert the assignments of values to guessed variables that lead to a conflict.

CDCL solvers heavily employ heuristics. They determine how to choose a variable for guessing (branching heuristics [14,19]), how to choose what learned clauses should be removed to find a compromise between the size of the database of learned clauses and the propagation performance [1], how to improve the quality of learned clauses [15], how to restart periodically the search in an attempt to find a more promising path, and so on. Typically, most heuristics are aimed at improving the effectiveness of CDCL on satisfiable or unsatisfiable instances, and sometimes on both. However, the distinction is far from being clear.

Essentially, the difference between two SAT solvers boils down to the difference between the employed heuristics and/or the difference between the parameter settings for those heuristics. Nevertheless, it quite often happens that the performance of relatively similar solvers on a specific family of instances can be very different. This fact has spurred the interest in metaparameter tuning for SAT solvers (see, e.g., [13]). However, due to the enormous computational costs, metaparameter tuning is employed quite rarely in practice.

2.2   On SAT-Based Cryptanalysis

SAT-based cryptanalysis is a broad term that encompasses all applications of SAT solvers in cryptography. In the context of the present paper, we are mainly interested in the evaluation of the cryptographic resistance of particular ciphers to attacks employing SAT solvers. Usually, such attacks belong to the class of guess-and-determine attacks. The problem in those attacks is tackled in two stages: in the first stage, which corresponds to the "guess" part of the name, the original problem is split into a large number of subproblems in such a manner that each one is essentially a copy of the initial problem, in which the values of the variables from a small set are fixed according to a specific assignment. After solving all subproblems, it is possible to efficiently reconstruct the solution to the initial problem. The number of subproblems usually coincides with the cardinality of the set of all possible assignments of a set of guessed variables. Typically, if the resulting problems can be solved by a polynomial algorithm, this division allows one to split the estimated runtime of a guess-and-determine attack into exponential and polynomial parts.

If the subproblems constructed in the course of a guess-and-determine attack can not be solved by any known polynomial algorithm, then we can tackle them by one of the methods for solving algebraic equations, including SAT solvers. In this case, however, the estimation of the attack runtime has to be carried out by the Monte Carlo method (see, e.g., [21,22]).

In the remainder of the paper, we will use the following notations. Let C be a CNF encoding a particular cryptanalysis problem, and let X be the set of its Boolean variables. Assume that $X^{in} \subseteq X$ is the set of Boolean variables that correspond to the inputs of the initial cryptanalysis problem, for example, to a secret key. We refer to the set $B = \{x_{i_1}, \ldots, x_{i_k}\}$, $B \subset X^{in}$, as the *decomposition set* and to the set of subproblems

$$D(B,C) = \left\{ C \wedge x_{i_1}^{\alpha_1} \wedge \ldots \wedge x_{i_k}^{\alpha_k}, \ (\alpha_1, \ldots, \alpha_k) \in \{0,1\}^k \right\}$$

as the *decomposition family* induced by B. Here, by x^0 we denote the literal $\neg x$ and by x^1 the literal x.

Thus, the components of a guess-and-determine attack on some cipher include the CNF C that encodes the cryptanalysis instance of the cipher, the decomposition set B, and the SAT solver A used to tackle the subproblems from the decomposition family induced by B. All three components have a major impact on the effectiveness of the resulting attack. If the attack can not be realistically implemented (e.g., because the size of B is too large), we can rely on the Monte Carlo method in the form described in [21,22] to estimate the runtime of the SAT-based attack that uses the CNF C, the SAT solver A, and the decomposition set B. Informally speaking, the Monte Carlo method consists in constructing a sample of N subproblems from the decomposition family $D(B,C)$, measuring the average runtime of the solver A on each one of the N SAT instances, and scaling the average runtime to the size of $D(B,C)$. Usually, the main question addressed in many research papers is how to choose the best B such that the estimated attack runtime is minimal. In the next section, we consider the supplementary problem, namely to find the best combination of a CNF C and a solver A for a fixed decomposition set.

3   Adapting SAT Solvers to Specific Instances

First of all, we outline the problems of cryptanalysis of the Bivium [5] and the Grain_v1 [10] ciphers, which we will use in experiments throughout this and the following sections.

Both Bivium and Grain_v1 were proposed in the course of the Estream project, aimed at discovering new-generation stream ciphers. Bivium is a weakened version of the Trivium cipher; it is often analyzed using SAT solvers [8,18,21]. Grain_v1 is a corrected version of the Grain cipher with significantly improved cryptographic resistance; it is also a frequent target for SAT-based attacks [22,23]. For both ciphers, we consider the *state recovery attack*, which implies that, given a keystream fragment, we need to determine the correct initial values of cipher registers. We consider a keystream fragment of size 200 for

Bivium and 160 for Grain_v1. The size of the initial state is 177 for Bivium and 160 for Grain.

In the first stage of the experiments, which is described in this section, we concentrated on Bivium. During testing, we used a methodology similar to that from [20], with several changes. To encode the Bivium cryptanalysis to SAT, we used the Transalg system[2] and the default TA-program for Bivium[3]. As the decomposition set for the Bivium cryptanalysis, we used the set of variables corresponding to the last 30 bits of the initial state

$$B_{\text{Bivium}} = \{x_{148}, \ldots, x_{177}\}.$$

However, unlike [20], we considered a sample of unsatisfiable instances constructed as follows. We randomly generated 200 keystream fragments of size 200 bits, assigned the corresponding values to variables in 200 copies of the initial CNF, and then, for each constructed CNF, additionally assigned the randomly generated values to the variables corresponding to B_{Bivium}. As a result, we obtained 200 unsatisfiable CNFs. We refer to this set of instances as the Bivium_30_sample. The reason for considering only unsatisfiable instances is simple: if we follow the methodology suggested in [21], then most likely there is exactly one satisfiable instance in the whole decomposition family of 2^{30} problems for B_{Bivium}. Thus, the vast majority of problems to solve are unsatisfiable.

3.1 Choosing the Right Solver

To choose the best solver, we ran several contestants on Bivium_30_sample. For the role of solvers, we chose the winners of SAT Competitions from 2016 to 2020 and the rokk SAT solver, which showed good results in [20]. The list of solvers looked as follows:

- kissat, the winner of the 2020 SAT Competition;
- Relaxed_LCMDCBDL_newTech, second-place winner of the 2020 SAT Competition;
- Cryptominisat5, third-place winner of the 2020 SAT Competition;
- MapleLCMDistChronoBT-DL-v3, the winner of the 2019 SAT Race;
- MapleLCMDistChronoBT, the winner of the 2018 SAT Competition;
- MapleLCMDist, the winner of the 2017 SAT Competition;
- MapleCOMSPS, the winner of the 2016 SAT Competition;
- rokk, a participant in the 2014 SAT Competition.

The solvers were launched on a PC with an AMD Ryzen 9 3950x and 32 Gb RAM with a time limit of 5000 s. The results of the experiment are depicted by the graph in Fig. 1.

The peculiar fact is that rokk, despite being the oldest solver, showed the best results. Also, we noticed that MapleLCMDistChronoBT-DL-v3 yielded worse

---

[2] https://gitlab.com/transalg/.
[3] https://gitlab.com/satencodings.

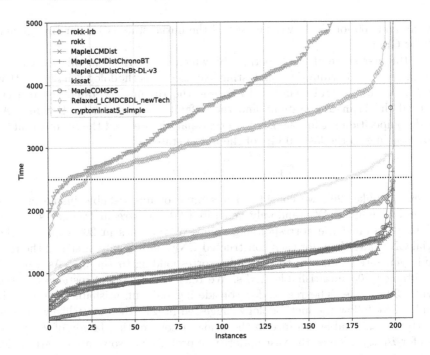

Fig. 1. Comparison of the performance of modern CDCL SAT solvers on Bivium_30_sample

results compared to `MapleLCMDistChronoBT`, `MapleLCMDist`, and `MapleCOMSPS`. The main difference between `MapleLCMDistChronoBT-DL-v3` and the other three solvers is that the latter use LRB branching heuristics [14] for the first 2500 s and then switch to VSIDS [19], while `MapleLCMDistChronoBT-DL-v3` switches between heuristics much more frequently. It was natural to assume that the LRB heuristics is the one to thank for the higher performance in this situation. Taking into account the fact that `rokk` relies solely on VSIDS heuristics, we decided to replace the latter in `rokk` with LRB and evaluate the performance of the resulting `rokk-lrb` solver. As it can be seen from Fig. 1, it turned out that `rokk-lrb` is almost twice as fast as `rokk` on the considered tests.

Thus, in the remainder of this section, we will use the `rokk-lrb` solver as a basis and see whether it is possible to tune its performance to become even more impressive by other means.

3.2 Choosing the Best Encoding

An often overlooked fact is that the same initial problem usually can be transformed into SAT form in many different ways. As the results in [20] show, different tools for encoding the cryptanalysis to SAT yield SAT instances with different degrees of difficulty. In the present paper, we employ the `Transalg` tool to construct different propositional encodings for the Bivium cryptanalysis problem.

In particular, we constructed four encodings that differed in the balance between the number of variables and the number of literals in the constructed CNFs. Usually, the less the number of variables is, the larger the number of literals (and the size of the CNF in megabytes) we obtain. However, there are many nuances. Informally speaking, the constructed encodings differ in the way Boolean variables are introduced to store auxiliary values. The programs can be obtained from a repository[4]. In Table 1, we give the results of the comparison. The first encoding is the default. It introduces no auxiliary Boolean variables apart from those that are necessary. The second encoding follows the opposite approach by introducing lots of auxiliary variables. It achieves the smallest overall size in kilobytes. The third and fourth encodings can be viewed as hybrids of the first and the second. It was quite surprising to see that the smallest encoding (the second) turned out to be the worst, while the largest one is the best. Therefore, we use the first encoding in the remainder of the paper.

Table 1. Comparison of the effectiveness of the `rokk-lrb` SAT solver with different SAT encodings for Bivium cryptanalysis

Encoding number	Variables	Clauses	Size (Kb)	Avg. solving time
1	642	9560	235	465.58
2	1507	5715	99	639.50
3	1172	7175	149	489.03
4	1107	7955	170	476.47

3.3 Parameterization

Parameterization or parameter tuning is a popular procedure to improve the performance of solving algorithms on specific classes of problems. The SAT solvers are not an exception to this empirical rule since they have many heuristics that can be manipulated. In the present research, we decided to manually modify several parameters instead of using specialized metaparameter tuning algorithms such as SMAC [12]. The motivation, in this case, is quite simple. SMAC-like tools generally use one of the machine learning models to approximate the black-box function that maps the metaparameter configurations to some measure of effectiveness. Not having any prior knowledge, they must gradually build a model of this function by performing numerous experiments involving many computations. In our case, the black-box function would represent the average runtime of a solver with tuned parameters over a sample of, say, 100 CNFs. From Table 1, it can be seen that it is likely that computing the value of this function at a point (corresponding to one configuration of parameters) requires about 13 CPU hours. Typically, SMAC would traverse at least several hundred or, better, thousands of points to achieve a meaningful result with the obtained speedup

---

[4] https://github.com/veinamond/PAVT2021.

under 20%. At the current stage of research, such an expenditure of computing resources is deemed to be unreasonable.

We chose the following parameters:

- *Initial step size* (`is`), default value: 0.4.
- *Step size decrement* (`sd`), default value: 0.000001.
- *Minimal step size* (`ms`), default value: 0.06.
- *Variable decay rate*(`vd`), default value: 0.8
- *Restart interval increase factor* (`ri`), default value: 2.

In the next experiment, the value of a single parameter was varied slightly to see whether the performance of the solver increases. The results are summed up in Table 2.

Table 2. Results of the parameterized variants of `rokk-lrb` on Bivium_30_sample

Solver configuration	is	sd	ms	vd	ri	Avg. time
rokk-lrb	0.4	0.000001	0.06	0.95	2	465.58
rokk-lrb-ms1	0.4	0.000001	0.01	0.95	2	410.95
rokk-lrb-ms01	0.4	0.000001	0.001	0.95	2	417.04
rokk-lrb-ms2	0.4	0.000001	0.02	0.95	2	417.31
rokk-lrb-ms1-vd08	0.4	0.000001	0.01	0.8	2	421.62
rokk-lrb-ms01-vd08	0.4	0.000001	0.06	0.8	2	424.49
rokk-lrb-vd08	0.4	0.000001	0.06	0.8	2	458.58
rokk-lrb-vd09	0.4	0.000001	0.06	0.9	2	459.55
rokk-lrb-is05	0.5	0.000001	0.06	0.95	2	468.85
rokk-lrb-sd05	0.4	0.0000005	0.05	0.95	2	470.50
rokk-lrb-is06	0.6	0.000001	0.06	0.95	2	475.48
rokk-lrb-sd02	0.4	0.000002	0.06	0.95	2	477.71
rokk-lrb-vd099	0.4	0.000001	0.06	0.99	2	502.88
rokk-lrb-ri3	0.4	0.000001	0.06	0.95	2	540.81

It turned out that reducing the minimal step size and increasing the variable decay rate exert a somewhat good effect on solver performance, but ultimately the best results were achieved with the `rokk-lrb-ms1` version having the minimal step size, namely 0.01, compared to the default 0.06. On the considered sample, it was about 12% better than the default `rokk-lrb`. Thus, from all the configurations we considered, `rokk-lrb-ms1` was the best performing one.

3.4   Preprocessing

Preprocessing is a popular technique for improving the effectiveness of modern SAT solvers by applying to an input CNF special techniques aimed at making it easier to tackle. It was largely popularized by [7], and today, the majority of solvers employ preprocessing in one way or another. However, different solvers rely on different methods. In particular, the Cadical solver [3] has one of the best and most up-to-date collections of preprocessing methods. We decided to apply it to Bivium_30_sample formulas and verify whether the results of preprocessing plus solving are better than just solving the formula upfront. We launched Cadical in simplification mode for 1, 10, 30, and 60 s and compared the performance of rokk, rokk-lrb, rokk-lrb-ms1, and kissat with that on unprocessed CNFs. The details are given in Table 3.

Table 3. Evaluation of the impact of preprocessing on the performance of CDCL solvers in Bivium_30_sample. The average runtime of a solver does not include the time spent on preprocessing.

Solver	Preprocessing time (seconds)				
	0	1	10	30	60
rokk	1012.53	978.77	965.89	988.42	964.23
rokk-lrb	465.58	424.70	420.16	422.49	419.76
rokk-lrb-ms1	410.95	384.72	384.50	387.66	380.93
kissat	1877.054	1858.61	1845.77	1837.95	1832.03

From the analysis of these data, it is obvious that preprocessing greatly benefits solvers' performance. However, the sweet spot lies somewhere between 1 and 10 s. Even taking the preprocessing time into account, the gain can be up to 10% of the average runtime.

3.5   Adapting the rokk Solver to Grain_v1 Cryptanalysis

Another problem we considered was the cryptanalysis of Grain_v1 cipher with the following decomposition set of 103 variables:

$$B_{\text{Grain}} = \{58, \ldots, 160\}$$

We constructed 200 unsatisfiable instances for the cryptanalysis of Grain_v1 via B_{Grain} in a manner similar to the one described above. We refer to the resulting set of instances as Grain_v1_103_sample. To our surprise, rokk-lrb was the best solver, the default encoding was overall the best, and the rokk-lrb-ms1 configuration yielded better results than the initial one. The results of the considered solver configurations, including preprocessing, are given in Table 4.

In the following sections, we apply the constructed solvers in an attempt to improve the estimates known for the resistance of Bivium and Grain_v1 to SAT-based cryptanalysis.

Table 4. Evaluation of the impact of preprocessing on the performance of CDCL solvers in Grain_v1_103_sample. The average runtime of a solver does not include the time spent on preprocessing.

Solver	Preprocessing time (seconds)				
	0	1	10	30	60
rokk	1182.19	1236.58	1191.48	1183.26	1193.45
rokk-lrb	675.88	673.28	650.23	647.43	645.25
rokk-lrb-ms1	641.75	656.03	633.69	635.43	632.71
kissat	1329.87	1303.06	1285.65	1293.23	1291.48

4   Improving the SAT-Based Guess-and-Determine Attack on Bivium

To better align the results with those in the literature, the experiments described in this and the next sections were conducted on a single node of the "Academician V. M. Matrosov" computing cluster of the Irkutsk Supercomputer Center [17]. The node is equipped with two 18-core Intel Xeon E5-2695 CPUs and 128 GB DDR4 RAM. The solvers were launched in 36 simultaneous threads.

To the best of the author's knowledge, the best estimates of the resistance of the Bivium cipher to SAT-based cryptanalysis were published in [21], where a decomposition set of 50 variables with numbers

$$B_{\text{Bivium}}^{\text{Splus}} = \{5, 19, 20, 22, 23, 31, 32, 34, 35, 45, 46, 47, 49, 50, 58, 59, 61, 62, 64,$$
$$74, 76, 77, 86, 88, 101, 113, 115, 116, 127, 128, 129, 130, 131, 133, 140,$$
$$142, 143, 144, 145, 146, 154, 155, 156, 157, 158, 160, 161, 170, 172, 173\}.$$

is used. Upon detailed examination, it turned out that $B_{\text{Bivium}}^{\text{Splus}}$ has a serious flaw, which was found via an automatic procedure that does not account for the features of the original problem. Indeed, if we look at the Bivium algorithm, we can see that the first keystream bits are formed by way of the following equations:

$$ks_1 = x_{162} \oplus x_{177} \oplus x_{66} \oplus x_{93},$$
$$\cdots\cdots\cdots\cdots\cdots\cdots\cdots\cdots\cdots\cdots\cdots\cdots$$
$$ks_{47} = x_{116} \oplus x_{131} \oplus x_{20} \oplus x_{47},$$
$$\cdots\cdots\cdots\cdots\cdots\cdots\cdots\cdots\cdots\cdots\cdots\cdots$$

Note that the four variables x_{20}, x_{47}, x_{116}, and x_{131} belong to $B_{\text{Bivium}}^{\text{Splus}}$. Recall that, in a SAT instance corresponding to the cryptanalysis of Bivium, the keystream bits are fixed. What happens when we construct a decomposition family using $B_{\text{Bivium}}^{\text{Splus}}$ is that the equation

$$ks_{47} = x_{116} \oplus x_{131} \oplus x_{20} \oplus x_{47}$$

has five known variables out of five. Thus, for half of the possible assignments of the variables x_{20}, x_{47}, x_{116}, and x_{131}, we know in advance that the SAT instance is unsatisfiable. It is trivial to extract this information and avoid launching a SAT solver on such instances. However, a better way is to simply remove one of the four variables from the decomposition set. A careful analysis of $B_{\text{Bivium}}^{\text{Splus}}$ shows that it is possible to remove more than five variables from this set.

By taking this feature into account and using a technique similar to that suggested in [21], we constructed a decomposition set of 41 variables,

$$B_{\text{Bivium}}^{41} = \{5, 7, 19, 20, 22, 23, 31, 32, 34, 35, 46, 47, 49, 50, 58, 59, 61, 62, 73, 74,$$
$$76, 77, 86, 88, 89, 90, 95, 101, 103, 107, 113, 121, 127, 128, 129, 130,$$
$$140, 144, 154, 155, 156\},$$

with a significantly better runtime estimate. However, intuitively, to better leverage all the benefits of SAT solvers and preprocessing, it is preferable when the average solving time for a subproblem from a decomposition family is more than just a few seconds. Thus, we manually experimented with B_{Bivium}^{41} and managed to somewhat prune it. The result was the following set:

$$B_{\text{Bivium}}^{28} = \{5, 7, 19, 20, 22, 31, 32, 34, 35, 46, 47, 49, 50, 58, 59, 61, 62, 73,$$
$$74, 76, 77, 88, 89, 101, 103, 127, 128, 130\}.$$

In Table 5, we give both the average solving time for problems from the random sample constructed for all three sets and the estimated time for the corresponding guess-and-determine attack. We constructed two random samples: one containing 1000 problems for the first two sets and one of 100 problems for B_{Bivium}^{28}.

Table 5. Runtime estimates for guess-and-determine attacks on Bivium

Set	Solver	Avg. time (s)	Runtime estimate (s)
$B_{\text{Bivium}}^{\text{Splus}}$	rokk	0.108	1.21e+14
	rokk-lrb-ms1	0.108	1.21e+14
	kissat	0.091	1.02e+14
B_{Bivium}^{41}	rokk	0.36	7.91e+11
	rokk-lrb-ms1	0.8	1.2e+12
	kissat	0.34	7.4e+11
B_{Bivium}^{28}	rokk-pre10	727.91	1.95e+11
	rokk-lrb-ms1-pre10	330.27	8.86e+10
	kissat-pre10	508.73	1.36e+11

Note that the runtime estimate given in [21] for $B_{\text{Bivium}}^{\text{Splus}}$ is 3.769e+10. It was computed on cluster nodes with about twice less powerful CPUs. However, taking into account the flaws of $B_{\text{Bivium}}^{\text{Splus}}$ outlined above, it is very likely that the random sample used for computing the runtime estimate of a guess-and-determine attack based on $B_{\text{Bivium}}^{\text{Splus}}$ contains many trivially resolvable formulas, thus making the sample unrepresentative. We should recall that, for obtaining the estimate 3.769e+10, the time to solve an individual subproblem would have to be equal to $\frac{3.769e+10}{2^{50}} = 0.0000334$ s, which is only possible if the SAT solver is invoked strictly inside RAM and it does not have to load a CNF, but even then, the solution of the problem would have to take little to no time. Therefore, we strongly believe that our estimate is correct, whereas that in [21] is too optimistic.

5   Improving the SAT-Based Guess-and-Determine Attack on Grain_v1

The cryptanalysis of Grain_v1 is another problem often considered in the SAT context. As far as we are aware, the best runtime estimate of a SAT-based attack on Grain is given in [24]. However, the employed decomposition set was not disclosed. Therefore, we took the previously best-known result from [23]. The corresponding decomposition set looks as follows:

$$
\begin{aligned}
B_{\text{Grain}}^{\text{OMS}} = \{ & 2, 3, 5, 6, 7, 9, 10, 12, 13, 14, 15, 16, 17, 18, 19, 20, 21, 22, 23, 24, \\
& 25, 26, 27, 28, 29, 30, 31, 32, 33, 34, 35, 36, 37, 39, 40, 41, 42, 43, \\
& 44, 45, 48, 49, 50, 51, 52, 53, 54, 55, 56, 58, 59, 60, 61, 63, 65, 66, \\
& 67, 68, 69, 70, 71, 72, 73, 74, 75, 76, 78, 79, 82, 83, 85, 86, 87, 89, \\
& 91, 92, 93, 94, 96, 97, 103, 104, 106, 107, 109, 110, 111, 112, 113, \\
& 120, 121, 125, 127, 128, 131, 132, 134, 135, 141, 144, 145, 148, 150, \\
& 151, 152, 153, 155, 160 \}.
\end{aligned}
$$

Following the same motivation as in the case of Bivium, we manually pruned the set so that SAT instances from the decomposition family were solved longer on average. The resulting set is

$$
\begin{aligned}
B_{\text{Grain}}^{91} = \{ & 2, 3, 5, 6, 7, 9, 10, 12, 13, 14, 15, 16, 17, 18, 19, 20, 21, 22, 23, 24, \\
& 25, 26, 27, 28, 29, 30, 31, 32, 33, 34, 35, 36, 37, 39, 40, 41, 42, 43, \\
& 44, 45, 48, 49, 50, 51, 52, 53, 54, 55, 56, 58, 59, 60, 61, 63, 65, 66, \\
& 67, 68, 69, 70, 71, 72, 73, 74, 75, 76, 78, 79, 82, 85, 87, 91, 93, 95, \\
& 97, 103, 105, 107, 109, 111, 113, 125, 127, 131, 135, 141, 144, 148, \\
& 151, 153, 160 \}.
\end{aligned}
$$

Table 6, which is similar to Table 5, contains both the average solving time for problems from the random sample constructed for the two sets considered and the estimated time for the corresponding guess-and-determine attacks. We constructed two random samples: one 1000 problems for $B_{\text{Grain}}^{\text{OMS}}$ and one of 100 problems for B_{Grain}^{91}.

The runtime estimate given in [24] is 1.63e+30, which, evidently, is larger than the one obtained for B_{Grain}^{91}.

Table 6. Runtime estimates for guess-and-determine attacks on Bivium

Set	Solver	Avg. time (s)	Runtime estimate (s)
$B_{\mathrm{Grain}}^{\mathrm{OMS}}$	rokk	0.160	5.19e+31
	rokk-lrb-ms1	0.201	6.50e+31
	kissat	0.106	3.40e+31
B_{Grain}^{91}	rokk-pre10	1253.49	3.10e+30
	rokk-lrb-ms1-pre10	553.71	1.37e+30
	kissat-pre10	1200.78	2.97e+30

6   Discussion and Related Work

In the present study, we aimed to emphasize the significance of considering all possible technical means for improving the performance of the implemented approach if we want to construct the best possible estimates of SAT-based guess-and-determine attacks on cryptographic constructions. It is plainly obvious from the results presented in previous sections that picking the correct encoding can easily provide a net gain of approximately 30% of performance or more. Moreover, instead of just choosing the best performing solver, it is highly advisable to compare the performance of several solvers on the considered problem and determine whether it is possible to improve even more the best one by manipulating the heuristics in the algorithm. Finally, the value of preprocessing should not be underestimated: even 10 s of preprocessing can save several dozens of seconds of solving time per subproblem, which adds up if we consider large families of subproblems.

To the best of the author's knowledge, there are two popular methods for adapting a SAT solver to a specific set of problems. One of them is somewhat *external* and consists in picking the best performing solver among many and, sometimes, tuning it by metaparameter tuning algorithms. For more information on this approach, refer to [13]. The other method implies that the additional knowledge of the interconnection between the original problem and its SAT encoding is exploited in some way. It consists of internal manipulations performed on the CDCL heuristics so that the algorithms that employ them behave better only with problems of this particular kind. Examples of this approach can be found in [2,6]. The approach considered in the present paper is closer to external methods with minor inclusions of internal ones.

As for the quality of the obtained results from the point of view of cryptanalysis, it should be noted that the SAT-based approach represents only a small portion of cryptanalysis methods and, therefore, its results rarely beat those of the most recent methods. In the case of Bivium, the best runtime estimate to date was given in [11] and is 3.7e+9, that is, about 24 times better than ours. We believe that it is possible to improve this SAT-based estimate by searching for a better decomposition set. In the case of Grain_v1, the constructed SAT-based attack is the best known. However, it is still inferior to brute-force key recovery attacks.

7   Conclusions

We showed that by careful experimentation and manipulation on CDCL heuristics, it is possible to improve significantly the performance of SAT solvers on specific cryptanalysis instances and, owing to this, achieve rather better estimates of SAT-based cryptanalysis. We believe that combining this approach with automated methods for finding decomposition sets is a promising direction for future research.

Acknowledgements. The author thanks Oleg Zaikin for fruitful preliminary discussions.

References

1. Audemard, G., Simon, L.: Predicting learnt clauses quality in modern SAT solvers. In: IJCAI, pp. 399–404 (2009)
2. Avellaneda, F., Petrenko, A.: Learning minimal DFA: taking inspiration from RPNI to improve SAT approach. In: Ölveczky, P.C., Salaün, G. (eds.) SEFM 2019. LNCS, vol. 11724, pp. 243–256. Springer, Cham (2019). https://doi.org/10.1007/978-3-030-30446-1_13
3. Biere, A.: CaDiCaL at the SAT race 2019. In: Proceedings of SAT Race 2019, vol. B-2019-1, pp. 8–9 (2019)
4. Biere, A., Heule, M., van Maaren, H., Walsh, T. (eds.): Handbook of Satisfiability. Frontiers in Artificial Intelligence and Applications, vol. 185. IOS Press, Amsterdam (2009)
5. De Cannière, C., Preneel, B.: TRIVIUM. In: Robshaw, M., Billet, O. (eds.) New Stream Cipher Designs. LNCS, vol. 4986, pp. 244–266. Springer, Heidelberg (2008). https://doi.org/10.1007/978-3-540-68351-3_18
6. De, D., Kumarasubramanian, A., Venkatesan, R.: Inversion attacks on secure hash functions using SAT solvers. In: Marques-Silva, J., Sakallah, K.A. (eds.) SAT 2007. LNCS, vol. 4501, pp. 377–382. Springer, Heidelberg (2007). https://doi.org/10.1007/978-3-540-72788-0_36
7. Eén, N., Biere, A.: Effective preprocessing in SAT through variable and clause elimination. In: Bacchus, F., Walsh, T. (eds.) SAT 2005. LNCS, vol. 3569, pp. 61–75. Springer, Heidelberg (2005). https://doi.org/10.1007/11499107_5
8. Eibach, T., Pilz, E., Völkel, G.: Attacking Bivium using SAT solvers. In: Kleine Büning, H., Zhao, X. (eds.) SAT 2008. LNCS, vol. 4996, pp. 63–76. Springer, Heidelberg (2008). https://doi.org/10.1007/978-3-540-79719-7_7
9. Erkök, L., Matthews, J.: High assurance programming in cryptol. In: Fifth Cyber Security and Information Intelligence Research Workshop, CSIIRW 2009, p. 60. ACM (2009)
10. Hell, M., Johansson, T., Meier, W.: Grain: a stream cipher for constrained environments. Int. J. Wire. Mob. Comput. **2**(1), 86–93 (2007)
11. Huang, Z., Lin, D.: Attacking bivium and trivium with the characteristic set method. In: Nitaj, A., Pointcheval, D. (eds.) AFRICACRYPT 2011. LNCS, vol. 6737, pp. 77–91. Springer, Heidelberg (2011). https://doi.org/10.1007/978-3-642-21969-6_5

12. Hutter, F., Hoos, H.H., Leyton-Brown, K.: Sequential model-based optimization for general algorithm configuration. In: Coello, C.A.C. (ed.) LION 2011. LNCS, vol. 6683, pp. 507–523. Springer, Heidelberg (2011). https://doi.org/10.1007/978-3-642-25566-3_40

13. Hutter, F., Lindauer, M., Balint, A., Bayless, S., Hoos, H., Leyton-Brown, K.: The configurable sat solver challenge (CSSC). Artif. Intell. **243**, 1–25 (2017). https://doi.org/10.1016/j.artint.2016.09.006

14. Liang, J.H., Ganesh, V., Poupart, P., Czarnecki, K.: Learning rate based branching heuristic for SAT solvers. In: Creignou, N., Le Berre, D. (eds.) SAT 2016. LNCS, vol. 9710, pp. 123–140. Springer, Cham (2016). https://doi.org/10.1007/978-3-319-40970-2_9

15. Luo, M., Li, C., Xiao, F., Manyà, F., Lü, Z.: An effective learnt clause minimization approach for CDCL SAT solvers. In: IJCAI, pp. 703–711 (2017)

16. Marques-Silva, J.P., Lynce, I., Malik, S.: Conflict-driven clause learning SAT solvers. In: Biere et al. [4], pp. 131–153

17. Irkutsk Supercomputer Center of SB RAS. http://hpc.icc.ru

18. Mcdonald, C., Charnes, C., Pieprzyk, J.: Attacking Bivium with MiniSat. Technical report 2007/040, ECRYPT Stream Cipher Project (2007)

19. Moskewicz, M.W., Madigan, C.F., Zhao, Y., Zhang, L., Malik, S.: Chaff: engineering an efficient SAT solver. In: Proceedings of the 38th Annual Design Automation Conference, DAC 2001, pp. 530–535 (2001)

20. Semenov, A., Otpuschennikov, I., Gribanova, I., Zaikin, O., Kochemazov, S.: Translation of algorithmic descriptions of discrete functions to SAT with applications to cryptanalysis problems. Log. Meth. Comput. Sci. **16** (2020)

21. Semenov, A., Zaikin, O.: Algorithm for finding partitionings of hard variants of boolean satisfiability problem with application to inversion of some cryptographic functions. Springerplus **5**(1), 1–16 (2016)

22. Semenov, A.A., Zaikin, O., Otpuschennikov, I.V., Kochemazov, S., Ignatiev, A.: On cryptographic attacks using backdoors for SAT. In: AAAI, pp. 6641–6648. AAAI Press (2018)

23. Zaikin, O., Kochemazov, S.: On black-box optimization in divide-and-conquer SAT solving. Optim. Methods Softw., 1–25 (2019). https://doi.org/10.1080/10556788.2019.1685993

24. Zaikin, O., Kochemazov, S.: Improving effectiveness of neighborhood-based algorithms for optimization of costly pseudo-boolean black-box functions. In: Kononov, A., Khachay, M., Kalyagin, V.A., Pardalos, P. (eds.) MOTOR 2020. LNCS, vol. 12095, pp. 373–388. Springer, Cham (2020). https://doi.org/10.1007/978-3-030-49988-4_26

FRaGenLP: A Generator of Random Linear Programming Problems for Cluster Computing Systems

Leonid B. Sokolinsky$^{(\boxtimes)}$ and Irina M. Sokolinskaya

South Ural State University (National Research University), 76, Lenin prospekt,
Chelyabinsk 454080, Russia
{leonid.sokolinsky,irina.sokolinskaya}@susu.ru

Abstract. The article presents and evaluates a scalable FRaGenLP
algorithm for generating random linear programming problems of large
dimension n on cluster computing systems. To ensure the consistency of
the problem and the boundedness of the feasible region, the constraint
system includes $2n + 1$ standard inequalities, called support inequalities. New random inequalities are generated and added to the system in
a manner that ensures the consistency of the constraints. Furthermore,
the algorithm uses two likeness metrics to prevent the addition of a new
random inequality that is similar to one already present in the constraint
system. The algorithm also rejects random inequalities that cannot affect
the solution of the linear programming problem bounded by the support
inequalities. The parallel implementation of the FRaGenLP algorithm
is performed in C++ through the parallel BSF-skeleton, which encapsulates all aspects related to the MPI-based parallelization of the program. We provide the results of large-scale computational experiments
on a cluster computing system to study the scalability of the FRaGenLP
algorithm.

Keywords: Random linear programming problem · Problem
generator · FRaGenLP · Cluster computing system · BSF-skeleton

1 Introduction

The era of big data [1,2] has generated large-scale linear programming (LP)
problems [3]. Such problems arise in economics, industry, logistics, statistics,
quantum physics, and other fields. To solve them, high-performance computing
systems and parallel algorithms are required. Thus, the development of new parallel algorithms for solving LP problems and the revision of current algorithms
have become imperative. As examples, we can cite the works [4–9]. The development of new parallel algorithms for solving large-scale linear programming

I. M. Sokolinskaya—The reported study was partially funded by the Russian Foundation for Basic Research (project No. 20-07-00092-a) and the Ministry of Science and
Higher Education of the Russian Federation (government order FENU-2020-0022).

© Springer Nature Switzerland AG 2021
L. Sokolinsky and M. Zymbler (Eds.): PCT 2021, CCIS 1437, pp. 164–177, 2021.
https://doi.org/10.1007/978-3-030-81691-9_12

problems involves testing them on benchmark and random problems. One of the most well-known benchmark repositories of linear programming problems is Netlib-Lp [10]. However, when debugging LP solvers, it is often necessary to generate random LP problems with certain characteristics, with the dimension of the space and the number of constraints being the main ones. The paper [11] suggested one of the first methods for generating random LP problems with known solutions. The method allows generating test problems of arbitrary size with a wide range of numerical characteristics. The main idea of the method is as follows. Take as a basis an LP problem with a known solution and then randomly modify it so that the solution does not change. The main drawback of the method is that fixing the optimal solution in advance significantly restricts the random nature of the resulting LP problem.

The article [12] describes the GENGUB generator, which constructs random LP problems with a known solution and given characteristics, such as the problem size, the density of the coefficient matrix, the degeneracy, the number of binding inequalities, and others. A distinctive feature of GENGUB is the ability to introduce generalized upper bound constraints, defined to be a (sub)set of constraints in which each variable appears at most once (i.e., has at most one nonzero coefficient). This method has the same drawback as the previous one: by preliminarily fixing the optimal solution, one significantly restricts the random nature of the resulting LP problem.

The article [13] suggests a method for generating random LP problems with a preselected solution type: bounded or unbounded, unique or multiple. Each of these structures is generated using random vectors with integer components whose range can be given. Next, an objective function that satisfies the required conditions, i.e., leads to a solution of the desired type, is obtained. The LP problem generator described in [13] is mainly used for educational purposes and is not suitable for testing new linear programming algorithms due to the limited variety of generated problems.

In the present paper, we suggest an alternative method for generating random LP problems. The method has the peculiarity of generating feasible problems of a given dimension with an unknown solution. The generated problem is fed to the input of the tested LP solver, and the latter outputs a solution that must be validated. The validator program (see, for example, [14]) validates the obtained solution. The method we suggest for generating random LP problems is named FRaGenLP (Feasible Random Generator of LP) and is implemented as a parallel program for cluster computing systems. The rest of the article is as follows. Section 2 provides a formal description of the method for generating random LP problems and gives a sequential version of the FRaGenLP algorithm. In Sect. 3, we discuss the parallel version of the FRaGenLP algorithm. In Sect. 4, we describe the implementation of FRaGenLP using a parallel BSF-skeleton and give the results of large-scale computational experiments on a cluster computing system. The results confirm the efficiency of our approach. Section 5 summarizes the obtained results and discusses plans to use the FRaGenLP generator in the development of an artificial neural network capable of solving large LP problems.

2 Method for Generating Random LP Problems

The method suggested in this paper generates random feasible bounded LP problems of arbitrary dimension n with an unknown solution. To guarantee the correctness of the LP problem, the constraint system includes the following *support inequalities*:

$$\begin{cases} x_1 & \leqslant \alpha \\ \quad x_2 & \leqslant \alpha \\ \quad \ddots & \dots\dots \\ \quad\quad x_n & \leqslant \alpha \\ -x_1 & \leqslant 0 \\ \quad -x_2 & \leqslant 0 \\ \quad \ddots & \dots\dots \\ \quad\quad -x_n \leqslant 0 \\ x_1 \;+x_2 \cdots +x_n \leqslant (n-1)\alpha + \alpha/2 \end{cases} \tag{1}$$

Here, the positive constant $\alpha \in \mathbb{R}_{>0}$ is a parameter of the FRaGenLP generator. The number of support inequalities is $2n+1$. The number of random inequalities is determined by a parameter $d \in \mathbb{Z}_{\geqslant 0}$. The total number m of inequalities is defined by the following equation:

$$m = 2n + 1 + d. \tag{2}$$

The coefficients of the objective function are specified by the vector

$$c = \theta\,(n, n-1, n-2, \dots, 1), \tag{3}$$

where the positive constant $\theta \in \mathbb{R}_{>0}$ is a parameter of the FRaGenLP generator that satisfies the following condition:

$$\theta \leqslant \frac{\alpha}{2}. \tag{4}$$

From now on, we assume that the LP problem requires finding a feasible point at which the maximum of the objective function is attained. If the number d of random inequalities is zero, then FRaGenLP generates an LP problem that includes only the support inequalities given in (1). In this case, the LP problem has the following unique solution:

$$\bar{x} = (\alpha, \dots, \alpha, \alpha/2). \tag{5}$$

If the number d of random inequalities is greater than zero, the FRaGenLP generator adds the corresponding number of inequalities to system (1). The coefficients $a_i = (a_{i1}, \dots, a_{in})$ of the random inequality and the constant term b_i on the right side are calculated through the function $\mathrm{rand}(l, r)$, which generates a random real number in the interval $[l, r]$ $(l, r \in \mathbb{R}; l < r)$, and the function rsgn(), which randomly selects a number from the set $\{1, -1\}$:

$$
\begin{aligned}
a_{ij} &:= \mathrm{rsgn}() \cdot \mathrm{rand}(0, a_{\max}), \\
b_i &:= \mathrm{rsgn}() \cdot \mathrm{rand}(0, b_{\max}).
\end{aligned}
\tag{6}
$$

Here, $a_{\max}, b_{\max} \in \mathbb{R}_{>0}$ are parameters of the FRaGenLP generator. The inequality sign is always "$\leqslant$". Let us introduce the following notations:

$$
f(x) = \langle c, x \rangle;
\tag{7}
$$

$$
h = (\alpha/2, \ldots, \alpha/2);
\tag{8}
$$

$$
\mathrm{dist}_h(a_i, b_i) = \frac{|\langle a_i, h \rangle - b_i|}{\|a_i\|};
\tag{9}
$$

$$
\pi(h, a_i, b_i) = h - \frac{\langle a_i, h \rangle - b_i}{|a_i|^2} a_i.
\tag{10}
$$

Equation (7) defines the objective function of the LP problem. Here and further on, $\langle \cdot, \cdot \rangle$ stands for the dot product of vectors. Equation (8) defines the central point of the *bounding hypercube* specified by the first $2n$ inequalities of system (1). Furthermore, Eq. (9) defines a function $\mathrm{dist}_h(a_i, b_i)$ that gives the distance from the hyperplane $\langle a_i, x \rangle = b_i$ to the center h of the bounding hypercube. Here and below, $\| \cdot \|$ denotes the Euclidean norm. Equation (10) defines a vector-valued function that expresses the orthogonal projection of the point h onto the hyperplane $\langle a_i, x \rangle = b_i$.

To obtain a random inequality $\langle a_i, x \rangle \leqslant b_i$, we calculate the coordinates of the coefficient vector a_i and the constant term b_i using a pseudorandom rational number generator. The generated random inequality is added to the constraint system if and only if the following conditions hold:

$$
\langle a_i, h \rangle \leqslant b_i;
\tag{11}
$$

$$
\rho < \mathrm{dist}_h(a_i, b_i) \leqslant \theta;
\tag{12}
$$

$$
f\left(\pi\left(h, a_i, b_i\right)\right) > f\left(h\right);
\tag{13}
$$

$$
\forall l \in \{1, \ldots, i - 1\} : \neg \mathrm{like}(a_i, b_i, a_l, b_l).
\tag{14}
$$

Condition (11) requires that the center of the bounding hypercube be a feasible point for the considered random inequality. If the condition does not hold, then the inequality $-\langle a_i, x \rangle \leqslant -b_i$ is added instead of $\langle a_i, x \rangle \leqslant b_i$. Condition (12) requires that the distance from the hyperplane $\langle a_i, x \rangle = b_i$ to the center h of the bounding hypercube be greater than ρ but not greater than θ. The constant $\rho \in \mathbb{R}_{>0}$ is a parameter of the FRaGenLP generator and must satisfy the condition $\rho < \theta$, where θ, in turn, satisfies condition (4). Condition (13) requires that the objective function value at the projection of the point h onto the hyperplane $\langle a_i, x \rangle = b_i$ be greater than the objective function value at the point h. This condition combined with (11) and (12) cuts off constraints that cannot affect the solution of the LP problem. Finally, condition (14) requires that the new inequality be *dissimilar* from all previously added ones, including the support ones. This condition uses the Boolean function "like", which determines the *likeness* of the inequalities $\langle a_i, x \rangle \leqslant b_i$ and $\langle a_l, x \rangle \leqslant b_l$ through the following equation:

$$\text{like}(a_i, b_i, a_l, b_l) = \left\| \frac{a_i}{\|a_i\|} - \frac{a_l}{\|a_l\|} \right\| < L_{\max} \wedge \left| \frac{b_i}{\|a_i\|} - \frac{b_l}{\|a_l\|} \right| < S_{\min}. \tag{15}$$

The constants $L_{\max}, S_{\min} \in \mathbb{R}_{>0}$ are parameters of the FRaGenLP generator. In this case, the parameter $L_{\max}$ must satisfy the condition

$$L_{\max} \leqslant 0.7 \tag{16}$$

(we will explain the meaning of this constraint below). According to (15), inequalities $\langle a_i, x \rangle \leqslant b_i$ and $\langle a_l, x \rangle \leqslant b_l$ are *similar* if the following two conditions hold:

$$\left\| \frac{a_i}{\|a_i\|} - \frac{a_l}{\|a_l\|} \right\| < L_{\max}; \tag{17}$$

$$\left| \frac{b_i}{\|a_i\|} - \frac{b_l}{\|a_l\|} \right| < S_{\min}. \tag{18}$$

Condition (17) evaluates the measure of parallelism of the hyperplanes $\langle a_i, x \rangle = b_i$ and $\langle a_l, x \rangle = b_l$, which bound the feasible regions of the corresponding inequalities. Let us explain this. The unit vectors $e_i = a_i / \|a_i\|$ and $e_l = a_l / \|a_l\|$ are normal to the hyperplanes $\langle a_i, x \rangle = b_i$ and $\langle a_l, x \rangle = b_l$, respectively. Let us introduce the notation $\delta = \|e_i - e_l\|$. If $\delta = 0$, then the hyperplanes are parallel. If $0 \leqslant \delta < L_{\max}$, then the hyperplanes are considered to be *nearly parallel*.

Condition (18) evaluates the *closeness* of the parallel hyperplanes $\langle a_i, x \rangle = b_i$ and $\langle a_l, x \rangle = b_l$. Indeed, the scalar values $\beta_i = b_i / \|a_i\|$ and $\beta_l = b_l / \|a_l\|$ are the normalized constant terms. Let us introduce the notation $\sigma = |\beta_i - \beta_l|$. If $\sigma = 0$, then the parallel hyperplanes coincide. If the hyperplanes are nearly parallel and $0 \leqslant \sigma < S_{\min}$, then they are considered to be *nearly concurrent*.

Two linear inequalities in $\mathbb{R}^n$ are considered *similar* if the corresponding hyperplanes are nearly parallel and nearly concurrent.

The constraint (16) for the parameter $L_{\max}$ is based on the following proposition.

Proposition 1. *Let the two unit vectors $e, e' \in \mathbb{R}^n$ and the angle $\varphi < \pi$ between them be given. Then,*

$$\|e - e'\| = \sqrt{2(1 - \cos \varphi)}. \tag{19}$$

Proof. By the definition of the norm in Euclidean space, we have

$$\|e - e'\| = \sqrt{\sum_j (e_j - e'_j)^2} = \sqrt{\sum_j (e_j{}^2 - 2e_j e'_j + e'_j{}^2)}$$

$$= \sqrt{\sum_j e_j{}^2 - 2\sum_j e_j e'_j + \sum_j e'_j{}^2} = \sqrt{1 - 2\langle e_j, e'_j \rangle + 1}.$$

Thus,

$$\|e - e'\| = \sqrt{2\left(1 - \langle e_j, e'_j \rangle\right)}. \tag{20}$$

By the definition of the angle in Euclidean space, we have, for unit vectors,

$$\langle e_j, e'_j \rangle = \cos \varphi.$$

Substituting in (20) the expression obtained, we have

$$\|e - e'\| = \sqrt{2\left(1 - \cos \varphi\right)}.$$

The proposition is proven.

It is reasonable to consider that two unit vectors e, e' are nearly parallel if the angle between them is less than $\pi/4$. In this case, according to (19), we have

$$\|e - e'\| < \sqrt{2\left(1 - \cos \frac{\pi}{4}\right)}.$$

Taking into account that $\cos(\pi/4) \approx 0.707$, we obtain the required estimate:

$$\|e - e'\| < 0.7.$$

An example of a two-dimensional LP problem generated by FRaGenLP is shown in Fig. 1. The purple color indicates the line defined by the coefficients of the objective function; the black lines correspond to the support inequalities, and the red lines correspond to the random inequalities. For the sake of clarity, we use green dashed lines to plot the large and the small circles defined by the equations $(x_1 - 100)^2 + (x_2 - 100)^2 = 100^2$ and $(x_1 - 100)^2 + (x_2 - 100)^2 = 50^2$. According to condition (12), any random line must intersect the large green circle but not the small green circle. The semitransparent red color indicates the feasible region of the generated LP problem.

Algorithm 1 represents a sequential implementation of the described method. Step 1 assigns zero value to the counter k of random inequalities. Step 2 creates an empty list A to store the coefficients of the inequalities. Step 3 creates an empty list B to store the constant terms. Step 4 adds the coefficients and constant terms of the support inequalities (1) to the lists A and B, respectively. Step 5 generates the coefficients of the objective function according to (3). If the parameter d, which specifies the number of random inequalities, is equal to zero, then Step 6 passes the control to Step 19. Steps 7 and 8 generate the coefficients

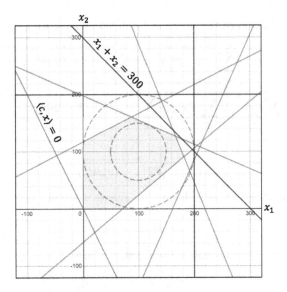

Fig. 1. Random LP problem with $n = 2$, $d = 5$, $\alpha = 200$, $\theta = 100$, $\rho = 50$, $S_{\min} = 100$, $L_{\max} = 0.35$, $a_{\max} = 1000$, and $b_{\max} = 10\,000$

and the constant term of the new random inequality. Step 9 checks condition (11). If the condition does not hold, then the signs of the coefficients and the constant term are reversed (Steps 10, 11). Step 12 checks condition (12). Step 13 checks condition (13). Step 14 checks condition (14). Step 15 appends the coefficients of the new random inequality to the list A (++ denotes the concatenation of lists). Step 16 appends the constant term of the new random inequality to the list B. Step 17 increments the counter of added random inequalities by one. If the number of added random inequalities has not reached the given quantity d, then Step 18 passes the control to Step 7 to generate the next inequality. Step 19 outputs the results. Step 20 stops computations.

3   Parallel Algorithm for Generating Random LP Problems

Implicit loops generated by passing the control from Steps 12–14 to Step 7 of Algorithm 1 can result in high overheads. For example, during the generation of the LP problem represented in Fig. 1, there were 112 581 returns from Step 12 to label 7, 32 771 from Step 13, and 726 from Step 14. Therefore, generating a large random LP problem on a commodity personal computer can take many hours. To overcome this obstacle, we developed a parallel version of the FRaGenLP generator for cluster computing systems. This version is presented as Algorithm 2. It is based on the BSF parallel computation model [15, 16], which assumes the master–slave paradigm [17]. According to the BSF model, the master node serves

Algorithm 1. Sequential algorithm for generating a random LP problem

Parameters: $n, d, \alpha, \theta, \rho, S_{\min}, L_{\max}, a_{\max}, b_{\max}$

1: $k := 0$
2: $A := [\,]$
3: $B := [\,]$
4: AddSupport(A, B)
5: **for** $j = n \ldots 1$ **do** $c_j := \theta \cdot j$
6: **if** $d = 0$ **goto** 19
7: **for** $j = 1 \ldots n$ **do** $a_j := \text{rsign}() \cdot \text{rand}(0, a_{\max})$
8: $b := \text{rsign}() \cdot \text{rand}(0, b_{\max})$
9: **if** $\langle a, h \rangle \leqslant b$ **goto** 12
10: **for** $j = 1 \ldots n$ **do** $a_j := -a_j$
11: $b := -b$
12: **if** $\text{dist}_h(a, b) < \rho$ **or** $\text{dist}_h(a, b) > \theta$ **goto** 7
13: **if** $\text{f}(\pi(h, a, b)) \leqslant \text{f}(h)$ **goto** 7
14: **for all** $(\bar{a}, \bar{b}) \in (A, B)$ **do if** $\text{like}(a, b, \bar{a}, \bar{b})$ **goto** 7
15: $A := A +\!\!+ [a]$
16: $B := B +\!\!+ [b]$
17: $k := k + 1$
18: **if** $k < d$ **goto** 7
19: **output** A, B, c
20: **stop**

as a control and communication center. All slave nodes execute the same code but on different data.

Let us discuss Algorithm 2 in more detail. First, we look at the steps performed by the master node. Step 1 assigns zero value to the counter of random inequalities. Step 2 creates an empty list A_S to store the coefficients of the support inequalities. Step 3 creates an empty list B_S to store the constant terms of the support inequalities. Step 4 adds the coefficients and constant terms of the support inequalities (1) to the lists A_S and B_S, respectively. Step 5 generates the coefficients of the objective function according to (3). Step 6 outputs the coefficients and constant term of the support inequalities. If the parameter d, which specifies the number of random inequalities, is equal to zero, then Step 7 passes the control to Step 36, which terminates the computational process in the master node. Step 8 creates an empty list A_R to store the coefficients of the random inequalities. Step 9 creates an empty list B_R to store the constant terms of the random inequalities. In Step 18, the master node receives one random inequality from each slave node. Each of these inequalities satisfies conditions (11)–(13) and is not similar to any of the support inequalities. These conditions are ensured by the slave nodes. In the loop consisting of Steps 19–32, the master node checks all received random inequalities for similarity with the random inequalities previously included in the lists A_R and B_R. The similar new inequalities are rejected, and the dissimilar ones are added to the lists A_R and B_R. In this case, the inequality counter is increased by one each time some inequality

Algorithm 2. Parallel algorithm for generating a random LP problem

Parameters: $n, d, \alpha, \theta, \rho, S_{\min}, L_{\max}, a_{\max}, b_{\max}$

Master	Slave (l=1,...,L)
1: $k := 0$	1: **if** $d = 0$ **goto** 36
2: $A_S := [\,]$	2: $A_S := [\,]$
3: $B_S := [\,]$	3: $B_S := [\,]$
4: AddSupport(A_S, B_S)	4: AddSupport(A_S, B_S)
5: **for** $j = n \ldots 1$ **do** $c_j := \theta \cdot j$	5: **for** $j = 1 \ldots n$ **do**
6: **output** A_S, B_S, c	6: $\quad a_j^{(l)} := \mathrm{rsign}() \cdot \mathrm{rand}(0, a_{\max})$
7: **if** $d = 0$ **goto** 36	7: **end for**
8: $A_R := [\,]$	8: $b^{(l)} := \mathrm{rsign}() \cdot \mathrm{rand}(0, b_{\max})$
9: $B_R := [\,]$	9: **if** $\langle a^{(l)}, h \rangle \leq b^{(l)}$ **goto** 12
10:	10: **for** $j = 1 \ldots n$ **do** $a_j^{(l)} := -a_j^{(l)}$
11:	11: $b^{(l)} := -b^{(l)}$
12:	12: **if** $\mathrm{dist}_h(a^{(l)}, b^{(l)}) < \rho$ **goto** 5
13:	13: **if** $\mathrm{dist}_h(a^{(l)}, b^{(l)}) > \theta$ **goto** 5
14:	14: **if** $\mathrm{f}(\pi(h, a^{(l)}, b^{(l)})) \leqslant \mathrm{f}(h)$ **goto** 5
15:	15: **for all** $(\bar{a}, \bar{b}) \in (A_S, B_S)$ **do**
16:	16: $\quad$ **if** $\mathrm{like}(a^{(l)}, b^{(l)}, \bar{a}, \bar{b})$ **goto** 5
17:	17: **end for**
18: **RecvFromSlaves** $a^{(1)}, b^{(1)}, ..., a^{(L)}, b^{(L)}$	18: **SendToMaster** $a^{(l)}, b^{(l)}$
19: **for** $l = 1 \ldots L$ **do**	19:
20: $\quad$ $isLike := false$	20:
21: $\quad$ **for all** $(\bar{a}, \bar{b}) \in (A_R, B_R)$ **do**	21:
22: $\quad\quad$ **if** $\mathrm{like}(a^{(l)}, b^{(l)}, \bar{a}, \bar{b})$ **then**	22:
23: $\quad\quad\quad$ $isLike := true$	23:
24: $\quad\quad\quad$ **goto** 27	24:
25: $\quad\quad$ **end if**	25:
26: $\quad$ **end for**	26:
27: $\quad$ **if** $isLike$ **continue**	27:
28: $\quad$ $A_R := A_R + [a^{(l)}]$	28:
29: $\quad$ $B_R := B_R + [b^{(l)}]$	29:
30: $\quad$ $k := k + 1$	30:
31: $\quad$ **if** $k = d$ **goto** 33	31:
32: **end for**	32:
33: **SendToSlaves** k	33: **RecvFromMaster** k
34: **if** $k < d$ **goto** 18	34: **if** $k < d$ **goto** 5
35: **output** A_R, B_R	35:
36: **stop**	36: **stop**

is added to the lists. If the required number of random inequalities has already been reached, then Step 31 performs an early exit from the loop. Step 33 sends the current number of added random inequalities to the slave nodes. If this quantity is less than d, then Step 34 passes the control to Step 18, which requests a new portion of random inequalities from the slave nodes. Otherwise, Step 35 outputs the results, and Step 36 terminates the computational process in the master node.

Let us consider now the steps performed by the l-th slave node. If the parameter d, which specifies the number of random inequalities, is equal to zero, then Step 1 passes the control to Step 36, which terminates the computational process in the slave node. Otherwise, Steps 2 and 3 create the empty lists A_S and B_S to store the support inequalities. Step 4 adds the coefficients and constant terms of the support inequalities (1) to the lists A_S and B_S, respectively. Steps 5–8 generate a new random inequality. Step 9 checks condition (11). If this condition does not hold, then the signs of the coefficients and the constant term are reversed (Steps 10 and 11). Steps 12–14 check conditions (12) and (13). Steps 15–17 check the similarity of the generated inequality to the support inequalities. If any one of these conditions does not hold, then the control is passed to Step 5 to generate a new random inequality. If all conditions hold, then Step 18 sends the constructed random inequality to the master node. In Step 33, the slave receives from the master the current number of obtained random inequalities. If this quantity is less than the required number, then Step 34 passes the control to Step 5 to generate a new random inequality. Otherwise, Step 36 terminates the computational process in the slave node.

4   Software Implementation and the Computational Experiments

We implemented the parallel Algorithm 2 in C++ through the parallel BSF-skeleton [18], which is based on the BSF parallel computation model [15] and encapsulates all aspects related to the parallelization of the program using the MPI library [19].

The BSF-skeleton requires the representation of the algorithm in the form of operations on lists using the higher-order functions *Map* and *Reduce*, defined by the Bird–Meertens formalism [20]. The required representation can be constructed as follows. Set the length of the *Map* and *Reduce* lists equal to the number of slave MPI processes. Define the *Map* list items as empty structures:

struct PT_bsf_mapElem_T{ } .

Each element of the *Reduce* list stores the coefficients and the constant term of one random inequality $\langle a, x \rangle \leqslant b$:

struct PT_bsf_reduceElem_T{ float a[n]; float b} .

Each slave MPI process generates one random inequality using the *PC_bsf_MapF* function, which executes Steps 5–17 of Algorithm 2. The slave

Table 1. Specifications of the "Tornado SUSU" computing cluster

Parameter	Value
Number of processor nodes	480
Processor	Intel Xeon X5680 (6 cores, 3.33 GHz)
Processors per node	2
Memory per node	24 GB DDR3
Interconnect	InfiniBand QDR (40 Gbit/s)
Operating system	Linux CentOS

MPI process stores the inequality that satisfies all conditions to its local *Reduce* list consisting of a single item. The master MPI process receives the generated elements from the slave MPI processes and places them in its *Reduce* list (this code is implemented in the problem-independent part of the BSF-skeleton). After that, the master MPI process checks each obtained inequality for similarity with the previously added ones. If no matches are found, the master MPI process adds the inequality just checked to its local *Reduce* list. These actions, corresponding to Steps 19–32 of Algorithm 2, are implemented as the standard function *PC_bsf_ProcessResults* of the BSF-skeleton. The source code of the FRaGenLP parallel program is freely available on the Internet at https://github.com/leonid-sokolinsky/BSF-LPP-Generator.

Using the program, we conducted large-scale computational experiments on the cluster computing system "Tornado SUSU" [21]. The specifications of the system are given in Table 1. The computations were performed for several dimensions, namely $n = 3000$, $n = 5500$, and $n = 15\,000$. The total numbers of inequalities were, respectively, 6301, 10001, and 31501. The corresponding numbers of random inequalities were 300, 500, and 1500, respectively. Throughout the experiments, we used the following parameter values: $\alpha = 200$ (the length of the bounding hypercube edge), $\theta = 100$ (the radius of the large hypersphere), $\rho = 50$ (the radius of the small hypersphere), $L_{\max} = 0.35$ (the upper bound of *near parallelism* for hyperplanes), $S_{\min} = 100$ (the minimum acceptable closeness for hyperplanes), $a_{\max} = 1000$ (the upper absolute bound for the coefficients), and $b_{\max} = 10\,000$ (the upper absolute bound for the constant terms).

The results of the experiments are shown in Fig. 2. Generating a random LP problem with 31501 constraints with a configuration consisting of a master node and a slave node took 12 min. Generating the same problem with a configuration consisting of a master node and 170 slave nodes took 22 s. The analysis of the results showed that the scalability bound (the maximum of the speedup curve) of the algorithm significantly depends on the dimension of the problem. For $n = 3000$, the scalability bound was 50 processor nodes approximately. This bound increased up to 110 nodes for $n = 5000$, and to 200 nodes for $n = 15\,000$. A further increase in problem size causes the processor nodes to run

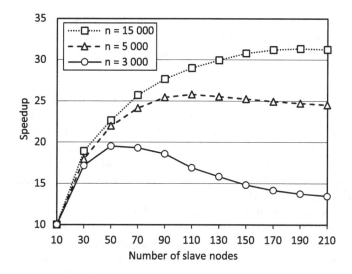

Fig. 2. Speedup curves of the FRaGenLP parallel algorithm for various dimensions

out of memory. It should be noted that the scalability bound of the algorithm significantly depends on the number of random inequalities too. Increasing this number by a factor of 10 resulted in a twofold reduction of the scalability bound. This is because an increase in the number of slave nodes results in a significant increase in the portion of sequential computations performed by the master node in Steps 19–32, during which the slave nodes are idle.

5   Conclusions

In this paper, we described the parallel FRaGenLP algorithm for generating random feasible bounded LP problems on cluster computing systems. In addition to random inequalities, the generated constraint systems include a standard set of inequalities called *support inequalities*. They ensure the boundedness of the feasible region of the LP problem. In geometric terms, the feasible region of the support inequalities is a hypercube with edges adjacent to the coordinate axes, and the vertex that is farthest from the origin is cut off. The objective function is defined in such a manner that its coefficients decrease monotonically. The coefficients and constant terms of the random inequalities are obtained using a random number generator. If the feasible region of a randomly generated inequality does not include the center of the bounding hypercube, then the sign of the inequality is reversed. Furthermore, not every random inequality is included in the constraint system. The random inequalities that cannot affect the solution of the LP problem for a given objective function are rejected. The inequalities, for which the bounding hyperplane intersects a small hypersphere located at the center of the bounding hypercube are also rejected. This ensures the feasibility of the constraint system. Moreover, any random inequality that is "similar" to at least one of the inequalities already added to the system (including the support ones) is also rejected. To define the "similarity" of inequalities, two formal metrics are introduced for bounding hyperplanes: the measure of parallelism and the measure of closeness.

The parallel algorithm is based on the BSF parallel computation model, which relies on the master–slave paradigm. According to this paradigm, the master node serves as a control and communication center. All slave nodes execute the same code but on different data. The parallel implementation was performed in C++ through the parallel BSF-skeleton, which encapsulates all aspects related to the MPI-based parallelization of the program. The source code of the FRaGenLP generator is freely available on the Internet at https://github.com/leonid-sokolinsky/BSF-LPP-Generator.

Using this implementation, we conducted large-scale computational experiments on a cluster computing system. As the experiments showed, the parallel FRaGenLP algorithm demonstrates good scalability, up to 200 processor nodes for $n = 15\,000$. Generating a random LP problem with 31 501 constraints takes 22 s with a configuration consisting of 171 processor nodes. Generating the same problem with a configuration consisting of a processor node takes 12 min. The program was used to generate a dataset of 70 000 samples for training an artificial neural network capable of quickly solving large LP problems.

References

1. Jagadish, H.V., et al.: Big data and its technical challenges. Commun. ACM **57**(7), 86–94 (2014). https://doi.org/10.1145/2611567
2. Hartung, T.: Making big sense from big data. Front. Big Data. **1**, 5 (2018). https://doi.org/10.3389/fdata.2018.00005
3. Sokolinskaya, I., Sokolinsky, L.B.: On the solution of linear programming problems in the age of big data. In: Sokolinsky, L., Zymbler, M. (eds.) PCT 2017. CCIS, vol. 753, pp. 86–100. Springer, Cham (2017). https://doi.org/10.1007/978-3-319-67035-5_7
4. Sokolinsky, L.B., Sokolinskaya, I.M.: Scalable method for linear optimization of industrial processes. In: Proceedings – 2020 Global Smart Industry Conference, GloSIC 2020, pp. 20–26. Article number 9267854. IEEE (2020). https://doi.org/10.1109/GloSIC50886.2020.9267854
5. Sokolinskaya, I., Sokolinsky, L.B.: Scalability evaluation of NSLP algorithm for solving non-stationary linear programming problems on cluster computing systems. In: Voevodin, V., Sobolev, S. (eds.) Supercomputing, RuSCDays 2017. Communications in Computer and Information Science, vol. 793. pp. 40–53. Springer, Cham (2017). https://doi.org/10.1007/978-3-319-71255-0_4
6. Mamalis, B., Pantziou, G.: Advances in the parallelization of the simplex method. In: Zaroliagis, C., Pantziou, G., Kontogiannis, S. (eds.) Algorithms, Probability, Networks, and Games. LNCS, vol. 9295, pp. 281–307. Springer, Cham (2015). https://doi.org/10.1007/978-3-319-24024-4_17
7. Huangfu, Q., Hall, J.A.J.: Parallelizing the dual revised simplex method. Math. Program. Comput. **10**(1), 119–142 (2018). https://doi.org/10.1007/s12532-017-0130-5

8. Tar, P., Stagel, B., Maros, I.: Parallel search paths for the simplex algorithm. Central Eur. J. Oper. Res. **25**(4), 967–984 (2017). https://doi.org/10.1007/s10100-016-0452-9

9. Yang, L., Li, T., Li, J.: Parallel predictor-corrector interior-point algorithm of structured optimization problems. In: 3rd International Conference on Genetic and Evolutionary Computing, WGEC 2009, pp. 256–259 (2009). https://doi.org/10.1109/WGEC.2009.68

10. Gay, D.M.: Electronic mail distribution of linear programming test problems. Math. Program. Soc. COAL Bull. **13**, 10–12 (1985)

11. Charnes, A., Raike, W.M., Stutz, J.D., Walters, A.S.: On generation of test problems for linear programming codes. Commun. ACM **17**(10), 583–586 (1974). https://doi.org/10.1145/355620.361173

12. Arthur, J.L., Frendewey, J.O.: GENGUB: a generator for linear programs with generalized upper bound constraints. Comput. Oper. Res. **20**(6), 565–573 (1993). https://doi.org/10.1016/0305-0548(93)90112-V

13. Castillo, E., Pruneda, R.E., Esquivel, Mo.: Automatic generation of linear programming problems for computer aided instruction. Int. J. Math. Educ. Sci. Technol. **32**(2), 209–232 (2001). https://doi.org/10.1080/00207390010010845

14. Dhiflaoui, M., et al.: Certifying and repairing solutions to large LPs how good are LP-solvers? In: SODA03: Proceedings of the Fourteenth Annual ACM-SIAM Symposium on Discrete Algorithms, pp. 255–256. Society for Industrial and Applied Mathematics, USA (2003)

15. Sokolinsky, L.B.: BSF: a parallel computation model for scalability estimation of iterative numerical algorithms on cluster computing systems. J. Parallel Distrib. Comput. **149**, 193–206 (2021). https://doi.org/10.1016/j.jpdc.2020.12.009

16. Sokolinsky, L.B.: Analytical estimation of the scalability of iterative numerical algorithms on distributed memory multiprocessors. Lobachevskii J. Math. **39**(4), 571–575 (2018). http://dx.doi.org/10.1134/S1995080218040121

17. Sahni, S., Vairaktarakis, G.: The master-slave paradigm in parallel computer and industrial settings. J. Glob. Optim. **9**(3–4), 357–377 (1996). https://doi.org/10.1007/BF00121679

18. Sokolinsky, L.B.: BSF-skeleton. User manual. arXiv:2008.12256 [cs.DC] (2020)

19. Gropp, W.: MPI 3 and beyond: why MPI is successful and what challenges it faces. In: Träff, J.L., Benkner, S., Dongarra, J.J. (eds.) EuroMPI 2012. LNCS, vol. 7490, pp. 1–9. Springer, Heidelberg (2012). https://doi.org/10.1007/978-3-642-33518-1_1

20. Bird, R.S.: Lectures on constructive functional programming. In: Broy, M. (ed.) Constructive Methods in Computing Science. NATO ASI Series F: Computer and Systems Sciences, vol. 55, pp. 151–216. Springer, Heidlberg (1988). https://doi.org/10.1007/978-3-642-74884-4_5

21. Kostenetskiy, P., Semenikhina, P.: SUSU supercomputer resources for industry and fundamental science. In: Proceedings – 2018 Global Smart Industry Conference, GloSIC 2018, art. no. 8570068, p. 7. IEEE (2018). https://doi.org/10.1109/GloSIC.2018.8570068

Application of the AmgX Library
to the Discontinuous Galerkin Methods
for Elliptic Problems

N. M. Evstigneev$^{(\boxtimes)}$ (iD) and O. I. Ryabkov

Federal Research Center "Computer Science and Control"
of the Russian Academy of Sciences, Moscow, Russia

Abstract. We consider an application of the AmgX library by NVIDIA as the preconditioner or solver for discrete elliptic problems expressed through Discontinuous Galerkin methods (DG) with various formulations. The effect of poor geometric multigrid performance on the elliptic DG formulation has been discussed in a recent paper by Fortunato, Rycroft, and Saye. In the present study, we check the 'out-of-the-box' performance of the Algebraic Multigrid Method (AMG) implemented in the open-source variant of the AmgX library. Four different DG discretization schemes are considered, namely local DG, compact DG, Bassi–Rebay-2 scheme, and internal penalty methods, including symmetric and nonsymmetric formulations. The local DG scheme is considered in its dual form; the rest are considered in primal form. All these methods yield a block matrix with a compact stencil, which is passed to the AmgX library (or Krylov-subspace methods with the AmgX library used as a preconditioner) for the solution of the linear system. We show that the library requires some code adjustments and additions before we can apply it to the block matrices by hand. It is also shown that the convergence of the AMG and Krylov-AMG methods is relatively poor and requires a reformulation of the problem. Further research is expected.

Keywords: Discontinuous Galerkin methods · Elliptic problems · Darcy problem · Multigrid methods · AmgX library

1 Introduction

The Discontinuous Galerkin method (DG) is a classic numerical method [22] initially applied to hyperbolic-type partial differential equations and systems of conservation laws [6,7]. It is considered a generalization of the finite volume method (for zero degree of polynomials) to high-order approximations. It is now one of the common methods to be used for high-order simulations of conservation laws in fluid and gas dynamics [5,17]. The method is also applied to elliptic

The reported study was funded by the Russian Foundation for Basic Research and the National Science Foundation of Bulgaria (NSFB) (project No. 20-51-18001).

L. Sokolinsky and M. Zymbler (Eds.): PCT 2021, CCIS 1437, pp. 178–193, 2021.
https://doi.org/10.1007/978-3-030-81691-9_13

and parabolic problems that may develop large gradients in the solutions (see [2,3,23] for more details). The benefit of the DG is that most of its discrete variants produce block matrices with a local stencil (unlike common finite element methods) which is beneficial in terms of communication loading in parallel implementations [4]. A detailed review of the DG would require considering a vast number of papers. We refer the reader to the cited papers.

A stable and consistent DG scheme for elliptic problems can be formulated in different ways leading to different properties of the resulting linear operators [2] by choosing a particular form of numerical fluxes. Thus, it is important to analyze different DG formulations and draw conclusions about them in terms of performance with multigrid methods. For example, in [16], a Geometric Multigrid Method (GMG) is applied to a Stokes system discretized with a divergence-free conforming DG. The DG scheme is the Internal Penalty (IP) method. A divergence-free subspace allows one to avoid the formation of the pressure Schur complement approximation. The smoothers for this GMG are of overlapping Schwarz-type, and a local Helmholtz decomposition is employed. The restriction and prolongation operators use the fact that discretization provides nested divergence-free subspaces. It has been demonstrated that such GMG possesses mesh-independent properties in terms of reduction of the residual. However, such a good convergence behavior of GMG is not always the case for DG methods. In theory, a GMG is an asymptotically optimal method for elliptic problems [15]. However, the application of a multigrid method directly for a primal DG discretization form can result in convergence problems. Let us review the current research status on the matter. One can divide multigrid methods into black-boxed ones (which apply DG operators or matrices obtained from DG discretization) and crafted ones (which are specially designed to work with DG methods). The former approach is the easiest one (e.g., the Algebraic Multigrid Method or AMG) but can lead to poor performance; the latter one is the hardest but can provide higher or even optimal performance (e.g., GMG). It is now the cutting-edge area of research in the field of computationally efficient fully implicit DG algorithms.

The deficiency of multigrid methods for elliptic problems with DG discretization is considered in [12]. The paper is dedicated to the analysis and experiments with the GMG method applied to the Local DG (LDG) scheme for the Poisson model equation. An h-p adaptation is used to construct the sequence of meshes and form a V-cycle. The abbreviation h-p stands for the standard method used to change the dimension of the finite element space (i.e., the mesh diameter h and, accordingly, the number of mesh elements) or the order p of the polynomials used. An example is brought up here for a better understanding of the problem since it appears counterintuitive. Let us consider the zero boundary Dirichlet problem for the Poisson equation with a given right-hand side (RHS) function $f \in L_2(\Omega)$ in the domain $\Omega \subset \mathbb{R}^d$:

$$\begin{aligned} -\triangle u &= f, \\ u|_{\partial\Omega} &= 0. \end{aligned} \tag{1}$$

This is called the initial problem. Let us consider also an equivalent dual form of (1) by introducing a gradient vector function σ:

$$\begin{aligned}
\sigma &= \nabla u, \\
-\nabla \cdot \sigma &= f, \\
u|_{\partial\Omega} &= 0.
\end{aligned} \tag{2}$$

It is shown in [12] that the traditional multigrid coarsening of the primal formulation leads to poor and suboptimal multigrid performance. However, it was noticed that the coarsening of the dual formulation leads to optimal convergence. Both LDG formulations are constructed out of the dual form (2). Nevertheless, the initial problem form (1) is used when LDG is considered in the primal form. The LDG primal form is simply the linear system $Ax = b$, where A is the matrix from the bilinear form of the LDG discretization, vector b is the functional of the LDG discretization, and x is the vector of unknown expansion coefficients of the desired solution. The dual form of the DG discretization is formulated in direct regard to (2) as

$$\begin{pmatrix} M & -G \\ -D & P \end{pmatrix} \begin{pmatrix} \sigma \\ u \end{pmatrix} = \begin{pmatrix} 0 \\ b \end{pmatrix}, \tag{3}$$

where M is the mass matrix, G is the gradient matrix, D is the divergence matrix, and P is the penalty matrix used to stabilize the discretization. The vector b is the discretization of the RHS function. The primal form now can be constructed as the Schur complement $(-DM^{-1}G + P)u = b$, and the variable σ is eliminated. This reduced discrete formulation is equivalent to the primal discrete form, but two formulations have different implications for multigrid methods. Applying standard operator coarsening to the discrete primal formulation results in poor multigrid performance; coarsening the discrete flux formulation in both σ and u before taking the Schur complement results in optimal multigrid performance and is equivalent to a pure geometric multigrid application to the discrete problem.

To show this, we introduce some notations regarding multigrid methods, assuming that the reader is familiar with the concepts of the multigrid approach (refer, for instance, to [25]). Let the operator I_c^f be an interpolation operator that maps piecewise polynomial functions from a coarse mesh to a fine mesh. For high order methods, one can construct operators that change the polynomial order; we refer to them as p-operators. Furthermore, traditional operators that work on coarse and fine meshes are called h-operators. Thus, the h-interpolation is an operator that maps piecewise polynomial function on the coarse mesh into the fine mesh without changing the polynomial degree. Correspondingly, the p-interpolation is an operator that sets first expansion coefficients in a higher-order polynomial approximation space by taking the polynomial from a lower-order approximation space. The restriction operator R_f^c is an adjoint operator to the interpolation, that is, $(R_f^c x_f, x_c)_c = (x_f, I_c^f x_c)_f$, where the dot product is computed on appropriate levels. One can notice that such operations are $L_2(\Omega)$ projections in embedded finite-dimensional functional spaces of different dimensions. Using the basis functions on each level, we can construct a restriction operator in a discrete space as $R_f^c := M_c^{-1}(I_c^f)^\mathsf{T} M_f$, which means that $M_c = (I_c^f)^\mathsf{T} M_f I_c^f$. Note that $R_f^c I_c^f = E_c$, where E is the identity matrix. The coarse operator L_c of a discrete problem can be constructed as $(L_c u_c, u_c)_c = (L I_c^f u_c, I_c^f u_c)_f$ or, in the discrete space, as $L_c = M_c^{-1}(I_c^f)^\mathsf{T} M_f L I_c^f = R_f^c L I_c^f$. This is called the "RAT" property [26], which defines the coarsening operator $\mathcal{C}(L) := R_f^c L I_c^f$. The application of GMG to the discrete system yields

$$A_c = -\mathcal{C}(D)\mathcal{C}(M^{-1})\mathcal{C}(G) + \mathcal{C}(P). \tag{4}$$

The coarsening of the discrete Laplace operator is expressed as

$$\mathcal{C}(A) := \mathcal{C}(-DM^{-1}G) + \mathcal{C}(P). \tag{5}$$

We can notice that the two results are not equal since $\mathcal{C}(DM^{-1}G) \neq \mathcal{C}(D)\mathcal{C}(M^{-1})\mathcal{C}(G)$. The coarsening process in (5) works as the composition $R_f^c DM^{-1}G I_c^f$, in which the discrete divergence and gradient operators act on a fine grid. On the other hand, the coarsening process in (4) works as a step-by-step composition $R_f^C D I_c^f R_f^c M^{-1} I_c^f R_f^c G I_c^f$ of interpolations and prolongations with the composition $I_c^f R_f^c \neq E$.

The coarsening property in the dual problem formulation (3), however, fulfills the "RAT" property of the direct application of GMG to the discrete form (4), namely

$$\begin{pmatrix} R_f^c & 0 \\ 0 & R_f^c \end{pmatrix} \begin{pmatrix} M & -G \\ -D & P \end{pmatrix} \begin{pmatrix} I_c^f & 0 \\ 0 & I_c^f \end{pmatrix} = \begin{pmatrix} M_c & -G_c \\ -D_c & P_c \end{pmatrix}.$$

The projected Schur complement $A_c = -\mathcal{C}(D)\mathcal{C}(M^{-1})\mathcal{C}(G) + \mathcal{C}(P)$ coincides with the direct GMG formulation (4) for the problem (2). Thus, it is shown in [12] that the convergence of GMG applied to the discrete dual form of LDG is optimal. And yet that formulation is far from optimal in terms of memory consumption since one needs $(d + 1)$ variables instead of one variable in the case of a scalar Poisson problem.

The application of AMG methods to different DG discretizations can also lead to poor convergence for DG. In addition to the problems we have outlined, we have to face the challenge of an inconsistent smoothed aggregation procedure in AMG (the algorithm to define the I_c^f and R_f^c operators for AMG). The standard aggregation cannot effectively aggregate or smooth the prolongation operator in the high-order DG discretization because of the complicated non-M-matrix stencil and a drastically rising condition number as p increases. It is shown in [20] that a special form of smoothed aggregation is required to correctly formulate prolongation operators. Such aggregation methods must take into consideration the strength of the connection between different nodes (or quadrature points) and thus require some geometric information about the original problem. It should be noted that the authors of the mentioned paper failed to achieve the p-independence and considered only the IP method and the dual form of LDG $((d + 1)$ variables for the scalar Poisson problem).

An updated smoothed aggregation algorithm is proposed in [1], where a variant of the AMG solver for the IP DG for the Poisson equation is considered.

The authors employ a new aggregation procedure based on block-aggregation; it removes the redundancy of degrees of freedom associated with the same grid point. The aggregation algorithm uses a new block-aggregation method on the finest level while the coarser levels are aggregated using the smoothed aggregation suggested in [20]. The finest level aggregation is built through the analysis of the matrix entries associated with each degree of freedom. Two-dimensional numerical experiments demonstrated that the suggested AMG method is uniformly convergent with respect to all the discretization parameters, namely the mesh size and the polynomial approximation degree using standard Jacobi and conjugate gradient smoothers. It is obvious that the proposed aggregation implies that the internal penalty methods rely on large values of the penalty parameter. There is no guarantee that such methods would work for other DG formulations (see the discussion above).

New hybrid combined matrix-free GMG and matrix-based AMG methods were developed in late 2019–2020. Those methods can also be applied to the solution of elliptic DG problems. Their advantage is the application of parallel efficient matrix-free GMG as much as possible. A matrix-free hybrid variant of multigrid methods is considered in [11]. The idea is to use a standard finite element p-h adaptation to perform a deeper V-cycle construction of the GMG (using the p-adaptation up to the lowest possible order and the h-adaptation to the lowest available coarse mesh) and then switch to the AMG solver on the lowest level of the GMG V-cycle with the lowest possible polynomial order. In [11], it is shown that this strategy, depending on a particular sequence of h and/or p prolongations/restrictions and particular smoothers, can lead to optimal convergence rates. However, the construction of the coarse meshes is still required at least as deep as one or two levels coarser before turning to the AMG black-box application. Thus, such methods should be considered as substantially dependent on the coarse mesh construction. An efficient implementation on Intel Xeon Phi is demonstrated for this approach while solving the Poisson equation on an irregular domain triangulated by an unstructured mesh.

The mentioned studies provide no information on the application of AMG methods to elliptic DG discretization for Graphics Processing Units (GPUs). Nevertheless, it seems to be an interesting task to tackle. The following is a list of freely available GPU-oriented and multiple GPU-oriented AMG libraries:

- AmgX [19]. This is a library designed and distributed by the NVIDIA Corporation. It comes with two variants of code: the proprietary one, available after a license is purchased, and the open-source one, distributed through GitHub. The open-source variant is used in this study.
- AMGCL [8–10]. This is a free and open-source library designed and distributed by D. Demidov via GitHub. It has been successfully tested and applied to various problems, including fluid flow simulations (see [9] for more details).
- SPARSH-AMG [13]. This is a fresh (2020) free and open-source AMG library aimed at multiple GPU computational architectures and distributed via GitHub.

In this work, we consider the AmgX library for being the easiest one to apply to CUDA-based software. The performance of other libraries is to be tested elsewhere. Our purpose was to test the performance of the AmgX library for different DG discretizations out of the box with as minimum modifications to the library as possible.

The paper has the following structure. First, we formulate the problems that are to be tested using the AmgX library. This includes the description of the governing equations and their discretization using DG with different formulations. Next, the AmgX library is considered more closely. Here, we discuss some of its features along with code modifications that make it possible to solve large block-matrix systems. In the following section, we demonstrate the results obtained by using the said library and estimate its efficiency. Finally, in the last section, we discuss the results and draw some preliminary conclusions.

2   Problem Formulation

Consider a simply connected bounded domain $\Omega \subset \mathbb{R}^d$, $d = 2$, having a piecewise smooth boundary $\Gamma = \partial \Omega$ with an outward normal vector n, Dirichlet and Neumann boundary conditions (designated "D" and "N", respectively) and $\Gamma_D \neq \varnothing$, $\Gamma_D \cap \Gamma_N = \varnothing$. On the domain Ω, we consider two problems: 1) the Poisson problem with nontrivial boundary conditions and coefficient matrix and 2) the Darcy flow problem. These problems are expressed as

1. Assume that $f \in L_2(\Omega)$, $g_D \in L_2(\Gamma_D)$, $g_N \in L_2(\Gamma_N)$, and K is a symmetric positive definite (SPD) matrix. The governing equations are the following:

$$-\nabla \cdot (K\nabla u) = f, u|_{\Gamma_D} = g_D, \quad n \cdot \nabla u|_{\Gamma_N} = g_N. \tag{6}$$

2. Assume that $f, q \in L_2(\Omega)$, $s_D \in L_2(\Gamma_{s_D})$, $s_N \in L_2(\Gamma_{s_N})$, $p_D \in L_2(\Gamma_{p_D})$, and $p_N \in L_2(\Gamma_{p_N})$. The governing equations corresponding to the total pressure–saturation formulation of the nonstationary linearized Darcy flow (see [23]) can be expressed as

$$\begin{cases} -\nabla \cdot (K_1 \nabla p) & = q, \\ \nabla \cdot (K_2 \nabla p) - \nabla \cdot (K_3 \nabla s) + \frac{\partial s}{\partial t} & = f, \\ p|_{\Gamma_{p_D}} = p_D, n \cdot \nabla p|_{\Gamma_{p_N}} = p_N, \\ s|_{\Gamma_{s_D}} = s_D, n \cdot \nabla s|_{\Gamma_{s_N}} = s_N. \end{cases} \tag{7}$$

where K_j are SPD matrices.

We introduce a tessellation of Ω into N simplexes defined as $\mathcal{T}_h$, where h is the simplex diameter. The broken Sobolev spaces of scalar and vector-valued functions are defined as usually:

$$\mathbb{H}^m(\mathcal{T}_h) := \{\phi \in L_2(\Omega) : \phi \in \mathbb{H}^m(k), \forall k \in \mathcal{T}_h\},$$
$$[\mathbb{H}^m]^d(\mathcal{T}_h) := \{\phi \in [L_2(\Omega)]^d : \phi \in [\mathbb{H}^m]^d(k), \forall k \in \mathcal{T}_h\}.$$

We also consider the finite-dimensional spaces

$$
\begin{aligned}
V_h &:= \{\phi \in L_2(\Omega) : \phi \in \mathbb{P}(k), \forall k \in T_h\}, \\
V_h^d &:= \{\phi \in [L_2(\Omega)]^d : \phi \in \mathbb{P}^d(k), \forall k \in T_h\},
\end{aligned}
\tag{8}
$$

where $\mathbb{P}^d$ and $\mathbb{P}$ are spaces of polynomials formed by the span of affine Legendre orthogonal (under the L_2 inner product) polynomials of degree $p \geq 1$ defined on the canonical simplex. The polynomials are sufficiently smooth, so we have the inclusion $V^d \subset [\mathbb{H}^m(T_h)]^d, d = \{1,2\}$. We consider the values $m = 1$ and $m = 2$. The choice of the basis functions in this manner yields the modal DG. Following [2], we introduce a few more notations and operators. A face of two simplexes is defined as $e = \partial k^+ \cap \partial k^-$ for any two adjacent simplexes in T_h, along with their outward unit normal vectors $n^\pm$ to $\partial k^\pm$. The union of all internal faces is denoted by Γ_I. Let the traces of $\tau \in V_h^d$ and $u \in V_h$ on e be defined as $\tau^\pm$ and $u^\pm$, respectively. Then, we can define the average and jump operators as

$$
\begin{aligned}
\{\tau\} &= (\tau^+ + \tau^-)/2, & [\tau] &= (\tau^+ \cdot n^+ + \tau^- \cdot n^-), \\
\{u\} &= (u^+ + u^-)/2, & [u] &= (u^+ n^+ + u^- n^-).
\end{aligned}
$$

They are used to derive the bilinear forms of DG relative to faces. Finally, we define the broken operator ∇_h as an operator whose action on each simplex k equals that of the ordinary operator ∇.

Weak forms of (6) are formulated in terms of bilinear forms as described below.

Problem 1. *Find* $u \in V_h$ *such that*

$$
\hat{b}_h(u, v)^S = F(v)^S, \forall v \in V_h.
\tag{9}
$$

The unified formulation for the primal bilinear form $\hat{b}_h(u, v)^S$ is given depending on the particular choice of the DG discretization S. In what follows, we omit the obvious integral measure for the sake of brevity.

The bilinear form and the linear bounded functional (which is valid since functions in the functional are from the appropriate space) for both IP DG formulations under consideration (SIPG and NIPG) [2] are defined as follows:

$$
\begin{aligned}
\hat{b}_h(u, v)^{IP} &:= \int_\Omega K\nabla_h u \cdot \nabla_h v + \int_{\Gamma_I \cup \Gamma_D} (\theta[u] \cdot \{K\nabla_h v\} - \{K\nabla_h u\} \cdot [v]) \\
&+ \int_{\Gamma_I \cup \Gamma_D} C_{IP}[u] \cdot [v], \\
F(v)^{IP} &:= \int_\Omega fv + \int_{\Gamma_D} \theta g_D n \cdot \nabla_h v + \int_{\Gamma_D} C_{IP} g_D v + \int_{\Gamma_N} g_N v,
\end{aligned}
$$

where $C_{IP} = Cp^d/h$ is a penalty parameter function (C is a problem-dependent positive constant that we will change in the experiments), while $\theta = -1$ for SIPG and $\theta = 1$ for NIPG.

The bilinear form and the linear functional for the Bassi–Rebay-2 (BR2) scheme [5] are defined as follows:

$$
\begin{aligned}
\hat{b}_h(u, v)^{BR2} &:= \int_\Omega K\nabla_h u \cdot \nabla_h v + \int_{\Gamma_I \cup \Gamma_G} (-[u] \cdot \{K\nabla_h v\} - \{K\nabla_h u\} \cdot [v]) \\
&+ \sum_{e \in \Gamma_I \cup \Gamma_D} C_{BR2} \int_\Omega (R_0^e([u]) \cdot R_0^e([v])), \\
F(v)^{BR2} &:= \int_\Omega fv - \sum_{e \in \Gamma_D} \int_e g_D n \cdot (K\nabla_h v + C_{BR2} R_0^e([v])) + \int_{\Gamma_N} g_N v.
\end{aligned}
$$

Here, C_{BR2} is a problem-independent constant [5] equal to the maximum number of faces in a single simplex ($C_{BR2} = 3$ for a triangle). Moreover, $R_0^e(v)$ is a local lifting operator [5] with respect to the face e, which is defined implicitly, i.e. $R_0^e(\phi) \colon [L_2(\Gamma)]^d \to \mathbb{V}_h^d$, and is a solution to the problem $\int_\Omega R_0^e(\phi) \cdot \tau = -\int_e \phi \cdot \{\tau\}$ for all $\tau \in \mathbb{V}_h^d$ and $e \in \Gamma_I \cup \Gamma_D$. Such lifting operators serve penalty purposes on jumps of the function traces on faces and are expressed as matrices contributing to the elements that share a face e. Thus, the locality of the stencil is preserved.

The bilinear form and the linear functional for the Compact DG (CDG) scheme [21] are defined as follows:

$$\hat{b}_h(u,v)^{CDG} := \int_\Omega K\nabla_h u \cdot \nabla_h v + \int_{\Gamma_I \cup \Gamma_G} \left(-[u] \cdot \{K\nabla_h v\} - \{K\nabla_h u\} \cdot [v]\right)$$
$$+ \int_{\Gamma_I} \left(-C_{12} \cdot [u][K\nabla_h v] - [K\nabla_h u]C_{12} \cdot [v]\right)$$
$$+ \sum_{e \in \Gamma_I \cup \Gamma_D} C_{BR2} \int_\Omega \left((R_0^e([u]) + L_0^e(C_{12} \cdot [u])) \cdot (R_0^e([v]) + L_0^e(C_{12} \cdot [v]))\right)$$
$$+ \int_{\Gamma_D} \left(-K\nabla_h u \cdot nv - un \cdot K\nabla_h v\right) + \int_{\Gamma_I \cup \Gamma_D} C_{11}[u] \cdot [v],$$
$$F(v)^{CDG} := \int_\Omega fv + \sum_{e \in \Gamma_D} \int_e \left(g_D n \cdot K\nabla_h v - vn \cdot R_0^e(g_D n)\right)$$
$$+ \int_{\Gamma_N} g_N v + \int_{\Gamma_D} C_{11} g_D v,$$

where additional local lifting operators are defined as $L_0^e(v) \colon L_2(\Gamma) \to \mathbb{V}_h^d$, [21]. They are solutions to the problem $\int_\Omega L_0^e(v) \cdot \tau = -\int_e v[\tau]$ for all $\tau \in \mathbb{V}_h^d$ and $e \in \Gamma_I \cup \Gamma_D$. The vector-function C_{12} and the constant C_{11} are taken from the LDG method [6] (see below). This method also provides local stencil discretization and can be more suited to multigrid methods but, obviously, it is more complicated and requires more computational work in terms of the assembly of multiple lifting operators. Note that an additional boundary lifting operator can be absorbed into R_0^e if jump operators are formulated by definition on the boundary.

For all primal forms of scalar equations, the bilinear form in a finite-dimensional space is a block matrix. Each block is of size $BS \times BS$; the linear size is defined through the binomial coefficients $BS = \binom{p+d}{p}$.

Problem 2. *Find* $(\sigma, u) \in \mathbb{V}_h^d \times \mathbb{V}_h$ *such that*

$$\begin{cases} \hat{a}_h^{LDG}(\sigma, \tau) + \hat{d}_h^{LDG}(u, K\tau) &= F_1^{LDG}(K\tau), \forall \tau \in \mathbb{V}_h^d. \\ -\hat{d}_h^{LDG}(v, \sigma) + \hat{c}_h^{LDG}(u, v) &= F_2^{LDG}(v), \forall v \in \mathbb{V}_h. \end{cases} \tag{10}$$

The bilinear forms $\hat{a}_h^{LDG}$, $\hat{d}_h^{LDG}$, $\hat{c}_h^{LDG}$, and the bounded linear functionals in (10) are based on the LDG method and defined (see [6]) as follows:

$$\hat{a}_h^{LDG}(\sigma, \tau) := \int_\Omega \sigma \cdot \tau,$$
$$\hat{d}_h^{LDG}(\sigma, \tau) := -\int_\Omega \tau \cdot (\nabla_h u) + \int_{\Gamma_I} ([u] \cdot \{\tau\} - \{C_{12} \cdot [u]\}[\tau]) + \int_{\Gamma_D} un \cdot \tau,$$
$$\hat{c}_h^{LDG}(u, v) := \int_{\Gamma_I} C_{11}[u] \cdot [v] + \int_{\Gamma_D} C_{11} uv,$$
$$F_1^{LDG}(\tau) := \int_{\Gamma_D} g_D n \cdot \tau,$$
$$F_2^{LDG}(v) := \int_\Omega fv + \int_{\Gamma_D} (1 + C_{11}) g_D v + \int_{\Gamma_N} g_N v,$$

where C_{12} is a switching vector function and C_{11} is a positive constant [6]; both provide an appropriate penalty on jumps of solution functions across faces of simplexes. These functions are problem-independent; their definition can be found in [6]. Note that this formulation defines appropriate matrices in (3). The provided dual form has a compact stencil in terms of the block-matrix structure, where the size of each matrix block is $(d+1)BS \times (d+1)BS$.

The weak form of (7) in terms of bilinear forms is formulated for the primal formulation as follows.

Problem 3. *Find $(p, s) \in \mathbb{V}_h \times \mathbb{V}_h$ such that*

$$\begin{cases} -\hat{A}_h(p, v) & = F_1(v), \forall v \in \mathbb{V}_h. \\ \hat{B}_h(p, v) - \hat{C}_h(s, v) + \hat{M}\mathrm{d}s/\mathrm{d}t & = F_2(v), \forall v \in \mathbb{V}_h. \end{cases} \tag{11}$$

We apply the IP and BR2 DG methods to this problem. The bilinear forms are similar to those from the Poisson problem. Notice that the time derivative is now a full derivative since we consider the semidiscrete form. In this paper, we use the implicit Euler's method to approximate the derivative $\mathrm{d}s/\mathrm{d}t$.

A particular set of boundary conditions is considered in the Results section, where we discussed the results of the experiments.

3   Properties of the AmgX Library

The description of the AMG library was given in [19] and it has not changed much since then. We only outline important features for our testing. The AmgX library implements both classical (for scalar matrices) and aggregation-based (for scalar and block matrices) AMG methods with different selector and interpolation strategies, along with a variety of smoothers and preconditioners, including block-Jacobi, Gauss–Seidel, and incomplete-LU factorizations. The smoothers and preconditioners often rely on parallel graph-coloring algorithms. The library contains the most popular Krylov-subspace solvers, which can be used with a backup of AMG preconditioners. The process of its execution involves three steps: loading the matrix and the RHS vector into the AmgX (GPU-GPU transfer), analysis of the matrix and formation of interpolation and restriction operators, and solution of the linear system using either the AMG solver itself or a Krylov-subspace solver with the AMG preconditioner. In the last stage, the selected smoother operator is used.

Unfortunately, the library is poorly documented. The available AmgX reference manual PDF from GitHub contains incorrect references to the functions and an inconsistent list of parameters. Most advanced functions are not listed in the documentation and require one to analyze the code. All matrices from DG discretization have a block structure with a narrow stencil. An example of such matrices for the BR2 and dual LDG methods is given in Fig. 1 after the application of the block Reverse Cuthill–McKee permutation. The block structure can be seen clearly.

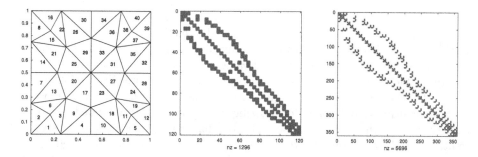

Fig. 1. Mesh example with numbered simplexes (left), the skeleton of the matrix for BR2 (center), and the LDG dual form (right) using $p = 1$

The AmgX library only allows one to use an aggregation algorithm to form the I_f^c and R_c^f operators without employing estimation of strong connections for block matrices. We were unable to successfully apply AmgX for DG matrices unless another undocumented feature was used: mesh geometric information. It is supplied to the library by setting the ``selector'': ``GEO'' switch in the aggregation algorithm parameters and supplying mesh information through the function `matrix_attach_geometry<CASE>(mtx, geox, geoy, geoz, n, dimension)` in the `base/src/amgx_c.cu` file. Plain dynamic arrays `geox, geoy, geoz` contain the coordinates of the centers for each simplex from 1 to `n`, and `dimension` is $d = 2$ or 3. In this case, the library uses the information supplied to perform more problem-oriented aggregation of the matrix.

Other modifications require the implementation of block functions that are not supported in the library. By default, only blocks of sizes 2–5, 8, and 10 are partially supported for colored block methods (such block-Jacobi, Gauss–Seidel, and block DILU methods). To implement other block sizes (6, 7, and 9 for $p = 1$ in LDG, and 3 for $p = 2$ in other methods), one needs to edit the source files in `core/src/aggregation/` and subfolders for the related algorithms, and the LU dense solver in `base/src/amgx_cusparese.cu` and `core/src/solvers/dense_lu_solver.cu` to modify the method as a means to support the required block sizes. After that, the library was tested on simple generated symmetric block matrices with block-diagonal domination having a pentadiagonal block structure. This allowed us to test block-Jacobi and multicolored Gauss–Seidel smoothers for all block sizes from 2 to 10 successfully, resulting in a residual reduction rate around 0.45 to 0.52.

Due to the restriction of supported block sizes, we were unable to test the dual LDG form of the method for $p > 1$ because the resulting block size was 9 for $p = 1$.

4   Results

To measure the performance of the AMG method, we used the classical definition of the residual reduction rate [24]. Let us solve the system $Ax = b$ using a multigrid method. Let $r^n = Ax^n - b$ be the residual vector at the n-th full iteration of the multigrid method. The residual reduction rate is defined as $\rho^n = \|r^{n+1}\|/\|r^n\|$, where $n \geq 1$, so that the initial residual is excluded. The mean residual reduction rate is the averaged value $\rho = \langle \rho^n \rangle$.

All problems were tested on the following hardware: Intel Xeon E5-2697V2 Ivy Bridge with up to six K40 Nvidia GPUs installed in a chassis. All tests were performed using double-precision floating-point format. We intended to use a single GPU for the test to measure the baseline for further comparisons with multiple-GPU executions. However, the performance we obtained forced us to stop multi-GPU tests (see Discussion). The maximum mesh size was selected in such a way that it would fit into a single GPU 6 GB memory for the maximum used polynomial degree $p = 3$. The mesh was constructed out of triangles; the domain was subdivided by the Delaunay method using the latest GMSH unstructured mesh generator [14]. Some adaptation was used to refine the mesh near singularities.

We performed multiple tests with different parameters and determined that the best converging combination for all problems was the GMRES Krylov solver with AMG preconditioner executed over the V-cycle, where aggregation was performed using geometric information. The best smoother was the diagonal ILU solver (DILU) used in multicolored mode. We applied the $\mathtt{min} - \mathtt{max}$ matrix coloring scheme with 0 pre-sweeps and 5 post-sweeps on each mesh level for the smoothers. The use of the preconditioned conjugate gradient solver resulted in a unit residual reduction rate, which seemed weird since all matrices were symmetric. This fact requires further research. All IP methods require the application of the inverted diagonal block to obtain the best convergence. Other methods were insensitive to this operation in terms of residual reduction. All the results were obtained on matrices with an inverted diagonal block.

Poisson Problem. The first boundary-value problem for (6) is considered in the domain $\Omega := [0,1] \times [0,1]$ with $K = E$ and the exact solution $u(x,y) = 2^{4a}x^a(1-x)^a y^a(1-y)^a$, where a is an integer parameter taken as $a = 2$, while E is the 2×2 identity matrix. The RHS function is replaced to satisfy the problem. All boundary values are zero Dirichlet conditions. The final residual reduction is taken to be $1.0 \cdot 10^{-10}$. The results are given in Table 1.

Table 1. Mean residual reduction rate for the solution of the first problem for the Poisson equation

Mesh	SIPG/NIPG			LDG	BR2			CDG		
	$p=1$	$p=2$	$p=3$	$p=1$	$p=1$	$p=2$	$p=3$	$p=1$	$p=2$	$p=3$
64K	0.631	0.836	0.867	0.412	0.875	0.898	0.928	0.894	0.925	0.939
120K	0.653	0.889	0.903	0.396	0.881	0.908	0.931	0.896	0.924	0.942
240K	0.652	0.891	0.923	0.398	0.891	0.914	0.965	0.899	0.932	0.951

The second boundary-value problem for (6) is considered in the domain $\Omega = [-1, 1] \times [-1, 1]$ with a triangle removed. The domain along with the DG solution is portrayed in Fig. 2. The problem is taken from [18] and represents a reentrant corner in the domain. This introduces a source of singularities in the solution, i.e., $u(x, y) \in \mathbb{H}^{1+\alpha-\varepsilon}$, $\varepsilon > 0$, $\alpha = \pi/\omega$, and ω is the angle shown in the figure. The solution is given as $u(x, y) = (x^2 + y^2)^{\alpha/2} \sin\left(\alpha \tan^{-1}(-y/x)\right)$ with $f(x, y) = 0$ and $\omega = \pi(2 - 1/10)$.

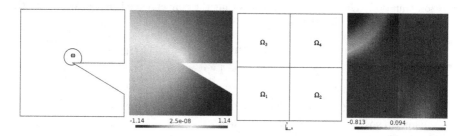

Fig. 2. From left to right: reentrant corner problem domain with $\omega = \pi(2 - 1/10)$; the solution by the BR2 method, $p = 2$; the domain for the nonlinear problem with a large variation of the coefficient matrices and the solution by the BR2 method, $p = 2$

The results for the residual reduction in the second problem are given in Table 2.

Table 2. Mean residual reduction rate for the solution of the second problem for the Poisson equation

Mesh	SIPG/NIPG			LDG	BR2			CDG		
	$p = 1$	$p = 2$	$p = 3$	$p = 1$	$p = 1$	$p = 2$	$p = 3$	$p = 1$	$p = 2$	$p = 3$
64K	0.711	0.893	0.945	0.492	0.895	0.955	0.986	0.899	0.985	0.993
120K	0.701	0.899	0.956	0.459	0.891	0.951	0.968	0.902	0.989	0.992
240K	0.705	0.903	0.966	0.468	0.898	0.949	0.974	0.909	0.988	0.993

The third boundary-value problem for (6) is defined in the domain $\Omega := ([-1, 0] \times [-1, 0]) \cup ([0, 1] \times [-1, 0]) \cup ([-1, 0] \times [0, 1]) \cup ([0, 1] \times [0, 1]) = \Omega_1 \cup \Omega_2 \cup \Omega_3 \cup \Omega_4$ (see Fig. 2). This is the Dirichlet–Neumann problem with nonlinear discontinuous coefficient matrices defined as $K := K_j(1 + u^2)$, where $K_1 = K_4 = 1000A$, $K_2 = K_3 = 0.1A$, and matrix $A = \begin{pmatrix} 1 & 0.5 \\ 0.5 & 1 \end{pmatrix}$. The RHS function is defined as $f(x, y) = x \sin(y)$. Zero Neumann conditions $g_N = 0$ are given on all external boundaries, except for the Dirichlet boundary: $g_D = 1$ on $x = 1, y \in [-1, 1]$. The problem is solved by Newton's method, where each iteration invokes a linear problem. It usually takes three or four Newton iterations to obtain the solution, which is shown in Fig. 2, with tolerance up to $1.0 \cdot 10^{-10}$. The total residual reduction for the linear system solver is set to $1.0 \cdot 10^{-6}$ on each Newton's method iteration. The test also verifies the ability of AmgX to update matrix entries without analyzing the matrix structure over successive Newton iterations. The results for the residual reduction are given in Table 3.

Table 3. Mean residual reduction rate for the solution of the third problem for the Poisson equation. The sign "—" indicates that the convergence is not achieved for the maximum number of GMRES iterations (500).

Mesh	SIPG/NIPG			LDG	BR2			CDG		
	$p=1$	$p=2$	$p=3$	$p=1$	$p=1$	$p=2$	$p=3$	$p=1$	$p=2$	$p=3$
64K	0.872	0.934	—	0.654	0.892	0.976	—	0.905	—	—
120K	0.894	0.956	—	0.693	0.904	—	—	0.914	—	—
240K	0.898	—	—	0.712	0.912	—	—	0.915	—	—

Darcy Problem. Two problems are considered, both derived from a smooth analytical solution. The domain is $\Omega = [0, 1] \times [0, 1]$. The analytical solution is given as $p(t, x, y) = 1 + txy(1 - x)(1 - y)$, $s(t, x, y) = 1/2 + txy(1 - x)(1 - y)$. The Dirichlet boundary conditions are constant along the whole Γ and are given as $p_G = 1$ and $s_G = 1/2$. The initial conditions are prescribed to s as a constant $s = 1/2$ in the whole domain. The nonlinearity is given in the coefficients, namely $K_1 = K$, $K_2 = 3/4K$, and $K_3 = 3K/16(2 - 2s)$, which corresponds to the prescribed capillary pressure function $p_c = 2s - s^2$. The matrices K define two distinct problems and are given below. The RHS function is used to balance the equation as $q(t, x, y) = 2t((x - 1)x + (y - 1)y)$, and $f(t, x, y)$ is calculated using symbolic arithmetics. All problems are solved only for $p = 1$ due to the restrictions on the block size (the resulting block size for $p = 1$ is 6, and for $p = 2$ is 12 when $d = 2$).

The first problem uses the uniform distribution of $K = E$ over the whole domain. The solution is shown in Fig. 3 (the two left figures). The second problem uses four different matrices $K \in \{10E, E, 0.1E, 0.01E\}$ in four different regions, similarly to the third Poisson problem. The solution is depicted in Fig. 3 (the two right figures).

The resulting residual reduction rate for both problems is given in Table 4.

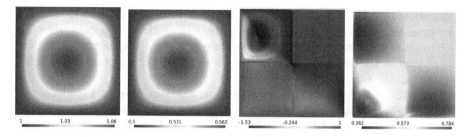

Fig. 3. Solution of the two Darcy problems (from left to right): (p, s) for the first problem, (p, s) for the second problem. The BR2 DG method was applied on a 64K mesh.

Table 4. Mean residual reduction rate for the solution of the two problems for the Darcy flow system. The sign "—" indicates that the convergence is not achieved for the maximum number of GMRES iterations (500) during a step of Newton's method linear solver.

Mesh	SIPG, problem 1	SIPG, problem 2	BR2, problem 1	BR2, problem 2
	$p = 1$	$p = 1$	$p = 1$	$p = 1$
64K	0.823	0.986	0.921	0.998
120K	0.889	—	0.964	—
240K	0.903	—	0.968	—

5   Discussion

First, we would like to stress that the AmgX library is poorly suited to solve systems having matrices with large blocks. The limitation on the supported block size greatly diminishes the application range of the library. However, since the project is open-source, one can adjust it in any direction as required, as we did by adding more supported block sizes directly into the source code.

Second, the residual reduction rates obtained for the Poisson equation problems indicate the following. On smooth solutions with no discontinuities in the coefficients, it is satisfactory for the LDG method. We obtained almost h-independent reduction rates. This complies with the conclusions drawn in [12] and the analysis in the Introduction section. The LDG scheme is the only one that satisfies the "RAT" property. However, the residual reduction rates for the nonlinear problem with discontinuities show a considerable mesh dependency, as can be seen from Table 3.

The residual reduction rates for IP methods (both SIPG and NIPG) are worse than those obtained for the LDG dual form method. We can definitely assert that h-independent rates are relatively achieved for $p = 1$, but no p-independence is achieved. The application of AmgX to the problem with discontinuous coefficients resulted in poor convergence rates or no convergence at all (see Table 3). This is the echo of the problem described in [20], which means that a special aggregation procedure is required to correctly take into account higher order discretization. The BR2 and CDG methods both performed poorly, showing the highest reduction rates and failing to converge in the nonlinear problem for $p > 1$. That is the joint action of an inconsistent "RAT" property and poorly constructed aggregations.

Third, the application to the Darcy problem was considered as a model of use in a real-world situation. The limitation on the supported block size forced us to use a first-order polynomial basis and only the primal form of DG discretization. We observed that the reduction rates for the smooth problem are satisfactory but highly nonoptimal, especially for the BR2 scheme. The second nonlinear problem with discontinuous coefficients yielded very poor performances for both methods, which failed to converge for all mesh sizes, except for the 64K mesh.

Further work will focus on testing other libraries mentioned in this paper and finding the best library that can be modified to include correct aggregation methods for DG discretization.

References

1. Antonietti, P.F., Melas, L.: Algebraic multigrid schemes for high-order nodal discontinuous Galerkin methods. SIAM J. Sci. Comput. **42**(2), A1147–A1173 (2020). https://doi.org/10.1137/18m1204383
2. Arnold, D.N., Brezzi, F., Cockburn, B., Marini, L.D.: Unified analysis of discontinuous Galerkin methods for elliptic problems. SIAM J. Numer. Anal. **39**(5), 1749–1779 (2002). https://doi.org/10.1137/0036142901384162
3. Babuška, I., Zlámal, M.: Nonconforming elements in the finite element method with penalty. SIAM J. Numer. Anal. **10**(5), 863–875 (1973). https://doi.org/10.1137/0710071
4. Baggag, A., Atkins, H., Keyes, D.: Parallel implementation of the discontinuous Galerkin method. In: Parallel Computational Fluid Dynamics 1999, pp. 115–122. Elsevier (2000). https://doi.org/10.1016/b978-044482851-4.50015-3
5. Bassi, F., Rebay, S.: Numerical evaluation of two discontinuous Galerkin methods for the compressible Navier-Stokes equations. Int. J. Numer. Methods Fluids **40**(1–2), 197–207 (2002). https://doi.org/10.1002/d.338
6. Cockburn, B., Shu, C.W.: The Runge–Kutta discontinuous Galerkin method for conservation laws V. J. Comput. Phys. **141**(2), 199–224 (1998). https://doi.org/10.1006/jcph.1998.5892
7. Cockburn, B., Shu, C.W.: J. Sci. Comput. **16**(3), 173–261 (2001). https://doi.org/10.1023/A:1012873910884
8. Demidov, D.: AMGCL: an efficient, flexible, and extensible algebraic multigrid implementation. Lobachevskii J. Math. **40**(5), 535–546 (2019). https://doi.org/10.1134/S1995080219050056
9. Demidov, D.: AMGCL - a C++ library for efficient solution of large sparse linear systems. Softw. Impacts **6**, 100037 (2020). https://doi.org/10.1016/j.simpa.2020.100037
10. Demidov, D., Shevchenko, D.: Modification of algebraic multigrid for effective GPGPU-based solution of nonstationary hydrodynamics problems. J. Comput. Sci. **3**(6), 460–462 (2012). https://doi.org/10.1016/j.jocs.2012.08.008

11. Fehn, N., Munch, P., Wall, W.A., Kronbichler, M.: Hybrid multigrid methods for high-order discontinuous Galerkin discretizations. J. Comput. Phys. **415**, 109538 (2020). https://doi.org/10.1016/j.jcp.2020.109538

12. Fortunato, D., Rycroft, C.H., Saye, R.: Efficient operator-coarsening multigrid schemes for local discontinuous Galerkin methods. SIAM J. Sci. Comput. **41**(6), A3913–A3937 (2019). https://doi.org/10.1137/18m1206357

13. Ganesan, S., Shah, M.: SParSH-AMG: A library for hybrid CPU-GPU algebraic multigrid and preconditioned iterative methods. ArXiv abs/2007.00056 (2020)

14. Geuzaine, C., Remacle, J.F.: Gmsh: A 3-d finite element mesh generator with built-in pre- and post-processing facilities. Int. J. Numer. Methods Eng. **79**(11), 1309–1331 (2009). https://doi.org/10.1002/nme.2579

15. Gholami, A., Malhotra, D., Sundar, H., Biros, G.: FFT, FMM, or multigrid? A comparative study of state-of-the-art poisson solvers for uniform and nonuniform grids in the unit cube. SIAM J. Sci. Comput. **38**(3), C280–C306 (2016). https://doi.org/10.1137/15m1010798

16. Kanschat, G., Mao, Y.: Multigrid methods for Hdiv-conforming discontinuous Galerkin methods for the stokes equations. J. Numer. Math. **23**(1) (2015). https://doi.org/10.1515/jnma-2015-0005

17. Krasnov, M.M., Kuchugov, P.A., Ladonkina, M.E., Tishkin, V.F.: Discontinuous Galerkin method on three-dimensional tetrahedral grids: using the operator programming method. Math. Models Comput. Simul. **9**(5), 529–543 (2017). https://doi.org/10.1134/s2070048217050064

18. Mitchell, W.F.: A collection of 2D elliptic problems for testing adaptive grid refinement algorithms. Appl. Math. Comput. **220**, 350–364 (2013). https://doi.org/10.1016/j.amc.2013.05.068

19. Naumov, M., et al.: AmgX: a library for GPU accelerated algebraic multigrid and preconditioned iterative methods. SIAM J. Sci. Comput. **37**(5), S602–S626 (2015). https://doi.org/10.1137/140980260

20. Olson, L.N., Schroder, J.B.: Smoothed aggregation multigrid solvers for high-order discontinuous Galerkin methods for elliptic problems. J. Comput. Phys. **230**(18), 6959–6976 (2011). https://doi.org/10.1016/j.jcp.2011.05.009

21. Peraire, J., Persson, P.O.: The compact discontinuous Galerkin (CDG) method for elliptic problems. SIAM J. Sci. Comput. **30**(4), 1806–1824 (2008). https://doi.org/10.1137/070685518

22. Reed, W.H., Hill, T.R.: Triangular mesh methods for the neutron transport equation (1973)

23. Rivière, B.: Discontinuous Galerkin Methods for Solving Elliptic and Parabolic Equations. Society for Industrial and Applied Mathematics (2008). https://doi.org/10.1137/1.9780898717440

24. Schaffer, S.: Higher order multi-grid methods. Math. Comput. **43**(167), 89 (1984). https://doi.org/10.1137/1.9780898717440

25. Vassilevski, P.S.: Lecture notes on multigrid methods (2010). https://doi.org/10.2172/983392

26. Xu, J.: Iterative methods by space decomposition and subspace correction. SIAM Rev. **34**(4), 581–613 (1992). https://doi.org/10.1137/1034116

Conjugate Direction Methods for Parallel Deflation

Yana Gurieva and Valery Il'in[(✉)]

Institute of Computational Mathematics and Mathematical Geophysics SB RAS,
Novosibirsk State University, Novosibirsk, Russia
ilin@sscc.ru

Abstract. We consider parallel iterative processes in Krylov subspaces
for solving symmetric positive definite systems of linear algebraic equations (SLAEs) with sparse ill-conditioned matrices arising under grid
approximations of multidimensional initial-boundary value problems.
Furthermore, we research the efficiency of the methods of moments for
choosing an initial guess and constructing a projective-type preconditioner based on a known basis formed by the direction vectors. As a
result, the reduction in the number of iterations implies an increase in
their computational complexity, which is effectively minimized by parallelizing vector operations. The approaches under consideration are relevant for the multiple solution of SLAEs with the same matrices and
different sequentially determined right-hand sides. Such systems arise
in multilevel iterative algorithms, including additive domain decomposition and multigrid approaches. The efficiency of the suggested methods is
demonstrated by the results of numerical experiments involving methodological examples.

Keywords: Iterative algorithms · Krylov subspaces · Conjugate
directions · Deflation · Preconditioning matrix · Numerical experiments

1 Introduction

One of the topical problems of computational algebra is the high-performance
solution of large systems of linear algebraic equations (SLAEs) with sparse matrices having a large-block structure. Such systems arise from approximations of
multidimensional initial-boundary value problems for systems of partial differential equations on unstructured grids when using methods of finite differences,
finite volumes, finite elements, and discontinuous Galerkin algorithms of various
orders of accuracy [1]. Problems of that kind frequently arise in the mathematical modeling of processes and phenomena from electromagnetism, fluid dynamics, elastic-plasticity, multiphase filtration in porous media, as well as in many
interdisciplinary problems. Typical examples are saddle-point problems obtained
from classical or generalized mixed formulations.

Among the most effective methods for solving SLAEs, we can mention iterative processes with large-block preconditioning matrices, the inversion of which

© Springer Nature Switzerland AG 2021
L. Sokolinsky and M. Zymbler (Eds.): PCT 2021, CCIS 1437, pp. 194–207, 2021.
https://doi.org/10.1007/978-3-030-81691-9_14

is supposed to be carried out approximately using some "internal" iterations. As a result, we arrive at two-level algorithms. Such approaches are employed in additive domain decomposition methods, which are the main tools in scalable parallelization of computations, multigrid algorithms with asymptotically optimal intensity in terms of the number of resources used (the required amount of computations is proportional to the number of unknowns), and various block-type factorizations (see [2–7] and the works cited therein).

An important aspect in the implementation of two-level iterative methods is the construction of economical approaches for multiple (recycling) solutions of SLAEs (at the lower level) with the same matrices but different sequentially determined right-hand sides. There are quite a lot of studies on this topic based on methods of deflation or augmentation, which consist in complementing the Krylov subspaces according to the information obtained during the solution of the first algebraic system (or that of the first several SLAEs). Those methods lead to a reduction in the number of iterations due to the complication of the preconditioning matrix, which can be varied and somehow optimized (see reviews in [8–14]). It should be borne in mind that methods of conjugate directions are used for symmetric matrices, and algorithms for semiconjugate directions or generalized minimal residuals with long recursions are employed for asymmetric matrices, which significantly increases the complexity of computations (see [15–19]).

Achieving high performance is a key point in the numerical solution of SLAEs. In the considered approaches, this is accomplished through the scalable parallelization of deflation algorithms and their mapping to the architecture of a supercomputer with distributed and hierarchical shared memory. The main tools for the corresponding implementations are based on the hybrid programming with MPI, OpenMP, and the use of vectorization of operations (AVX instructions). With all the variety of such tools, we mainly mean the utilization of multithreaded technologies for the algorithms under consideration.

The paper is structured as follows. Section 2 provides a specification of the problem statement and some preliminary information. Section 3 is devoted to the description of deflation iterative processes in Krylov subspaces with the extension of their bases by using precalculated direction vectors. In Sect. 4, we examine a parallelization of the suggested methods and discuss some estimates of the corresponding speedup. Section 5 gives the results of numerical experiments for one model problem. Section 6 contains the conclusions.

2   Two-Level Methods of Conjugate and Semiconjugate Directions

The subject of our research is the study of high-performance iterative methods for solving large SLAEs of the form

$$Au = f, \quad A \in \mathcal{R}^{N,N}; \quad u, f \in \mathcal{R}^N, \tag{1}$$

where the matrix A is assumed at first, for the sake of simplicity, to be real and symmetric positive definite (s.p.d.); possible generalizations will be mentioned below. Some peculiarities of the matrix A are its high order (10^8 to 10^{11}, and even higher), and such properties as ill-conditioning, large-block structure, and compressed sparse storage format (for example, Compressed Sparse Row (CSR)), which imposes its own requirements upon the implementation and optimization of the program code.

An example of an algebraic system with a block structure is a saddle-point SLAE,

$$Ku \equiv \begin{bmatrix} A_{1,1} & C^{\mathsf{T}} \\ C & 0 \end{bmatrix} \begin{bmatrix} u_a \\ u_c \end{bmatrix} = \begin{bmatrix} f_a \\ f_c \end{bmatrix} \equiv f, \tag{2}$$

where $A_{1,1} \in \mathcal{R}^{N_1,N_1}$ is an s.p.d. matrix, $C \in \mathcal{R}^{N_2,N_1}$, and $K \in \mathcal{R}^{N,N}, N = N_1 + N_2$. Using the Schur complement $S = CA_{1,1}^{-1}C^{\mathsf{T}}$, the matrix K can be factorized as

$$K = \begin{bmatrix} A_{1,1} & 0 \\ C & -S \end{bmatrix} \begin{bmatrix} I & A_{1,1}^{-1}C^{\mathsf{T}} \\ 0 & I \end{bmatrix}.$$

Thus, using various approximations of the matrices $A_{1,1}$ and S, it is possible to construct preconditioned iterative processes for solving (1), including two-level ones, if the preconditioning matrix is inverted approximately using its own iterative algorithm.

An arbitrary SLAE can be represented in a block form,

$$A_{q,q}u_q + \sum_{r \in \Omega_q} A_{q,r}u_r = f_q, \quad q = 1, \dots, P, \tag{3}$$

$$A = \{A_{q,r}\}, \quad A_{q,r} \in \mathcal{R}^{N_q,N_r}, \quad f_q \in \mathcal{R}^{N_q}, \quad N_1 + \dots + N_P = N,$$

where Ω_q is the set of numbers of matrix rows that make up the q-th block row of A, and P is its block order. It seems that the most feasible to solve such algebraic systems is to use the block Jacobi method, which, in a somewhat generalized form, is written as

$$B_{q,q}u_q^{n+1} \equiv (A_{q,q} + \theta D_q)u_q^{n+1} = f_q + \theta D_q u_q^n - \sum_{r \in \Omega_q} A_{q,r}u_r^n, \quad q = 1, \dots, P.$$

Here, $\theta \in [0,1]$ is an iterative (compensating) parameter, and D_q is a diagonal matrix determined from the equality

$$D_q e = \sum_{r \in \Omega_q} A_{q,r}e, \quad e = (1, \dots, 1)^{\mathsf{T}} \in \mathcal{R}^{N_q},$$

which is called the compensation condition or filtering (sometimes the introduction of the matrix D_q is called lumping). Such block iterative algorithms underlie additive parallel domain-decomposition methods.

Preliminarily, we consider a rather general form of preconditioned methods of conjugate directions for solving SLAEs (1). More precisely, we investigate the symmetric system obtained from (1) using two-sided preconditioning, namely

$$\bar{A}\bar{u} = \bar{f}, \quad \bar{A} = L_B^{-1}AU_B^{-1}, \quad \bar{u} = U_B u, \quad \bar{f} = L_B^{-1}f. \tag{4}$$

Here L_B and U_B are the factors for the factorization of the nondegenerate preconditioning matrix

$$B = L_B U_B, \quad B^{-1} = U_B^{-1} L_B^{-1}. \tag{5}$$

To solve the preconditioned SLAE (4) with a symmetric positive definite matrix $\bar{A} = \bar{A}^{\mathsf{T}}$, we consider iterative processes of the following form:

$$\bar{r}^0 = \bar{f} - \bar{A}\bar{u}^0, \quad \bar{p}^0 = \bar{r}^0, \quad n = 0, 1, \ldots :$$
$$\bar{u}^{n+1} = \bar{u}^n + \alpha_n \bar{p}^n = \bar{u}^0 + \alpha_0 \bar{p}^0 + \ldots + \alpha_n \bar{p}^n, \tag{6}$$
$$\bar{r}^{n+1} = \bar{f} - \bar{A}\bar{u}^{n+1} = \bar{r}^n - \alpha_n \bar{A}\bar{p}_n = \bar{r}^0 - \alpha_0 \bar{A}\bar{p}^0 - \ldots - \alpha_n \bar{A}\bar{p}^n,$$

where $\bar{p}^n$ are some direction vectors, α_n are iteration parameters, $\bar{u}^0 = U_B u^0$ and $\bar{r}^0$ are, respectively, the preconditioned vectors of the initial guess and the residual, and $\bar{u}^0$ is an arbitrary vector.

Assuming in formulas (6) that the vectors $\bar{p}^n$ possess the orthogonality properties

$$\left(\bar{A}^\gamma \bar{p}^n, \bar{p}^k\right) \equiv (\bar{p}^n, \bar{p}^k)_\gamma = \rho_n^{(\gamma)} \delta_{k,n}, \quad \rho_n^{(\gamma)} = (\bar{p}^n, \bar{p}^n)_\gamma, \tag{7}$$

where $\gamma = 1, 2$, and $\delta_{k,n}$ is the Kronecker delta, we conclude that if the coefficients α_n in the residual functional

$$\Phi_\gamma\left(\bar{r}^{n+1}\right) \equiv \left(\bar{r}^{n+1}, \bar{r}^{n+1}\right)_{\gamma-2}$$
$$= (\bar{r}^0, \bar{r}^0)_{\gamma-2} - \sum_{k=0}^{n} \left[2\alpha_k \left(\bar{r}^0, \bar{p}^k\right)_{\gamma-1} - \alpha_k^2 \left(\bar{p}^k, \bar{p}^k\right)_\gamma\right] \tag{8}$$

are defined as

$$\alpha_n = \sigma_n^{(\gamma)} / \rho_n^{(\gamma)}, \quad \sigma_k = \left(\bar{r}^0, \bar{p}^k\right)_{\gamma-1}, \tag{9}$$

then the values $\Phi_\gamma\left(\bar{r}^{n+1}\right) = (A^{\gamma-2}\bar{r}^{n+1}, \bar{r}^{n+1})$ attain a minimum in the Krylov subspaces

$$\mathcal{K}_{n+1}\left(\bar{r}^0, \bar{A}\right) = \mathrm{Span}\left\{\bar{r}^0, \bar{A}\bar{r}^0, \ldots, \bar{A}^n\bar{r}^0\right\}. \tag{10}$$

To ensure that the orthogonality conditions (7) are fulfilled, the vectors $\bar{p}^n$ are determined from the recursions

$$\bar{p}^0 = \bar{r}^0, \quad \bar{p}^{n+1} = \bar{r}^{n+1} + \beta_n \bar{p}^n, \quad \beta_n = -\left(\bar{r}^{n+1}, \bar{p}^n\right)_\gamma / \rho_n^{(\gamma)}. \tag{11}$$

In this case, the additional properties

$$\left(\bar{r}^k, \bar{r}^n\right)_{\gamma-1} = \|\bar{r}^n\|_{\gamma-1} \delta_{k,n}, \quad \left(\bar{r}^n, \bar{p}^k\right)_{\gamma-1} = 0, \quad k < n, \tag{12}$$

of vector orthogonality are fulfilled, and also the equality $(\bar{r}^0, \bar{p}^n)_{\gamma-1} = (\bar{r}^n, \bar{r}^n)_{\gamma-1}$ is valid, from which new formulas for the coefficients $\sigma_n^{(\gamma)}$ and β_n follow, namely

$$\sigma_n^{(\gamma)} = (\bar{r}^n, \bar{r}^n)_{\gamma-1}, \quad \beta_n = \sigma_{n+1}/\sigma_n. \tag{13}$$

Below, the index "γ" of the coefficients α_n and β_n is omitted for the sake of brevity.

The described conjugate directional algorithms for solving SLAE (4) for $\gamma = 1, 2$ are called the conjugate gradient method and the conjugate residual method, respectively (CG and CR; see [12, 20, 21] and the works cited therein). The above relations for $\gamma = 1, 2$ yield the following formulas in terms of the matrices A and B:

– for the conjugate gradient method:

$$r^0 = f - Au^0, \quad p^0 = B^{-1}r^0, \quad \alpha_n = \sigma_n/\rho_n,$$
$$u^{n+1} = u^n + \alpha_n p^n, \quad r^{n+1} = r^n - \alpha_n Ap^n, \quad p^{n+1} = B^{-1}r^{n+1} + \beta_n p^n, \quad (14)$$
$$\sigma_n = (r^n, p^n) = \left(B^{-1}r^n, r^n\right), \quad \rho_n = (Ap^n, p^n), \quad \beta_n = \sigma_{n+1}/\sigma_n;$$

– for the conjugate residual method:

$$r^0 = f - Au^0, \quad \hat{r}^0 = \hat{p}^0 = B^{-1}r^0, \quad \alpha_n = \sigma_n/\rho_n,$$
$$u^{n+1} = u^n + \alpha_n \hat{p}^n, \quad \hat{r}^{n+1} = \hat{r}^n - \alpha_n B^{-1}A\hat{p}^n, \quad \hat{p}^{n+1} = \hat{r}^{n+1} + \beta_n \hat{p}^n, \quad (15)$$
$$\sigma_n = \left(B^{-1}\hat{r}^n, A\hat{p}^n\right) = (A\hat{r}^n, \hat{r}^n), \quad \rho_n = \left(B^{-1}A\hat{p}^n, A\hat{p}^n\right), \quad \beta_n = \sigma_{n+1}/\sigma_n.$$

The most commonly used criterion for the termination of the iterations is the following inequality for the residual:

$$\|r^n\| \leq \varepsilon_e \|f\|, \quad \varepsilon_e \ll 1, \quad \|\cdot\| = \|\cdot\|_0. \quad (16)$$

Moreover, the number $n(\varepsilon)$ of iterations required to satisfy (16) for $\varepsilon = \varepsilon_e$ and for exact computations in (14) and (15) (including cases in which B^{-1} or A is a positive semidefinite matrix), can be estimated by the inequality

$$n(\varepsilon) \leq \frac{1}{2}\left|\ln\frac{\varepsilon}{2}\right|(\text{cond}_r(B^{-1}A)^{1/2} + 1),$$

where $\text{cond}_r(B^{-1}A) = \frac{\lambda_{max}}{\lambda_{mnz}}$ is the so-called reduced or effective condition number, and λ_{mnz} is the minimal nonzero eigenvalue of the matrix $B^{-1}A$. If the product by the matrix B^{-1} is computed approximately using some iterative process, then we carry out these "internal" iterations in the same manner but choosing some other accuracy parameter $\varepsilon_i \ll 1$.

For example, the approximate initial direction vector $\bar{p}^0$ is determined from the solution of the system $B\bar{p}^0 = r^0$ as indicated hereunder:

$$\delta^0 = r^0 - B p^0, \quad \bar{p}^0 = B^{-1}(r^0 - \delta^0), \quad \|\delta^0\| \leq \varepsilon_i \|r^0\|. \quad (17)$$

It should be noted that if the internal iterations are carried out using some Krylov-type method, then, in fact, the preconditioning matrix is a nonlinear operator that depends on the initial data, and to make sure that the orthogonality conditions (7) hold, the direction vectors p^n must be calculated not from

the two-term expressions (11) but by long recursions with dynamic preconditioners. A relevant example is the flexible conjugate gradient method [18]. As
a direct generalization of formulas (14) and (15), we can mention the multipreconditioned algorithms of semiconjugate directions [6], which may be written in
the general case (including asymmetric SLAEs) as follows:

$$r^0 = f - Au^0, \quad n = 0, \ldots : \quad u^{n+1} = u^n + P_n \bar{\alpha}_n,$$

$$r^{n+1} = r^n - AP_n \bar{\alpha}_n = r^q - AP_q \bar{\alpha}_q - \cdots - AP_n \bar{\alpha}_n, \quad 0 \leq q \leq n, \quad (18)$$

$$P_n = (p_1^n, \ldots, p_{M_n}^n) \in \mathcal{R}^{N, M_n}, \quad \bar{\alpha}_n = (\alpha_{n,1}, \ldots, \alpha_{n, M_n})^\mathsf{T} \in \mathcal{R}^{M_n},$$

where $p_1^n, \ldots, p_{M_n}^n$ are direction vectors that form the matrix P_n at the n-th
iteration, and $\bar{\alpha}_n$ is the vector of iteration parameters. Regarding the vectors p_k^n
in (18), we only assume that the orthogonality conditions are fulfilled:

$$(p_k^n, A^\gamma p_{k'}^{n'}) = \rho_{n,k}^{(\gamma)} \delta_{n,n'}^{k,k'}, \quad \rho_{n,k}^{(\gamma)} = (p_k^n, A^\gamma p_k^n),$$
$$\gamma = 1, 2, \quad n' = 0, 1, \ldots, n-1, \quad k, k' = 1, 2, \ldots, M_n. \quad (19)$$

However, if the coefficients $\bar{\alpha}_n = \{\alpha_{n,l}\}$ in this case are determined by the
formulas

$$\alpha_{n,l} = \sigma_{n,l} / \rho_{n,n}^{(\gamma)}, \quad \sigma_{n,l} = (r^0, A^\gamma \bar{p}_l^n), \quad (20)$$

then we obtain from (18) the following expressions for the residual functionals:

$$\Phi_n^{(\gamma)}(r^{n+1}) \equiv (r^{n+1}, A^{\gamma-2} r^{n+1}) =$$
$$= (r^q, A^{\gamma-2} r^q) - \sum_{k=q}^{n} \sum_{l=1}^{M_n} (r^q, A^\gamma p_l^k)^2 / \rho_{k,l}^{(\gamma)}, \quad q = 0, 1, \ldots, n, \quad (21)$$

which reach their minima in the Krylov block subspaces

$$\mathcal{K}_M = \text{Span}\{p_1^0, \ldots, p_{M_0}^0, Ap_1^1, \ldots, Ap_{M_1}^1, \ldots, Ap_1^n, \ldots, Ap_{M_n}^n\},$$
$$M = M_0 + M_1 + \cdots + M_n, \quad (22)$$

for $\gamma = 2$, and also for $\gamma = 1$ in the case of a symmetric matrix A. It should be
noted that the application of the algorithms for $\gamma = 1$ in the case of nonsymmetric matrices is actually limited to SLAEs with matrices having a symmetric
positive definite part $A_s = 0.5(A + A^\mathsf{T})$ (indeed, for a skew-symmetric matrix,
we have, for example, $(Au, u) = 0$ for $u = \{1\}$).

The orthogonality properties (19) are fulfilled if the direction vectors are
defined by "multipreconditioned" recursive relations in which each vector p_l^{n+1}
corresponds to its "own" preconditioning matrix $B_{n+1,l}$:

$$p_l^0 = B_{0,l}^{-1} r^0, \quad p_l^{n+1} = B_{n+1,l}^{-1} r^{n+1} - \sum_{k=0}^{n} \sum_{l=1}^{M_k} \beta_{n,k,l}^{(\gamma)} p_l^k$$

$$B_{n,l} \in \mathcal{R}^{N,N}, \quad \gamma = 1, 2,$$

$$\bar{\beta}_{n,k}^{(\gamma)} = \{\beta_{n,k,l}^{\gamma}\} = \left(\beta_{n,k,1}^{(\gamma)} \cdots \beta_{n,k,M_n}^{(\gamma)}\right)^{\mathsf{T}} \in \mathcal{R}^{M_n}, \tag{23}$$

$$\beta_{n,k,l}^{(\gamma)} = -\left(A^\gamma p_l^k, B_{n+1,l}^{-1} r^{n+1}\right) / \rho_{n,l}^\gamma,$$

$$n = 0, 1, \ldots, \quad k = 0, \ldots, n, \quad l = 1, \ldots, M_n.$$

If the matrix A is symmetric, then, instead of a long recursion, we obtain a two-term one and arrive at the methods of conjugate gradients or conjugate residuals ($\gamma = 1, 2$, respectively, in the multipreconditioned or the classical version). In the case of asymmetric SLAEs, these algorithms are called semiconjugate gradients and semiconjugate residuals (SCG and SCR methods).

3 Deflation and Augmentation Algorithms in Krylov Subspaces

In this section, we consider the reduction of the number of iterations in conjugate direction methods for multiple solution of SLAEs with the same matrices but different sequentially determined right-hand sides. These techniques will be used in the next section to construct parallel iterative algorithms.

Consider the solution of the first SLAE after $n_1(\varepsilon)$ iterations, and assume that $m \leq n_1$ direction vectors p^k and the same number of vectors Ap^k, $k = 0, 1, \ldots, m - 1$, are saved. Then, for each of the following systems, we can determine the initial guess u^0 and the corresponding residual $r^0 = f - Au^0$ using the formulas

$$u^0 = u^{-1} + c_0 p^0 + \cdots + c_{m-1} p^{m-1} = u^{-1} + Pc, \quad c \in \mathcal{R}^m,$$
$$r^0 = r^{-1} - c_0 Ap^0 - \cdots - c_{m-1} Ap^{m-1} = r^{-1} - APc, \quad P \in \mathcal{R}^{N,m}, \tag{24}$$

where u^{-1} is an arbitrary vector, the vectors p^k are assumed to be A^γ-orthogonal, $\gamma = 1, 2$ (for the sake of brevity, the index γ of the coefficients c_k is omitted), and P is a full-rank rectangular matrix, in which m columns are the direction vectors p^k.

By requiring the $A^{\gamma-1}$-orthogonality of the vectors r^0 and p^k, we obtain the following nondegenerate algebraic system for the vector of coefficients c, with a diagonal matrix:

$$A_\gamma c \equiv P^{\mathsf{T}} A^{\gamma-1} Pc = P^{\mathsf{T}} A^{\gamma-1} r^{-1}. \tag{25}$$

The solution of this system provides the minimum of the residual functional

$$\Phi_\gamma(r^0) = (A^{\gamma-2} r^0, r^0), \quad r^0 = Qr^{-1}, \quad Q = I - APA_\gamma^{-1} P^{\mathsf{T}} A^{\gamma-1}. \tag{26}$$

Note that, in this case, the error vectors

$$z^k = u - u^k = A^{-1} r^k, \quad k = -1, 0, \tag{27}$$

satisfy the relations

$$z^0 = Tz^{-1}, \quad T = I - PA_\gamma^{-1}P^T A^\gamma, \tag{28}$$

and for the matrices Q and T, which are projectors ($Q^2 = Q$, $T^2 = T$), the following relation holds:

$$QA = AT. \tag{29}$$

It is worth noting that the definitions of the initial guess u^0 and the residual r^0 for u^{-1} correspond in fact to the application of the method of moments in Krylov subspaces (see [19]).

The sought solution u can be written as

$$u = Tu + (I - T)u, \tag{30}$$

where the second term is easily calculated using the formula

$$(I - T)u = PA_\gamma^{-1}P^T A^{\gamma-1}Au = PA_\gamma^{-1}P^T A^{\gamma-1}f. \tag{31}$$

Therefore, as a consequence of (29), we have

$$ATu = QAu \equiv \widetilde{A}u = Qf \equiv \widetilde{f}.$$

Hence, denoting by $\widetilde{u}$ the solution of the singular consistent SLAE

$$\widetilde{A}\widetilde{u} = \widetilde{f}, \quad \widetilde{A} = QA, \quad \widetilde{f} = Qf, \tag{32}$$

it follows from (30) and (31) that the final solution is written as

$$u = T\widetilde{u} + PA_\gamma^{-1}P^T A^{\gamma-1}f.$$

Thus, within this approach, the most laborious operation is the solution of SLAE (32) with the degenerate preconditioning matrix $B^{-1} = Q = I - APA_\gamma^{-1}P^T A^{\gamma-1}$.

Note that both the preconditioning matrix B in the conjugate residual method ($\gamma = 2$) and the preconditioned matrix $\widetilde{A} = QA = B^{-1}A$ in the conjugate gradient method are symmetric.

When $\gamma = 1$, i.e., in the conjugate gradient algorithm, the symmetric preconditioning matrix can be constructed differently using the orthogonality condition

$$P^T Ap^0 = 0 \tag{33}$$

for the initial direction vector. This condition can be easily verified if we assume that

$$p^0 = r^0 - AP(P^T A^2 P)^{-1}P^T Ar^0 = B_1^{-1}r^0,$$
$$B_1^{-1} = I - APA_2^{-1}P^T A. \tag{34}$$

Using the orthogonality conditions and the recursive relations for the column vectors of the matrix P, we can show that the matrix A_2 in (34) is tridiagonal and can be easily inverted. It is easy to prove that if the vectors r^0 and p^0 for the conjugate gradient method in (14) are determined in conformity with (26) and (34) for $\gamma = 1$ and $B = B_1$, then the orthogonality relations

$$P^T r^k = 0, \quad P^T Ap^k = 0, \quad k = 0, 1, \ldots, n,$$

are valid in each iteration.

4   Estimates of Parallelization Efficiency

As we can see from the above formulas, if the deflation and augmentation methods operate with the rectangular dense matrices P and AP computed and saved during the solution of the first SLAE, then the complexity of iterations for subsequent algebraic systems significantly increases, especially for large values of $\bar{m}$. The salutary effect, in this case, is that the additional operations of multiplication of rectangular matrices by vectors are easily parallelized through multithreaded computing technologies with such system tools as OpenMP. It is obvious that the direct multiplication of a vector by a dense preconditioning matrix is too resource-consuming.

General issues related to the parallelization of the solution of large SLAEs are considered in [20]. In the case examined here, it is enough to study the features of the achievable scalability of parallel implementations for the following pair of typical sequentially performed operations:

$$v = Pq, \quad s = P^{\mathsf{T}}w, \quad v, w \in \mathcal{R}^{N}, \quad q, s \in \mathcal{R}^{m}, \tag{35}$$

which are the most essential, for example, when the matrix Q is multiplied by a vector in (26). The first operation in (35) is called the extension of the vector, while the second, which is the dual of the first, is called the restriction of the vector. Let us make the natural assumption that $m \ll N$ (for example, the values $m = 100$ and $N = 10^8$ can be considered as having average complexity) and denote the number of used computational threads by R. We assume for simplicity that each thread is executed on its own processor core. Let the number of threads be $R = R_1 R_2$. Furthermore, we suppose that the dimension and the number of vectors are multiples of the numbers R_1 and R_2, namely

$$N = N_1 R_1, \quad m = N_2 R_2.$$

To be specific, we assume that $N_1 > N_2$. The total number of computations (multiplications and additions) in (35) is

$$N^a = 4mN - m - N. \tag{36}$$

To parallelize them, it is natural to split the matrix P into $R_1 \cdot R_2$ rectangular blocks with the same number $N_1 N_2$ of elements:

$$P = \left\{ P_{k,l} \in \mathcal{R}^{N_1, N_2} \right\}, \quad k = 1, 2, \dots, R_1, \quad l = 0, 1, \dots, R_2 - 1.$$

Accordingly, we split the vectors in (35) into subvectors

$$v = \{v_k \in \mathcal{R}^{N_1}, k = 1, \dots, R_1\}, \quad q = \{q_l \in \mathcal{R}^{N_2}, l = 1, \dots, R_2\},$$
$$w = \{w_k \in \mathcal{R}^{N_1}, k = 1, \dots, R_1\}, \quad s = \{s_l \in \mathcal{R}^{N_2}, l = 1, \dots, R_2\}.$$

The direct and dual operations in (35) are performed sequentially, one after another, on R threads or cores, each of which synchronously implements the multiplication of submatrices $P_{k,l}$ or $P_{k,l}^{\mathsf{T}}$ for the corresponding subvectors:

$$v_k = \sum_{l=0}^{R_2-1} P_{k,l} q_l, \quad s_l = \sum_{k=1}^{R_1} (P_{k,l})^{\mathsf{T}} w_k, \quad k = 1, \ldots, R_1, \; l = 0, 1, \ldots, R_2 - 1.$$

$$(37)$$

Each term in (37) is a direct or dual (expanding or restricting) reduced (low dimension) vector-matrix multiplication performed on one processor. In the first case, it is required to compute N_1 dot products of vectors of dimension N_2, and the same in the second case but replacing N_1 with N_2, and vice versa. Therefore, the corresponding volumes of computations are

$$\widehat{N}_{k,l}^a = N_1(2N_2 - 1), \quad \check{N}_{k,l}^a = N_2(2N_1 - 1).$$

Since each subvector v_k is computed on R_2 cores and each subvector s_l on R_1 cores, the amounts of time required for their computation using the doubling scheme for parallel implementation of the summation are, respectively, expressed as

$$\widehat{T}_k^a \cong N_1(2N_2 + \log_2 R_2)\tau_a, \quad \check{T}_l^a \cong N_2(2N_1 + \log_2 R_1)\tau_a, \quad (38)$$

where τ_a denotes the average time for the execution of one arithmetic operation. Since all subvectors v_k in (37) are computed simultaneously, each on its "own" processor (the same applies to the subvectors s_l), the total time required for the execution of a pair of operations (35) on R threads is determined by the sum of $\widehat{T}_k^a$ and $\check{T}_l^a$ from (38):

$$T_R^a \cong (4N_1N_2 + N_1 \log_2 R_2 + N_2 \log_2 R_1)\tau_a. \quad (39)$$

Thus, taking into account (36), we conclude that the speedup of parallel computations for the implementation of the deflation preconditioning operator Q on $R \gg 1$ threads is asymptotically almost linear:

$$S_R = T_1^a / T_R^a \approx R \left(1 + \frac{\log_2 R_2}{R_2} + \frac{\log_2 R_1}{R_1}\right)^{-1}, \quad (40)$$

where T_1^a is the execution time of a pair of operations (35) on one computational thread.

The computational and time expenditures hitherto considered are only associated with deflation approaches and are supplementary to the resources required to execute the classical Krylov methods. At each of the two levels of the iterative process, this requires one multiplication of a vector by the matrix of the original SLAE, possibly an approximate (iterative) solution of an auxiliary system that carries out the "usual" preconditioning, and also three or four vector operations, including semiparallelizable inner products (see formulas (14), (15)).

5   Examples of Numerical Experiments

We discuss in this section the results of numerical experiments with some of the deflation approaches to the conjugate gradient method and the conjugate residual method we have previously considered. The computations were conducted on model grid SLAEs obtained from standard five-point approximations of second-order accuracy on square grids with $N \times N$ cells for the two-dimensional Poisson equation with Dirichlet boundary conditions in the square domain $\Omega = [0, 1]^2$. In each experiment, we considered two algebraic systems with the same matrices but different right-hand sides obtained for distinct exact solutions to differential problems. The right-hand side of the first SLAE corresponds to the exact solution of the Poisson equation $u(x, y) = 1$. The initial guess for the iterative process at the grid nodes $(x_i = ih, y_j = jh, h = 1/N)$ was $u^0 = \{u^0_{i,j} = x^2_i + y^2_j\}$. The right-hand side of the second SLAE was determined by multiplying the exact solution of the Dirichlet problem $u(x, y) = x^2 + y^2$ by the matrix of the first SLAE; the initial guess u^{-1} was assumed to be zero. All computations were carried out with standard double precision on sequentially refined grids with numbers of nodes $N^2 = 8^2, 16^2, 32^2, \ldots, 256^2, 512^2$. Everywhere, the iteration termination parameter in (16) was $\varepsilon_e = 10^{-7}$.

Table 1 shows the results of a series of computations with the CR method to solve the second SLAE using the A^2-orthogonal vectors p^n obtained during the solution of the first SLAE, as deflation vectors for the method (15) with $B = I$ (the number of iterations for the first SLAE is denoted by n_1). The deflation approach for the second SLAE was implemented either for the initial guess along with the vector of the initial residual corrected according to (24), or for a complete set of direction vectors p^n as columns of the matrix P. These vectors are obtained while solving the first SLAE by the CR method. The corresponding numbers of iterations in the solution of the second SLAE are denoted by n_2 and n_3.

Similar data are given in Table 2 for the CG method.

Table 1. Number of iterations for the CR method with $\varepsilon = 10^{-7}$: n_1 – in the solution of the first SLAE without deflation; n_2 – in the solution of the second SLAE with deflation of the initial guess and the initial residual only; n_3 – in the solution of the second SLAE with deflation and preconditioning by a complete set of direction vectors

N	8	16	32	64	128	256	512
n_1	21	42	82	158	302	573	1081
n_2	11	36	73	150	284	564	1113
n_3	2	19	38	73	148	256	577

As we can see from the tables, the deflation applied only to the initial guess when solving the second SLAE gives an insignificant effect in the CR method. In the CG algorithm, however, the reduction in the number of iterations reaches a value of 1.5 or more. The use of a "deflation" preconditioner in both algorithms gives approximately the same additional acceleration, i.e., the n_1/n_2 ratio reaches a value of 2 or more, and this effect is approximately the same for different grids.

Table 2. Number of iterations for the CG method with $\varepsilon = 10^{-7}$: n_1 – in the solution of the first SLAE without deflation; n_2 – in the solution of the second SLAE with deflation of the initial guess and the initial residual only; n_3 – in the solution of the second SLAE with deflation and preconditioning by a complete set of direction vectors

N	8	16	32	64	128	256	512
n_1	21	42	83	141	314	611	1186
n_2	10	26	53	96	190	351	745
n_3	2	18	37	75	148	280	557

We should emphasize that these preliminary results have been obtained for only one sufficiently large number m of direction vectors (equal to the number of iterations for the first SLAE). Undoubtedly, it would be interesting to study how the acceleration depends on m and examine the actual reduction of the computation time when using multithreaded parallelization for deflation operations. We plan to address these issues in further research.

6   Conclusions

The preliminary results of numerical experiments demonstrate a rather good acceleration effect for the deflation approaches to the conjugate gradient method and the conjugate residual method. The study of the suggested algorithms can be continued in several directions: with different numbers of additional deflation vectors, with approximate eigenvectors for the original matrix instead of the direction vectors p^k, using deflation in some combination with the "classic" preconditioning of SLAEs, analysis of the actual parallelization of iterative processes on various supercomputer platforms, and others.

We can see from this list that the problem considered in the paper is a complex one: it is associated not only with a wide variety of algorithmic approaches but also with significant specific features from various applications, for which it is ultimately desirable to have practical recommendations to automate the selection of optimal methods of solution in specific situations. It is obvious that achieving significant results in these areas requires theoretical and experimental computational research with the involvement of machine learning technologies based on cognitive principles, leading eventually to creating an active base of mathematical knowledge.

Acknowledgements. The theoretical part of the study was carried out under a government contract with the ICMMG SB RAS (0315-2019-0008). The computational experiments were supported by the Russian Foundation for Basic Research (project No. 18-01-00295).

References

1. Il'in, V.P.: Mathematical Modeling. Part I. Continuous and Discrete Models, SBRAS, Novosibirsk (2017). (in Russian)
2. Dolean, V., Jolivet, P., Nataf, F.: An Introduction to Domain Decomposition Methods: Algorithms, Theory and Parallel Implementation. SIAM, Philadelphia (2015). https://doi.org/10.1137/1.9781611974065
3. Vassilevski, Y.V., Olshanskii, M.A.: Short Course on Multi-Grid and Domain Decomposition Methods. MAKS Press, Moscow (2007)
4. Vassilevski, P.S.: Multi-Level Block Factorization Preconditioners. Springer, New York, (2008). https://doi.org/10.1007/978-0-387-71564-3
5. Gurieva, Y.L., Il'in, V.P., Petukhov, A.V.: On multigrid methods for solving two-dimensional boundary-value problems. J. Math. Sci. **249**(2), 118–127 (2020). https://doi.org/10.1007/s10958-020-04926-7
6. Il'in, V.P.: Multi-preconditioned domain decomposition methods in the Krylov subspaces. In: Dimov, I., Farago, I., Vulkov, L. (eds.) Numerical Analysis and Its Applications. NAA 2016. Lecture Notes in Computer Science, vol. 10187, pp. 95–106. Springer, Cham Springer (2017). https://doi.org/10.1007/978-3-319-57099-0_9
7. Il'in, V.P.: Parallel shifts triangular iterative methods in the Krylov subspaces. Zapiski POMI **496**, 104–119 (2020). (in Russian)
8. Tang, J.M., Nabben, R., Vuik, C., Erlangga, Y.A.: Comparison of two-level preconditioners derived from deflation, domain decomposition and multigrid methods. J. Sci. Comput. **39**, 340–370 (2009). https://doi.org/10.1007/s10915-009-9272-6
9. Saad, Y., Yeung, M., Erhel, J., Guyomarc'h, F.: A deflated version of conjugate gradient algorithm. SIAM J. Sci. Comput. **24**, 1909–1926 (2000). https://doi.org/10.1137/s1064829598339761
10. Kolotilina, L.Y.: Preconditioning of systems of linear algebraic equations by means of twofold deflation. I. Theory. J. Math. Sci. **89**, 1652–1689 (1998). https://doi.org/10.1007/bf02355371
11. Il'in, V.P.: Two-level least squares methods in Krylov subspaces. J. Math. Sci. **232**(6), 892–902 (2018). https://doi.org/10.1007/s10958-018-3916-8
12. Gaul, A., Gutknecht, M.H., Liesen, J., Nabben, R.: A framework for deflated and augmented Krylov subspace methods. SIAM J. Anal. Appl. **34**, 495–518 (2013). https://doi.org/10.1137/110820713
13. Gurieva, Y.L., Il'in, V.P.: On conjugate directions methods for multiple SLAE solving. Zapiski POMI **496**, 26–42 (2020). (in Russian)
14. Neuenhofen, M.P., Greif, C.: MSTAB: stabilized inducted dimension reduction for Krylov subspace recycling. SIAM J. Sci. Comput. **40**(2), 554–571 (2018). https://doi.org/10.1137/16m1092465
15. Saad, Y.: Iterative Methods for Sparse Linear Systems, 2nd edn., SIAM, Philadelphia (2003). https://doi.org/10.1137/1.9780898718003
16. Il'in, V.P.: Finite Element Methods and Technologies. ICMMG SBRAS, Novosibirsk (2007).(in Russian)
17. Olshanskii, M.A., Tyrtyshnikov, E.E.: Iterative Methods for Linear Systems. Theory and Applications. SIAM, Philadelphia (2014). https://doi.org/10.1137/1.9781611973464
18. Notay, Y.: Flexible conjugate gradients. SIAM J. Sci. Comput. **22**(4), 1444–1460 (2000). https://doi.org/10.1137/s1064827599362314

19. Il'in, V.P.: On methods of moments in Krylov subspaces. Doklady RAS Math. Informat. Manag. Process. **495**, 38–43 (2020). (in Russian)
20. Il'in, V.P.: Problems of parallel solution of large systems of linear algebraic equations. J. Math. Sci. **216**(6), 795–804 (2016). https://doi.org/10.1007/s10958-016-2945-4

Supercomputer Simulation

Research of the Mechanism of External Hormonal Regulation of the Development of Phyto- and Zooplankton Populations Using Supercomputer Technologies

Alexander I. Sukhinov[1], Alexander E. Chistyakov[1], Yulia Belova[1], Alexander Epifanov[1], and Alla V. Nikitina[2,3(✉)]

[1] Don State Technical University, Rostov-on-Don, Russia
[2] Supercomputers and Neurocomputers Research Center, Taganrog, Russia
[3] Southern Federal University, Rostov-on-Don, Russia

Abstract. The paper is devoted to modeling the dynamics of phyto- and zooplankton populations in coastal systems, taking into account the mechanism of external hormonal regulation and relying on NVIDIA Tesla K80 graphics accelerators. The mathematical model of the dynamics of plankton populations is based on a system of non-stationary equations of convection-diffusion-reaction with nonlinear terms. We carry out the linearization of the continuous problem and construct its discrete analog by splitting the original three-dimensional problem into a two-dimensional problem and a one-dimensional problem, in conformity with the linearized model. To construct the discrete two-dimensional model, we use a linear combination of the Upwind and the Standard Leapfrog difference schemes, which makes it possible to increase the modeling accuracy in the case of large values of the grid Péclet number. We introduce into the model of ectocrine regulation of interacting phytoplankton species a nonlinear dependence between the phytoplankton growth rate and the concentration of metabolites. By doing so, we manage to describe the ability of algal metabolites to control their growth, even under conditions of an excess of nutrients, which corresponds to modern concepts on the functioning of hydrobiocenosis. The solution to the problem is numerically implemented on a graphics accelerator for massively parallel computations, which significantly reduces the operating time of the software module. We study a parallel computing model on a GPU on a sequence of thickening grids with different numbers of threads.

Keywords: Plankton populations · External hormonal regulation · Coastal system · Parallel algorithm · Software package · GPU

The reported study was funded by the RFBR (project No. 20-01-00421).

L. Sokolinsky and M. Zymbler (Eds.): PCT 2021, CCIS 1437, pp. 211–227, 2021.
https://doi.org/10.1007/978-3-030-81691-9_15

1   Introduction

Much of current hydrobiological research of aquatic ecosystems and trophic chains is intended to analyze the transformation of matter and energy in ecosystems. This kind of research in hydrobiology has paved the path for major advances in the understanding of the mechanisms that govern aquatic ecosystems. Along with direct trophic interactions, indirect (chemical) interactions are also possible (e.g., the action of waste products from individual organisms). This has to do with the fact that the aquatic environment makes the spread of waste products easier and, accordingly, favors both intra- and interspecific chemical interactions [1].

Chemical interactions in ecosystems are not limited to populational interactions, intraspecific or interspecific interactions within one level of the food chain: on the contrary, they often play an important role in the interaction of organisms belonging to different levels but, as a rule, trophically related to each other. Phytoplankton is the base of the trophic pyramid, and together with zooplankton, it is the basis of fish and benthos nutrition. Chemoreception affects the development of zooplankton. The potential toxicity of blue-green algae, a food source for zooplankton, has been studied by several scientists, such as DeMott W. R. and Moxter F. [2], Iörgensen G. [3], Wang W. [4], and others. J. Findeneg divides all the factors that exert an effect on phytoplankton into the following groups: physical (directly or indirectly associated with solar radiation), chemical or the content of nutrients, and biological or mutual influence of organisms [5].

During the life process of phytoplankton populations, a biologically active metabolite is released which affects the growth of algal cells. The quantitative and qualitative composition of metabolites in the medium, being for the cell a source of information about the state of the entire population, can act as a regulator of the community density according to the feedback principle. Such metabolite-mediated regulation of the number of populations composing the phytoplankton may turn out to be the main mechanism for the formation of the latter's structure, being even more significant than food competition [6].

The action of blue-green algae on other representatives of the algal flora of water bodies is the best studied. Developing in massive quantities, these algae (first of all *Microcystis aeruginosa*) produce biologically active substances that suppress the growth processes in other algae, primarily green ones, and enable the producer species to take a dominant position in the biocenosis. There is evidence that the long-term intake of microcystis toxins through the food chain by humans leads to cancer. Coastal systems such as the Azov Sea and the Taganrog Bay are, undoubtedly, areas of possible ecological disaster since the quantitative development of *M. aeruginosa* at those locations is extreme and, reaching during some years 400 g/m^3.

It should be noted that, at the present stage of development of mathematical modeling of aquatic ecosystems, mediated chemical interactions are practically neglected. The overwhelming number of investigations on this topic is devoted to the study of the mechanisms of direct trophic interactions and the transformation of matter and energy in ecosystems using mathematical models of various degrees of complexity [7].

To discretize the posed problem of biological kinetics, we use a uniform rectangular grid. The advantages of this approach can be attributed to its wide and universal application [8]. Discretization on such grids can lead to an error when solving model problems at the boundary of the computational domain, but this drawback can be practically eliminated by using the method of partial filling of computational cells, which increases the accuracy of modeling the problems of biological kinetics of coastal systems [9]. We construct the discrete model using a linear combination of the Upwind and the Standard Leapfrog difference schemes. This approach increases the accuracy of modeling in the case of large values of the grid Péclet number. The large amount of computational work that needs to be done on grids containing millions of computational nodes with a complex geometry of the computational domain determines the need to develop parallel algorithms for the numerical solution of the problems.

Our study of the mechanism of external hormonal regulation of interacting phytoplankton populations through mathematical modeling is based on a scenario approach [10]. The software implementation is done on the NVIDIA Tesla K80 graphics accelerator. The high computing power of this GPU shall be attributed to the features of the architecture. It is known that modern CPUs contain a small number of cores, whereas GPUs were originally designed as multithreaded structures with many cores. The architecture of the CPU assumes sequential processing of information, while the GPU was historically intended for processing computer graphics, therefore, it is designed for massively parallel computations [11]. An analysis of both architectures shows that the CPU works better with sequential tasks; on the other hand, the GPU has an obvious advantage when a large amount of information needs to be processed. There is only one condition: parallelism must be present in the problem, and happily, this is just what happens in the case of problems of hydrobiology of the coastal system.

The rest of the paper is structured as follows. Section 2 is devoted to the development of a mathematical model that describes the dynamics of phyto- and zooplankton populations, taking into account the mechanism of external hormonal regulation; here, we also give the formulation of an initial-boundary value problem. In Sect. 3, we describe the construction of a discrete model based on splitting schemes. Section 4 deals with the parallel implementation of the biological kinetics problem on a graphics accelerator. In Sect. 5, we describe a numerical experiment in which four possible scenarios of the development of phyto- and zooplankton in a coastal system are modeled. In the Conclusions section, we summarize the results of the study and indicate some possible directions for future research.

2   The Problem Statement

The spatially inhomogeneous model of biological kinetics used to study the mechanism of external hormonal regulation in the summer is based on works by Dombrovsky Yu. A., Markman G. S., and Tyutyunov Yu. A. et al. [12], and Matishov G. G. and Ilyichev V. G. [13]. It can be described using the following equations:

$$\frac{\partial S_i}{\partial t} + u\frac{\partial S_i}{\partial x} + v\frac{\partial S_i}{\partial y} + (w - w_{gi})\frac{\partial S_i}{\partial x} = \mu_i \Delta S_i + \frac{\partial}{\partial z}\left(\nu_i \frac{\partial S_i}{\partial z}\right) + \psi_i, \quad (1)$$

$$\psi_1 = \alpha_1 \varphi_1 (S_4) \chi_1 (C, T) S_1 - g_1 (S_1, S_3) - \theta_1 S_1 S_2 - \varepsilon_1 S_1,$$

$$\psi_2 = \alpha_2 \varphi_2 (S_4) \chi_2 (C, T) S_2 - g_2 (S_2, S_3) - \theta_2 S_1 S_2 - \varepsilon_2 S_2,$$

$$\psi_3 = \varphi_3 (S_1, S_2) \chi_3 (C, T) S_3 - \lambda (S_6) S_3,$$

$$\psi_4 = \varepsilon_1 S_1 + \varepsilon_2 S_2 - \varphi_4 (S_1, S_2) S_4 + \lambda (S_6) S_3 + B(\tilde{S}_4 - S_4) + f,$$

$$\psi_m = k_l S_l - \varepsilon_m S_m, \ l \in \{1, 2\}, \ m \in \{5, 6\}.$$

System (1) includes equations to describe the changes in the concentrations of phyto- and zooplankton, their metabolites, and impurities polluting the coastal system, which include biogenic substances (compounds of nitrogen, phosphorus, and silicon). The index i indicates the type of substance; S_i is the concentration of the i-th substance, $i = \overline{1,6}$; S_l, $l \in \{1,2\}$, denote the concentrations of green (*Chlorella vulgaris*) and blue-green algae (*M. aeruginosa*), respectively; S_3 is the zooplankton concentration (*Bosmina longirostris*); S_4 is the concentration of nutrient (nitrogen or phosphorus); S_m is the concentration of the metabolite of the l-th type of alga, $m \in \{5,6\}$; C and T stand for the salinity and the temperature of the aquatic environment, respectively; μ_i and ν_i are the diffusion coefficients in the horizontal and vertical directions, respectively, for the substance S_i; α_l, $l \in \{1,2\}$, denotes the growth function of the l-th species of phytoplankton due to metabolites; α_3 is the zooplankton growth rate; ξ_m, $m = \overline{1,3}$, are the functions that describe the growth rate of plankton populations depending on salinity and temperature; $g_l (S_l, S_3)$, $l \in \{1,2\}$, is the function of absorption of phytoplankton of the l-th species by zooplankton; $\varphi_3 (S_1, S_2)$ is the function that describe the growth of S_3 due to consumption of algae of types S_1 and S_2; $\varphi_4 (S_1, S_2)$ is the function of nutrient consumption by algae; $\tilde{S}_4$ denotes the maximum possible concentration of nutrients; f is the function of the source of nutrient (pollution); B is the rate of nutrient inflow; ε_l, $l \in \{1,2\}$, are the mortality rates of the l-th species of phytoplankton; the function $\lambda (S_6)$ describes the reduction of zooplankton concentration due to fish, gelatinous plankton, and mortality, including the risk of extermination due to the metabolite of blue-green algae; k_l, $l \in \{1,2\}$, is the coefficient of excretion of the l-th species of phytoplankton; ε_m, $m = \{3,4\}$, are the coefficients of decomposition of the metabolite; θ_l, $l \in \{1,2\}$, denotes the coefficient of interspecific competition of the l-th species of phytoplankton; $\mathbf{u}_{0i}$ stands for the sedimentation rate of the i-th substance; $\mathbf{u}$ is the field of water flow velocities, and $\mathbf{U} = \mathbf{u} + \mathbf{u}_{0i}$, $i = \overline{1,6}$, is the rate of convective transfer of matter.

We assume that $\varphi_l (S_4) = S_4$, $l \in \{1,2\}$; $\varphi_3 (S_1, S_2) = p_1 S_1 + p_2 S_2$; $g_l (S_l, S_3) = \delta_l S_l S_3$; $\lambda (S_6) = \varepsilon_3 + \gamma_3 S_6$, where γ_3 is a parameter that represents the effect of the metabolite of blue-green algae on zooplankton; $\varphi_4 (S_1, S_2) = s_{n1} \alpha_1 S_1 + s_{n2} \alpha_2 S_2$, where s_{nl} is a normalizing factor for the content of nutrients in the organic matter of phytoplankton of the l-th species; p_l is a coefficient that corresponds to the processed biomass of algae of the l-th species in the biomass of zooplankton; δ_l is a coefficient that corresponds to the biomass loss of the l-th species of algae due to zooplankton feeding on it; ψ_i, $i = \overline{1,6}$, is a chemical-biological source (sink) or a term describing aggregation if the corresponding component is a suspension.

The functions that describe how the growth rate of plankton populations depends on the temperature and salinity are expressed as follows:

$$\chi_m\left(C,T\right) = \exp\left(-\alpha_m((T - T_{\mathrm{opt}})/T_{\mathrm{opt}})^2 - \beta_m((C - C_{\mathrm{opt}})/C_{\mathrm{opt}})^2\right), \ m = \overline{1,3}$$

where T_{opt} and C_{opt} are, respectively, the temperature and salinity optimal for a given type of plankton; and $\alpha_m > 0$ and $\beta_m > 0$ are the coefficients of the width of the plankton tolerance range to temperature and salinity, respectively.

The initial conditions are as follows:

$$S_i\left(x,y,z,0\right) = S_{i0}\left(x,y,z\right), \ i \in \overline{1,6}, \ (x,y,z) \in \bar{G}, \ t = 0. \tag{2}$$

The computational domain G is a closed basin bounded by a cylindrical lateral surface σ, by the undisturbed surface of the reservoir Σ_0, and by the bottom $\Sigma_H = \Sigma_H(x,y)$. Let $\Sigma = \Sigma_0 \cup \Sigma_H \cup \sigma$ be the piecewise-smooth boundary of the domain G for $0 < t \leq T_0$.

Let us set the following boundary conditions:

$$\begin{aligned} S_i = 0 \text{ on } \sigma \text{ if } u_n < 0; \qquad &\frac{\partial S_i}{\partial n} = 0 \text{ on } \sigma \text{ if } u_n \geq 0; \\ \frac{\partial S_i}{\partial z} = \eta\left(S_i\right) \text{ on } \Sigma_0; \qquad &\frac{\partial S_i}{\partial z} = -\xi_i S_i \text{ on } \Sigma_H, \ i = \overline{1,6}. \end{aligned} \tag{3}$$

where ξ_i are non-negative constants, namely ξ_1 and ξ_2 take into account the sinking of algae to the bottom and their submersion, ξ_3 accounts for the elimination of zooplankton and its sinking to the bottom, while ξ_4, ξ_5, and ξ_6 reflect the absorption of nutrients and metabolites of green and blue-green algae by bottom sediments. The scheme of the multi-species model (1)–(3) is depicted in Fig. 1 in the form of a digraph.

The model of phytoplankton dynamics (1)–(3) considers the mechanisms of ectocrine regulation and also takes into account the movement of the water flow, microturbulent diffusion, gravitational deposition of pollutants and plankton, nonlinear interaction of plankton populations, biogenic, temperature, and oxygen regimes; the influence of salinity. The model enables us to study the mechanism of external hormonal regulation. Based on the model, it is possible to study the process of allelopathy, i.e., the influence of some algae on others through a change in the environment by releasing their metabolites into it [14].

By taking into account the changes in the qualitative composition of the environment chemical background formed by metabolites, we modify the dependence between the specific growth rate of phytoplankton and the concentration of metabolites. A nonlinear form for this dependence is more realistic since it takes into account the changes in both the chemical composition of the aquatic environment and the reaction of aquatic organisms [15].

We investigated the three-dimensional model (1)–(3) in the absence of a mechanism of external hormonal regulation ($\gamma_l = 0$, $l \in \{1,2\}$, the growth of

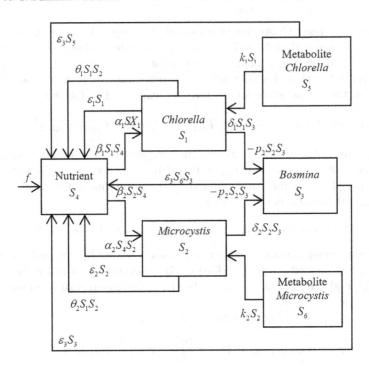

Fig. 1. Model diagram

algae is limited by biogenic substances) and obtained sufficient conditions for the existence and uniqueness of its solution. The following theorems are the result of this research.

Theorem 1. Assume that $S_i(x, y, z, t)$, $\psi_i \in C^2(W_t) \cap C(\overline{W}_t)$, $W_t = G \times (0 < t < T_0)$, $\mu_i = \text{const} > 0$, $\mathbf{U} = (u, v, w - w_{gi})$, $\nu_i(z) \in C^1(\bar{G})$, and $S_{i0} \in C(\bar{G})$, $i = \overline{1, 6}$. Furthermore, assume that the inequality

$$\max_G \{\mu_i, \nu_i\} - \frac{1}{\lambda_0} \max_G \{|p_i|\} > 0$$

holds for each $i = \overline{1, 6}$, and $\psi_i = p_i(S_j) S_i + \bar{\psi}_i$, $i \neq j$, where

$$\bar{\psi}_i = LS_i - DS_i - p_i S_i,$$

$$LS_i = \frac{\partial S_i}{\partial t} + \text{div}(S_i \mathbf{U}_i),$$

$$DS_i = \mu_i \Delta S_i + \frac{\partial}{\partial z}\left(\nu_i \frac{\partial S_i}{\partial z}\right),$$

$$\lambda_0 = \pi^2 \left(\frac{1}{l_x^2} + \frac{1}{l_y^2} + \frac{1}{l_z^2}\right),$$

and l_x, l_y, and l_z are the maximum spatial dimensions of the computational domain. Then, the biological kinetics problem (1)–(3) has a solution.

Theorem 2. Assume that $S_i(x, y, z, t)$, $\psi_i \in C^2(W_t) \cap C(\overline{W}_t)$, $\mu_i = \text{const} > 0$, and $\mathbf{U}, \nu_i(z) \in C^1(\bar{G})$, $i = \overline{1,6}$. Assume also that the inequalities

$$2\mu_i \left(\frac{1}{l_x^2} + \frac{1}{l_y^2} \right) + 2\frac{v_i}{l_z^2} \geq \varphi_i, \quad i = \overline{1,6},$$

are valid for the functions φ_i, determined by the sources of the pollutant. Then, the biological kinetics problem (1)–(3) has a unique solution.

3   The Method of Solution of the Problem

In [16], a splitting algorithm of a special type is constructed and investigated. The algorithm is based on explicit-implicit schemes with weights for multidimensional diffusion-convection problems and is applied for the numerical implementation of a 3D model of transport of suspended matter in coastal water systems. The splitting scheme (into a two-dimensional problem horizontally and a one-dimensional problem along the vertical direction) makes it possible to minimize the number of information exchanges occurring between adjacent streams during the transition from a time layer to another in a parallel manner at the boundary nodes of subdomains with a geometric decomposition of the three-dimensional grid by vertical planes.

Consider the approximation of the two-dimensional problem taking as an example the homogeneous diffusion-convection equation

$$c_t' + uc_x' + vc_y' = (\mu c_x')_x' + (\mu c_y')_y' \tag{4}$$

with boundary conditions:

$$c_n'(x, y, t) = \alpha_n c + \beta_n, \tag{5}$$

where u and v are the components of the velocity vector of the aquatic environment, and μ is the coefficient of turbulent exchange.

Let us carry out the discretization of the two-dimensional problem obtained by splitting the three-dimensional problem (1)–(3). For this, we embed the computational domain in a rectangle [17]. For the numerical implementation of the mathematical model, we introduce a uniform grid:

$$w_h = \{t^n = n\tau, \ x_i = ih_x, \ y_j = jh_y; \ n = \overline{0, N_t}, \ i = \overline{0, N_x}, \ j = \overline{0, N_y};$$

$$N_t\tau = T, \ N_x h_x = l_x, \ N_y h_y = l_y\},$$

where τ is the time step, h_x and h_y are the space steps, N_t is the upper time bound, N_x and N_y are the upper space bounds. To approximate homogeneous Eq. (4) for large grid Péclet numbers, we use the splitting schemes in space:

$$\frac{c^{n+1/2} - c^n}{\tau} + u(c^n)_x' = (\mu(c^n)_x')_x', \tag{6}$$

$$\frac{c^{n+1} - c^{n+1/2}}{\tau} + v(c^{n+1/2})_y' = (\mu(c^{n+1/2})_y')_y'. \tag{7}$$

To approximate the system of Eqs. (6), (7), we use a scheme that is the result of a linear combination of the Upwind and the Standard Leapfrog difference schemes, with weight coefficients 2/3 and 1/3, respectively, which are attained by minimizing the order of the approximation error and describe more accurately the behavior of the solution to diffusion-convection-reaction problems in the case of large grid Péclet numbers [18]. We now take into account the function for filling the calculation cells [19]:

– the difference scheme for Eq. (6), which describes the transport along the direction Ox, is written as

$$\frac{2q_{2,i,j} + q_{0,i,j}}{3} \frac{c_{i,j}^{n+1/2} - c_{i,j}^n}{\tau} + 5u_{i-1/2,j}q_{2,i,j} \frac{c_{i,j}^n - c_{i-1,j}^n}{3h_x}$$

$$+ u_{i+1/2,j} \min(q_{1,i,j}, q_{2,i,j}) \frac{c_{i+1,j}^n - c_{i,j}^n}{3h_x} + \frac{2\Delta_x c_{i-1,j}^n q_{2,i,j} \Delta_x c_{i,j}^n q_{0,i,j}}{3}$$

$$= 2\mu_{i+1/2,j}q_{1,i,j} \frac{c_{i+1,j}^n - c_{i,j}^n}{h_x^2} - 2\mu_{i-1/2,j}q_{2,i,j} \frac{c_{i,j}^n - c_{i-1,j}^n}{h_x^2}$$

$$- |q_{1,i,j} - q_{2,i,j}| \mu_{i,j} \frac{\alpha_x c_{i,j}^n + \beta_x}{h_x}, \quad u_{i,j} \geq 0; \quad (8)$$

$$\frac{2q_{1,i,j} + q_{0,i,j}}{3} \frac{c_{i,j}^{n+1/2} - c_{i,j}^n}{\tau} + 5u_{i+1/2,j}q_{1,i,j} \frac{c_{i+1,j}^n - c_{i,j}^n}{3h_x} +$$

$$+ u_{i-1/2,j} \min(q_{1,i,j}, q_{2,i,j}) \frac{c_{i,j}^n - c_{i-1,j}^n}{3h_x} + \frac{2\Delta_x c_{i+1,j}^n q_{1,i,j} + \Delta_x c_{i,j}^n q_{0,i,j}}{3}$$

$$= 2\mu_{i+1/2,j}q_{1,i,j} \frac{c_{i+1,j}^n - c_{i,j}^n}{h_x^2} - 2\mu_{i-1/2,j}q_{2,i,j} \frac{c_{i,j}^n - c_{i-1,j}^n}{h_x^2}$$

$$- |q_{1,i,j} - q_{2,i,j}| \mu_{i,j} \frac{\alpha_x c_{i,j}^n + \beta_x}{h_x}, \quad u_{i,j} < 0, \quad \text{where } \Delta_x c_{i,j}^n = \frac{c_{i,j}^{n-1/2} - c_{i,j}^{n-1}}{\tau};$$

– the difference scheme for Eq. (7), which describes the transport along the direction Oy, can be written as

$$\frac{2q_{4,i,j} + q_{0,i,j}}{3} \frac{c_{i,j}^{n+1} - c_{i,j}^{n+1/2}}{\tau} + 5v_{i,j-1/2}q_{4,i,j} \frac{c_{i,j}^{n+1/2} - c_{i,j-1}^{n+1/2}}{3h_y}$$

$$+ v_{i,j+1/2} \min(q_{3,i,j}, q_{4,i,j}) \frac{c_{i,j+1}^{n+1/2} - c_{i,j}^{n+1/2}}{3h_y} + \frac{2\Delta_y c_{i,j-1}^{n+1/2} q_{4,i,j} + \Delta_y c_{i,j}^{n+1/2} q_{0,i,j}}{3}$$

$$= 2\mu_{i,j+1/2}q_{3,i,j} \frac{c_{i,j+1}^{n+1/2} - c_{i,j}^{n+1/2}}{h_y^2} - 2\mu_{i,j-1/2}q_{4,i,j} \frac{c_{i,j}^{n+1/2} - c_{i,j-1}^{n+1/2}}{h_y^2}$$

$$- |q_{3,i,j} - q_{4,i,j}| \mu_{i,j} \frac{\alpha_y c_{i,j}^{n+1/2} + \beta_y}{h_y}, \quad v_{i,j} \geq 0; \quad (9)$$

$$\frac{2q_{3,i,j} + q_{0,i,j}}{3} \frac{c_{i,j}^{n+1} - c_{i,j}^{n+1/2}}{\tau} + 5v_{i,j+1/2}q_{3,i,j} \frac{c_{i,j+1}^{n+1/2} - c_{i,j}^{n+1/2}}{3h_y}$$

$$+ v_{i,j-1/2} \min\left(q_{3,i,j}, q_{4,i,j}\right) \frac{c_{i,j}^{n+1/2} - c_{i,j-1}^{n+1/2}}{3h_y} + \frac{2\Delta_y c_{i,j+1}^{n+1/2} q_{3,i,j} + \Delta_y c_{i,j}^{n+1/2} q_{0,i,j}}{3}$$

$$= 2\mu_{i,j+1/2}q_{3,i,j} \frac{c_{i,j+1}^{n+1/2} - c_{i,j}^{n+1/2}}{h_y^2} - 2\mu_{i,j-1/2}q_{4,i,j} \frac{c_{i,j}^{n+1/2} - c_{i,j-1}^{n+1/2}}{h_y^2}$$

$$- \left|q_{3,i,j} - q_{4,i,j}\right| \mu_{i,j} \frac{\alpha_y c_{i,j}^{n+1/2} + \beta_y}{h_y}, \quad v_{i,j} < 0, \text{ where } \Delta_y c_{i,j}^{n+1/2} = \frac{c_{i,j}^n - c_{i,j}^{n-1/2}}{\tau}.$$

4 Parallel Implementation of the Biological Kinetics Problem

We developed parallel algorithms for the numerical implementation of the inter-related mathematical models of hydrodynamics and biological kinetics. The algorithms are adapted for hybrid computer systems using the NVIDIA CUDA architecture [20]. The NVIDIA Tesla K80 graphics accelerator offers high computing performance and supports both closed (CUDA) and open (OpenCL, DirectCompute) technologies. Its specifications are as follows: 560 MHz GPU frequency, 24 GB of GDDR5 video memory, 5000 MHz video memory frequency, and 768-bit video memory bus. The NVIDIA CUDA platform specifications are as follows: Windows 10 (x64) operating system, CUDA Toolkit v11.1, Intel Core i5-6600 3.3 GHz processor, 32 GB DDR4 RAM, NVIDIA GeForce GTX 750 Ti graphics card with 2 GB and 640 CUDA cores.

Computing system specifications:

- number of GPU Cores: 2;
- CUDA driver version: 11.1;
- CUDA Compute Capability index: 3.7;
- number of multiprocessors: 13;
- number of CUDA cores per multiprocessor: 192;
- total number of CUDA cores: 2496;
- maximum GPU clock frequency: 824 MHz;
- total amount of constant memory: 65 536 bytes;
- total amount of total memory per block: 49 152 bytes;
- total amount of shared memory per multiprocessor: 11 4688 bytes;
- maximum number of threads per multiprocessor: 2048;
- maximum number of threads per block: 1024.

Each computational node is allocated to one GPU thread to implement a parallel algorithm for solving a two-dimensional problem of biological kinetics. The technology of dividing computational areas into thread blocks is used for computational grids exceeding the maximum allowable number of GPU threads. The block diagram of the parallel calculation algorithm is shown in Fig. 2.

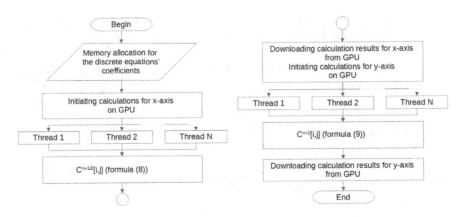

Fig. 2. Flowchart of the parallel algorithm for GPU

Table 1 contains the results of the numerical solution to the two-dimensional problem of biological kinetics for different numbers of employed flows in the implementation of the parallel algorithm using CUDA. The size of the computational grid varies from 100×100 to $10\,000 \times 10\,000$ computational nodes for experiments 1–6.

Figure 3 portrays a comparison of the running time (in seconds) of the parallel algorithm (vertical axis) on a sequence of grids (experiments 1–6 on the horizontal axis). The number of involved threads is taken equal to 512.

The results of the numerical experiments on a graphics accelerator show the advantage of the parallel algorithm when increasing the size of the computational grid. A comparison of the parallel implementation of the solution to the two-dimensional convection-diffusion-reaction problem on a GPU controlled by the CUDA system with the classical implementation on a CPU is given in [21], where it is shown that such a powerful tool as CUDA is ineffective for grids of small dimensions (100×100 computational nodes) and, in the case of more

Table 1. Results of the algorithm on a GPU

Experiment number, N	1	2	3	4	5	6
N_x	100	500	1000	2000	5000	10 000
N_y	100	500	1000	2000	5000	10 000
N_t	10	10	10	10	10	10
Time, s ($p = 128$)	0.004296	0.0704	0.26099	0.95916	6.4114	23.892
Time, s ($p = 256$)	0.004252	0.0705	0.25349	0.97414	6.4082	24.393
Time, s ($p = 512$)	0.004301	0.0716	0.25046	0.95707	6.546	24.981
Time, s ($p = 1024$)	0.00408	0.0745	0.25876	0.9798	6.4035	24.993

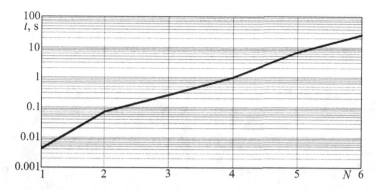

Fig. 3. Running time t of the parallel algorithm on a GPU, for a sequence of thickening grids

detailed computational grids (1000×1000 computational nodes), it reduces the computation time by an order of magnitude.

5 Results of Numerical Experiments on the Research of Allelopathy of Phytoplankton Populations

We used the developed software package on a graphics accelerator for numerical experiments in which we studied the problem of biological kinetics (1)–(3), the influence of nutrients on the growth of green algae (*C. vulgaris*), blue-green algae (*M. aeruginosa*), and zooplankton (*B. longirostris*) in a real area of complex shape (coastal system – Sea of Azov). The modeling took into account the influence of abiotic factors (salinity and temperature) on the development of plankton populations [22]. The input data sets were based on expeditionary data and an electronic atlas prepared by the SSC RAS in 2018 [23]. We considered several scenarios of dynamics of interacting phytoplankton algae, which enabled us to study the mechanism of ectocrine regulation. We used data from expeditionary studies and literature sources when carrying out the numerical experiments based on the scenario approach.

Scenario 1. Consider an observation model expressed in the form of a functional dependence: $\alpha_1 = \alpha_{01} + \gamma_1 S_5$, $\alpha_2 = \alpha_{02} + \gamma_2 S_6$, where α_{0l} is the phytoplankton growth rate in the absence of a metabolite and γ_l is the impact parameter of the l-th species of algae, $l \in \{1, 2\}$. Assume that $\gamma_l > 0$, which corresponds to a stimulating effect of metabolites secreted by algae. Set the following values of the parameters: $\alpha_{01} = 0.3$, $\alpha_{02} = 0.5$, $\gamma_1 = 0.08$, $\gamma_2 = 0.05$, $f = 0.15$.

Figure 4 shows the simulation results for Scenario 1. Figures 4(a)–(c) portray a three-dimensional distribution (surface layer) showing changes in plankton concentration over time at a fixed point of the reservoir surface at optimal salinity. Figure 4(d) shows temporal changes in plankton concentration at fixed a point of the reservoir surface at optimum salinity. The initial concentrations were as follows: green algae—2.5 mg/l, blue-green algae—2.6 mg/l, zooplankton—0.1 mg/l. The distribution is uniform.

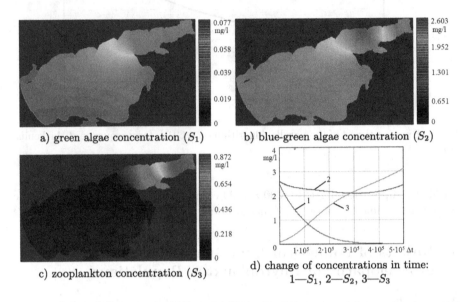

a) green algae concentration (S_1)

b) blue-green algae concentration (S_2)

c) zooplankton concentration (S_3)

d) change of concentrations in time:
1—S_1, 2—S_2, 3—S_3

Fig. 4. Results of the numerical experiment (Scenario 1)

The experiment with the given input parameters of the system showed that *Chlorella* algae are rather quickly consumed by zooplankton (this type of green algae is preferred in the feeding regime), while the concentration of blue-green algae increases, due, among other things, to stimulation by the metabolite.

Scenario 2. Suppose that the metabolite secreted by green algae has a multidirectional effect on their dynamics: on the one hand, it increases the growth rate, on the other hand, it increases their mortality: $\alpha_1 = \alpha_{01} + \gamma_1 S_5$, $\varepsilon_1 = \varepsilon_0 + \gamma_3 S_5$, where ε_1 is the specific mortality of the phytoplankton, which linearly depends on the latter's density. The parameters have the following values: $\alpha_{01} = 0.3$, $\gamma_1 = 0.08$, $\varepsilon_0 = 0.5$, $\gamma_3 = 0.08$. This scenario gives a model with unstable dynamics. Continue modeling under the condition that different metabolites increase and restrict the growth rate of the phytoplankton.

Scenario 3. Assume that $\alpha_1 = \alpha_{01} + \gamma_1 S_5 - \gamma_2 S_6$, $\alpha_2 = \alpha_{02} + \gamma_2 S_6$. If $\gamma_l > 0$, $l \in \{1, 2\}$, then the metabolites of the first species of algae have a stimulating effect on them, whereas the metabolites of the second species of algae stimulate their own growth (blue-green algae) and have a restraining effect on the first species (green algae). The parameters have the following values: $\varepsilon_1 = 0.5$, $\varepsilon_2 = 0.3$, $f = 0.52$, $\alpha_{01} = 0.3$, $\alpha_{02} = 0.5$, $\gamma_1 = 0.08$, $\gamma_2 = 0.05$, $k_1 = 0.5$, $k_2 = 0.4$.

Scenario 4. Consider a parabolic dependence for the concentration of blue-green algae: $\alpha_2 = \alpha_2^{\max} - \left(S_6 - S_6^{\mathrm{opt}} \right)^2$, where $\alpha_2^{\max}$ stands for the specific growth rate of blue-green phytoplankton at a unit concentration of nutrients and optimal level of metabolite S_6^{opt} in the environment. At low concentrations of the metabolite, there is a stimulating effect, at high concentrations, an inhibitory effect. The parameters take on the following values: $\varepsilon_1 = 0.5$, $\varepsilon_2 = 0.3$, $f = 0.15$, $\alpha_{01} = 2$, $\alpha_2^{\max} = 2.8$, $S_6^{\mathrm{opt}} = 0.1$, $\gamma_1 = 0.08$, $\gamma_2 = 0.05$, $k_1 = 0.015$, $k_2 = 0.015$. This is a rather "optimistic" scenario for the functioning of the biosystem under lack of food.

Figure 5 shows the fluctuations in the density of blue-green phytoplankton for a nonlinear dependence of its growth rate on the metabolite concentration, as per Scenario 4 of the model of ectocrine regulation of phytoplankton dynamics (1)–(3) with a model area of regular shape.

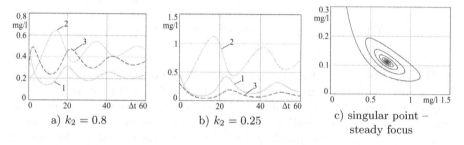

a) $k_2 = 0.8$ b) $k_2 = 0.25$ c) singular point – steady focus

Fig. 5. Functional dependencies of fluctuations in density: 1—phytoplankton (S_2), 2—biogenic substance (S_4) (mineral nutrition), 3—metabolite (S_6). A projection of the phase portrait on the coordinate planes: along the abscissa axis—biogenic substance (S_4); along the ordinate axis—blue-green algae metabolite (S_6)

Figure 6 shows the simulation results for Scenario 4. Figures 6(a)–c) portray the three-dimensional distributions (surface layer) of the concentrations of green and blue-green algae. Figure 6(d) displays the changes in plankton concentrations over time at a fixed point of the reservoir surface at optimum salinity.

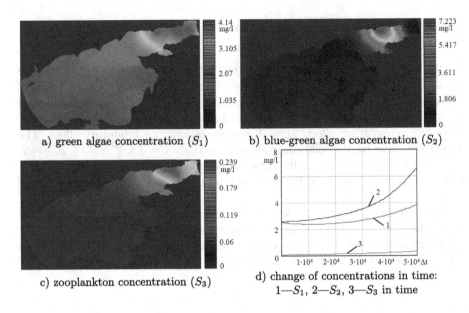

a) green algae concentration (S_1)   b) blue-green algae concentration (S_2)

c) zooplankton concentration (S_3)   d) change of concentrations in time:
1—S_1, 2—S_2, 3—S_3 in time

Fig. 6. Results of the numerical experiment (Scenario 4)

The experiment with the given input parameters of the system showed that the optimal value of the metabolite concentration S_6^{opt} is 0.1 mg/l. At greater or smaller values, the concentration of blue-green algae decreases rapidly. The results we obtained agree well with data from literature and field observations.

The experiments show that Scenario 1 is valid for the typical development of green and blue-green algae in the summer in the Sea of Azov. This scenario allows analyzing the influence of both biotic and external factors, including salinity and temperature, on the production and destruction processes of phyto- and zooplankton. Starting in the second half of July, the concentration of blue-green algae becomes quite high, especially in Taganrog Bay.

Scenario 2 assumes that the metabolite secreted by green algae has a multidirectional effect on their dynamics: on the one hand, it promotes an increase in the growth rate and, on the other, it increases their mortality. This scenario gives a model with unstable dynamics.

The study of Scenario 3, under the condition that different metabolites increase and restrict the growth rate of phytoplankton, shows that it is more realistic.

Scenario 4, with a nonlinear dependence between the growth rate of phytoplankton and the metabolite concentration, is in agreement with modern concepts on the functioning of hydrobiocenosis. It allows describing the ability of algal metabolites to control their growth even under conditions of an excess of nutrients.

6 Conclusions

We developed several modifications of the spatial-temporal multi-species model of plankton dynamics, which connects changes in the densities of the considered species of phyto- (green and blue-green algae) and zooplankton with the concentration of biogenic substances (compounds of nitrogen, phosphorus, and silicon). The model makes it possible to study the effect of various metabolites secreted by phytoplankton on their kinetics.

One of the considered scenarios assumes that the metabolite secreted by green algae has a multidirectional effect on their dynamics (it increases the growth rate but, at the same time, increases their mortality) and leads to a model with unstable dynamics. It became necessary to study a scenario with the condition that different metabolites increase and restrict the growth rate of the phytoplankton. This scenario proved more realistic. The introduction of a nonlinear dependence between the growth rate of phytoplankton and the metabolite concentration in the model of ectocrine regulation of the phytoplankton dynamics made it possible to describe the ability of algal metabolites to control their growth even under conditions of an excess of nutrients. This fact is in agreement with modern concepts on the functioning of hydrobiocenosis. Under this scenario, stable fluctuations in the concentrations of phytoplankton and nutrients are observed.

The splitting of the initial three-dimensional problem (1)–(3) into a two-dimensional problem horizontally and a one-dimensional one vertically makes it possible to minimize the number of information exchanges occurring between adjacent streams during the transition from a time layer to another in a parallel manner at the boundary nodes of subdomains with a geometric decomposition of the three-dimensional grid by vertical planes. The discretization of the developed model problem of aquatic ecology, which is part of the software package, is based on a linear combination of the Upwind and the Standard Leapfrog difference schemes, taking into account the partial filling of the calculated cells. This makes it possible to significantly reduce the solution error in computational domains of complex shapes.

We developed parallel algorithms to solve the problem of biological kinetics on a sequence of thickening grids. We analyzed their efficiency for different numbers of employed flows. The development of efficient parallel algorithms for the numerical solution of the posed biological kinetics problem was oriented to the NVIDIA Tesla K80 graphics accelerator and made it possible to study both intra- and interspecific chemical communications between planktonic populations of a coastal system (the Azov Sea) in limited time mode. This is very important in case of ecological situations of catastrophic nature.

References

1. Novikov, M.A., Kharlamova, M.N.: Transbiotic factors in the aquatic environment (review). J. Gen. Biol. **61**(1), 22–46 (2000). (in Russian)
2. DeMott, W.R., Moxter, F.: Foraging on cyanobacteria by copepods: responses to chemical defenses and resources abundance. Ecology. **72**, 1820–1834 (1991). https://doi.org/10.2307/1940981

3. Iörgensen, G.: Growth-inhibing substances formed by algae. Physiol, Plant. **9**, 712–717 (1956). https://doi.org/10.1111/j.1399-3054.1956.tb07833.x

4. Wang, W.: Chromate ion as a referense toxicant for aquatic phytotoxicity tests. Environ. Toxicol, Chem. **6**(12), 953–960 (1987)

5. Findeneg, J.: Factors controlling primary productivity, especially with regard to water replenishment, stratification and mixing. In: Proceendings of the 1BP Symposium on Prymary Productivity in Aquatic Enviroments. Pallanza. vol. 18, pp. 105–119 (1965)

6. Zimina, L.M., Sazykina, T.G.: Isolation of exometabolites by microalgae as a mechanism of population density regulation. Hydrobiol. J. **23**(4), 50–55 (1987). (in Russian)

7. Dombrovsky Yu., A., Markman, G.S.: Spatial and Temporal Ordering in Ecological and Biochemical Systems, p. 120. Rostov-on-Don, Rostov University Publishing House, Rostov-on-Don (1983). (in Russian)

8. Samarskiy, A.A., Vabishchevich, P.N.: Finite-difference approximations to the transport equation II. Diff. Equ. **36**(7), 1069–1077 (2000). https://doi.org/10.1007/BF02754509

9. Sukhinov, A.A., Chistyakov, A.E., Alekseenko, E.V.: Numerical realization of the three-dimensional model of hydrodynamics for shallow water basins on a high-performance system. Math. Models Comput. Simul. (Translation of RAS) **3**(5), 562–574 (2011). https://doi.org/10.1134/S2070048211050115

10. Matishov, G.G., Ilyichev, V.G., Semin, V.L., Kulygin, V.V.: On adaptation of populations to the temperature regime of the environment. Results of computer experiments.. Rep. Acad. Sci. **420**(2), 282–285 (2008). (in Russian)

11. Sanders J., Kendroth, E.: CUDA Technology in Examples: An Introduction to GPU Programming, 232 p. DMK Press, Moscow (2018). (in Russian)

12. Tyutyunov, Yu., V., Zagrebneva, A.D., Azovsky, A.I.: Spatiotemporal pattern formation in a prey-predator system: the case study of short-term interactions between diatom microalgae and microcrustaceans. Mathematics **8**(7), 1065–1080 (2020). https://doi.org/10.3390/math8071065

13. Matishov, G.G., Kovaleva, G.V., Yasakova, O.N.: Abnormal salinization in the Taganrog estuary and the Don delta. Sci. South Russia (Bull. Southern Sci. Center). **12**(1), 43–50 (2016). (in Russian)

14. Zhdanova, O.L., Abakumov, A.I.: Modeling the dynamics of phytoplankton taking into account the mechanisms of ectocrine regulation. Math. Biol. Bioinform. **10**(1), 178–192 (2015). (in Russian)

15. Alekseenko, E., Roux, B., Fougere, D., Chen, P.G.: The effect of wind induced bottom shear stress and salinity on Zostera noltii replanting in a Mediterranean coastal lagoon. Estuar. Coast. Shelf Sci. **187**, 293–305 (2017). https://doi.org/10.1016/j.ecss.2017.01.010

16. Sukhinov, A.I., Chistyakov, A.E., Sidoryakina, V.V., Protsenko, E.A.: Economical explicit-implicit schemes for solving multidimensional diffusion-convection problems. Comput. Mech. Cont. Media **12**(4), 435–445 (2019). (in Russian)

17. Chetverushkin, B.N., Savelyev, A.V., Savelyev, V.I.: Modeling of magnetohydrodynamic problems on high-performance computing systems. Math. Model. **32**(12), 3–13 (2020). https://doi.org/10.20948/mm-2020-12-01

18. Sukhinov, A.I., Chistyakov, A.E., Belova, Y.V.: The difference scheme for the two-dimensional convection-diffusion problem for large Peclet numbers. MATEC Web Conf. **226**, 04030 (2019)

19. Sukhinov, A.I., Chistyakov, A.E., Ugol'nitskii, G.A., Usov, A.B., Nikitina, A.V., Puchkin, M.V., Semenov, I.S.: Game-theoretic regulations for control mechanisms of sustainable development for shallow water ecosystems. Autom. Rem. Control **78**(6), 1059–1071 (2017). https://doi.org/10.1134/S0005117917060078
20. Boreskov, A.V., Kharlamov, A.A.: Basics of working with CUDA technology. 232 p., M., DMK Press, Moscow (2019). (in Russian)
21. Chistyakov A.E., Strazhko A.V., Atayan A.M., Protsenko S.V.: Software development for calculating the polluted by suspension and other impurities zones volumes on the basis of graphics accelerator. IOP Conf. Ser. Mater. Sci. Eng. **1029**, 012084 (2020). https://doi.org/10.1088/1757-899X/1029/1/012084
22. Nikitina, A., Belova, Y., Atayan, A.: Mathematical modeling of the distribution of nutrients and the dynamics of phytoplankton populations in the Azov Sea, taking into account the influence of salinity and temperature. In: AIP Conference Proceedings, vol. 2188 (2019). https://doi.org/10.1063/1.5138454
23. Electronic atlas prepared by the SSC RAS (2018). http://atlas.iaz.ssc-ras.ru/sitemap-ecoatlas.html. (in Russian)

Luthien: A Parallel PIC Code for Modeling the Interaction of Focused Electron Beams with Plasma

Evgeny Berendeev[✉] ⓘ and Evgeniia Volchok[✉] ⓘ

Institute of Computational Mathematics and Mathematical Geophysics SB RAS, Novosibirsk, Russia

Abstract. The paper presents a parallel PIC code for simulating the electromagnetic emission from a focus of electron beams injected into a plasma. The code aims to study the method of efficient generation of terahertz radiation by kiloampere electron beams capable of focusing to mm-scale spots. Luthien uses an axially symmetric 2D3V kinetic plasma model based on the particle-in-cell method and implements open boundary conditions allowing for the continuous injection of high-power colliding electron beams into a plasma. The article discusses in detail the mathematical model used and describes the structure of the code, the basic numerical algorithms, and their parallel implementation. The performance of the code on various parallel computing systems is studied by considering as an example the collision of two Gaussian electron beams with different focal spot sizes in a plasma.

Keywords: High-performance computing · Kinetic plasma simulations · Particle-in-cell method · Beam-plasma interaction · Sources of terahertz electromagnetic radiation

1 Introduction

The generation of gigawatt terahertz (THz) emission is a relevant problem in a very wide range of fundamental and applied research in physics, chemistry, biology, and medicine, and also in security and THz location systems. The greatest success has been achieved with free-electron lasers. However, the need to accelerate electrons to ultrarelativistic energies in those devices means that they must be large, and therefore, such facilities are scarcely available. In our opinion, one of the most promising ways to achieve gigawatt THz emissions consists in using the collective interaction of kiloampere electron beams of relatively low energy (from 1 to 2 MeV) with plasma. In previous studies [20], we showed that the emission efficiency in a beam-plasma system can reach very high values (5 to 10%) if the beam size is comparable to the radiation wavelength. This means that the efficient generation of THz waves requires beams with a characteristic transverse size of the order of 1 mm. The linear induction accelerators that

© Springer Nature Switzerland AG 2021
L. Sokolinsky and M. Zymbler (Eds.): PCT 2021, CCIS 1437, pp. 228–242, 2021.
https://doi.org/10.1007/978-3-030-81691-9_16

have been developed at the Budker Institute of Nuclear Physics (BINP, Siberian Branch of the Russian Academy of Sciences) allow focusing electron beams to such a size at a current of 2 kA and energy of several megaelectronvolts [16]. The combination of such small sizes and multi-gigawatt beam power paves the way for generating gigawatt electromagnetic (EM) radiation in the terahertz frequency range.

The full-scale numerical simulation of this problem makes it possible to carry out a large amount of preliminary work to search for the most efficient radiation regimes before real experiments are set up. In combination with subsequent laboratory studies, this will open the way to creating powerful and compact terahertz sources. There are many high-performance plasma simulation codes based on different models. The most realistic results can be obtained using the particle-in-cell model implying simulations ab initio. The use of a 2D3V axially symmetric model can significantly reduce the number of computations and yield a sufficient number of computational experiments in a reasonable amount of time.

Several leading research groups, both in Russia and abroad, are successfully developing numerical codes based on the particle-in-cell method. In Russia, it is worth mentioning the work of A. N. Andrianov and K. N. Efimkin (Keldysh Institute of Applied Mathematics) [1], the PICADOR code (I. B. Meerov and S. I. Bastrakov, University of Nizhny Novgorod) [17], the KARAT code (V. P. Tarakanov, Moscow Institute of Physics and Technology) [19], and the UMKA code (V. A. Vshivkov and G. I. Dudnikova, Institute of Computational Mathematics and Mathematical Geophysics, Siberian Branch of the RAS) [12]. Among the codes developed in other countries, we can mention OSIRIS [9], SMILEI [10], FBPIC [13], SHARP [15], and WARP-X [21]. The abundance of numerical codes and models based on the particle method is a consequence of the fact that solving each specific problem requires modifying standard algorithms, changing boundary conditions, and taking into account various physical effects. The use of a single solution for a wide range of problems is computationally ineffective. The most versatile and, at the same time, the most effective code is OSIRIS, which is designed for both cylindrical and Cartesian geometries and provides a wide range of tools to suppress the numerical disadvantages of the particle-in-cell method. Unfortunately, OSIRIS is a proprietary code. We should also note our work [5], which relies on a code to simulate open traps in cylindrical geometry; however, the code was developed for low-temperature nonrelativistic plasmas. The code [2,3] allows simulations of continuous beam injection into plasma but is designed only for Cartesian geometry.

The main goal of the present work is to create a tool for modeling the interaction of continuously injected electron beams with a plasma, in the framework of an axially symmetric geometry. We have developed Luthien, a code that allows the user to make real-scale simulations of the problem under consideration. It is a development of the code given in [2,3] and also implements continuous beam injection through open boundaries. Moreover, a self-consistent formation of a plasma channel is taken into account in this version. The code presented here is written in C++ using the MPI library, has an object-oriented structure, and allows users to easily add their own implementations of the main methods. To demonstrate the capabilities of the Luthien code, we will consider, as an example, the interaction of high-current counter-propagating electron beams focused to spots of different sizes.

The article is structured as follows. Section 2 is devoted to the description of the model used and its main features. In Sect. 3, we consider the code structure and software implementation. In the Conclusions, we sum up the main points of the study.

2   The Mathematical Model and Its Implementation

Let us consider the construction of a model for the interaction of focusing electron beams with a plasma. A distinctive feature of electron beams used at the BINP SB RAS is their long duration. The widely used infinite plasma model is not suitable for numerical simulations of the injection process. In the infinite model, the beam has a fixed energy content and is thus capable of pumping plasma oscillations only for a limited time before being trapped by the most unstable resonant wave. The subsequent evolution of the quasi-stationary non-linear Bernstein–Green–Kruskal waves (BGK waves) takes place in the absence of realistic beam pumping. In a real problem of continuous injection, the non-linear stage of the beam-plasma interaction is significantly different from such a scenario. Therefore, we need a model that allows studying the processes during long-term continuous injection of a relativistic particle beam into the plasma and investigating in detail the EM radiation generated in such a system. The main difficulty here lies in the selection of the necessary boundary conditions for the most complete compliance with the conditions of laboratory experiments. In this case, the electron beam entering the plasma through one boundary and leaving it through the other provides continuous pumping of plasma oscillations. Such a formulation requires the simulation of a sufficiently lengthy plasma domain to accommodate the whole region within which the beam is captured by the field of the excited wave. In the transverse direction, it is proposed to restrict the plasma to a vacuum region and set absorbing boundary conditions, which makes it possible to compare the fluxes of radiation emerging from the plasma with experimental data. Also, it is necessary to create at the plasma boundary some mechanism for maintaining the distribution of particles, thereby providing an imitation of plasma continuity at the boundary. Figure 1 shows a diagram of the computational domain with typical system parameters.

We characterize electron beams by the size of the focal spot, the distribution of density and velocity at the focus, and the focusing distance. We will set these parameters close to those of real physical experiments.

To describe unstable regimes of interaction between a relativistic electron beam and a plasma, we consider a numerical kinetic model that allows one to study the dynamics of the considered processes ab initio. The evolution of plasma can be most fully described by the Vlasov equation for the distribution functions $f_\alpha(\mathbf{r}, \mathbf{v}, t)$ of charged particles,

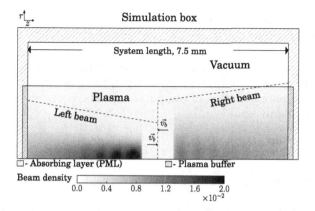

Fig. 1. The simulation layout

$$\frac{\partial f_\alpha}{\partial t} + \mathbf{v}\frac{\partial f_\alpha}{\partial \mathbf{r}} + q_\alpha\left(\mathbf{E} + \frac{1}{c}[\mathbf{v}, \mathbf{B}]\right)\frac{\partial f_\alpha}{\partial \mathbf{p}} = 0, \tag{1}$$

and the system of Maxwell's equations for electromagnetic fields,

$$\operatorname{rot}\mathbf{B} = \frac{4\pi}{c}\mathbf{J} + \frac{1}{c}\frac{\partial \mathbf{E}}{\partial t} = \frac{4\pi}{c}\sum_\alpha q_\alpha\int f_\alpha\mathbf{v}d\mathbf{v} + \frac{1}{c}\frac{\partial \mathbf{E}}{\partial t}, \tag{2}$$

$$\operatorname{rot}\mathbf{E} = -\frac{1}{c}\frac{\partial \mathbf{B}}{\partial t}, \tag{3}$$

$$\operatorname{div}\mathbf{E} = 4\pi\rho = 4\pi\sum_\alpha q_\alpha\int f_\alpha d\mathbf{v}, \tag{4}$$

$$\operatorname{div}\mathbf{B} = 0, \tag{5}$$

where α is a label for the type of particles, and q_α is the charge of the particles of that type.

We suggest the use of the particle-in-cell (PIC) method to solve these equations. According to the PIC method, the plasma is represented by a set consisting of a large number of model particles. Thus, the real particle distribution function f is replaced by the distribution function $\tilde{f}$ of model particles, namely

$$\tilde{f}(\mathbf{r}, \mathbf{v}, t) = \int f(\mathbf{r}', \mathbf{v}, t)S(\mathbf{r}, \mathbf{r}')d\mathbf{r}' = \sum_j S(\mathbf{r}, \mathbf{r}_j(t))\delta(\mathbf{v} - \mathbf{v}_j(t)). \tag{6}$$

Here, $\mathbf{r}_j$ and $\mathbf{v}_j$ are the coordinate and velocity of the particle with index j. Model particles have a spatial charge distribution characterized by the shape function $S(\mathbf{r}, \mathbf{r}_j)$ and interact with each other only by means of the computational grid, thereby contributing to the current and charge density:

$$\rho(\mathbf{r}, t) = \sum_j q_j S(\mathbf{r}, \mathbf{r}_j(t)), \quad \mathbf{J}(\mathbf{r}, t) = \sum_j q_j\mathbf{v}_j S(\mathbf{r}, \mathbf{r}_j(t)). \tag{7}$$

The fields and currents calculated in this manner are taken into account when solving Maxwell's equations. Thus, the particles move in self-consistent electro-magnetic fields.

The equations of motion coincide with the equations of characteristics of the Vlasov kinetic Eq. 1 and are solved independently for each model particle, thereby allowing parallelization of computations. The equations can be written in the following form:

$$\frac{d\mathbf{p}_j(t)}{dt} = q_j\left(\mathbf{E}_j + \frac{1}{c}[\mathbf{v}_j, \mathbf{B}_j]\right), \quad \frac{d\mathbf{r}_j(t)}{dt} = \mathbf{v}_j, \tag{8}$$

where $\mathbf{E}_j$ and $\mathbf{B}_j$ are the electric and magnetic fields acting on a particle with index j.

We compute the motion of model particles according to the Boris scheme [7]. This scheme is well suited for describing the motion of relativistic particles, allows the use of axially symmetric geometry, and is the de facto standard in the particle method.

We solve Maxwell's equations by the finite-difference scheme proposed in [18]. The components of all grid quantities in this scheme are computed on grids shifted relative to each other by half a step in time and space. All derivatives in the equations are written in terms of central differences, which ensures a level of accuracy of the second order in time and space. We define the divergence and curl grid operators in axially symmetric geometry in the following manner:

$$\mathrm{div}_h(F_r, F_\phi, F_z) \tag{9}$$
$$= \left(\frac{r_{l+1}(F_r)_{l+1,k+1/2} - r_l(F_r)_{l,k+1/2}}{r_{l+1/2}h_r} + \frac{(F_z)_{l+1/2,k+1} - (F_z)_{l+1/2,k}}{h_z}\right),$$

$$\mathrm{rot}_h(F_r, F_\phi, F_z) = \left(-\frac{(F_\phi)_{l,k+1} - (F_\phi)_{l,k}}{h_z},\right.$$
$$\frac{(F_r)_{l+1/2,k+1} - (F_r)_{l+1/2,k}}{h_z} + \frac{(F_z)_{l+1,k+1/2} - (F_z)_{l,k+1/2}}{h_r},$$
$$\left.\frac{r_{l+1}(F_\phi)_{l+1,k} - r_l(F_\phi)_{l,k}}{r_{l+1/2}h_r}\right). \tag{10}$$

Thus, Eqs. 2–5 can be rewritten in terms of these central differences:

$$\frac{\mathbf{E}^{m+1/2} - \mathbf{E}^{m-1/2}}{\tau} = c\,\mathrm{rot}_h\,\mathbf{B}^m - 4\pi\mathbf{J}^{m+1/2}, \tag{11}$$

$$\frac{\mathbf{B}^{m+1} - \mathbf{B}^m}{\tau} = -c\,\mathrm{rot}_h\,\mathbf{E}^{m+1/2}, \tag{12}$$

$$\mathrm{div}_h\,\mathbf{E}^{m+1/2} = 4\pi\rho, \tag{13}$$

$$\mathrm{div}_h\,\mathbf{B}^m = 0. \tag{14}$$

As an alternative to the proposed method, we can use the spectral approach for solving the field equations proposed in [13]. However, it is shown in [14] that the correct choice of temporal and spatial steps in the classical scheme 11–14 is comparable in accuracy to these methods. Hence, the preference was given to the finite-difference scheme. Nevertheless, Luthien makes provisions to incorporate custom field solvers if the need arises.

To compute the currents, we use the scheme suggested in [11] but adapted to the cylindrical geometry. It automatically satisfies the difference equation of continuity and, therefore, accurately fulfills Gaussian difference law 4. Also, the scheme admits the use of arbitrary particle shapes.

2.1   Features of the Axial-Cylindrical Geometry

Unlike 2D3V Cartesian geometry, where the grid cell is an infinitely elongated parallelepiped along one direction, grid cells in 2D3V RZ axially symmetric geometry are rings of finite volume. In the case of a uniform grid step along the system axis direction, the volume of the ring V increases as the cell moves away from the center:

$$V_i = \pi h_z h_r r_{i+1/2},\tag{15}$$

where V_i is the volume of the cell number i counting from the system axis, h_r and h_z are the grid steps in the r and z directions, and $r_i + 1/2$ is the radial coordinate of the cell center.

Thus, to obtain a uniform distribution density of particles in such a space, it is necessary to distribute the particles in such a manner that a larger radius corresponds to a larger number of particles in the cell. This ratio depends on the radius of the cell as follows:

$$\rho_{l,k} = \frac{1}{V_{l,k}} \sum_j q_j S'(\mathbf{r}_{l,k}, \mathbf{r}'_j),\tag{16}$$

where l is the radial cell index, $r_{l,k}$ is the radius vector of the cell center, and S' is the grid shape of the particle that distributes the charge among the nodes. For example, the second-order kernel $S'(\mathbf{r}_{l,k}, \mathbf{r}'_j) = S'(r_l, r'_l)S'(r_k, r'_k)$:

$$S'(r, r') = \begin{cases} 3/4 - (r - r')^2/h, & \text{if } 0 \le |r - r'| < h/2, \\ \dfrac{(3 - 2|r - r'|)^2}{8h}, & \text{if } h/2 \le |r - r'| < 3h/2, \\ 0 & \text{otherwise.} \end{cases}\tag{17}$$

In this case, the computational accuracy will suffer in cells near the axis that contain few particles, while the computational load will increase manyfold in distant cells. Since each model particle represents a certain number of real particles, the solution to this problem can be the establishment of different values for the concentration of real particles in the model. That concentration is determined when the background plasma particles (background electrons and ions) are initially distributed and it is set up proportionally to the radius of the model particle position. Thus, model particles that are close to the axis represent a smaller number of real particles than distant ones. This approach allows one to specify a uniform distribution of model particles over the grid cells.

2.2   Focusing the Beams

In the model, we reproduce the focusing of the beams as close as possible to the observed one in the experiments performed at the BINP SB RAS. The beams are focused from a distance of 10 cm into a spot of 1 mm. In this case, the velocity and density distribution functions of the beam particles at the focus are Gaussian. The dispersion of these distributions is determined by the distance and focusing angle used in the experiment. To accurately reproduce this distribution and avoid unnecessary errors in 2D3V axially symmetric geometry, we focus the beam according to the following algorithm:

1. Assign to the beam particles the required distribution in the focusing region in 3D Cartesian geometry.
2. Compute the intersection of the region boundary and the trajectory of the backward motion of the beam particle per the present velocities and coordinates.
3. Transform the coordinates and velocities of the particles from 3D Cartesian to 2D3V axially symmetric geometry.
4. Place the particles of the beam at the distribution points found and start each step from there with the obtained velocities.

We should note that the approach to changing the concentration of real particles in a model particle is not suitable for focusing beams. Particles with a higher concentration, moving towards the axis, create significant jumps in density which lead to numerical errors. Therefore, all the particles of the beam represent the same number of real particles.

2.3   Boundary Conditions

The open boundaries are the main feature of the simulated problem. It makes it possible to implement continuous injection of beams into the plasma. We use the open boundary conditions described in detail in [2,3]. The longitudinal electric field (transverse to the boundary) is set as continuous at the boundaries $z = 0$ and $z = L_z$. To implement it, the buffer cells are placed beyond the plasma boundary, left and right. All outgoing particles are removed from the computational domain, but at each time step, we clone the distributions of particles from the boundary plasma cells to the buffer cells outside the domain boundary. Thus, charged particles in the buffer cells move in the same field as the boundary particles in the plasma. At the top and bottom of the computational domain, we set absorbing boundary conditions for electromagnetic waves. The code implements two types of absorbing conditions: PML [6] and simple absorbing layer [4].

3   Software Implementation and Code Structure

Let us consider in detail the structure of the code. First of all, we will emphasize the object-oriented structure and composition of the main elements, and then consider the implementation of the parallel algorithm. The code is based on the ideas described in [8]. The main objects used in the model are particles and a simulation space with a computational grid superimposed on it. Accordingly, it is logical to distinguish them as two main base classes.

3.1 Simulation Space

The class World contains information about the computational domain and the main parameters of the system. This class contains a special method, split, which is responsible for the domain decomposition and the topology of the distributed memory. After the decomposition, each process receives information about its position in the topology and new boundary conditions describing the communication between subdomains. This approach makes it possible to manage the topology and load balance in a flexible manner. There are several approaches to distributing the computational load. The most universal approach uses the balance between the cells and the particles contained in them [1]. In this task, we consider, however, the computational load is approximately uniform, so we will focus on the simplest linear decomposition along the Z direction. Such a decomposition usually has two levels. At the first level, the domain is decomposed into subdomains along the selected direction. A group of processors is assigned to each subdomain. Each group has information about electromagnetic fields and particles that have got into the subdomain. At each step, both the particles that move between the subdomains and the boundary grid cells, which contain information about the boundary current density and electromagnetic fields, should be exchanged between the groups of processors. The exchange occurs only between neighboring groups, so it occurs synchronously, which makes it possible to scale this approach to a very large number of groups. At the second level, we divide all the subdomain particles between the processors of the group. In this case, it is necessary to exchange information within the group about the current density on the entire computational grid of the subdomain. In this case, the exchange is made according to the all-with-all scheme and is scaled as a binary tree within the framework of the function MPI_AllReduce.

Figure 2 shows the decomposition and communication diagram. It is necessary to exchange particles and boundary values of fields between groups. The computational grid is larger by several cells than a subdomain because of the selection of overlapping regions, which is sent. Certainly, the particle has a spatial size, and if it is in the boundary cell, it affects the current density in the nodes located outside the boundary. The advantage of the chosen scheme consists in its high theoretical scalability since communication is made in parallel. The grid for electromagnetic fields is stored in the World class as arrays. This allows one to automatically perform subdivision and assign each group its own computational grid.

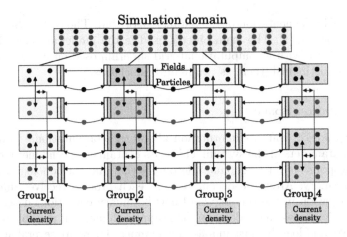

Fig. 2. Decomposition and communication scheme.

We would like to draw special attention to the additional class `EM_Solver`, which is directly related to the modeling space and the computational grid. This is the class of solvers for Maxwell's equations. It includes the FDTD scheme and special border processing, either a PML or a simple absorbing layer. Solvers are not tied to a parallel algorithm, all communication is taken over by the `World` class; therefore, `EM_Solver` contains a reference to this class and uses its methods for communication. It is enough to specify which data need to be received from neighboring processors in the form of boundary conditions, after which the `World` methods automatically determine the transfer map based on the topology. Of course, more work is assigned to the groups that must handle the boundaries of the modeling domain, but this is not significant when compared with the total amount of computations.

The `class ParticlesArray` is a container for the array of particles-objects of a given type, the parameters of this type of particles, the solvers of motion equations, functions for computing the main characteristics of the particles (such as density and energy), and functions for adding and removing particles. Also, the class can store various space-dependent quantities as density or total charge in a cell. To modify spatially dependent data, the `ParticlesArray` class stores a reference to `class World` and, for these data, it calls the functions of this class, in which the communication topology is enclosed. Thus, the particle class is also not tied to the parallel algorithm. In the main program, we use an array of pointers to the base `class Particle`, for each element of which we compute the movement of particles and their main characteristics. This makes it easier to define inherited classes with their own methods, which can be type-specific. Thus, we can easily add the necessary properties of a type, such as a concentration that depends on the coordinate or the need to use a buffer to maintain the density at the boundary.

The current density can be calculated by several methods that make it possible to satisfy the charge conservation equation and avoid the solution of Eqs. 13–14. We based Luthien on the scheme given in [11] because it was important for us not only to keep the code independent from the choice of the kernel form factor but also to have a straightforward performance algorithm. The main share of the computational load corresponds to the interpolation of the electromagnetic field at the position of the particle and the computation of the current at grid nodes. This procedure can be simplified by vectorization over several nodes depending on the particle kernel form. In the case of a simple PIC kernel of the first order, we have three nodes. For kernels of the third and fourth orders, we have five and seven nodes in each direction, respectively. For this reason, the method suggested in [11] allows vectorizing the computations for a given number of nodes (along one direction, the data are linearly stored in the memory). The use of local arrays can also improve the vectorization of [22]. We should also note that, depending on the used particle shapes, we are forced to increase the number of overlapping cells when decomposing the domain. This is because the particle affects the current density in a larger number of nodes. This increases the number of exchanges between groups during the decomposition, so this fact should be taken into account when testing the code performance.

Now we proceed to the performance test.

3.2 Performance of the Code

Let us consider a typical simulation. The task parameters are as follows:

– Number of cells: $N_z = 6400$, $N_r = 2000$. Grid step: $h_r = h_z = 0.02\,c/\omega_p$. Time step: $\tau = 0.01\,\omega_p^{-1}$ ($\omega_p = \sqrt{4\pi n_0 e^2/m_e}$ is the plasma frequency). Number of time steps: 10^5.
– Total number of particles: $10^9 - 10^{10}$ (depending on the type of simulation).
– Plasma density: $n_0 = 5 \cdot 10^{15}$ cm^{-3}.
– The beams are injected from a distance of 10 cm. Beam velocity: $v_b = 0.979c$.
– Left beam density: $n_b = 0.02 n_0$, focal spot size: 0.5 mm.
– Right beam density is $n_b = 0.01 n_0$, focal spot size: 1 mm.

Figure 3 shows the particle density and the z-component of the electric field to demonstrate the electromagnetic emission at different moments.

Figure 4 portrays a two-dimensional histogram of the distribution of the number of all model particles (electrons and beam particles) over the cells. As we

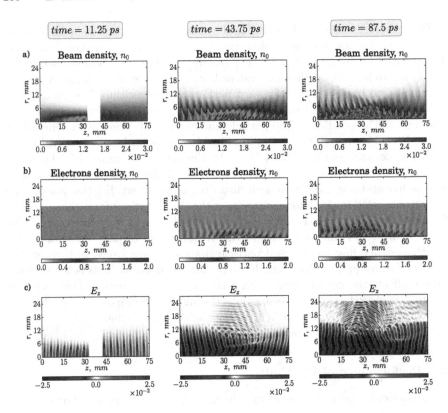

Fig. 3. Simulation results.

can see, the axial symmetry of the system implies that the pattern of the distribution density of the particles and the distribution of the particles over the cells are significantly different. However, the distribution along the z direction after the beams finally arrive is relatively uniform, which makes it possible to use a straightforward linear decomposition.

Let us consider the operation timing distribution of the main functions (see Fig. 5) We can see that most time is spent, as expected, on the movement of the particles. We can efficiently reduce this time during the decomposition into groups along the z axis by simply increasing the number of processors at the second level of decomposition (i.e., increasing the number of processors in a group without changing the number of groups). Let us examine the scalability of the code. Figure 6 shows the speedup when the domain is decomposed into 64 subdomains. The computations were carried out on NKS-1P Broadwell processors. The node is equipped with two CPU Intel Xeon E5-2697A v4 (2.6 GHz, 16 cores) and 128 GB of RAM. As Fig. 6 shows, the acceleration is close to ideal for up to 16 nodes in the case of particle shapes of the second and fourth orders. Note that we actually increased only the number of processors in the group without changing the division of the domain into subdomains. As we increase the number

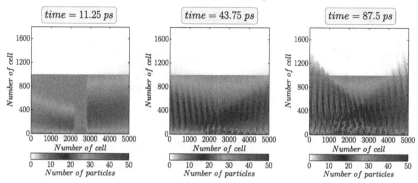

Fig. 4. Number of model particles

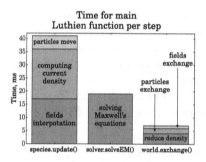

Fig. 5. Time for main functions

Fig. 6. Acceleration efficiency

of subdomains during the decomposition, we will quickly encounter limitations, namely, load imbalance due to different numbers of particles in subdomains and an increase in the share of exchanges (we reduce the grid size and leave the number of exchanges approximately the same).

We determined the efficiency of further scaling by estimating the communication time between groups and within a group. To calculate the communication time within a group, we considered a partition into 32 subdomains and then increase the number of processors within the group. To calculate the communication time between groups, we also considered a partition into 32 subdomains as the basic version, after which we increased the number of subdomains while keeping the number of processors within the group constant. Thus, we used one node (32 cores) for the initial computations in both cases. The results are shown in Fig. 7.

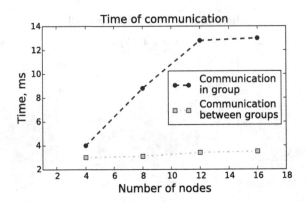

Fig. 7. Time of communications

We can see that, as expected, an increase in the number of processors in a group does not lead to a significant slowdown, since all-to-all communication occurs through a binary tree. If the number of groups increases, then the time of communication between them also increases but by no more than a few percent. Thus, the code shows fairly good scalability results.

We also tested the performance of the code on individual nodes. We considered four types of nodes based on processors with or without avx-512 support:

- Node 1: two Intel Xeon E5-2697A v4 (2.6 GHz, 16 cores);
- Node 2: Intel Xeon Phi 7290 KNL (1.5 GHz, 72 cores);
- Node 3: two Intel Xeon Platinum 8268 (2.9 GHz, 24 cores, avx512);
- Node 4: two 12-core 2.7 (3.8) GHz IBM POWER9 processors.

The performance of the algorithm is calculated as the number of full steps, including particle motion, processing of boundary conditions, computation of current density, and computation of electromagnetic fields. For each node, the performance is determined as the average of four identical computations with 1000 steps each. The average number of particles in the calculation was $6 \cdot 10^7$. Table 1 shows the performance in time-steps/s for different nodes.

Table 1. The performance in time-steps/s for different nodes

Intel Xeon node (peak performance 1331.2 Gflop/s)	Intel Xeon Phi node (peak performance 3456 Gflop/s)	Intel Platinum node (peak performance 4454.4 Gflop/s)	IBM Power9 node (peak performance 1037 Gflop/s)
2.2	3.8	6.1	1.64

As we can see, the performance on modern Xeon Platinum nodes is the highest thanks to the high clock speed and avx-512 instructions. It allows us to process about $3.66 \cdot 10^8$ particles per second.

4   Conclusions

In the paper, we considered a 2D3V axially symmetric code Luthien for simulating the generation of electromagnetic radiation in the interaction of focused electron beams with a plasma. Luthien can be used for real-scale modeling of the considered task with up to 10^{10} model particles in the simulation. The article also offers a computation example with beams having different densities and focal spot sizes.

We tested the parallel two-level decomposition algorithm on the supercomputer of the Shared Computing Center SSCC ICM&MG SB RAS, using sixteen 32-core nodes equipped with Broadwell Intel Xeon E5-2697A v4 processors. The code showed close to linear scalability. In the article, we also described the performance of the code on Intel Xeon Phi 7290 KNL and Intel Xeon Platinum 8268 processors with avx-512 technology. The test showed that vectorization of computations gives a significant increase in performance for the movement of model particles with a fourth-order form factor. The overall performance of the code, despite the difficulties of using an axially symmetric geometry, was at a fairly high level. This was achieved through an object-oriented structure, by inheriting the unique properties of the particle type from the base class and applying an individual concentration for the background plasma particles. The basic algorithms for particle motion, current density computation, and electromagnetic field dynamics were obtained from the basic algorithms for Cartesian geometry by adding appropriate changes to the derivatives in the radial direction.

Luthien is successfully used to find the optimal regimes for the generation of electromagnetic radiation in plasma with counter streaming relativistic electron beams.

Acknowledgements. The work was supported by the Russian Science Foundation (project 19-71-00054). We gratefully acknowledge the support given by the Siberian Supercomputer Center, the Irkutsk Supercomputing Center, and the Novosibirsk State University Computer Center, which provided their supercomputer facilities for our research.

References

1. Andrianov, A.N., Efimkin, K.N.: Approach to parallel implementation of the particles in cell method. Keldysh Institute Preprints (009), 20 (2009)
2. Annenkov, V.V., Berendeev, E.A., Timofeev, I.V., et al.: High-power terahertz emission from a plasma penetrated by counterstreaming different-size electron beams. Phys. Plasmas (11), 113,110. https://doi.org/10.1063/1.5048245
3. Annenkov, V.V., Timofeev, I.V., Volchok, E.P.: Simulations of electromagnetic emissions produced in a thin plasma by a continuously injected electron beam. Phys. Plasmas (5), 053,101. https://doi.org/10.1063/1.4948425
4. Berendeev, E., Dudnikova, G., Efimova, A., et al.: A simple absorbing layer for EM-radiation from a beam-plasma interaction system. Math. Methods Appl. Sci. (18), 9276–9282. https://doi.org/10.1002/mma.5253

5. Berendeev, E.A., Dimov, G.I., Dudnikova, G.I., et al.: Mathematical and experimental simulation of a cylindrical plasma target trap with inverse magnetic mirrors. J. Plasma Phys. (5), 495810,512. https://doi.org/10.1017/S0022377815000896

6. Berenger, J.P.: A perfectly matched layer for the absorption of electromagnetic waves. J. Comput. Phys. (2), 185–200. https://doi.org/10.1006/jcph.1994.1159

7. Boris, J.P.: Relativistic plasma simulation-optimization of a hybrid code. In: Proceeding of Fourth Conference on Numerical Simulations of Plasmas (1970)

8. Brieda, L.: Plasma Simulations by Example. CRC Press, Boca Raton (2019)

9. Davidson, A., Tableman, A., An, W., et al.: Implementation of a hybrid particle code with a PIC description in RZ and a gridless description in ϕ into OSIRIS. J. Comput. Phys. 1063–1077. https://doi.org/10.1016/j.jcp.2014.10.064

10. Derouillat, J., Beck, A., Pérez, F., et al.: SMILEI: a collaborative, open-source, multi-purpose particle-in-cell code for plasma simulation. Comput. Phys. Commun. 351–373. https://doi.org/10.1016/j.cpc.2017.09.024

11. Esirkepov, T.: Exact charge conservation scheme for Particle-in-Cell simulation with an arbitrary form-factor. Comput. Phys. Commun. (2), 144–153. https://doi.org/10.1016/S0010-4655(00)00228-9

12. Grigoryev, Y.N., Vshivkov, V.A., et al.: Numerical "Particle-in-Cell" Methods. DE GRUYTER, Berlin, Boston. https://doi.org/10.1515/9783110916706

13. Lehe, R., Kirchen, M., Andriyash, I.A., et al.: A spectral, quasi-cylindrical and dispersion-free Particle-In-Cell algorithm. Comput. Phys. Commun. 66–82. https://doi.org/10.1016/j.cpc.2016.02.007

14. Lu, Y., Kilian, P., Guo, F., et al.: Time-step dependent force interpolation scheme for suppressing numerical Cherenkov instability in relativistic particle-in-cell simulations. J. Comput. Phys. 109388. https://doi.org/10.1016/j.jcp.2020.109388

15. Shalaby, M., Broderick, A.E., Chang, P., et al.: SHARP: a spatially higher-order, relativistic particle-in-cell code. Astrophys. J. (1), 52. https://doi.org/10.3847/1538-4357/aa6d13

16. Starostenko, D.A., Logachev, P.V., Akimov, A.V., et al.: Results of operating LIA-2 in radiograph mode. Phys. Particles Nuclei Lett. (5), 660–664. https://doi.org/10.1134/S1547477114050264

17. Surmin, I., Bastrakov, S., Efimenko, E., et al.: Particle-in-cell laser-plasma simulation on Xeon Phi coprocessors. Comput. Phys. Commun. 204–210. https://doi.org/10.1016/j.cpc.2016.02.004

18. Taflove, A., Hagness, S.C., Piket-May, M.: Computational electromagnetics: the finite-difference time-domain method. In: The Electrical Engineering Handbook, pp. 629–670. Elsevier. https://doi.org/10.1016/B978-012170960-0/50046-3

19. Tarakanov, V.: User's manual for code KARAT. Berkley Research, Springfield, VA (1992)

20. Timofeev, I.V., Berendeev, E.A., Dudnikova, G.I.: Simulations of a beam-driven plasma antenna in the regime of plasma transparency. Phys. Plasmas (9), 093,114. https://doi.org/10.1063/1.4995323

21. Vay, J.L., Almgren, A., Bell, J., et al.: Warp-X: a new exascale computing platform for beamplasma simulations. Nucl. Instrum. Meth. Phys. Res. Sect. A Accel. Spectr. Detectors Assoc. Equip. 476–479. https://doi.org/10.1016/j.nima.2018.01.035

22. Vincenti, H., Lobet, M., Lehe, R., et al.: An efficient and portable SIMD algorithm for charge/current deposition in Particle-In-Cell codes. Comput. Phys. Commun. 145–154. https://doi.org/10.1016/j.cpc.2016.08.023

Simulation of Heat and Mass Transfer in Open Geothermal Systems: A Parallel Implementation

Elena N. Akimova[1,2(✉)] , Mikhail Yu. Filimonov[1,2] ,
Vladimir E. Misilov[1,2] , Nataliia A. Vaganova[1,2] ,
and Arkadiy D. Kuznetsov[2]

[1] Krasovskii Institute of Mathematics and Mechanics, Ural Branch of RAS,
16 S. Kovalevskaya Street, Ekaterinburg, Russia
{aen,fmy,vna}@imm.uran.ru, v.e.misilov@urfu.ru
[2] Ural Federal University, 19 Mira Street, Ekaterinburg, Russia

Abstract. The paper is devoted to the study of algorithms for the simulation of heat and mass transfer in open geothermal systems. The systems considered in the paper consist of injection wells and production wells. The production wells extract hot water, whereas the injection wells return cold water to the aquifer. The parameters to be optimized are the pressure created by the pumps in both the production and the injection wells and the distance between them. By choosing the values of these parameters, we aim to ensure the longest possible period of effective operation of the geothermal system. We describe an efficient parallel implementation of the algorithm for graphics processors using CUDA technology and test its performance in a series of numerical experiments. Afterward, we compare the GPU implementation with the serial and OpenMP implementations for multicore CPUs. The experiments generated a 15-fold speedup compared to the serial program.

Keywords: Heat and mass transfer · Simulation · Numerical methods · Parallel computing · CUDA

1 Introduction

Geothermal energy is regarded as a promising kind of renewable energy [1–4]. Unlike solar and wind energy, which depend on weather and time, the heat from the Earth can be used constantly. A geothermal system is a heating system that utilizes the earth as the heat source. The methods of use of geothermal energy depend on the temperature of the water in the reservoir. A significant

The work was supported by the Russian Foundation for Basic Research (project No. 19-07-00435).

L. Sokolinsky and M. Zymbler (Eds.): PCT 2021, CCIS 1437, pp. 243–254, 2021.
https://doi.org/10.1007/978-3-030-81691-9_17

part of the territory of Russia is characterized by the presence of natural low- and medium-temperature (50 to 150 °C) aquifers lying at depths ranging from 200 to 3000 m.

In this paper, we consider an open geothermal system consisting of injection wells and production wells. The hot water from the production well is used and cools down; the injection well returns the cold water to the aquifer [5]. The cold water is filtered through porous soil toward the inflow of hot water of the production well. We need to describe the propagation of the cold front in the productive layer of water. Note that the description depends on different thermal parameters of the soil, and initial data are defined by the filtration rate in the productive layer. Moreover, it is necessary to determine the time of the system's effective operation. Usually, the operation of a geothermal system is stopped when the front of cold water reaches the inflow of the production well. In the countryside around Paris, for instance, there are 37 pairs (doublets) of wells that, owing to geothermal sources, have supplied several companies and more than 0.5 million people with heat and hot water for more than 30 years [6].

A model of an open geothermal system with multiple wells is considered in [7]. The system consists two types of wells: several production wells with hot water and several injection wells which return the cold water to the productive layer (aquifer). The model takes into account the thermophysical characteristics of the geothermal reservoir and the most significant technical parameters of the wells. These parameters determine the cost-effective operation of the geothermal system. It is believed that after 30 years of operation of the geothermal system, the temperature in the production well would not be less than the specified temperature. At the same time, the output of the production well should be sufficient to cover the specified economic needs. The fulfillment of these requirements obviously depends on the distance between the wells in the productive layer and the pressure difference created by the pumps of the production and injection wells. To determine these parameters, a series of numerical calculations is required to compute the water temperature in the production well.

The main problem is to determine the distance between the wells in the productive layer and the pressure difference for a two-well system [8]. Substantial computational resources are required to solve this problem in a complex three-dimensional domain. The computation time for a single task can often exceed several hours of machine time on a supercomputer.

A parallel algorithm is suggested in [9] for the simulation of an open geothermal system. Its implementation for multicore processors using OpenMP technology is considered therein.

In the current paper, we describe a parallel algorithm for NVIDIA graphics processors using CUDA technology and compare it against other implementations in terms of computation time.

The paper is structured as follows. Section 2 describes the mathematical model and the equations for the simulation problem. Section 3 presents the setup of the test problem and the results of the simulation. In Sect. 4, we outline the parallel algorithm for GPUs and compare the computation times for the parallel

programs. Section 5 concludes the study and offers a summary of plans related
to the topics considered in the paper.

2   Problem Statement and Mathematical Model

For the sake of simplicity, we consider a layer with water filtrating from the
injection well to the production one [8]. Let $T(t, x, y, z)$ be the temperature in
the aquifer. The aquifer is a complex system and, as a rule, includes underground
lakes and rivers, as well as different porous and waterproof layers, as shown in
Fig. 1. The thermal fluxes Γ_1 and Γ_2 provide heat to the geothermal reservoir.

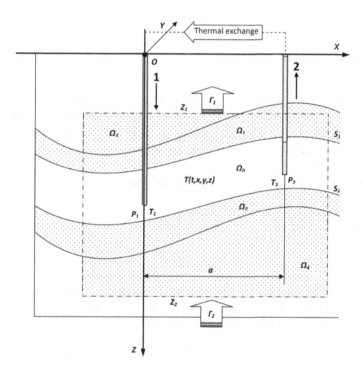

Fig. 1. An aquifer with two wells: (1) injection well, (2) production well

For the simulation of underground flows into the productive layer, we rely on
Darcy's law and the law of conservation of mass (the continuity equation) [10].
Consider the mathematical model [8] of an open geothermal loop system consisting of two fully penetrating wells: the injection well Ω_1, with water temperature
$T_1(t)$, and the production well Ω_2, with water temperature $T_2(t)$ $(T_1 < T_2(0))$
(see Fig. 2). For a system with several wells, the considerations are roughly the
same [7].

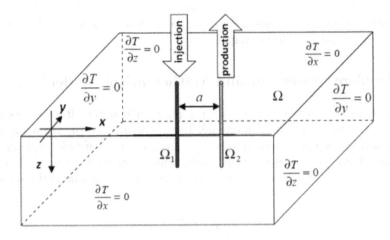

Fig. 2. A model of a geothermal open loop showing the boundary conditions

In the general case, the fluid motion in a geothermal aquifer Ω is described by the Navier–Stokes equations. In equations of underground hydrodynamics describing the motion of water in porous soil [10], it is assumed that the fluid velocity components $V = (u, v, w)$ and the derivatives with respect to the coordinates x, y, and z are small.

The thermal exchange is described by the equation

$$\frac{\partial T}{\partial t} + b\left(\frac{\partial T}{\partial x}u + \frac{\partial T}{\partial y}v + \frac{\partial T}{\partial z}w\right) = \lambda_0 \Delta T,$$

$$b = \sigma \rho c_f / (\rho_0 c_0 (1 - \sigma) + \rho c_f \sigma), \quad \lambda_0 = \kappa_0 / (\rho_0 c_0 (1 - \sigma) + \rho c_f \sigma),$$

(1)

where ρ_0 and ρ_f are the densities of the aquifer soil and the water, c_0 and c_f are the specific heats of the aquifer soil and the water, κ_0 stands for the thermal conductivity coefficient of the soil, and σ is the porosity.

The following are the equations of water filtration:

$$\begin{cases} \dfrac{\partial u}{\partial t} = -\dfrac{1}{\rho}\dfrac{\partial P}{\partial x} - \dfrac{g\sigma u}{k}, \\[2mm] \dfrac{\partial v}{\partial t} = -\dfrac{1}{\rho}\dfrac{\partial P}{\partial y} - \dfrac{g\sigma v}{k}, \\[2mm] \dfrac{\partial w}{\partial t} = -\dfrac{1}{\rho}\dfrac{\partial P}{\partial z} - \dfrac{g\sigma w}{k} - g. \end{cases}$$

(2)

We should also take into account the continuity equation:

$$\frac{\partial u}{\partial x} + \frac{\partial v}{\partial y} + \frac{\partial w}{\partial z} = 0.$$

In (2), we assume that the filtration coefficient k and the porosity σ in the aquifer are constant (we can use their average values), g is the standard gravity, and $P = P(t, x, y, z)$ is the pressure.

We also assume that the fluid in the productive layer is initially at rest, i.e.,

$$u(0, x, y, z) = v(0, x, y, z) = w(0, x, y, z) = 0. \tag{3}$$

System (2) is a consequence of the Navier–Stokes equations if the quadratic terms are neglected in view of their smallness. For a discussion and the justification of such linearization, refer to [10].

We assume that the aquifer Ω (see Fig. 1) is located between two impermeable layers bounded by the parallel planes $z = Z_1$ and $z = Z_2$. We set the boundary conditions for the pressure on these surfaces as

$$\left.\frac{\partial P}{\partial z}\right|_{z=Z_j} = 0, \quad j = 1, 2. \tag{4}$$

Similar conditions are given on the lateral surfaces of the computational domain:

$$\left.\frac{\partial P}{\partial x}\right|_{x=X_j} = \left.\frac{\partial P}{\partial y}\right|_{y=Y_j} = 0, \quad j = 1, 2. \tag{5}$$

By γ_1 and γ_2 ($Z_1 < z < Z_2$), we denote, respectively, the cylindrical surface of the injection well (whose radius is r_1) and that of the production well (whose radius is r_2). On these surfaces, we set the pressures as follows:

$$P(t, x, y, z)|_{\gamma_1} = P_1 - \rho g z, \quad P(t, x, y, z)|_{\gamma_2} = P_2 - \rho g z. \tag{6}$$

In Ω (excluding Ω_1 and Ω_2), the hydrostatic pressure and the pressure of the liquid column at a depth z are regarded as the initial pressure $P(0, x, y, z)$:

$$P(0, x, y, z) = -\rho g z. \tag{7}$$

To determine the pressure in Ω, we rely on the piezoconductivity equation [11,12]:

$$\frac{\partial P}{\partial t} = \omega \Delta P. \tag{8}$$

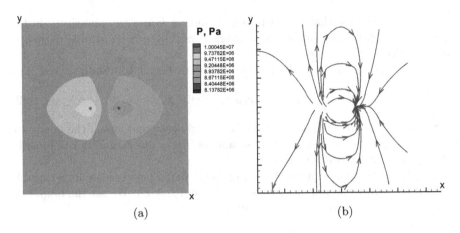

Fig. 3. (a) pressure, (b) streamlines

The boundary and initial conditions (4)–(7) for Eq. (8) are given. Equation (8) is solved together with system (2) and the initial condition (3). The pressure distribution in the aquifer Ω is obtained as a solution of the problem given by (2)–(8) and is used to determine the velocity field (u, v, w).

In simulations described by Eqs. (1) and (2), it is necessary to estimate the distance a between the injection well and the production well as a function of the production well temperature that is appropriate for the considered system. The velocity vector of the filtered water in the aquifer is determined after finding the pressure field.

3   Simulation Results

According to Samarsky's ideas expressed in [13], we use a finite-difference method with splitting along the spatial axes in a three-dimensional domain to solve the problem (1)–(6). We construct an orthogonal grid, uniform or condensing near the ground surface or the surfaces Ω_1 and Ω_2. The original equations for each spatial direction are approximated by an implicit central-difference scheme. Additionally, we use the three-point sweep method to solve the system of linear algebraic equations.

We assume that the computational domain is a parallelepiped containing the injection and production wells. The soil thermophysical parameters correspond to those of Khankala geothermal fields in the North Caucasus. These parameters are given in Table 1.

Table 1. Thermophysical parameters

Parameters	Medium (sandstone)	Fluid (water)
Thermal conductivity κ_0 [W/(m · K)]	2.0	—
Density ρ [kg/m^3]	—	1000
Specific heat capacity c_f [J/(K·kg)]	—	$4.18 \cdot 10^3$
Filtration speed k [m/s]	$1.7 \cdot 10^{-5}$	—
Porosity σ	0.241	—

The initial temperature of the water in the aquifer at a depth from 950 to 1000 m is 95 °C, the temperature of the injected water is 55 °C. In Fig. 3, we see a typical pressure distribution (a) and the distribution of streamlines (b) in the aquifer. The transition of the filtered water allows computing the temperature in the aquifer and determining how the cold injection well influences the production one.

The initial water temperature in the productive layer is 95 °C, the injection water temperature is 55 °C. The simulation was performed for a period of 30 years with a step equal to 1 day.

The numerical simulation allowed us to find the optimal distance between the wells: $a = 600$ m.

Table 2 contains data on the water temperature in the production well relative to the pressure difference between the wells. Figure 4 shows the temperature distribution in the (x, y)-plane at a depth $z = 975$ m, after 3, 5, 10, and 15 years of exploitation of the system.

4   Parallel Implementation for Graphics Processors

Numerical simulations focused on the long-term forecasting of thermal effects in technical systems require a considerable amount of computation time. One way to speed up the simulations is through the involvement of parallel computations. In previous research, the authors developed a parallel algorithm for the simulation of open geothermal loops and implemented it for multicore CPUs using OpenMP technology [9]. The parallel implementation reduced the computation time by 4.5 times compared to the serial program on a 6-core CPU.

In the current paper, we implement the parallel algorithm for the solution of the problem given by (1)–(6) on NVIDIA graphics processors using CUDA technology.

Table 2. The temperature in the production well

Year	Pressure difference between the wells [kPa]									
	100.00	200.00	300.00	400.00	500.00	600.00	700.00	800.00	900.00	1000.00
0	95.00	95.00	95.00	95.00	95.00	95.00	95.00	95.00	95.00	95.00
4	95.00	95.00	95.00	95.00	95.00	95.00	95.00	95.00	95.00	95.00
5	95.00	95.00	95.00	95.00	95.00	95.00	95.00	95.00	95.00	94.98
6	95.00	95.00	95.00	95.00	95.00	95.00	95.00	94.99	94.94	94.78
7	95.00	95.00	95.00	95.00	95.00	95.00	94.98	94.90	94.63	93.96
8	95.00	95.00	95.00	95.00	95.00	94.99	94.90	94.56	93.67	92.03
9	95.00	95.00	95.00	95.00	94.99	94.94	94.62	93.66	91.75	88.96
10	95.00	95.00	95.00	95.00	94.98	94.77	93.94	92.00	88.94	85.30
11	95.00	95.00	95.00	95.00	94.92	94.38	92.71	89.61	85.65	81.73
12	95.00	95.00	95.00	94.99	94.77	93.64	90.87	86.76	82.40	78.68
13	95.00	95.00	95.00	94.96	94.46	92.47	88.56	83.80	79.52	76.27
14	95.00	95.00	95.00	94.89	93.92	90.86	86.00	81.05	77.15	74.43
15	95.00	95.00	94.99	94.76	93.09	88.90	83.44	78.67	75.27	73.04
16	95.00	95.00	94.98	94.52	91.96	86.74	81.05	76.69	73.82	71.99
17	95.00	95.00	94.96	94.15	90.54	84.53	78.95	75.10	72.69	71.18
18	95.00	95.00	94.93	93.60	88.89	82.40	77.16	73.82	71.81	70.56
19	95.00	95.00	94.86	92.87	87.10	80.44	75.66	72.81	71.11	70.07
20	95.00	95.00	94.75	91.93	85.27	78.69	74.44	71.99	70.56	69.68
21	95.00	95.00	94.58	90.82	83.46	77.18	73.43	71.33	70.12	69.37
22	95.00	94.99	94.33	89.56	81.75	75.89	72.60	70.80	69.76	69.12
23	95.00	94.99	94.00	88.19	80.17	74.79	71.92	70.36	69.46	68.92
24	95.00	94.98	93.57	86.75	78.74	73.87	71.35	70.00	69.22	68.75
25	95.00	94.97	93.03	85.30	77.46	73.08	70.88	69.70	69.02	68.61
26	95.00	94.95	92.39	83.86	76.35	72.42	70.48	69.44	68.85	68.49
27	95.00	94.91	91.64	82.47	75.37	71.86	70.14	69.23	68.71	68.39
28	95.00	94.87	90.80	81.16	74.52	71.38	69.86	69.05	68.59	68.30
29	95.00	94.81	89.87	79.94	73.78	70.97	69.61	68.89	68.48	68.23
30	95.00	94.72	88.88	78.82	73.14	70.62	69.40	68.76	68.39	68.17
31	95.00	94.61	87.85	77.79	72.58	70.31	69.22	68.64	68.32	68.11

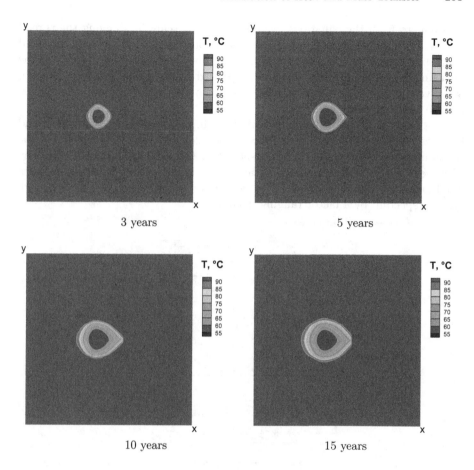

Fig. 4. The temperature in the aquifer for different years of exploitation, °C

The most expensive procedure is the computation of the temperature and pressure fields. Profiling results show that these two procedures take about 80% of the total computation time. Both procedures consist of three steps for forming and solving SLAEs and updating the fields in each spatial direction. The SLAEs for the one-dimensional scheme do not depend on each other. For example, when forming and solving the SLAEs along the X axis for each pair of YZ coordinates, we can solve each SLAE independently.

Thus, we split the computational algorithm into tasks, each consisting of forming an SLAE, solving it, and updating the field values for a single "scan line". This scheme of parallelization is shown in Fig. 5.

In the OpenMP implementation, we distributed the tasks among threads, and each thread performs its portion of tasks. This approach shows good performance for multicore CPUs, but unfortunately, such tasks are too complex for CUDA threads. For the GPU implementation, we need to further split the tasks.

First, to form the equations, we distribute the scan lines among the thread blocks and individual points of a scan line among the CUDA threads. To avoid warp divergence, we use separate kernels for the inner and outer points of the scan line. The computed coefficients are stored in the global memory. Second, we solve the systems, allocating each system to one CUDA thread. Finally, we update the field values.

The main problem of the numerical algorithm is the memory bandwidth and latency. The algorithm uses a complex pattern for accessing the elements of the three-dimensional arrays in the three spatial directions. This limits the efficiency of caches. In our implementation, we avoid this bottleneck by splitting the data into blocks and manually transferring them to the shared memory. This approach yields a speedup by a factor ranging from 3 to 4.

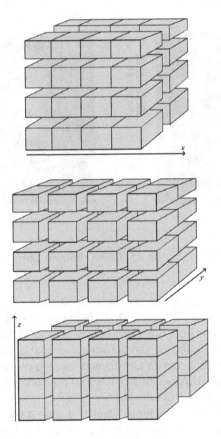

Fig. 5. The scheme of parallelization

The performance of the parallel implementations was tested on two problems with grids sizes of $237 \times 157 \times 21$ (781 389 nodes) and $539 \times 297 \times 41$ (6 563 403 nodes). The time interval is 30 years; the time step is 1 day.

Tables 3 and 4 contain the computation time T of the test problems on an 8-core Intel i7-10700k CPU and an NVIDIA GeForce RTX 3080 GPU. The tables also show the speedup coefficients $(S_m = T_{\text{serial}}/T)$ for comparing the parallel programs with the serial one.

Table 3. Computation time for the test problem on a grid of $237 \times 157 \times 21$ nodes

Algorithm and Processor	Computation time, minutes	Speedup
Serial, i7-10700k	19.45	1
OpenMP, 8 threads, i7-10700k	4.4	4.4
OpenMP, 16 threads, i7-10700k	4.2	4.6
CUDA, GeForce RTX 3080	1.75	11

Table 4. Computation time for the test problem on a grid of $539 \times 297 \times 41$ nodes

Algorithm and Processor	Computation time, minutes	Speedup
Serial, i7-10700k	187	1
OpenMP, 8 threads, i7-10700k	47	4
OpenMP, 16 threads, i7-10700k	38.5	4.8
CUDA, GeForce RTX 3080	12.5	15

5 Conclusions

The suggested parallel algorithm allows carrying out simulations of temperature fields in an aquifer for several kinds of open geothermal loops consisting of two or more wells. The dynamics of changes in temperature provided by the hot water production well depends on several parameters. The main ones are the distance between the wells in the productive layer and the pressure difference in a system of two wells.

The computations enable the choice of the optimal parameters for open geothermal systems. In particular, they make it possible to determine the appropriate distance between the injection well and the production well depending on the operating conditions of the geothermal system.

The parallel implementation of the algorithm was developed for graphics processors using CUDA technology.

The test problem with a grid of size $539 \times 297 \times 41$ yielded a 3-fold speedup compared to the OpenMP implementation on an 8-core CPU and a 15-fold speedup compared to the serial program.

We plan to develop models and parallel algorithms for the simulation of geothermal cyclic systems consisting of multiple partially penetrating wells in a plane-parallel geothermal reservoir. The corresponding models will require the construction of new computational grids with large numbers of nodes. The models and parallel algorithms will take into account various spatial configurations of the wells and require a large number of numerical experiments.

Acknowledgements. The work was performed on the URAN supercomputer at the IMM UrB RAS.

References

1. Bertani, R.: World Geothermal Generation in 2007. Geo-Heat Centre Q. Bull. Oregon Inst. Technol. **28**(3), 8–19 (2007)
2. Alkhasov, A.B.: Geothermal Power Engineering: Problems, Resources, Technologies. Fizmatlit, Moscow (2008)
3. Alekseenko, S.V., Borodulin, V.Y., Gnatus, N.A., Nizovtsev, M.I., Smirnova, N.N.: Problems and outlooks for petrothermal power engineering (*review*). Thermophys. Aeromech. **23**(1), 1–16 (2016). https://doi.org/10.1134/S0869864316010017
4. Vieira, A., Alberdi-Pagola, M., Christodoulides, P., Javed, S., Loveridg, F., et al.: Characterisation of ground thermal and thermo-mechanical behaviour for shallow geothermal energy applications. Energies **10**(12), 2044 (2017). https://doi.org/10.3390/en10122044
5. Vaganova, N.A., Filimonov, M.Yu.: Refinement of model of an open geothermal system. In: AIP Conference Proceedings, vol. 1789 (2016). https://doi.org/10.1063/1.4968441
6. Le Brun, M., Hamm, V., Lopez, V., et al.: Hydraulic and thermal impact modelling at the scale of the geothermal heating Doubletin the Paris basin, France. In: Proceedings, Thirty-Sixth Workshop on Geothermal Reservoir Engineering; Stanford University, Stanford (2011)
7. Vaganova, N.A., Filimonov, M.Y.: Simulation of optimal operation of a multiple wells open geothermal system. J. Phys. Conf. Ser. **1128** (2018). https://doi.org/10.1088/1742-6596/1128/1/012139
8. Vaganova, N.A., Filimonov, M.Y.: Simulation and numerical investigation of temperature fields in an open geothermal system. In: Dimov, I., Faragó, I., Vulkov, L. (eds.) FDM 2014. LNCS, vol. 9045, pp. 393–399. Springer, Cham (2015). https://doi.org/10.1007/978-3-319-20239-6_44
9. Misilov, V.E., Vaganova, N.A., Filimonov, M.Yu.: Parallel algorithm for solving the problems of heat and mass transfer in the open geothermal system. In: AIP Conference Proceedings, vol. 2312 (2020). https://doi.org/10.1063/5.0035531
10. Polubarinova-Kochina, P.Ya.: Theory of Ground Water Movement. Princeton University Press, Princeton (1962)
11. Rubinstein, I., Rubinstein, L.: Partial Differential Equations in Classical Mathematical Physics. Cambridge University Press, Cambridge (1994)
12. Nikolaevskij, N.N.: Mechanics of Porous and Fractured Media. Series in Theoretical and Applied Mechanics, 8. World Scientific, Singapore (1990)
13. Samarsky, A.A., Vabishchevich, P.N.: Computational Heat Transfer. The Finite Difference Methodology, vol. 2. Wiley, New York (1995)
14. Akimova, E.N., Filimonov, M.Yu., Misilov, V.E., Vaganova, N.A.: Supercomputer modelling of thermal stabilization processes of permafrost soils. In: 18th International Conference on Geoinformatics: Theoretical and Applied Aspects, Kiev, Ukraine (2019). https://doi.org/10.3997/2214-4609.201902035

Supercomputer-Based Simulation of the Hydrodynamics of River Mouth Areas

Alexander I. Sukhinov[1], Alexander E. Chistyakov[1], Alla V. Nikitina[2,3],
Inna Yu. Kuznetsova[2], Asya M. Atayan[1], Elena A. Protsenko[4],
and Vladimir N. Litvinov[1,5(✉)]

[1] Don State Technical University, Rostov-on-Don, Russia
[2] Southern Federal University, Rostov-on-Don, Russia
[3] Supercomputers and Neurocomputers Research Center, Taganrog, Russia
[4] A.P. Chekhov University of Taganrog, Taganrog, Russia
[5] Azov-Black Sea Engineering Institute of Don State Agrarian University,
Zernograd, Russia

Abstract. The article is devoted to the development and numerical implementation of a 3D hydrodynamic mathematical model intended for computing the movement velocity of the aquatic environment in river mouth areas. The equations in the hydrodynamic model of a shallow reservoir are approximated using the balance method and taking into account the fullness of control areas. This approach makes it possible to take into account the complex geometry of the coastline and the bottom and significantly increase the accuracy of computations. The numerical methods and algorithms we have developed are the basis of the software package that we tested on a supercomputer cluster using MPI technology. The package can simulate hydrodynamic processes that take place in shallow-water bodies. It is designed for computing systems with distributed memory. To test the functionality of the software package, we use the mathematical model to compute the rise in the water level of a river and its course in the mouth area. The geometry of the computational area is given in the form of a depth map. The computations for a rectangular grid with $1000 \times 1000 \times 60$ nodes on 24 processors yield an acceleration by more than a factor of 15.

Keywords: Mathematical modeling · 3D models · Hydrodynamics · River mouth area · Splitting schemes for physical processes · Parallel algorithms

1 Introduction

There are large-scale engineering projects aimed at ensuring the safety of navigation. This requires the use of predictive modeling to plan shipping routes

The reported study was funded by Russian Foundation for Basic Research (project No. 19-07-00623).

L. Sokolinsky and M. Zymbler (Eds.): PCT 2021, CCIS 1437, pp. 255–269, 2021.
https://doi.org/10.1007/978-3-030-81691-9_18

taking into account the consequences of siltation and synthetic disasters. For example, in November 2007, a storm of catastrophic proportions in the Kerch Strait wrecked more than 20 ships. Oil spills caused the pollution of the coastline and bottom with oil products and other harmful substances. Later, from 2008 to 2011, compounds of petroleum products in the form of bitumen and resins were found along a portion of more than 200 km of the coastline of the Black Sea and the Sea of Azov. The coastal areas of the Sea of Azov were flooded due to a storm, and the water level rose by more than four meters on September 24–25, 2014. This caused significant damage to the regional economy. The shallowing of the Sea of Azov off Taganrog shoreline and the Don River coast in November 2019 was associated with low precipitations in the basins of rivers flowing into the Sea of Azov and strong winds driving water away from the coast. There has been an unfavorable movement of bottom sediments from the estuary areas of the Don River in the western direction for a long time. This has led to the displacement of species of the local flora and fauna from the eastern part of the Taganrog Bay, intense water bloom, and reproduction of nonbiting midges (family Chironomidae) over vast water areas.

The analysis of existing hydrophysics mathematical models shows that they focus on hydrodynamic models that do not take into account many factors, such as the complex coastline and bottom geometry, surge phenomena, friction on the bottom, wind stresses, turbulent exchange, Coriolis force, river flows, evaporation, and others [1,2]. Some of the currently developed 3D hydrophysics models are implemented in such software packages as MARS 3D, POM (Princeton Ocean Models), CHTDM (Climatic Hydro Termo Dynamic Model), and NEMO (Nucleus for European Modeling of the Ocean). Oceanological models have proven themselves well able for studying the hydrodynamics of reservoirs of 50 to 100 m in depth but cannot be used to compute current fields in shallow water if the reservoir depth is comparable to the length of surface waves. As a rule, a hydrostatic approximation is used in oceanological models, which neglects the specificity of shallow water bodies, namely the significant effect of the bottom topography on the wave motion, due to which turbulent exchange in the vertical direction occurs [3–5]. Oceanological models often use a sigma coordinate system, which does not correctly describe neither the acceleration of the vertical movement of the water flow for significant depth differences in shallow water nor the coastal area drainage and flooding processes during surges, something that is typical of shallow water bodies. Grids with variable levels of the sigma coordinate system partially solve this problem. To study the movement of microparticles in the hydrosphere, we can rely on mathematical models with uniform rectangular grids given their wider application. These models can lead to errors in the solution at the boundary of the computational domain. This disadvantage can be eliminated to a large extent by using the method of partial fullness of cells, which improves the accuracy in hydrophysics problems related to shallow water bodies [6]. The computation algorithm that takes into account the partial fullness of cells is free from the drawback associated with the representation of a stepped boundary region on a rectangular grid [7].

The paper describes a 3D hydrophysical model of coastal systems and river mouth areas that takes into account bottom friction, complex bottom and coastline topography, and nonlinear microturbulent exchange in the vertical direction. We describe an approach to this model that considers the fullness of the control areas. The model is the basis of a software package aimed to describe hydrodynamic processes occurring in river mouth areas.

2   The Problem Statement

The model for computation of the 3D velocity vector of the aquatic environment movement is based on the hydrodynamics mathematical model of shallow-water bodies [8,9] and consists of the following equations:

– equations of motion (Navier–Stokes):

$$u'_t + uu'_x + vu'_y + wu'_z = -\frac{1}{\rho}P'_x + \left(\mu u'_x\right)'_x + \left(\mu u'_y\right)'_y + \left(\nu u'_z\right)'_z$$
$$+ 2\Omega(v\sin\theta - w\cos\theta), \quad (1)$$

$$v'_t + uv'_x + vv'_y + wv'_z = -\frac{1}{\rho}P'_y + \left(\mu v'_x\right)'_x + \left(\mu v'_y\right)'_y + \left(\nu v'_z\right)'_z - 2\Omega u\sin\theta, \quad (2)$$

$$w'_t + uw'_x + vw'_y + ww'_z = -\frac{1}{\rho}P'_z + \left(\mu w'_x\right)'_x + \left(\mu w'_y\right)'_y + \left(\nu w'_z\right)'_z$$
$$+ 2\Omega u\cos\theta + g\left(\rho_0/\rho - 1\right); \quad (3)$$

– continuity equation in case of variable density:

$$\rho'_t + (\rho u)'_x + (\rho v)'_y + (\rho w)'_z = 0; \quad (4)$$

– heat transfer equation:

$$T'_t + uT'_x + vT'_y + wT'_z = \left(\mu T'_x\right)'_x + \left(\mu T'_y\right)'_y + \left(\nu T'_z\right)'_z + f_T; \quad (5)$$

– salt transfer equation:

$$S'_t + uS'_x + vS'_y + wS'_z = \left(\mu S'_x\right)'_x + \left(\mu S'_y\right)'_y + \left(\nu S'_z\right)'_z + f_S, \quad (6)$$

where $\mathbf{V} = \{u, v, w\}$ is the velocity vector of the water flow in the shallow-water body; P is the hydrodynamic pressure; ρ stands for the aquatic environment density; μ and ν denote turbulent exchange coefficients in the horizontal and vertical directions, respectively; $\mathbf{\Omega} = \Omega\left(\cos v \cdot \mathbf{j} + \sin v \cdot \mathbf{k}\right)$ is the angular velocity of the Earth's rotation; θ is the latitude of the place; g denotes the acceleration due to gravity; f_T and f_S stand for heat and salt sources, respectively; T is the water temperature, and S is the water salinity.

We conditionally decompose the total hydrodynamic pressure into two components, namely the pressure of the liquid column and the hydrodynamic part [9]:

$$P(x, y, z, t) = p(x, y, z, t) + \rho_0 g z, \tag{7}$$

where p is the hydrostatic pressure of the undisturbed liquid, and ρ_0 is the density of fresh water under normal conditions.

The equation of state for the density can be expressed as

$$\rho = \tilde{\rho} + \rho_0, \tag{8}$$

where ρ_0 is the density of fresh water under normal conditions, and $\tilde{\rho}$ is determined according to the equation recommended by UNESCO, namely

$$
\begin{aligned}
\tilde{\rho} = \tilde{\rho}_w &+ (8.24493 \cdot 10^{-1} - 4.0899 \cdot 10^{-3} T + 7.6438 \cdot 10^{-5} T^2 \\
&- 8.2467 \cdot 10^{-7} T^3 + 5.3875 \cdot 10^{-9} T^4) S + (-5.72466 \cdot 10^{-3} \\
&+ 1.0227 \cdot 10^{-4} T - 1.6546 \cdot 10^{-6} T^2) S^{3/2} + 4.8314 \cdot 10^{-4} S^2, \quad (9)
\end{aligned}
$$

where $\tilde{\rho}_w$ is the density of freshwater, given by the polynomial [9]

$$
\begin{aligned}
\tilde{\rho}_w = 999.842594 &+ 6.793952 \cdot 10^{-2} T - 9.095290 \cdot 10^{-3} T^2 \\
&+ 1.001685 \cdot 10^{-4} T^3 - 1.120083 \cdot 10^{-6} T^4 + 6.536332 \cdot 10^{-9} T^5. \quad (10)
\end{aligned}
$$

Equation 9 applies to values of salinity in the range from 0 to 42‰ and temperatures between -2 and $40\,^\circ\mathrm{C}$.

The boundary conditions for Eqs. (1)–(6) are as follows:

– entrance:

$$\mathbf{V} = \mathbf{V}_1, \ P'_{\mathbf{n}} = 0, \ T = T_1, \ S = S_1; \tag{11}$$

– bottom boundary:

$$
\begin{aligned}
&\rho_v \mu \left(\mathbf{V}_\tau\right)'_{\mathbf{n}} = -\tau, \ \mathbf{V}_{\mathbf{n}} = 0, \ P'_{\mathbf{n}} = 0, \\
&T'_{\mathbf{n}} = 0, \ S'_{\mathbf{n}} = 0, \ f_T = 0, \ f_S = 0;
\end{aligned} \tag{12}
$$

– lateral boundary:

$$
\begin{aligned}
&\left(\mathbf{V}_\tau\right)'_{\mathbf{n}} = 0, \ \mathbf{V}'_{\mathbf{n}} = 0, \ P'_{\mathbf{n}} = 0, \\
&T'_{\mathbf{n}} = 0, \ S'_{\mathbf{n}} = 0, \ f_T = 0, \ f_S = 0;
\end{aligned} \tag{13}
$$

– upper boundary:

$$
\begin{aligned}
&\rho_v \mu \left(\mathbf{V}_\tau\right)'_{\mathbf{n}} = -\tau, \ w = -\omega - P'_t / (\rho g), \ P'_{\mathbf{n}} = 0, \\
&T'_{\mathbf{n}} = 0, \ S'_{\mathbf{n}} = 0, \ f_T = k(T_a - T), \ f_S = \frac{\omega}{h_z - \omega} S;
\end{aligned} \tag{14}
$$

– exit (Kerch Strait):

$$\mathbf{V'_n} = 0, \ P'_n = 0, \ T'_n = 0, \ S'_n = 0, \ f_T = 0, \ f_S = 0, \tag{15}$$

where ω is the rate of liquid evaporation, equal to $606\,\mathrm{m^3/s}$; $\mathbf{n}$ stands for the normal vector; $\mathbf{V_n}$ and $\mathbf{V_\tau}$ denote the normal and tangential components of the velocity vector, respectively; $\boldsymbol{\tau} = \{\tau_x, \tau_y, \tau_z, \}$ is the tangential stress vector; ρ is the water density; ρ_v denotes the suspension density; T_a is the atmospheric temperature; k is the coefficient of heat transfer between the atmosphere and the aquatic environment; h_z denotes the depth step, and $h_\omega = \omega\tau$ is the thickness of the liquid layer that evaporates during the time τ.

The tangential stress vector for the free surface is given by the formula

$$\boldsymbol{\tau} = \rho_a C d_s \, |\mathbf{V}| \, \mathbf{V},$$

where $\mathbf{V}$ is the wind velocity relative to the water, ρ_a denotes the atmosphere density, and $Cd_s = 0.0026$ is a dimensionless coefficient of surface resistance that depends on the wind speed and is in the range from 0.0016 to 0.0032 [9].

The tangential stress vector for the bottom has the form

$$\boldsymbol{\tau} = \rho C d_b \, |\mathbf{V}| \, \mathbf{V},$$

where $Cd_b = gK^2/h^{1/3}$; K denotes the group roughness coefficient, whose value is in the range from 0.025 to 0.2 (we considered the value 0.025 since the bottom of the Sea of Azov es predominantly covered with silty deposits; $h = H + \eta$ is the water area depth; H is the undisturbed surface depth, and η is the free surface elevation relative to the sea level.

The system of Equations (1)–(6) is considered under the following initial conditions:

$$\mathbf{V} = \mathbf{V_0}, T = T_0, S = S_0, \tag{16}$$

where $\mathbf{V_0}$, T_0, and S_0 are specified functions.

The turbulent viscosity is directly computed from the Navier–Stokes equations and naturally appears in the numerical simulation if the vertical resolution of the grid allows reproducing all mechanisms up to viscous dissipation with very small vortices. Thus, if the vertical size of the computational grid is rather large, similar to that of the areas studied, then the mechanisms of vertical turbulent exchange are suppressed, thereby making it necessary to choose a sufficiently small scale of vertical resolution. This is the idea of D. Smagorinsky's subgrid model, in which the turbulent viscosity is added to the molecular viscosity. The turbulent viscosity is determined through the mixing length, which corresponds to the size of small eddies: $\nu = C_s^2 \Delta^2 \bar{s}^{1/2}$, where C_s is a dimensionless empirical constant (Smagorinsky's constant), whose value is determined from the computation of the decay process of homogeneous isotropic turbulence and should ensure the compliance with experimental measurements; Δ is the characteristic scale of the grid, and $\bar{s}$ denotes the dissipation rate, which is expressed as $\bar{s} = 2\bar{s}_{ij} \cdot \bar{s}_{ij}$, with $\bar{s}_{ij}$ being the averaged strain rate tensor, $\bar{s}_{ij} \sim \varepsilon^{2/3} \Delta^{4/3}$, where ε denotes the average value of the dissipation rate of the turbulence energy per unit volume.

3   Physical Processes Splitting Schemes for Solving Hydrodynamic Problems

The computational domain is inscribed in a parallelepiped. For the numerical implementation of the discrete mathematical model corresponding to the posed hydrodynamic problem, a uniform grid is introduced as follows:

$$\overline{\omega}_h = \{t^n = n\tau, x_i = ih_x, y_i = jh_y, z_i = kh_z; n = \overline{0..N_t}, i = \overline{0..N_x},$$
$$j = \overline{0..N_y}, k = \overline{0..N_z}; N_t\tau = T, N_x h_x = l_x, N_y h_y = l_y, N_z h_z = l_z\},$$

where τ is the time step; h_x, h_y, and h_z denote the space steps; N_t is the number of time layers; T is the upper bound of the time coordinate; N_x, N_y, and N_z are the numbers of nodes by spatial coordinates, and l_x, l_y, and l_z stand for the space boundaries.

According to the pressure correction method, the original model of hydrodynamics is divided into three subtasks [10–13]. The first one is represented by the diffusion-convection equation, which is used to calculate the field components of the velocity vector of the water flow in an intermediate time layer:

$$\frac{\tilde{u} - u}{\tau} + u\overline{u}'_x + v\overline{u}'_y + w\overline{u}'_z = (\mu\overline{u}'_x)'_x + (\mu\overline{u}'_y)'_y + (\nu\overline{u}'_z)'_z + 2\Omega(v\sin\theta - w\cos\theta),$$

$$\frac{\tilde{v} - v}{\tau} + u\overline{v}'_x + v\overline{v}'_y + w\overline{v}'_z = (\mu\overline{v}'_x)'_x + (\mu\overline{v}'_y)'_y + (\nu\overline{v}'_z)'_z - 2\Omega u\sin\theta,$$

$$\frac{\tilde{w} - w}{\tau} + u\overline{w}'_x + v\overline{w}'_y + w\overline{w}'_z = (\mu\overline{w}'_x)'_x + (\mu\overline{w}'_y)'_y + (\nu\overline{w}'_z)'_z$$

$$+ 2\Omega u\cos\theta + g\left(\frac{\rho_0}{\rho} - 1\right), \quad (17)$$

where u, v, w are the components of the velocity vector in the previous time layer; $\tilde{u}, \tilde{v}, \tilde{w}$ are the components of the velocity vector at the intermediate time layer; $\overline{u} = \sigma\tilde{u} + (1 - \sigma)u$, and $\sigma \in [0, 1]$ stands for the scheme weight.

The computation of the pressure distribution (second subtask) is based on the Poisson equation:

$$P''_{xx} + P''_{yy} + P''_{zz} = \frac{\check{\rho} - \rho}{\tau^2} + \frac{(\check{\rho}\tilde{u})'_x}{\tau} + \frac{(\check{\rho}\tilde{v})'_y}{\tau} + \frac{(\check{\rho}\tilde{w})'_z}{\tau}. \quad (18)$$

The third subtask allows using explicit formulas to determine the distribution of the velocities in the next time layer:

$$\frac{\check{u} - \tilde{u}}{\tau} = -\frac{1}{\check{\rho}}P'_x, \quad \frac{\check{v} - \tilde{v}}{\tau} = -\frac{1}{\check{\rho}}P'_y, \quad \frac{\check{w} - \tilde{w}}{\tau} = -\frac{1}{\check{\rho}}P'_z, \quad (19)$$

where $\check{u}, \check{v}, \check{w}$ are the components of the velocity vector in the current time layer.

By $o_{i,j,k}$, we denote the volume of fluid (VOF) function of the cell (i, j, k), which is determined by the liquid column pressure inside this cell [9,10]. In the general case, the VOF can be computed by the following formula [4]:

$$o_{i,j,k} = \frac{P_{i,j,k} + P_{i-1,j,k} + P_{i,j-1,k} + P_{i-1,j-1,k}}{4\rho g h_z}. \quad (20)$$

The computation of an approximation of the velocity field of the aquatic environment movement in terms of spatial variables is carried out by the balance method and taking into account the coefficients of fullness for control areas.

4   Method for the Solution of Grid Equations

The most resource-intensive part of the software implementation is the function for solving a system of linear algebraic equations (SLAE). To speed up the computations, we developed a parallel algorithm based on a modified alternating triangular iterative method (MATM) for solving SLAEs and using MPI technology for information exchange between computers. In a finite-dimensional Hilbert space H, the operator equation is solved

$$Ax = f, \quad A\colon H \to H, \tag{21}$$

where A is a linear positive definite operator $(A > 0)$.

To find a solution to the problem (21), an implicit iterative process is used, namely

$$B\frac{x^{m+1} - x^m}{\tau_{m+1}} + Ax^m = f, \quad B\colon H \to H, \tag{22}$$

where m is the iteration number, $\tau > 0$ is an iterative parameter, and B denotes some invertible operator, called a preconditioner or stabilizer. The inversion of the operator B in (22) should be much simpler than the direct inversion of the original operator A in (21). The operator B is constructed from the additive representation of the operator A_0, which is the symmetric part of the operator A:

$$A_0 = R_1 + R_2, \quad R_1 = R_2^*, \tag{23}$$

where $A = A_0 + A_1$, $A_0 = A_0^*$, and $A_1 = -A_1^*$.

The preconditioner operator can be written in the form

$$B = (D + \omega R_1) D^{-1} (D + \omega R_2), \quad D = D^* > 0, \ \omega > 0 \tag{24}$$

where D is a certain operator.

If the operators R_1 and R_2 are defined, and the methods for determining the parameters τ_{m+1} and ω and the operator D are indicated, then relations (23) and (24) define a modified alternating triangular method (MATM) for solving grid equations [14].

The algorithm for computing the grid equations by the modified alternating triangular method of variational type is written as

$$r^m = Ax^m - f, \ B(\omega_m)w^m = r^m, \ \tilde{\omega}_m = \sqrt{\frac{(Dw^m, w^m)}{(D^{-1}R_2w^m, R_2w^m)}} \,,$$

$$s_m^2 = 1 - \frac{(A_0w^m, w^m)^2}{(B^{-1}A_0w^m)(Bw^m, w^m)}, \quad k_m^2 = \frac{(B^{-1}A_1w^m, A_1w^m)}{(B^{-1}A_0w^m, A_0w^m)}, \tag{25}$$

$$\theta_m = \frac{1 - \sqrt{\frac{s_m^2 k_m^2}{(1+k_m^2)}}}{1 + k_m^2 (1 - s_m^2)}, \tau_{m+1} = \theta_m \frac{(A_0 w^m, w^m)}{(B^{-1} A_0 w^m, A_0 w^m)},$$

$$x^{m+1} = x^m - \tau_{m+1} w^m, \omega_{m+1} = \tilde{\omega}_m,$$

where r^m denotes the residual vector, w^m is the correction vector, the parameter s_m stands for the rate of convergence of the method, and k_m is the ratio of the norm of the skew-symmetric part of the operator to the norm of the symmetric part.

For the method convergence rate, we have

$$\rho \le \frac{\nu^* - 1}{\nu^* + 1}, \tag{26}$$

where $\nu^* = \nu \left(\sqrt{1 + k^2} + k \right)^2$, and ν is the condition number of the matrix C_0, which is defined as $C_0 = B^{-1/2} A_0 B^{-1/2}$.

Furthermore, the value ω is optimal for

$$\omega = \sqrt{\frac{(Dw^m, w^m)}{(D^{-1} R_2 w^m, R_2 w^m)}}, \tag{27}$$

and the condition number of the matrix C_0 can be estimated as

$$\nu = \max_{y \ne 0} \left(\frac{1}{2} + \frac{\sqrt{(Dy, y)(D^{-1} R_2 y, R_2 y)}}{(A_0 y, y)} \right) \le \frac{1}{2} \left(1 + \sqrt{\frac{\Delta}{\delta}} \right) = \frac{1 + \sqrt{\xi}}{2\sqrt{\xi}},$$

where $\xi = \frac{\delta}{\Delta}$, $D \le \frac{1}{\delta} A_0$, and $R_1 D^{-1} R_2 \le \frac{\Delta}{4} A_0$.

5   The Software Implementation

We developed a software package written in C++ intended to compute the field of the velocity vector in a 3D water environment. The package takes into account such physical parameters as turbulent exchange, bottom and coastline complex geometry, wind currents, and bottom friction. Furthermore, it provides the following functions:

- computation of the velocity field without considering the pressure;
- computation of the hydrostatic pressure (used as an initial approximation to the hydrodynamic pressure);
- computation of the hydrodynamic pressure;
- computation of the velocity field of the 3D water flow.

The following blocks can be distinguished in the software package:

- a control block that loops over the time coordinate and calls the functions for the computation of the velocity field without taking into account the pressure, the hydrostatic pressure, the hydrodynamic pressure, the three-dimensional velocity field, and the water-data output;

- a block to input initial data required to compute currents and pressure; it is used to set the initial distribution of the velocity and pressure field, as well as the coordinates and values of water flows in the river mouth area;
- a block that constructs the grid equations for the velocity field neglecting the pressure, in compliance with the finite-difference scheme;
- a block that constructs the grid equations for the pressure field in the hydrostatic approximation;
- a block that constructs the grid equations for the hydrodynamic pressure field;
- a block that computes the velocity field taking into account the pressure (the result is the computation of the three-dimensional field of the velocity vector in the next time layer);
- a block that computes seven-diagonal grid equations by the modified alternating triangular method of steepest descent;
- a block that computes five-diagonal grid equations by the modified alternating triangular method of steepest descent;
- a block to output the values of the velocity field to files.

The software package is the basis of an information system that enables the solution of the following tasks [15]:

- computation of possible flood and drainage areas when waves run up onto the shore, by recalculating the fullness of the calculated cells during the implementation of the hydrodynamic model;
- determination of the concentration of the main types of pollutants, including biogenic substances (compounds of nitrogen, phosphorus, silicon), plastics and microplastics, and oil products;
- identification of reservoir areas with vortex structure of water flow currents, as well as the areas most susceptible to phenomena of primary and secondary pollution of the water environment and coastal areas in the basin of the Sea of Azov–Black Sea;
- identification of previously unexplored features of the transfer of chemical elements, oil and oil products, and plastics and microplastics in the catchment basins of rivers, their transformation in the zone where river water meets seawater, and the seasonal and long-term dynamics of sediment removal from the surface layer to deep-water zones;
- ingress and microplastics accumulation assessment into the organisms of the main commercial fish of the Sea of Azov (anchovy, so-iuy mullet), depending on the places of their spawning and feeding;
- assessment of the impact of dredging operations, including damage caused by the death of or the decrease in fish food organisms;
- forecasting of the distribution of suspended plumes in the aquatic environment, changes in bottom topography due to the deposition of suspended soil particles during the operation of dredging equipment.

The software implementation of the hydrodynamic model was written in C++ using MPI technology. It made it possible to carry out several computational experiments on a multiprocessor computing system at Sirius Science and

Technology University. The part of the cluster we used is based on an open stack of OpenHPC applications and equipped with 1440 processor cores at 2.3 GHz and 10.24 TB of RAM. The computational experiments confirmed the efficiency of the algorithm. In Fig. 1, we can see the dependence graph for the execution time of one step of the MATM algorithm for computational grids of $500 \times 500 \times 100$ and $1000 \times 1000 \times 60$ nodes with the computational domain divided into p parts along one spatial direction.

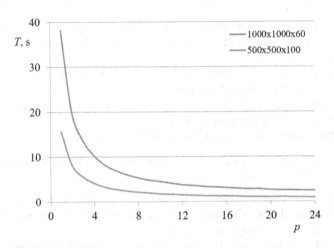

Fig. 1. Dependence between the execution time of a MATM step and the number of processors

To increase the efficiency of parallel computations, we decomposed the computational domain in two spatial directions (x and y). Table 1 shows the results yielded by the algorithm for several distributions of processors in the spatial directions of the computational domain.

Figure 2 describes how the simulation time depends on the distribution of the processors over the spatial directions.

The computations for a rectangular grid of $1000 \times 1000 \times 60$ nodes on 24 processors showed an acceleration by a factor of 15.2 (the execution time was 38.16 s for one processor and 2.51 s for 24 processors).

6   Results of the Numerical Experiments

The dimensions of the computational domain in the spatial directions X, Y, and Z were assumed to be 50 m, 50 m, and 2 m, respectively. The elevation level above the sea surface was taken equal to 2 m. The grid parameters were set as follows. The steps were 0.5 m in both horizontal directions and 0.1 m in the vertical direction. The time step was 0.25 s. The speed of the water flow in the river bed was assumed to equal 0.2 m/s. The incoming flow from the sea was set

Table 1. The results of the parallel algorithm depending on the decomposition of the computational domain in two spatial directions

$p = p_x p_y$	p_x	p_y	$500 \times 500 \times 100$	$1000 \times 1000 \times 60$
16	16	1	1.31	3.16
16	8	2	1.29	3.00
16	4	4	1.28	2.99
20	20	1	1.08	2.68
20	10	2	1.03	2.55
20	5	4	1.02	2.50
24	24	1	0.97	2.51
24	12	2	0.96	2.25
24	8	3	0.94	2.24
24	6	4	0.93	2.24

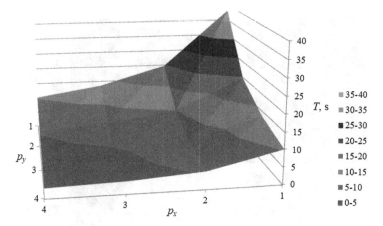

Fig. 2. Dependence of the simulation time on the distribution of the processors over the spatial directions

equal to $0.4\,\mathrm{m/s}$. The geometry of the computational domain was described for modeling purposes in the form of a depth map, shown in Fig. 3 (Table 1).

Figure 4 shows the change in the water level at different points in time. Figures 5 and 6 show the water flow velocity on the surface (XOY section, Fig. 5) and in a section passing through the center of the computational domain (XOZ section, Fig. 6). Figure 6 shows the flooding in the river mouth area. The horizontal line indicates the zero water level. We plan to make modifications to the software package to ensure high accuracy in the description of the processes occurring when the water flows of interconnected reservoirs meet each other and predict the penetration of saline waters into the river floodplain.

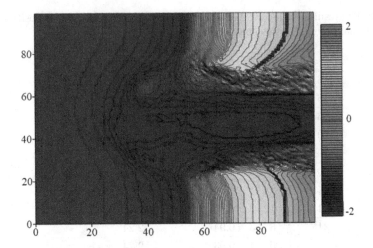

Fig. 3. Depth map of the computational domain

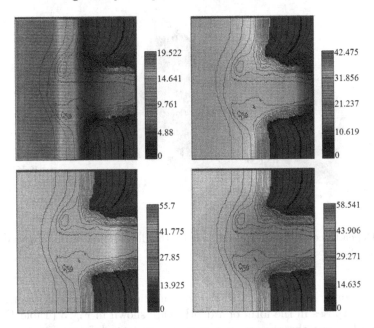

Fig. 4. Dynamics of the water level (in centimeters) after 5, 10, 15, and 20 s

For the verification of the model, we relied on the results from expeditionary research carried out by the team of authors in the Sea of Azov [11]. The relative deviation of the computed hydrophysical parameters obtained through modeling from those measured in field experiments is in the range of 15 to 20%. For the time being, we have developed and tested several algorithms to parameterize the model, including a filtering algorithm based on the Kalman filter, which allows

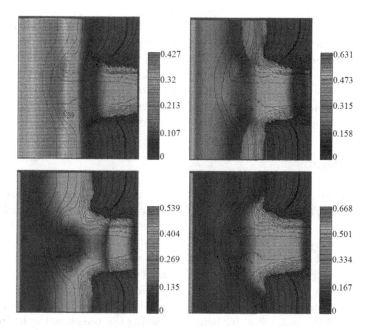

Fig. 5. Water flow speed on the surface (in meters per second) after 5, 10, 15, and 20 s

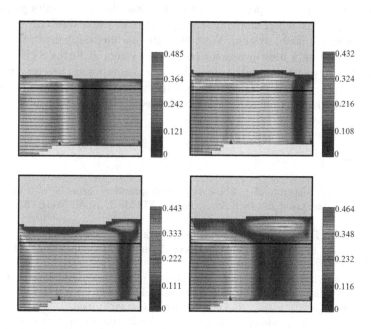

Fig. 6. Water flow speed (in meters per second) in the center of the computational domain after 5, 10, 15, and 20 s

getting rid of the noise level in expeditionary measurements of the water flow velocity vector. By comparing modeling results with those of field measurements for the coefficient of vertical turbulent exchange at different horizons of the reservoir, we concluded that the computed data yielded by the Smagorinsky turbulence subgrid model on turbulent processes in shallow reservoirs are in good agreement with field data. It should be noted that it is difficult to increase the model accuracy since the results of field experiments for some parameters may differ significantly from the mean values under the same conditions.

7   Conclusions

In this paper, we suggested a 3D hydrodynamic model of river mouth areas that makes it possible to compute the field of the velocity vector. The approximation of the continuous hydrodynamic model in terms of spatial variables is based on the balance method and takes into account the fullness of the calculated cells, thereby making it possible to consider coastlines with the complex geometry and, consequently, increase the accuracy of the model. For the numerical solution of the model, we developed a software package (in C++ using MPI technology) featuring functions for the computation of several physical factors, such as the velocity field of the water flow without considering the pressure, the hydrostatic pressure (used as an initial approximation to the hydrodynamic pressure), the hydrodynamic pressure, and the three-dimensional field of the water flow speed in an area of complex shape. The paper also describes the results yielded by the software package when modeling the dynamics of water flow currents in the estuary area of a coastal system. We tested the parallel implementation of the software package on a multiprocessor computer system at Sirius STU. To evaluate the efficiency of the parallel algorithm, we decomposed the computational domain in two spatial directions. The computations for a rectangular grid of $1000 \times 1000 \times 60$ nodes on 24 processors showed an acceleration by a factor of 15.21.

References

1. Oliger, J., Sundstorm, A.: Theoretical and practical aspects of some initial boundary-value problems in fluid dynamica SIAM. J. Appl. Math. **35**, 419–445 (1978)
2. Marchesiello, P., Mc.Williams, J.C., Shchepetkin A.: Open boundary conditions for long-term integration of regional oceanic models. Oceanic Model. J. **3**, 1–20 (2001)
3. Alekseenko, E., Roux, B.: Risk of wind-driven resuspension and transport of contaminated sediments in a narrow marine channel confluencing a wide lagoon. ECSS **237**, 106649 (2020). https://doi.org/10.1016/j.ecss.2020.106649
4. Shiganova, T., Alekseenko, E., Kazmin, A.: Predicting range expansion of invasive ctenophore Mnemiopsis leidyi A. agassiz 1865 under current environmental conditions and future climate change scenarios. Estuarine, Coastal Shelf Sci. **347** (2019). https://doi.org/10.1016/j.ecss.2019.106347

5. Alekseenko, E., Roux, B.: Numerical simulation of the wind influence on bottom shear stress and salinity fields in areas of Zostera noltei replanting in a Mediterranean coastal lagoon. Prog. Oceanogr. **163**, 147–160 (2018). https://doi.org/10.1016/j.pocean.2017.05.001

6. Marchuk, G.I., Kagan, B.A.: Dynamics of Oceans Tides. Hydrometeoizdat, Moscow (1983)

7. Matishov, G., et al.: Climatic Atlas of the Sea of Azov. NOAA Atlas NESDIS 59, U.S. Government Printing Office, Washington, D.C., p. 103 (2006)

8. Belotserkovskii, O.M.: Turbulence: New Approaches. Nauka, Moskow (2003)

9. Gushchin, V.A., Sukhinov, A.I., Nikitina, A.V., Chistyakov, A.E., Semenyakina, A.A.: A model of transport and transformation of biogenic elements in the coastal system and its numerical implementation. Comput. Math. Math. Phys. **58**(8), 1316–1333 (2018). https://doi.org/10.1134/S0965542518080092

10. Tran, J.K.: A predator-prey functional response incorporating indirect interference and depletion. Verh. Internat. Verein. Limnol. **30**, 302–305 (2008)

11. Alekseenko, E., Roux, B., Sukhinov, A.I., Kotarba, R., Fougere, D.: Coastal hydrodynamics in a windy lagoon. Comput. Fluids **77**, 24–35 (2013)

12. Samarskii, A.A., Vabishchevich, P.N.: Numerical methods for solving convection-diffusion problems. URSS, Moscow (2009)

13. Konovalov, A.N.: Method of rapid descent with adaptive alternately-triangular recondition. Differ. Equ. **40**(7), 953–963 (2004)

14. Sukhinov, A.I., Chistyakov, A.E.: Adaptive modified alternating triangular iterative method for solving grid equations with a non-self-adjoint operator. Math. Models Comput. Simul. **4**(4), 398–409 (2012)

15. Nikitina, A.V., Filina, A.A., Belova, Yu.V., Lyashchenko, T., Litvinov, V.N., Kravchenko, L.V.: The computational structure development for modeling hydrological shallow water processes on a graphics accelerator. In: AIP Conference Proceedings, vol. 2188, no. 1, p. 050025 (2019). https://doi.org/10.1063/1.5138452

System for the Visualization of Meshes of Big Size Obtained from Gas-Dynamic Simulations

Stepan Orlov[ID], Alexey Kuzin[ID], Alexey Zhuravlev$^{(\boxtimes)}$[ID],
Vyacheslav Reshetnikov[ID], Vladislav Kiev[ID], Egor Usik[ID],
and Andrey Pyatlin[ID]

Peter the Great St. Petersburg Polytechnic University, St. Petersburg, Russia
vlad@rwwws.ru , andrey@pyatlin.com

Abstract. The size of data obtained during the simulation of gas-dyna-mic problems may be extremely large. The visualization of those data, even using modern tools, is unacceptably slow. In the present paper, we describe the workflow of the system developed by the authors to enable visualization with tens of frames per second (FPS). The original data are converted into a special data structure based on the octree representation of spatial data. This structure provides the storage optimized in terms of memory usage and ease of access. After that, data are distributed among computational nodes. The visualization itself is performed by a set of components interacting with each other. The core of the system is a render server. The user manipulates a web interface that is directly connected with the render server and receives frames from the transporting server. The latter extracts the frames that are composed and recorded by the render server. The developed system can thus handle data with a size of up to 10^9 spatial nodes at frequencies higher than 20 FPS.

Keywords: Big data · Octree · Visualization system

1 Introduction

Today, there are many tools and methods intended to solve problems arising in different fields of mechanics. Some of those tools and methods are specially intended to be used in scientific disciplines like gas-dynamics. The data produced in this case frequently have a very large size, which is difficult to handle at postprocessing of the results. That is why the process of rendering may take an unacceptably long time. Modern visualization tools are, in most cases, unable to handle data with a convenient speed for engineers. Let us take a look at some of these tools.

Kitware ParaView is an open-source multi-platform visualization application. It was developed to visualize extremely large datasets through data distribution among remote computational nodes. It can be deployed both on supercomputers and on laptops with lower capabilities. Moreover, it supports the development

L. Sokolinsky and M. Zymbler (Eds.): PCT 2021, CCIS 1437, pp. 270–283, 2021.
https://doi.org/10.1007/978-3-030-81691-9_19

of specialized plugins that can be connected to the visualization system. An example using ParaView is given in [1].

NVIDIA IndeX [2] is another framework for remote visualization. It uses the computing capabilities of GPUs to work with big data. NVIDIA IndeX is intended for real-time visualization, owing to the distribution of the visualization tasks over a GPU-accelerated cluster. Also, a specialized plugin for ParaView has been developed and is intended to improve the performance of big data visualization. It is claimed that the framework has good scalability across GPU nodes. The performance of visualization with NVIDIA IndeX of a dataset containing $2.3 \cdot 10^9$ nodes ($1730 \times 3455 \times 384$) is considered in [3], where it is shown that one frame is processed in $1.48\,$s. However, the startup cost, taking into account the additional time required by ParaView to collect the data, is rather considerable, which is explained by the necessity of transferring data from the CPU to the GPU.

One more tool for visualizing scientific and engineering data is Tecplot 360 [4], which is mostly specialized in the visualization of simulation results from computational fluid dynamics. It is commercial software developed by the company Tecplot. The support of big data handling is provided through SZL Technology, which ensures the reduction of the file size, the processing time, and the required operating memory. It is claimed that visualization with SZL is about 7.3 times faster, and the peak memory use is 93% lower than that with traditional datafiles of PLT type.

There are visualization systems used in specific fields. One of them is Voxler [5]. It is mostly used by geophysicists, geologists, GIS professionals, and other researchers and engineers in environmental sciences. Voxler can work with different 3D models, such as boreholes, LiDAR data, point clouds, etc. An example is demonstrated in [6].

A thorough review of big data visualization and analysis tools is given in [7].

In this paper, we are presenting a new program intended for interactive visualization of spatial non-steady results of simulations in such fields as fluid and solid mechanics, and others. Interactivity means that the user can switch the displayed field and the level of an isosurface, perform pan-zoom-rotate actions, change the scale of deformations, and switch to another time layer when visualizing non-steady processes. Moreover, all these options are possible in real-time or with only a reasonable delay, thereby providing a comfortable interaction between the user and the visualization system. Because of the large size of the original datasets, the problem of achieving such interactivity during visualization becomes non-trivial. Some difficulties arise: it is impossible to operate with the whole dataset in RAM due to its huge size, the speed of data exchange with hard drives is insufficient even when SSDs are used, the amount of video memory is not enough, and so on. The visualization system and data storage should be able to solve all these issues.

The paper is organized as follows. In Sect. 2, we describe the architecture of the developed visualization system, its main structural elements, and the interaction between them. Section 3 describes the model of parallel rendering used in the system and its software implementation. Section 4 presents the test results of the system performance. Finally, in the Conclusions, we summarize the study and point out some possible directions for future research.

2   Visualization System Architecture

The architecture of the visualization system is portrayed in Fig. 1. It can be split into the following unequal components:

- visualization server;
- client application;
- preprocessing facilities.

Preprocessing facilities are not an essential part of the visualization system and are not shown in Fig. 1, but they are the key feature of the technology. The goal of preprocessing is to transform original data into a format suitable to be used by the visualization server. Also, the preprocessing stage includes the distribution of datasets among the nodes of the cluster where the visualization server is run. Preprocessing is performed only once before visualization; therefore, it is not necessary to carry out this stage in real-time: it is sufficient to do it in a reasonable time. The core algorithms of data preprocessing and storage data format, named *Sparse 3D mipmapping* (*s3dmm*), are described in [8] and, therefore, are not the subject of this article.

Presently, the preprocessing stage consists in converting the original results of the simulation into a dataset suitable for visualization, but it can also be part of the simulation. It is known that fluid mechanics problems of large size generate huge amounts of data that there is no need or possibility to store all the simulation results. Therefore, one can think of in situ preprocessing when a visualization dataset is generated during simulation.

The *visualization server* is the main and biggest part of the system. It contains the visualization controller, which renders the frame according to input commands from the client, such as time frame number, current transformation matrix, visualization mode (isosurface, raytracing, etc.), and so on. The resulting image is stored by the controller in shared memory and is read from there by the video stream service. The service is an HTTP server that reads shared memory periodically and streams the video to the client application. The current implementation provides the video stream as a sequence of JPEGs, but the authors are working on methods to stream compressed video (for example, with the help of `gstreamer`).

The interaction with the visualization server is done via a web interface. The layout of the web page is given in Fig. 2. The top area contains dropdown lists for setting the visualized problem and the physical field; the timeline and the corresponding buttons to change the time frame; buttons for changing the camera position; a button for controlling the colormap function; buttons for visualization stream sharing, settings, and finishing the visualization session.

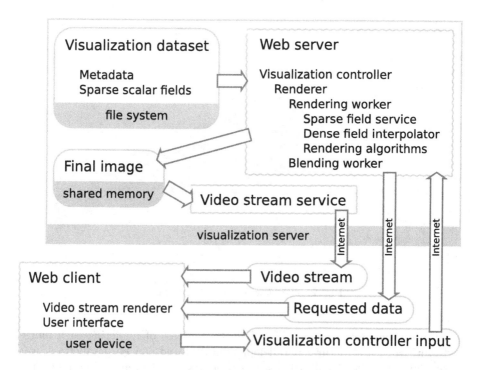

Fig. 1. Visualization system architecture

On the left-hand side, there is a dropdown list for selecting the field visualization mode. It also contains a button that calls the panel for controlling the clipping planes.

A web server is used to receive the HTML page with the corresponding scripts. It is based on the *Express JS* framework [9]. The web server directly operates the visualization server to enable the settings defined by the user through the web interface. The activation of settings is done with the help of the controller mentioned above. Since the controller is written in C++, whereas the interaction is done in JavaScript, there is a special add-on involved, which is based on the node-addon-api technology.

Let us briefly consider the work of the web interface. Its activity can be split between several services. The remote storage may store several visualization datasets. It is obvious that the work can not be started until the problem is selected. Therefore, the head service, which runs other services, is the problem service. When the problem is selected and the corresponding dataset is found among others, the remaining services are run. The remaining services encapsulate the control of the clipping planes, the camera transform, the field visualization mode, the displayed time frame, the colormap function, and other settings.

Sparse 3D mipmapping technology [8] ensures the mapping of the original computational mesh to the octree of structured meshes with different levels

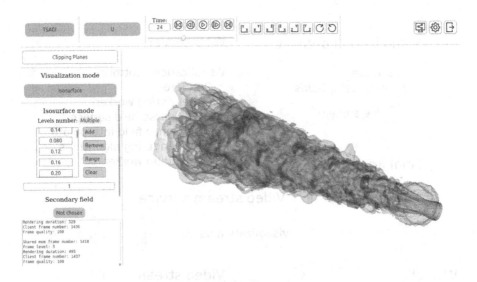

Fig. 2. The view of the web interface

of detail during preprocessing. Therefore, the process of rendering each image deals with such a structural parallelepipedal grid and can be parallelized over space. Currently, the visualization server supports parallel rendering on multiple NVIDIA GPUs. The authors plan to provide distributed rendering on several computational nodes of the cluster where the server resides. The present state of the rendering implementation is described in the next section.

3   Parallel Rendering Implementation

The renderer generates a 2D image using s3dmm data and input parameters received from the client's side. This takes place either when the input data is updated or in background mode (progressive rendering). The current renderer's implementation is intended to work on SMP machines and involves both GPUs and CPUs.

The s3dmm data of the frame image defined at the vertices of a structured parallelepipedal grid are divided into *blocks*. Each block is an octree of fixed depth d, usually, sparse. The grid is characterized by level l, which determines the number of blocks each edge of the grid is split into. Consequently, the grid of level l contains 2^{3l} blocks: level 0 consists of 1 block, level 1 consists of 8 blocks, and so on.

This structure suggests a natural way of parallelization of data for rendering. Each thread of execution processes its own block (or several blocks) and generates the part of the image from these data. These parts of the image are further blended. The tasks of rendering and blending form a directed graph of execution, which is below referred to as the *task graph*. An example of such a task graph with four rendering tasks is portrayed in Fig. 3. An upper level is formed by

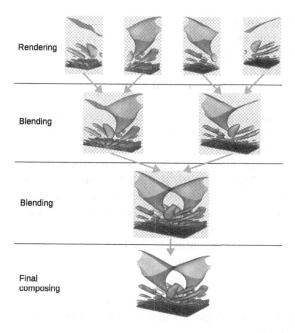

Fig. 3. An example of rendering a task graph, with four rendering tasks

the tasks of rendering, after that two layers of tasks of pair-wise blending take place. On blending, either a true blending of pixel colors (with the transparency of both components taken into account) or a selection of maximum value (in Maximal Intensity Projection mode) takes place. All these tasks are performed for an initially transparent background; the real background color is added at the stage of final composing. Obviously, if the number of rendering tasks is different, the number of levels of blending is also changed.

In the current implementation, rendering tasks are performed on an NVIDIA GPU using CUDA, while blending tasks are performed on the CPU.

The problem of initial balancing of workload between tasks of rendering is reduced to the problem of splitting the index cube of size $2^l \times 2^l \times 2^l$ to n maximally equal subdomains (n is the number of rendering tasks). The subdomains must satisfy an extra condition: they must allow ordering according to their z-order in the view direction. This is necessary for the correct blending of the image parts in the future. This problem a has simple solution when n is a power of 2. The current implementation of the renderer is restricted almost completely to this case. In this case, the workloads of rendering tasks are ideally balanced (of course, without taking into account the sparsity of the blocks!), and the workloads of blending tasks are determined automatically.

Since the process of rendering implies parallel execution of the task graph, for example, as it is shown in Fig. 3, the efficient development of rendering requires the use of specialized frameworks of task programming. In fact, the indirect use of low-level threads, such as, for example, provided by STL is time-consuming, error-prone, and requires a big amount of routine work. There are several technologies intended to reduce this work, for instance, the Taskflow framework [10]. This is a header-only library written in C++. It supports such features as graph execution, dynamic tasking, conditional tasking, loops, and can execute CUDA tasks.

Another possible solution is to use the library Intel Threading Building Blocks (TBB) [11], which also provides similar functionality but requires rather big efforts for learning.

Finally, another possible solution is to use the OpenMP's mechanism of *tasks* (pragma omp task). This approach is probably the most suitable when parallelism is to be introduced into existing code. However, if a piece of software is developed from scratch, it is often preferable to use the capabilities of the last C++ standards at a maximum.

The specifics of parallel execution of the task graph of rendering requires the framework to provide the following features:

1. Support for different types of tasks.
2. Execution of tasks both on GPUs and CPUs.
3. Cancelation of the graph processing due to internal causes and by a signal from the frontend.
4. Unified support for running tasks on remote nodes (given that distributed rendering on the cluster is planned).

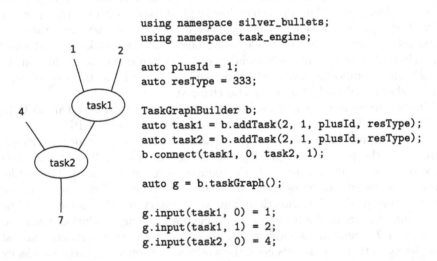

```
using namespace silver_bullets;
using namespace task_engine;

auto plusId = 1;
auto resType = 333;

TaskGraphBuilder b;
auto task1 = b.addTask(2, 1, plusId, resType);
auto task2 = b.addTask(2, 1, plusId, resType);
b.connect(task1, 0, task2, 1);

auto g = b.taskGraph();

g.input(task1, 0) = 1;
g.input(task1, 1) = 2;
g.input(task2, 0) = 4;
```

Fig. 4. A task graph representing the operation $(1+2)+4 = 7$, and the programming code for its generation using silver_bullets

Because of the presence of the last requirement, the authors decided to develop their own framework of task programming. It is a part of the library of auxiliary features (https://github.com/deadmorous/silver_bullets), which is distributed under the MIT license. The library is organized as a set of header files and developed according to the C++17 standard. It should be noted that task programming is one of many features that the library provides. This is not a specialized task programming framework and, therefore, does not provide such an advanced set of features as, for example, Taskflow. By way of example, it does not support loops and conditional tasking. But apart from that, all the requirements associated with the task graph processing listed above are met.

All the features of `silver_bullets` intended to work with task programming are collected in the namespace `silver_bullets::task_engine`. The common pattern of the task graph startup consists of the graph generation with the object `TaskGraphBuilder` at the preparation step and the subsequent run of the graph with the object `TaskGraphExecutor` equipped with instances of the `TaskExecutor` interface.

An example of the use of `TaskGraphBuilder` for the generation of a simple two-node graph for the evaluation of the operation $(1 + 2) + 4 = 7$ is given in Fig. 4. At this stage, one creates the nodes and edges of the graph and assigns input data to the input ports. The graph is not aware of the task function, it only knows its identifier (`plusId`) and the so-called *resource type* `resType`, which is an identifier of the type of the node. To understand it, let us refer to the task graph of rendering shown in Fig. 3). There are three resource types: rendering, blending, and final composition. It is natural that all render tasks have the same function identifier, but this is not necessary: one can think of different render functions for different nodes (even though it has no sense).

```
using TaskFunc = SimpleTaskFunc;
using TFR = TaskFuncRegistry<TaskFunc>;
using TTX = ThreadedTaskExecutor<TaskFunc>;
using TGX = TaskGraphExecutor<TaskFunc>;

auto plus = makeSimpleTaskFunc([](int a, int b) {
    std::this_thread::sleep_for(std::chrono::milliseconds(500));
    return a + b;
});

TFR taskFuncRegistry;
taskFuncRegistry[plusId] = plus;

TGX x;
for (auto i=0; i<10; ++i)
    x.addTaskExecutor(std::make_shared<TTX>(resType, &taskFuncRegistry));

auto cache = x.makeCache();
x.start(&g, cache).wait();
```

Fig. 5. Code for the execution of the task graph generated in Fig. 4, using `silver_bullets`

When the task graph is built, it can be executed as shown in Fig. 5 (the code snippet in Fig. 5 is the continuation of the one in Fig. 4). This process is straightforward: one defines the task function `plus` and creates ten objects of type `ThreadedTaskExecutor`, which implement the `TaskExecutor` interface by encapsulation of `std::thread`. Finally, one runs the graph execution and waits for completion. It is worth noting that the number of executors may be arbitrary. This means that the number of executors does not correlate with the number of nodes in the graph. The graph executor manages a pool of task executors and dynamically assigns vacant executors of the appropriate type to the task when all the inputs are ready. For example, the simple graph in Fig. 4 can involve only one executor at a time: its two nodes can be run only sequentially.

At the moment, `silver_bullets` provides two implementations of thread executors: `ThreadedTaskExecutor`, which executes the task in an in-process thread, and `RemoteTaskExecutor` to execute the tasks on remote nodes. The remote executor implementation is based on `grpc` and Protocol Buffers `protobuf`.

4   Tests and Discussion

The visualization system has been tested on several real-life problems. In this article, we present an example of visualization of simulation results in the problem of filtration in a porous medium. The view of this computational domain is displayed in Fig. 6(a). This is a parallelepipedal piece of a porous medium filled with fluid. The details of the physical formulation of the problem are not important for the purpose of visualization and, therefore, are not described here. The original computational dataset is defined on a grid of $702 \times 702 \times 702$ cells. It is preprocessed into an s3dmm octree that consists of 3 levels, the depth of the block is 8 ($d = 8$). The characteristics of s3dmm octree data are given in Table 1.

Table 1. Parameters of s3dmm data generated for the visualized problem

Level	Avg. nodes per block	Number of blocks	Total nodes	Avg. fill
0	$2.53 \cdot 10^6$	1	$2.53 \cdot 10^6$	0.1489
1	$1.57 \cdot 10^6$	8	$1.27 \cdot 10^7$	0.0928
2	$1.11 \cdot 10^6$	64	$7.08 \cdot 10^7$	0.0652

The first column is the index of the level. The second contains the average number of nodes per block. The third column corresponds to the number of blocks at each level, which equals 2^{3l}, where l is the level index. The fourth column is the total number of nodes in the whole grid of the corresponding level. The last column shows the average fill of the blocks of the level, which is computed as follows. For each block, the ratio N/N_0 is evaluated, where N is the number of nodes in the block and $N_0 = (2^d + 1)^3$ is the maximum number of nodes in

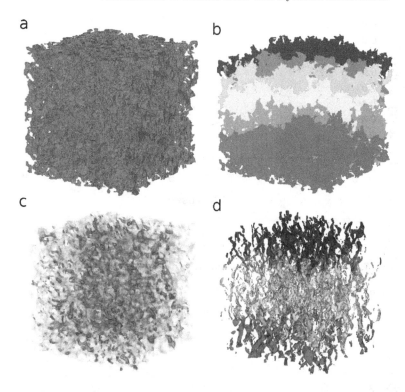

Fig. 6. Examples of modes supported by the visualization system: a) shape of a porous medium; b) Maximal Intensity Projection (MIP); c) colormap with transparency and per-sample lighting mode; d) isosurface with another field mapped

the block of depth d. Then, the average ratio among the blocks of the levels is computed. The value 1 corresponds to a dense grid with all nodes defined. As one can see from Table 1, the s3dmm grid of the model is rather sparse: the grid at level 0 contains only 15% of nodes, and the sparsity increases with the level index.

The visualization server is installed on an NVIDIA DGX-1 machine with 2 Intel(R) Xeon(R) CPU E5-2698 v4 @ 2.20 GHz (20 cores), 512 GB RAM, 8 V100-SXM2 GPUs (16 GB memory, 5120 CUDA cores per GPU).

The available visualization modes are shown in Fig. 6. These are examples of maximal intensity projection (MIP) (b), Colormap with per-sample lighting modes (c), and isosurfaces (d). All these modes have different requirements on computing capabilities, as it is shown below.

First of all, we tested the scalability of the renderer in isosurface mode. To make the rendering step heavier, each frame consisted of 20 isosurfaces of different levels. The resulting dataset was rather big. We measured the total time of the frame rendering. Such a large number of isosurfaces in one frame produces a longer rendering time, thereby decreasing the influence of random

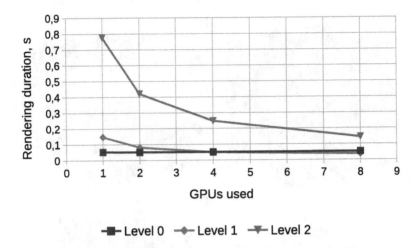

Fig. 7. Rendering duration as a function of the number of GPUs used

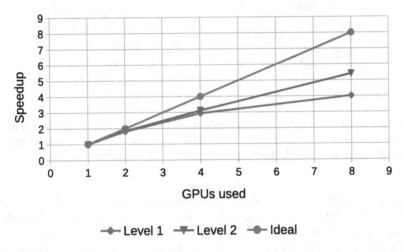

Fig. 8. Rendering relative speedup as a function of the number of GPUs used

fluctuations. The number of rendering tasks was equal to the number of GPUs employed, therefore, each rendering task was executed on a separate GPU in parallel.

The results of the rendering time measurement are shown in Fig. 7. We can see that the rendering duration for level 0 does not depend on the number of GPUs. This is obvious because the dataset of level 0 consists of only one block, and therefore, it can not be processed in parallel: only one GPU is used at a time.

Also, we can expect that the rendering times for levels 0 and 1 are equal when level 1 is rendered on eight GPUs because level 1 consists of eight blocks, and each GPU processes only one block. As we can see, the curve of level 1 is

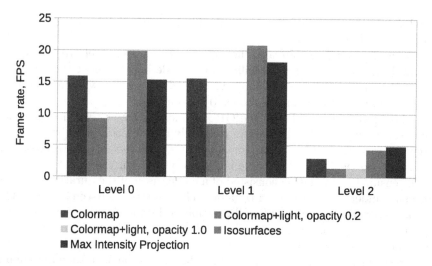

Fig. 9. Comparison of frame rates for different rendering modes. Four rendering tasks are used, one task per GPU

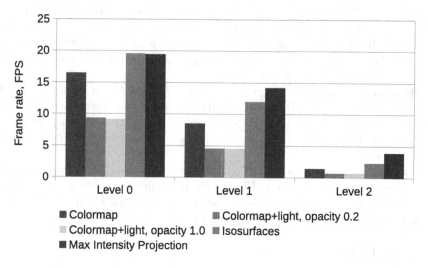

Fig. 10. Comparison of frame rates for different rendering modes. Four rendering tasks are used, two tasks per GPU

even under the one of level 0. This may occur because the blocks of level 1 are more sparse than those of level 0 and contain fewer nodes (see Table 1).

The curve of level 2 demonstrates the same behavior. In the case of, a single GPU all 64 blocks are processed sequentially, but the ratio of durations of level 2 to level 0 is only 14.8. In the case of eight GPUs, each one processes eight blocks at level 2 against one block at level 0, but the ratio of durations is only 2.74. This also should be explained as a consequence of the sparsity of the blocks at level 2: according to Table 1, they contain only $1.11 \cdot 10^6$ nodes, against $2.53 \cdot 10^6$ nodes per block at level 0.

The results from Fig. 7 are also shown in Fig. 8 as speedup relative to sequential run. It demonstrates the scalability of the rendering of levels 1 and 2 relative to the number of GPUs used. The curve of level 0 is not shown since the level consists of only one block and is rendered sequentially.

It should also be noted that the GPU memory is larger than necessary for a single rendering task. Therefore, we can study the situation when the number of rendering tasks is larger than that of GPUs, and the server starts several rendering tasks per GPU. This issue is a subject for future research.

The ensuing investigation consisted of a comparison of the duration of image processing under different rendering modes. The results can be seen in Fig. 9. The diagram shows the frame rates (in FPS) achieved by the visualization server for different modes at different levels. The rendering was performed on four GPUs, one rendering task per GPU.

As we can see, colormap with per-sample lighting is the most time-consuming mode, and the result does not depend on the opacity of the colormap (an opacity of 0.2 corresponds to rather transparent colors, whereas an opacity equal to 1.0 corresponds to fully opaque colors). The last result seems surprising but it may be explained by the relatively fast stage of blending the image parts. Also, we can notice that the rendering rates of level 0 and level 1 are almost the same. This correlates with the results given in Fig. 7 and, probably, comes from the relative sparsity of blocks at level 1.

The results displayed in Fig. 9 demonstrate that the frame rates under Colormap, Isosurfaces, and MIP modes are almost suitable for interactive visualization since they provide 15 to 20 FPS for levels 0 and 1. However, if per-sample lighting is enabled or if a more detailed dataset is used, then the frame rate is not appropriate.

The same tests were conducted on four rendering tasks, with two tasks per GPU. The results are shown in Fig. 10. Even though the amount of RAM on each GPU is enough for two threads, we see that the frame rate decreases at levels 1 and 2. This is an issue that requires additional research.

5   Conclusions

We presented a new system for the visualization of simulation results on large meshes. One of the key features of the system is the use of preprocessed data stored in a special format [8], which excludes the need to read the original dataset during visualization. The obtained dataset is small compared to the original dataset but enough for high-resolution progressive rendering and provides fast direct access to the required parts of data. At present, the visualization dataset (also called the s3dmm dataset) is created at the preprocessing stage. One of the future directions of research is a kind of in situ visualization, in which the s3dmm dataset is generated during simulation. This is a relevant feature since large-scale simulations do not store all the simulation results due to their extremely large size.

The current implementation of the visualization system provides a remote visualization server that supports parallel rendering on SMP machines using NVIDIA GPUs.

The user's frontend was developed as a web client. It is started in a browser and provides interactive handling of the displayed dataset.

The performance tests conducted with real-life datasets show rather good scalability of parallel rendering when isosurfaces are generated (see Fig. 8). Additional investigations are required for other modes of visualization.

Another important direction of research is the development of a distributed visualization server, where the rendering stage is distributed among the nodes of a cluster. At the moment, this work is in progress.

Acknowledgements. The authors express their gratitude to the Russian Science Foundation for the support of their investigations (grant No. 18-11-00245).

The authors also thank the Supercomputer Center Polytechnic of Peter the Great St. Petersburg Polytechnic University for granting access to the DGX-1 server.

References

1. Moreland, K., Rogers, D., Greenfield, J.: Large Scale Visualization on the Cray XT3 Using ParaView. In: Cray User Group 2008 (2008)
2. NVIDIA IndeX. https://developer.nvidia.com/nvidia-index
3. Favre, J., Blass, A.: A comparative evaluation of three volume rendering libraries for the visualization of sheared thermal convection. Parallel Comput. **88**, (2019). https://doi.org/10.1016/j.parco.2019.07.003
4. Tecplot 360. https://www.tecplot.com/products/tecplot-360
5. Voxler – 3D geologic and scientific modelling software. https://www.goldensoftware.com/products/voxler
6. Yasir, S. F., Jani, J., Mukri, M.: A dataset of visualization methods to assessing soil profile using RES2DINV and VOXLER software. Data Brief **24**, (2019). https://doi.org/10.1016/j.dib.2019.103821
7. Caldarola, E.G., Rinaldi, A.M.: Big data visualization tools: a survey – the new paradigms, methodologies and tools for large data sets visualization. In: Proceedings of the 6th International Conference on Data Science, Technology and Applications, Vol. 1, pp. 296–305. KomIS, Madrid, Spain (2017). https://doi.org/10.5220/0006484102960305
8. Ivanov, A., Levchenko, V., Korneev, B., Perepelkina, A.: Management of computations with LRnLA algorithms in adaptive mesh refinement codes. In: Voevodin, V., Sobolev, S. (eds.) RuSCDays 2020. CCIS, vol. 1331, pp. 25–36. Springer, Cham (2020). https://doi.org/10.1007/978-3-030-64616-5_3
9. Express JS framework. https://expressjs.com
10. Huang, T.-W., et al.: Cpp-Taskflow: fast task-based parallel programming using modern C++. In: IEEE International Parallel and Distributed Processing Symposium (IPDPS), pp. 974–983. Rio de Janeiro, Brazil (2019). https://doi.org/10.1109/IPDPS.2019.00105
11. Reinders, J.: Intel Threading Building Blocks. O'Reilly Media, Inc., Sebastopol (2007)

Finite Element Simulation
of the Influence of the Bending Roll
Profile on the Stress-Strain State
of Billets for Longitudinal-Welded
Rolled Pipes

Leonid M. Gurevich[1](✉) , Roman E. Novikov[1], Alexandr I. Bannikov[1] ,
Dmitriy Vladimirovich Pronichev[1] , and Dmitry B. Frunkin[2]

[1] Volgograd State Technical University, Volgograd, Russian Federation
[2] Volzhsky Pipe Plant, Volzhsky, Russian Federation

Abstract. In this paper, we describe 3D finite-element models for the study of billets used in pipe rolling and made of steel sheets thicker than 25 mm. Relying on 3D modeling with the MSC Marc software package, we study how several alternatives of lowering the upper roller of a traditional profile affect the geometry of the resulting pipe billet and, also, the distribution of deformations and stress during the bending process. We manage to reduce the computation time for a 3D model with a finite element mesh containing more than one million nodes, which is possible through multi-threaded computation distributed over the nodes of a computing cluster. The main load during the first pass of a bending tool with a traditional profile is exerted on local areas of the outer surface of the pipe billet. Those areas are located on the border of the edges and the chamfers of the weld groove. Plastic deformation occurs on them and leads to local thinning of the pipe billet. We suggest alternatives for changing the profile of the bending tool to create additional contact pads during the bending process.

Keywords: Longitudinal welded pipes · Finish bending · Finite element method · Bending roll shape · Parallel computations · Cluster · Stress-strain state

1 Production Schemes for Longitudinal-Welded Pipes

Straight-seam pipes of large diameter (over 426 mm) are intended for main pipelines of gas, oil, oil products, and also for water and steam pipelines. Welded pipes have the following advantages:

- the electric welding equipment is simpler than the one used for pipe rolling;
- the manufacture of welded tubes requires fewer steps than the production of seamless pipes;
- the cost of welded pipes is 15% to 20% lower than that of seamless pipes;

© Springer Nature Switzerland AG 2021
L. Sokolinsky and M. Zymbler (Eds.): PCT 2021, CCIS 1437, pp. 284–299, 2021.
https://doi.org/10.1007/978-3-030-81691-9_20

- higher quality of the steel sheet surface, no casting defects in surface layers;
- higher accuracy of pipe dimensions: there is practically no difference in wall thickness of pipes along the perimeter;

In the production of large diameter pipes, the following methods are the most commonly used when forming sheet blanks:

- on large presses, as per the so-called "UOE" scheme [1,2];
- step-by-step shaping, as per the "JCOE" scheme [3–5];
- forming of sheet stock by rolling in a three-roll machine with final bending of the edges on a sheet bending machine, as per the RBE (roll-bending-expansion) scheme [6,7].

A straight seam on a bent hot-rolled steel sheet is made by submerged-arc welding. Then, the calibration operation is carried out by expansion. Expansion is the final operation of forming a pipe billet; it reduces shape defects. During this operation, a synchronous radial expansion of the segments of the compound tool occurs at each step of the movement of the expander [8].

An important indicator of the quality of oil and gas pipelines is the degree of deviation of the cross-sectional geometry from a circle. The importance of this indicator increases for pipes of underwater crossings as it reduces the time spent on preparatory operations before welding the next assembly circumferential seam.

For projects of underwater crossings, the assignment of tolerances for the deviation of the geometry of pipe ends is regulated by the "Standards for Subsea Structures-Subsea Pipeline Systems" DNV-OS-F101 (Det Norske Veritas). The ovality of the ends should not exceed 3.0 mm for 50% of the pipes from the total volume. The fulfillment of such stringent geometry requirements can only be ensured by optimizing technological operations in the process of forming a billet in the sheet-tube redistribution.

The technology of forming billets for large-diameter pipes in a three-roll machine according to a scheme has several advantages when compared with other technologies. The main ones are the minimum power consumption of the process and the stability of the curvature in the main part of the cylindrical perimeter. Curvature stability is very important to ensure a minimum ovality of the pipe. It is for these reasons that this technology is used at two large pipe plants, namely the JSC Volzhsky Pipe Plant (Pipe Metallurgical Company), and the JSC Zagorsk Pipe Plant, for forming large-diameter pipes.

The complexity of the stress-strain state of pipes is due to the sequential displacement of local areas of deformation during pipe molding along (RBE scheme) or across the pipe axis (JUOE scheme). The traditional optimization of the production processes of pipe billets relied on the production of prototypes and empirical attempts to change the technological parameters of operation or calibration of the forming tool. The optimization of deformation processes using finite element modeling was hampered by the large number of mesh nodes required for the adequate modeling of large-sized pipe billets. Therefore, the modeling task used various assumptions, for instance, 2D modeling [9,10]. Mainly, 2D finite element modeling methods are used to analyze pipe forming by step-by-step shaping [11,12] or bending on a press as per the UOE scheme [13,14]. For these technological processes, the assumption was made that there were no deflections of technological tools along their axis, which had little effect on the reliability of the obtained simulation results, though. Much less adequate are the results of engineering calculations [15] or 2D modeling of expansion process [16,17], in which it is impossible to take into account how subsequent expansion cycles of the expander segments at a close distance from the already deformed section affect the shape of the workpiece.

Similarly, the analysis of elastic-plastic deformations in the process of pre-bending of edges on a press using 2D finite element modeling does not take into account the effect of the subsequent bending steps [23].

Improving the reliability of finite element modeling for operations associated with forming large-sized pipe billets became possible only after the creation of 3D finite element modeling packages that support parallel computations on multiprocessor computers [19,20].

The purpose of this article is to study sequential changes in the shape and stress-strain state of a pipe billet with a three-stage post-bending of the edges using 3D finite element modeling.

The rest of the paper consists of the following sections. In Sect. 2, we outline the 3D finite element model of the pipe bending process we are working with, as well as the principles used to simulate the process of plastic deformation. In Sect. 3, we go on to describe the mechanical characteristics of deformable materials and the kinematics of the movement of the main parts of the model. Deformations and stresses in the billet at various stages of bending are considered in Sect. 4. Finally, in Sect. 5, we give a summary of our findings.

2   A Finite Element Model of Bending Roll Profile

In the production of pipes, the parameters of edge bending determine several deviations in the shape of the workpiece from the required geometry, for example, decrease in wall thickness near the weld groove, out-of-roundness of the deformed pipe billet ends, the waviness and non-straightness of the weld groove. Manufacturers try to minimize the size of these defects by changing the geometry of the composite deforming tool elements and the amount of lowering of the upper roller. The amount of lowering of the upper roller can vary with both the distance from the ends of the pipe billet and during the three sequential technological stages.

We used the licensed software complex Marc (Mentat), developed by MSC Software Corporation, to accomplish the 3D finite element modeling task through parallel computations. The calculations were carried out on a 128-core node of the Volgograd State Technical University supercomputer. The Marc solver is based on the finite element method with an implicit integration scheme and, among other things, is designed to simulate nonlinear deformations of solid metal bodies occurring at moderate speeds. The Marc solver stands out by its high efficiency of parallelizing computations on a multiprocessor computer cluster, which significantly contributes to the implementation of the idea of "engineering analysis at design pace" [21]. MSC Software systems allow parallelization of computations on computer systems of all classes and types: Vector supercomputers, shared-memory parallel computers, distributed-memory parallel computers, hybrid systems, cluster systems, etc.etera. To parallelize computations, the MSC Software Marc solver applies geometric domain decomposition [22]. The various sources of nonlinearity, such as material, geometric and kinematic nonlinearities, as well as contact, need to be taken into consideration. Other requirements, distinct from linear analysis, are handling of multiple steps and step-by-step changing load balance at the stage of contact analysis. In general, stability plays a key role in the distributed implementation of MSC Software Marc. MSC Marc features an algorithm for obtaining a stable solution to nonlinear quasistatic boundary value problems that satisfy the sufficient conditions of uniqueness (stability).

We created a 3D finite element model (see Fig. 1), whose main elements (pipe billet, upper roller, take-up rollers, lower rollers [inner and outer barrels], guides) are located similarly to the real nodes of the technological equipment at the JSC Volzhsky Pipe Plant [19].

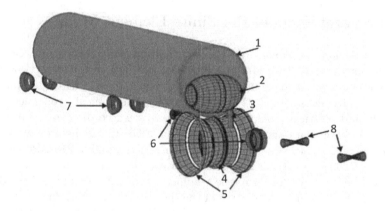

Fig. 1. General view of the edge post-bending model: 1–pipe billet; 2–upper roller; 3–upper roller clamping rod; 4–lower inner rolls; 5–lower outer rolls; 6–receiving rollers; 7–rear guides; 8–front guides.

We employed the basic relations of the theory of the plastic flow of a hardening material to simulate the process of plastic deformation of a steel sheet blank and considered the classical Huber–Mises hypothesis on the specific energy of deformation as a plasticity criterion. Moreover, we used a strain diagram for isotropically hardened pipe steel and applied both the Coulomb friction model with a constant coefficient and the gravity model.

The contact problem was formulated based on the following conditions:

$$g \equiv (x^2 - x^1) \cdot n \geq 0, \tag{1}$$

$$t_n \equiv t \cdot n \leq 0, \tag{2}$$

where x^1, x^2 denote the radius vectors of material points corresponding to two contact bodies in the current configuration, n is the unit normal vector to the contact surface, t is a vector of distributed contact forces, and t_n stands for distributed contact normal forces. The g value determines the normal clearance. When the bodies touch at the contact boundary, instead of the inequality in formula (1), we obtain an equality; when the bodies diverge, the inequality is strict.

When the external force exerted reaches a certain value, the material is in the plastic state, and the stress components satisfy the von Mises yield function. The equivalent stress is equal to the yield strength:

$$\bar{\sigma} = \frac{1}{\sqrt{2}} \sqrt{(\sigma_1 - \sigma_2)^2 + (\sigma_2 - \sigma_3)^2 + (\sigma_3 - \sigma_1)^2}, \tag{3}$$

where $\bar{\sigma}$ is the equivalent stress, and σ_1, σ_2, and σ_3 are the principal stresses [18].

3   The Parameters of the Finite Element Model

In the simulation, we considered the deformation and stresses of a pipe billet made out of an API 5L Grade X70 steel sheet 3681 mm wide and 30.9 mm thick. We employed a finite element mesh of constant size with quadrangular eight-node cells measuring 5.22×5.22 mm. The mechanical properties of the elastically and plastically deformable body were set according to the results of tests of samples cut in different directions from a hot-rolled sheet manufactured by Salzgitter AG (Germany), with an elastic modulus equal to 210 GPa and steel density of 7770 kg/m^3. The dependence between the yield stress and the deformation was set in a tabular form (the graphical representation of the dependency is shown in Fig. 2). The deformation of the sheet during the forming process was taken into account; therefore, the pipe blank had different values of the yield point in different areas. While post-bending the edges, the sign of the deformation does not change compared to the deformation after the forming process on a three-roll machine; because of this, we neglected the Bauschinger effect [24].

The elements of the composite deforming tool and the transporting system are discrete and rigid [25]. The axial movement of the pipe is ensured by rotating the lower inner rolls. The graph of the change in the rotation of the lower inner rolls throughout the post-bending process is shown in Fig. 3. The time of one pass is about 13 s. At each pass, the absolute value of the angular velocity of the lower inner rolls remained unchanged, and the direction of rotation at the end of the pass was reversed. The pipe billet moved in the axial direction and rotated

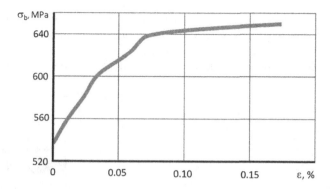

Fig. 2. Dependence between the yield point and the deformation

the upper roller and the lower outer rolls as a result of frictional forces. The coefficient of friction of the pipe billet on the upper roller and lower inner rolls was set equal to 0.29; for all other pairs of elements, the coefficient of friction was 0.1, which corresponds to the values usually attained during the processing of metals by pressure [26].

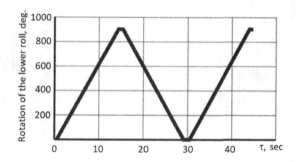

Fig. 3. Graph of changes in the rotation of the inner roll during the post-bending process. The analysis of the simulation results showed that the use of a standard geometry of the post-bending tool generates several defects (e.g., variations in the gap between the pipe edges along the axis of the billet, formation of vertical kinks, and local thinning of the edge near the weld groove), which hinders the successful accomplishment of subsequent operations (assembly and welding of pipe billets) [19].

Therefore, we considered a wide calibration of the post-bending tool when creating a new 3D model (see Fig. 4). The corresponding profile was suggested by specialists of the JSC Volzhsky Pipe Plant.

The movement pattern of the upper roller during the process of bending the edges (Fig. 5) included:

– a smooth lowering of the upper roller from the front and rear ends of the pipe
  billet on the first pass for 1 s, followed by a continuous lowering along the rest
  of the pipe;
– a continuous lowering of the upper roller during the second and third passes.

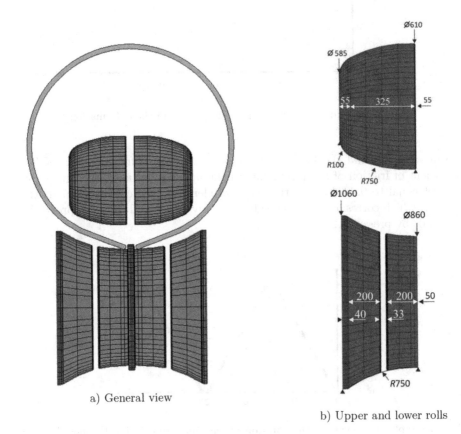

a) General view

b) Upper and lower rolls

Fig. 4. Geometrical parameters for wide calibration of the post-bending tool

4   Experimental Results of the Finite Element Simulation

Figures 6 and 7 depict the change in the position and shape of the contact
areas of the post-bending tool with a wide calibration at the inner and outer
surfaces of the pipe billet at different stages of the first pass, as obtained in the
3D finite element modeling. For the sake of convenience, only small fragments of
the pipe billet are shown, from different angles of view with the contour of the
deforming tool. The position of the pipe billet, deforming tool, support rollers,
and the angles of view are shown simultaneously in Figs. 6a and 7a.

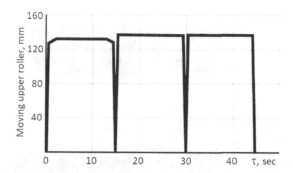

Fig. 5. Vertical movement of the upper roller in the 3D post-bending model with wide calibration of the post-bending tool

As we can see from Figs. 6 and 7, throughout the first pass, the inner surface of the billet contacts with the upper roll along a sufficiently long arc whose projection exceeds the width of the lower inner rolls. Additionally, a point of contact is observed in the region of the fillets of the upper roller with the inner surface of the pipe. Changing the contact area of the pipe outer surface with the lower rolls is much more difficult. The lower outer rolls did not come into contact with the outer surface of the pipes throughout the first pass. The contact area of the lower inner rolls with the outer surface of the pipe changes its shape as the pipe moves axially. Initially, a narrow contact area is visible at some distance from the boundary between the edge surface and the weld groove, which is associated with an annular groove on the surface of the lower inner roll.

The posterior advancement of this section of the pipe toward the deformation zone as the gap between the upper roller and the lower rolls decreases results in a gradual increase of the contact area until the contact extends to the entire width of the lower inner rolls. As the contact area gradually increases, two deformation processes occur at the same time: a) bending of both the edge and the entire pipe billet; b) partial crush of the pipe metal in the contact zone with the surface of the lower inner rolls near the annular groove.

When we consider the wide calibration of the upper roller in the simulation, the main pressure in the first pass on the outer surface at the moment of entering the deformation zone is exerted on local areas near the boundary of the surface of the edges and chamfers of the weld groove. Those areas are in contact with both the fillet of the annular groove and the single-radius surface of the lower inner rolls near the annular groove.

The wide calibration of the post-bending tool made it possible to stabilize the size of the gap between the edges of the pipe billet throughout the first pass. This stems from the fact that the proportion corresponding to the horizontal components of the reaction forces is relatively small at the points of contact of the surface of the billet with the upper roll and the lower rolls (see Fig. 8).

Upper roll

Lower roll

a) The position of the pipe billet, deforming
tool, support rollers, and angles of view

b) The light yellow region corresponds to the contact area
of the post-bending tool with the inner surface of the pipe
billet.

c) The light yellow region corresponds to the contact area
of the post-bending tool with the outer surface of the pipe
billet.

Fig. 6. The position of contact areas between the surface of the pipe and the deforming
tool with a wide calibration (first pass after processing 33% of the length of the pipe
billet) (Color figure online)

Figure 9 depicts the change in the gap between the edges along the length of
the pipe and the displacement of the points of the outer surface at the boundary
of the surface of the edges and the chamfers of the weld groove.

By comparing the reaction and frictional forces at the beginning of the first
pass, we found that significant forces acted on the inner surface of the pipe billet
from the end sections of the upper roller when using a traditional calibration.
They caused the expansion of the gap of the pipe billet, overcoming both the
rigidity of the billet and the frictional forces on the contact surfaces with the
post-bending tool.

After the first pass, we observed a slight difference in the gap and distortion
of the straightness of the edge ends. The gap width changed by no more than
25 mm, which allowed the end areas of the edges to remain within the annular
groove.

Upper roll

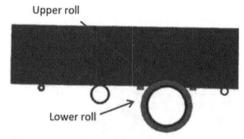

a) The position of the pipe billet, deforming
tool, support rollers, and angles of view

b) The light yellow region corresponds to the contact area
of the post-bending tool with the inner surface of the pipe
billet.

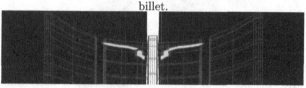

c) The light yellow region corresponds to the contact area
of the post-bending tool with the outer surface of the pipe
billet.

Fig. 7. The position of contact areas between the surface of the pipe and the deforming
tool with a wide calibration (first pass after processing 66% of the length of the pipe
billet) (Color figure online)

Figures 10 and 11 depict the variation in the deformation of areas on the
inner and outer surfaces of the pipe blank at different stages of the first pass.
The demonstrated stages of the first pass, the areas of the surface of the pipe
billet, and the angles of view correspond to those shown in Figs. 6 and 7.

The area of the contact surface of the edge with the fillet at the transition
of the annular groove to the single-radius surface of the lower inner roll became
large enough after a slight deformation of the pipe billet upon entering the
deformation zone, and the equivalent local von Mises stresses did not exceed the
yield stress. This deformation was found in two relatively narrow strips located
near the boundary of the edges and the chamfers of the weld groove. The width
of the deformation zone was no more than 30% of the generatrix of the lower

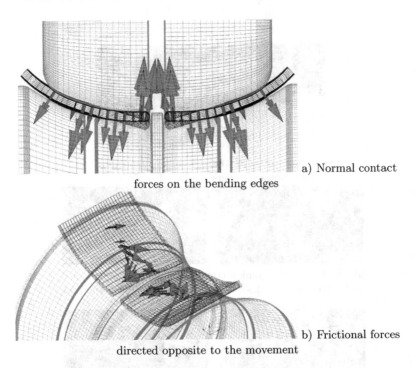

a) Normal contact forces on the bending edges

b) Frictional forces directed opposite to the movement

Fig. 8. Forces after the beginning of the first pass using a wide calibration of the post-bending tool

inner rolls. There was no contact between the outer surface of the pipe and the lower outer rolls, therefore, there was no significant deformation of the outer surface of the pipe billet in this section. Significantly wider bands of relatively low plastic deformation regions were located on the inner surface of the pipe billet. They corresponded to the projection position of the lower inner rolls. Two more narrow strips of plastic deformation were located on the inner surface of the pipe symmetrically to the gap in the pipe billet. They were located at the point of contact with 100 mm radius fillets at the outer ends of the upper roller. Thus, with the simulated post-bending option and a wide calibration of the upper roller, the latter was in contact with the pipe billet in the first pass over almost the entire surface, but the main load was applied to the local areas of the outer surface of the pipe near the weld groove chamfers. The plastic deformation occurs in this zone and results in local thinning of the pipe billet. The width of the plastic deformation area when using a wide calibration was greater than that under the traditional one without an annular groove on the lower inner roll. This should lead to less thinning of the pipe wall in these sections.

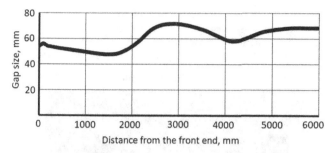

a) Change in the gap between the edges along the length of the pipe

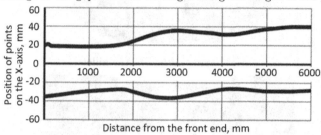

b) Displacement of the points of the outer surface

Fig. 9. Changing the geometry at the boundary of the surface of the left and right edges and the chamfers of the weld groove after the end of the first pass.

We also measured the change in thickness of the sheet on the right and left sides of the deformation zone at different distances from the front end. The measurement was made by determining the position of the points on the boundary of the surface of the edges and the weld groove. The results of modeling showed that the post-bending of the edges does not lead practically to any change in the thickness of the steel sheet along the entire length of the pipe billet. This is easily explained since the section of the pipe billet containing the measured points was constantly above the annular groove in the lower inner roll.

The previously discovered absence of significant horizontal components of the reaction forces at the points of contact of the billet with the upper and lower tools made it possible to maintain the position of the section containing the measured points above the annular groove throughout the first pass. However, the points on the outer surface of the edge, which were in actual contact with the surface of the lower inner roll, practically did not wrinkle. The explanation is that the contact surface of the edge with the fillet at the transition of the annular groove to the single-radius surface of the lower inner roll becomes large enough

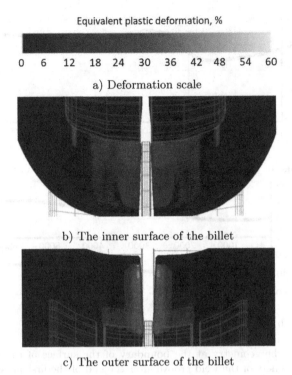

Equivalent plastic deformation, %

0   6   12   18   24   30   36   42   48   54   60

a) Deformation scale

b) The inner surface of the billet

c) The outer surface of the billet

Fig. 10. Deformation of areas on the inner and outer surfaces of the billet (first pass after processing 33% of the length of the pipe billet)

after a slight deformation of the pipe billet at the entrance of the deformation zone, and the equivalent local von Mises stresses do not exceed the yield stress.

Figure 9 shows the change in the profile along the length of the billet during the first pass of post-bending the edges. After the first pass, the edge becomes almost horizontal, and in some sections, there is even a deflection to the pipe axis (the so-called "apple" shape). The horizontality of the edge should ensure a good closure of the end surfaces of the weld groove.

Equivalent plastic deformation, %

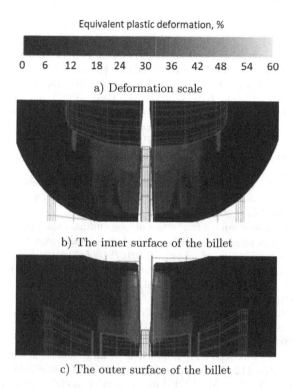

0   6   12   18   24   30   36   42   48   54   60

a) Deformation scale

b) The inner surface of the billet

c) The outer surface of the billet

Fig. 11. Deformation of areas on the inner and outer surfaces of the billet (first pass after processing 66% of the length of the pipe billet)

5   Conclusions

We simulated the post-bending of the edges using a wide calibration of the post-bending tool in the first pass. The main load on the outer surface at the entrance into the deformation area was exerted on the contact surface of the edge of the pipe billet with the fillet at the transition of the annular groove to the single-radius surface of the lower inner roll. The deformation extended to the entire contact strip with the surface of the lower inner rolls only after a slight deformation at the initial point. There was no contact with the surface of the lower outer roll in the first pass. Despite the locality of the initial contact of the edge surface with the lower bending tool, no significant steel crushing occurred. The area of the contact surface of the edge with the fillet at the transition of the annular groove to the single-radius surface of the lower inner roll became large enough after a slight deformation of the pipe billet upon entering the deformation zone, and the equivalent local von Mises stresses did not exceed the yield stress.

References

1. Herynk, M.D., Kyriakides, S., Onoufriou, A., Yun, H.D.: Effects of the UOE/UOC pipe manufacturing processes on pipe collapse pressure. Int. J. Mech. Sci. **49**(5), 533–553 (2007). https://doi.org/10.1016/j.ijmecsci.2006.10.001
2. Zou, T., Wu, G., Li, D., Ren, Q., Xin, J., Peng, Y.: A numerical method for predicting O-forming gap in UOE pipe manufacturing. Int. J. Mech. Sci. **98**, 39–58 (2015). https://doi.org/10.1016/j.ijmecsci.2015.04.006
3. Fan, L.-F., Yan, J.-X., Gao, Y., Yun, J.-B.: Research on deformation characteristics of JCOE forming in large diameter welding pipe. Adv. Manuf. **4**(3), 268–277 (2016). https://doi.org/10.1007/s40436-016-0154-5
4. Shinkin, V.N.: Calculation of technological parameters of O-forming press for manufacture of large-diameter steel pipes. CIS Iron Steel Rev. **13**, 33 (2017). https://doi.org/10.17580/cisisr.2017.01.07
5. Yang, Z.Z., et al.: Mechanical properties of longitudinal submerged arc welded steel pipes used for gas pipeline of offshore oil. Acta Metallurgica Sinica (Engl. Lett.) **21**(2), 85–93 (2008). https://doi.org/10.1016/S1006-7191(08)60024-1i
6. Il'ichev, V.G., Zalavin, Y.E.: Improving the roller shaping of large-diameter pipe from strip. Steel Transl. **46**(1) (2016). https://doi.org/10.3103/S0967091216010058i
7. Shinkin, V.N.: Asymmetric three-roller sheet-bending systems in steel-pipe production. Steel Transl. **47**(4), 235–240 (2017). https://doi.org/10.3103/S0967091217040106
8. Kolikov, A.P., Zvonarev, D.Y.: Expansion of large-diameter welded pipe. Steel Transl. **47**(3), 210–212 (2017). https://doi.org/10.3103/S0967091217030068
9. Delistoian, D., Chirchor, M.: UOE pipe numerical model: manufacturing process and Von Mises residual stresses resulted after each technological step. ACTA Universitatis Cibiniensis **69**(1), 113–120 (2017). https://doi.org/10.1515/aucts-2017-0014
10. Hillenbrand, H.G., Graef, M.K., Groß-Weege, J., Knauf, G., Marewski, U.: Development of linepipe for deep-water applications. In: The Twelfth International Offshore and Polar Engineering Conference. International Society of Offshore and Polar Engineers, January 2002
11. Gao, Y., Li, Q., Fan, L.: Finite element analysis of JCO forming process for longitudinal seam submerged arc welded pipes. Int. J. Model. Ident. Control **11**(3–4), 239–249 (2010). https://doi.org/10.1504/IJMIC.2010.037036
12. Chandel, J.D., Singh, N.L.: Formation of X-120 M line pipe through JCOE technique. Engineering **3**(4), 400–410 (2011). https://doi.org/10.4236/eng.2011.34046
13. Chatzopoulou, G., Karamanos, S.A., Varelis, G.E.: Finite element analysis of UOE manufacturing process and its effect on mechanical behavior of offshore pipes. Int. J. Solids Struct. **83**, 13–27 (2016). https://doi.org/10.1016/j.ijsolstr.2015.12.020
14. Raffo, J., Toscano, R.G., Mantovano, L., Dvorkin, E.N.: Numerical model Of UOE steel pipes: forming process and structural behavior. Mecanica Computacional 317–333 (2007)
15. Shinkin, V.N., Kolikov, A.P.: Engineering calculations for processes involved in the production of large-diameter pipes by the SMS Meer technology. Metallurgist **55**(11–12), 833–840 (2012). https://doi.org/10.1007/s11015-012-9510-2
16. Kyriakides, S., Herynk, M.D., Yun, H.: Optimization of UOE pipe manufacturing process for improved collapse performance under external pressure. In: International Pipe-Line Conference, vol. 42614 (2006). https://doi.org/10.1115/IPC2006-10614

17. Ren, Q., Zou, T., Li, D., Tang, D., Peng, Y.: Numerical study on the X80 UOE pipe forming process. J. Mater. Process. Technol. **215**, 264–277 (2015). https://doi.org/10.1016/j.jmatprotec.2014.08.013

18. Fan, L., Gao, Y., Li, Q., Xu, H.: Quality control on crimping of large diameter welding pipe. Chin. J. Mech. Eng. **25**(6), 1264–1273 (2012). https://doi.org/10.3901/CJME.2012.06.1264

19. Frunkin, D., Gurevich, L.M., Novikov, R.: A Simulation of the post-bending process of the pipe billets for welded pipe manufacturing. In: Solid State Phenomena, vol. 299. Trans Tech Publications Ltd. (2020). https://doi.org/10.4028/www.scientific.net/SSP.299.676

20. Frunkin, D.B., Gurevich, L.M., Novikov, R.E., Bannikov, A.I., Serov, A.G., Dyatlov, N.A.: Welded pipe geometry changing during the expanding process. In: IOP Conference Series: Materials Science and Engineering, vol. 450, no. 3, p. 032048, November 2018. https://doi.org/10.1088/1757-899X/450/3/032048

21. Javanbakht, Z., Öchsner, A.: Advanced Finite Element Simulation with MSC Marc. Springer, Cham (2017). https://doi.org/10.1007/978-3-319-47668-1

22. Komzsik, L., Rose, T.: Substructuring in MSC/NASTRAN for large scale parallel applications. Comput. Syst. Eng. **2**(2–3), 167–173. (1991). https://doi.org/10.1016/0956-0521(91)90017-y

23. Park, M.S., Lee, B.C.: Geometrically non-linear and elastoplastic three-dimensional shear flexible beam element of von-Mises-type hardening material. Int. J. Numer. Methods Eng. **39**(3), 383–408 (1996). https://doi.org/10.1002/(SICI)1097-0207(19960215)39:3⟨383::AID-NME859⟩3.0.CO;2-F

24. Chun, B.K., Jinn, J.T., Lee, J.K.: Modeling the Bauschinger effect for sheet metals, part I: theory. Int. J. Plast. **18**(5–6), 571–595 (2002). https://doi.org/10.1016/S0749-6419(01)00046-8

25. Bloch, A.M., Crouch, P.E., Marsden, J.E., Ratiu, T.S.: Discrete rigid body dynamics and optimal control. In: Proceedings of the 37th IEEE Conference on Decision and Control (Cat. No. 98CH36171), vol. 2, pp. 2249–2254. IEEE, December 1998. https://doi.org/10.1109/CDC.1998.758678

26. Domenech, A., Domenech, T., Cebrian, J.: Introduction to the study of rolling friction. Am. J. Phys. **55**(3), 231–235 (1987). https://doi.org/10.1119/1.15223

Digital Twins of Geological Objects: Development and Use

Galina Reshetova[1,2]([⊠]) [iD], Vladimir Cheverda[2] [iD], and Vadim Lisitsa[2] [iD]

[1] Institute of Computational Mathematics and Mathematical Geophysics SB RAS,
Novosibirsk 630090, Russia
kgv@nmsf.sscc.ru
[2] Trofimuk Institute of Petroleum Geology and Geophysics SB RAS,
Novosibirsk, Russia
{CheverdaVA,LisitsaVV}@ipgg.sbras.ru

Abstract. We describe the workflow associated with the construction of a digital twin for a realistic three-dimensional model of a carbonate field in the north of Eastern Siberia. It involves creating the skeleton of the geological object and a set of synthetic seismic data obtained by numerical simulations. To create synthetic data, we carry out finite-difference numerical simulations, which serve as a blind test to verify various techniques used for retrieving a reservoir structure on a subseismic scale. For the simulation of synthetic seismograms, we rely on an original finite-difference scheme based on a local grid refinement in time and space. To cope with the huge amounts of input/output data, we use high-performance computing systems with parallel architecture and a hybrid parallelization strategy for process optimization.

Keywords: Seismic waves · Numerical modeling · Carbonate reservoir · Finite-difference schemes · Local grid refinement · Domain decomposition

1 Introduction and Motivation

The construction of a comprehensive geological model of an object under study is necessary to ensure a successful seismic exploration and the subsequent development of hydrocarbon reservoirs. This stage is crucial when considering fields in carbonate environments, which are frequent in the north of Eastern Siberia, particularly in the Yurubcheno-Tokhomskaya zone. Indeed, such hydrocarbon reservoirs are characterized by an extremely complex internal structure, determined by the presence of multiple accumulations of subseismic objects, such as caverns, fractures, and fracture corridors. The corresponding definition and the technology for constructing a digital twin of a geological object are given hereunder.

A digital twin of a geological object, according to our understanding, is a set of data that determines its geometric and physical properties in conjunction with

L. Sokolinsky and M. Zymbler (Eds.): PCT 2021, CCIS 1437, pp. 300–311, 2021.
https://doi.org/10.1007/978-3-030-81691-9_21

the corresponding synthetic geophysical fields. In what follows, we construct a seismic digital twin of an object located in the Yurubcheno-Tokhomskaya zone.

For a detailed study of a carbonate reservoir, we need an extensive amount of varied geological and geophysical information, in which an important role is assigned to seismic data. This information should be able to explain the reservoir's internal structure and changes in its properties occurring in the interwell space. However, the fundamental physical properties of seismic wavefields impose very harsh restrictions upon solution methods based on reflected waves. Therefore, when it comes to fractured and fractured-cavernous reservoirs, standard seismic methods based on reflected waves are not as effective as in classical terrigenous reservoirs. A distinctive feature of carbonate reservoirs is the absence of sharp acoustic boundaries on their roof, which is due to the diffuse nature of the voids formed in the process of dissolution and leaching of rocks [1].

By attracting scattered/diffracted waves, it is possible to expand and deepen significantly the information obtained from seismic methods [2–6]. The presence of such waves indicates the existence of singular objects in the medium, such as faults, cracks, clusters, caverns, and so on. Therefore, the use of such waves opens up possibilities for a significant increase in information content and resolution of seismic methods for the study of the internal structure of media [7–11]. The requirement to perform a reliable validation of the developed approaches, allowing for independent verification, is one of the main issues here. The most reliable way to achieve this is to build a digital geological model of the reservoir, so to say, its digital twin, which describes the main geological elements of the object under study: its geometry, stratigraphy, lithologic characteristics of facies, net thickness, reservoir properties, and others. Knowing these characteristics is particularly important when developing carbonate reservoirs, which, as a rule, have a very complex structure of hollows. When developing reservoirs of this kind, we need to consider the uneven distribution of cracks and caves since they act as the main filtration paths for fluids (cracks) and form cavities in carbonate reservoirs. Such reservoirs are rather diverse and concentrate a significant part of the world's hydrocarbon reserves: up to 60% of oil and 40% of gas [12]. In the territory of the Russian Federation, such reservoirs are frequently found in such places as the Central Siberian Plateau, the Volga–Ural basin, the Timan Ridge–Pechora River basin, the Orenburg Oblast, the Ural Mountains, the Caspian Depression, and others.

Note that the construction of digital twins as an approach has been around for some time. It has been developed by the SEG Advanced Corporation, created under the SEG (Society of Exploration Geophysicists) Modelling Corporation (https://seg.org/News-Resources/Research-and-Data/SEAM), which, in collaboration with geologists from large oil companies, has designed typical synthetic models for solving various geological problems, such as

– the generation of subsalt imaging in tertiary basins (https://seg.org/News-Resources/SEG-Advanced-Modelling-SEAM/SEAM-Projects/Phase-I-Subsalt, 2011);

- land seismic (https://seg.org/SEAM/Phase2, 2018), including fractured reservoirs, desert areas with karst near-surface inclusions, foothills with complex topography of the free surface;
- reservoir pressure forecast based on seismic images (https://seg.org/News-Resources/SEG-Advanced-Modelling-SEAM/SEAM-Projects/Pressure-Prediction, 2017),

and others.

In Russia, however, this is perhaps the first experiment to attempt the creation of a digital twin of a field, including full-scale 3D elastic numerical simulations.

The rest of the paper is organized as follows. Section 2 is devoted to the construction of a digital twin for a geological object. In Sect. 3, we outline the stages of the 3D multiscale numerical simulation of seismic waves, including the mathematical formulation and the numerical method. In Sect. 4, we outline the corresponding parallel implementation. The final section summarizes the main conclusions and points out directions for further research.

2   Construction of a Digital Twin for a Geological Object

We chose one of the fields in the north of Eastern Siberia as the basis for a three-dimensional model. The main object was a carbonate reservoir of the Riphean age containing deposits of massive type, tectonically and lithologically screened. The field's reservoir is a complex structure with two kinds of voids: cavities and cracks. The reservoir is characterized by strong heterogeneity and anisotropy. It also combines low capacity (on average 1 to 2%) and high permeability (up to 4000 mD), mainly due to natural fracturing. The initial stage of modeling consists of the construction of the model skeleton, that is, the description of the interfaces between layers, built as a result of processing and interpreting 3D seismic data. The parameters of the elastic medium between these boundaries are determined from geophysical surveys of wells. A significant feature of the studied area is the existence of faults that split the reservoir into a series of blocks with displacement amplitudes reaching hundreds of meters. Today, it is becoming more and more accepted by specialists to understand a geological fault as a complex three-dimensional geological object [13,14]. For this reason, we consider faults as certain volumetric geological bodies consisting of rocks deformed by tectonic movements [15]. The latter are determined by a wide range of parameters, including the tectonic regime, the magnitude of a layer displacement, mechanical properties of surrounding rocks, and so forth [16,17].

To model the internal structure of faults, we relied on data from geophysical surveys of a horizontal well at the opening of a fault on the considered field. Of course, we are aware that data from a single well is insufficient for a detailed description of the tectonic breccia. Nevertheless, the velocities of P- and S-waves specified for the well and the density made it possible to calibrate the parameters used in the geomechanical model. This provided a close-to-realistic description of tectonic breccia filling geological faults (see Fig. 1). In addition to faults, the carbonate reservoir contains various proportions of fracture corridors and caverns, which are the main reservoir (cavities) and transport paths (cracks) for fluids. We introduced fracture zones in two multidirectional systems of subvertical fractures obtained by statistical modeling using spectral decomposition of random fields. In this manner, we could generate cracks from 5 to 300 m long, forming realistic fracture corridors. Additionally, we added to the model intervals of intense cavitation, regularly occurring on the field. According to data from core samples, these intervals, related to host rocks, possess increased cavitation, which reaches 15 to 20%, and small thickness, ranging from one to ten meters. To determine the parameters of cavitation zones, we conducted a statistical analysis of ten digital models of core samples built by X-ray computed tomography [18].

It is worth noting that the seismo-geological model given in Fig. 1 does not strive to describe each and every small crack being only a few millimeters thick. We built instead so-called fracture corridors [19] representing clusters of cracks with one or more selected orientations. Fracture corridors can extend for several hundred meters and have a height of the order of tens of meters and a thickness of a few meters. To construct the fracture corridors in the geological model, we relied on both the direct observation of outcrops and the results from downhole measurements. We based on previous results [7,11,13] describing the structure of such objects according to a statistical analysis of the results of full-scale observations, including the examination of outcrops and microscanner studies of the reservoir.

Figure 1 gives a general view of the frame of the constructed three-dimensional model, with faults and other small-scale irregularities. The framework is specified as a set of reflective boundaries, geological faults, fracture corridors, and zones with increased cavernosity. To determine the elastic properties of the medium filling the wireframe model, we used the results of velocity analysis, measurements of the borehole parameters, and data yielded by laboratory measurements of the composition of core samples. Thus, we constructed a digital twin of the geological object for numerical simulation of seismic wavefields. The results of full-scale numerical simulations served as synthetic data to verify various techniques used for restoring the reservoir structure on a subseismic scale. The use of different-scale geological and geophysical data provided a reliable blind test for approbation and verification of different approaches employed to retrieve the geological internal structure of reservoirs and determine the optimal strategy for their development in carbonate environments.

3   3D Multiscale Numerical Simulation of Seismic Wavefields

Apart from the creation of the model skeleton, the construction of a digital twin for a geological object involves the determination of various attributes. One of the main attributes is the synthetic seismogram for this digital twin. It makes possible a thorough analysis of wave processes and the development of new technologies to reconstruct a carbonate reservoir. Moreover, it provides the means to conduct fully controlled numerical experiments to verify the

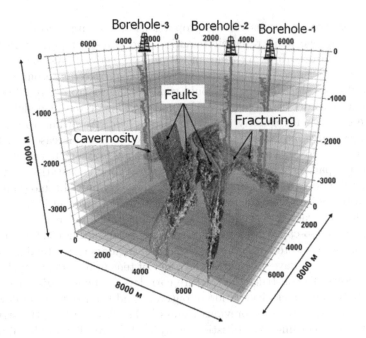

Fig. 1. Seismo-geological model framework (digital twin of the geological object). Half-tone images correspond to regular reflective surfaces.

developed methods for retrieving the reservoir structure on a subseismic scale, the localization of both fracture and cavity accumulations, and the distribution of micro-inhomogeneities. This information ensures the choice of an optimal strategy for the development of reservoirs in carbonate environments.

The generation of seismograms implies rather time-consuming procedures consisting of multisource numerical simulations of seismic wavefields for a 3D digital model. The main steps are described below.

3.1   The Mathematical Statement

For the description of seismic waves propagating in elastic or viscoelastic media, we use the Generalized Standard Linear Solid (GSLS) model described by the following equations:

$$\rho \frac{\partial u}{\partial t} = \nabla \cdot \sigma,$$

$$\frac{\partial \varepsilon}{\partial t} = \left(\nabla u + \nabla u^T \right),$$

$$\frac{\partial \sigma}{\partial t} = C_1 \varepsilon + \sum_{l=1}^{L} r^l,$$

$$\tau_{\sigma,l} \frac{\partial r^l}{\partial t} = -C_2 \varepsilon - r^l,$$

(1)

where u is the velocity vector, ρ is the mass density, σ stands for the stress tensor, ε denotes the strain tensor, C_1 and C_2 are fourth-order tensors defining the model properties; r^l, $l = 1, \ldots, L$, are memory variables, and L denotes the number of memory variables, typically equals two or three. Proper initial and boundary conditions are assumed.

The tensor C_2 is zero for an elastic media. In the case of zero initial conditions, this means that the solution of the last equation is trivial, and the memory variables can be excluded from the equations. The system turns into that for an ideal velocity-stress-elasticity system, so there is no need to allocate random-access memory (RAM) for the memory variables in the ideally elastic parts of the model.

3.2   Model Parameters and Acquisition

The formal parameters of the model and acquisition are as follows. The model fills a parallelepiped of $8\,\text{km} \times 8\,\text{km} \times 4\,\text{km}$ with uniform grid cells of $5\,\text{m} \times 5\,\text{m} \times 5\,\text{m}$ everywhere except for the localization of small-scale heterogeneities. Within areas with small-scale inhomogeneities such as damaged areas, clusters of caves, and fracture corridors, we use a locally refined grid with cells of 0.05 meters to describe the variability of the elastic properties with higher accuracy. The acquisition is a rectangle of $8\,\text{km} \times 8\,\text{km}$ with

- three component receivers uniformly placed on a grid of $25\,\text{m} \times 25\,\text{m}$;
- vertical-force point sources placed along lines with a step of $50\,\text{m}$ (the distance between the lines is $300\,\text{m}$);
- 5280 sources at all;
- the source function is a Ricker wavelet with a dominant frequency $40\,\text{Hz}$;
- the recording time interval for each receiver is $4\,\text{s}$, with samples of 2 ms.

3.3   The Numerical Method

Existing numerical methods for seismic waves simulation in complicated geological media cannot always be realized, even with the most powerful high-performance computing systems. As a rule, explicit finite-difference schemes oriented to uniform grids with a spatial cell size equal to 0.1–0.2 dominant wavelength, which is usually 5–10 m, while the characteristic dimensions of the irregularities are 0.01–0.1 m. For modeling the interaction of seismic wavefields with such inhomogeneities, we need a spatial step comparable to their size. However, the use of a step of $0.05\,\text{m}$ throughout the target area (reference model) would require colossal computing resources: terabytes of RAM and a performance level of teraFLOPS. To avoid the need for such unrealistic resources, we used a multiscale approach based on finite-difference schemes with local space-time refinement of the grid in regions with clusters of small-scale irregularities [20–22]. In this case, we used grids with varying space and time steps to represent correctly different components of the model: a relatively large step to describe the three-dimensional heterogeneities of the reference model, and a much smaller step to describe them inside the reservoir.

The results of numerical simulations for one source are shown in Fig. 2. The graph demonstrates a typical seismogram of the velocity displacement z-component for a source of a volumetric type excited in the center of the model and recorded on the receiver lines passing through the source.

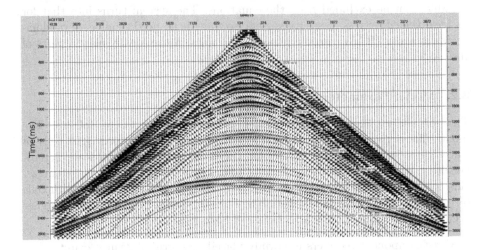

Fig. 2. Seismogram of the velocity displacement z-component for a source of a volumetric type excited in the center of the model

4   The Parallel Implementation

We conducted a numerical simulation of seismic wave propagation in a 3D heterogeneous multiscale medium (digital twin) using an explicit-in-time finite-difference technique with staggered grids locally refined in time and space [21]. We tried to organize the parallel computations to ensure the uniform load of computing resources with small and large spatial steps. Considering our algorithm's main features, the most reasonable approach to parallelization is to use two groups of processes to perform simulations separately on fine and coarse grids (see Fig. 3). The approach to dividing computations into two groups allows you to avoid uneven loading of processor units and achieve a balance during computations. The parallelization strategy for each group is based on a static decomposition of the computational domain.

The two-level parallel scheme is described as follows:

- **First level.** The reference medium on a coarse mesh is computed by the first group of processes, while the second group of processes computes the reservoir on a fine mesh. Although the physical dimensions of the reservoir can be several times smaller than those of the reference medium, the numerical simulations for the reservoir (second group of processes) are performed on a fine grid and therefore can be much more computationally labor-intensive than those for the reference medium. During the computations, at each time step, data exchange is required both within each group of processes and between groups to ensure the exchange of the necessary data in the computation procedure.

- **Second level.** Each group of processes works with its own sufficiently large computational area. A domain decomposition method is used to organize parallel computations within each group. This technique requires data exchange between adjacent processes at each time step. To optimize the exchange, data transferring is carried out using the nonblocking MPI operations Isend/Irecv.

- **Two-group communications.** Data exchange between groups (between the first and second levels) is carried out using MPI procedures applied to the interpolation data transmitted from coarse to fine (or fine to coarse) grids on the plane interfaces coupled with the group areas. The data transfer scheme depends on the group and is performed by the Master Processes (MP) assigned to each group.

While transferring data from the first to the second group, the MP join together the processes containing the grid points of contact with the fine grid and gathers the computed current values of displacements/stresses. The collected data are processed using the Fast Fourier transform (FFT), and a part of the spectrum is sent to the corresponding MP of the second group (see Fig. 4). In turn, the obtaining process performs the interpolation to the fine grid by inverse FFT and sends the interpolated data to each process in its subgroup. Note that we send/receive not all data in our parallel data exchange algorithm but only the data corresponding to the coefficients of the Fourier expansion. This allows reducing significantly the amount of send/receive data, thereby decreasing the idle time and increasing the algorithm efficiency.

Transferring data from the second to the first group is somewhat different. The MP for each face of the fine grid block is identified. This MP collects data from the relevant face, performs the FFT, and sends a part of the spectrum to the corresponding MP of the first group (a coarse grid). Formally, the FFT can be excluded, and the data to be exchanged can be obtained as a projection of the fine grid solution onto the coarse grid. However, truncated spectrum reduces the amount of data to be exchanged and ensures stability since it acts as a high-frequency filter. Finally, the interpolated data are sent to the processes that need these data.

We should emphasize that the number of independent simulations equals the number of sources. In our case, the number of sources is 5280, which means that we must solve the three-dimensional dynamic seismic problem describe above 5280 times. It is possible to consider parallelization across sources as the third level of parallelism.

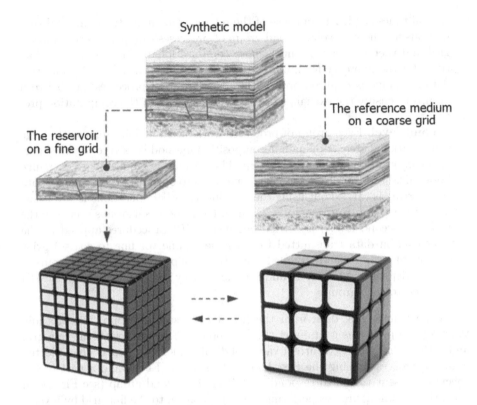

Fig. 3. Decomposition of the model into two components and their loading on various computational processes

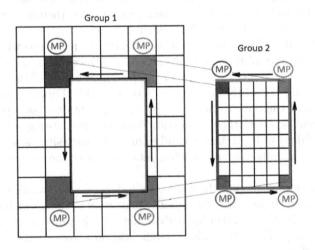

Fig. 4. Two-group communications. The exchange scheme for processor units for a coarse grid (left) and a fine grid (right).

4.1   Scalability and Efficiency

The use of two groups of processes and the nonblocking procedures Isend/Irecv allows overlapping communications within and between groups, thus significantly reducing the idle time and increasing the efficiency of our parallel algorithm. For determining the parallel scaling of jobs, the strong and the weak scalings are usually measured to estimate the parallel efficiency.

We cannot provide here the results of the strong scaling due to the large dimension of the problem and the impossibility of solving it on a small number of processes. However, we can estimate the weak scalability by increasing both the model size and the number of processing elements. Our implementation efficiency for one source and the described above medium model is close to 93% for up to 4000 core samples (see Fig. 5).

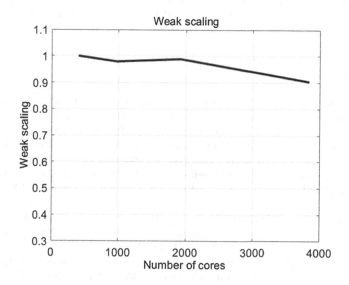

Fig. 5. Weak scaling of the parallel algorithm

5   Conclusions

The current development level of technologies for processing seismic data and interpretation of the results obtained requires thorough testing of new developments. At the initial stage, the approbation should be conducted in well-known objects. Synthetic models that describe thoroughly real geological objects are the best suited for this purpose. Recently, such datasets have come to be called digital twins. Using digital twins at all stages of data processing and interpretation of the obtained results, it is possible to provide full control over the retrieval of the studied geological objects. This opens up an opportunity for determining the optimal excitation, the data acquisition system, and the boundaries of applicability of the suggested method for solving specific problems.

In this work, we described the construction of a synthetic model which is a digital twin of a realistic three-dimensional model of a carbonate field in Eastern Siberia. It involves creating the skeleton of the geological object and a set of synthetic data obtained by numerical simulations. We carried out a series of full-scale numerical simulations to test the mathematical methods for retrieving the internal structure of the medium on real data. The obtained synthetic data serve as a blind test to verify various techniques used for retrieving a reservoir structure on a subseismic scale. To cope with the huge amounts of input/output data, we used high-performance computing systems with parallel architecture and a hybrid two-level parallelization strategy for process optimization.

Acknowledgements. This work was supported by the Russian Science Foundation (project 20-11-20112, "Development of a modeling system for analyzing the current state and assessing the future trends in the environment of the Siberian Shelf Seas"). We thank the Joint Supercomputer Center of RAS and the Siberian Supercomputer Center for granting access to their HPC facilities during our research.

References

1. Levyant, V.B., et al.: Methodological Recommendations for the Use of Data Ceismic Surveys for Calculating Hydrocarbon Reserves in Carbonate Rocks with Porosity of fissure-cavernous Type. TsGE, Moscow (2010). (in Russian)
2. Berkovitch, A., et al.: Diffraction imaging by multifocusing. Geophysics **74**(6), WCA75–WCA81 (2009). https://doi.org/10.1190/1.3198210
3. Dell, S., Gajewski, D.: Common-reflection-surface based workflow for diffraction imaging. Geophysics **76**(5), S187–S195 (2011). https://doi.org/10.1190/geo2010-0229.1
4. Merzlikin, D., et al.: Diffraction imaging of high-resolution 3D P-cable data from the gulf of Mexico using azimuthal plane-wave destruction. First Break **35**(2), 35–41 (2017). https://doi.org/10.3997/1365-2397.2017002
5. Bakulin, I., Silvestrov, I., Dmitriev, M.: Nonlinear beamforming for enhancement of 3D prestack land seismic data. Geophysics **85**(3), V283–V296 (2020). https://doi.org/10.1190/geo2019-0341.1
6. Landa, E.I.: The role of the diffraction component of the wave field at construction of seismic images. Tekhnol. Seysmorazvedki **1**, 5–31 (2013). (in Russian)
7. Petrov, D.A., Melnik, A.A., Shilikov, V.V..: Identification of fractured-cavernous reservoirs based on the interpretation of seismic scattered waves using the Gaussian method bundles. Neftyanoye khozyaystvo **1**, 6–10 (2019). https://doi.org/10.24887/0028-2448-2019-1-6-10. (in Russian)
8. Pozdnyakov, V.A., Cheverda, V.A.: Focusing seismic transformations data for areal stationary systems. Geol. Geophy. **3**, 328–338 (2005). (in Russian)
9. Bondarev, V.I.: Seismic Survey, USGU, Yekaterinburg (2007). (in Russian)
10. Kharakhinov, V.V., Shlenkin, S.I.: Fractured Reservoirs of Oil and Gas. Nauchnyy mir, Moscow (2015). (in Russian)
11. Kozyayev, A.A., Merzlikina, A.S., Petrov, D.A.: Identification of zones with improved filtration and storage properties in carbonate cavernous fractured reservoir by the scattered component of the seismic wave field. Neftyanoye khozyaystvo **11**, 20–25 (2017)

12. Schlumberger: Characterization of Fractured Reservoirs (2007). https://www.slb.com/-/media/files/theme/brochure/cb-characterization-09os0003.ashx

13. Kolyukhin, D.R., Lisitsa, V.V., Protasov, M.I..: Seismic imaging and statistical analysis of fault facies models. Interpretation **5**(4), SP71–SP82 (2017). https://doi.org/10.1190/INT-2016-0202.1

14. Vishnevsky, D.M.: Correlation analysis of the statistical facies model fault zone. Dokl. RAN **473**(6), 719–723 (2017). https://doi.org/10.7868/S0869565217120209. (in Russian)

15. Faulkner, D.R., Jackson, A.L., Lunn, R.: A review of recent developments concerning the structure, mechanics and fluid flow properties of fault zones. J. Struct. Geol. **32**(11), 1557–1575 (2010). https://doi.org/10.1016/j.jsg.2010.06.009

16. Hardy, S., Finch, E.: Discrete-element modelling of detachment folding. Basin Res. **17**(4), 507–520 (2005). https://doi.org/10.1111/j.1365-2117.2005.00280.x

17. Hardy, S., Finch, E.: Mechanical stratigraphy and the transition from Trishear to kink-band fault-propagation fold forms above blind basement thrust faults: A discrete-element study. Mar. Petrol. Geol. **24**, 75–90 (2007). https://doi.org/10.1016/j.marpetgeo.2006.09.001

18. Bazaikin, Y., Gurevich, B., Iglauer, S., et al.: Effect of CT image size and resolution on the accuracy of rock property estimates. J. Geophys. Res. Solid Earth **122**(5), 3645–3647 (2017). https://doi.org/10.1002/2016JB013575

19. Questiaux, J.-M., Gary, D., Couples, G.D., et al.: Fractured reservoirs with fracture corridors. Geophys. Prospect. **58**, 279–295 (2010). https://doi.org/10.1111/j.1365-2478.2009.00810.x

20. Landa, E., Reshetova, G., Tcheverda, V.: Modeling and imaging of multiscale geological media: exploding reflectors revisited. Geosciences **8**(12), 1–19 (2018). https://doi.org/10.3390/geosciences8120476'

21. Kostin, V.I., Lisitsa, V.V., Reshetova, G.V.: Local time-space mesh refinement for simulation of elastic wave propagation in multi-scale media. J. Comput. Phys. **281**, 669–689 (2015). https://doi.org/10.1016/j.jcp.2014.10.047

22. Kostin, V.I., et al.: Finite difference simulation of elastic wave propagation through 3D heterogeneous multiscale media based on locally refined grids. Numer. Analys. Appl. **6**, 40–48 (2013). https://doi.org/10.1134/S1995423913010059

A Parallel Algorithm to Compute the Transport of Suspended Particles Based on 3D Models

Asya M. Atayan[1,2(✉)] and Inna Yu. Kuznetsova[3]

[1] Don State Technical University, Rostov-on-Don, Russia
[2] Sirius Science and Technology University, Sochi, Russia
[3] Southern Federal University, Rostov-on-Don, Russia

Abstract. We consider 2D and 3D models dealing with the transport of suspended particles. The approximation of 2D and 3D models that describe the transport of suspended particles is considered on the example of the two-dimensional diffusion-convection equation. We use discrete analogs of convective and diffusion transfer operators on the assumption of partial filling of cells. The geometry of the computational domain is described based on the filling function. We solve the problem of transport of suspended particles using a difference scheme that is a linear combination of the Upwind and the Standard Leapfrog difference schemes with weight coefficients obtained from the condition of minimization of the approximation error. The scheme is designed to solve the problem of transfer of impurities for large grid Péclet numbers. We have developed some parallel algorithms for the solution of this problem on multiprocessor systems with distributed memory. The results of numerical experiments give us grounds to draw conclusions about the advantages of 3D models of transport of suspended particles over 2D ones.

Keywords: Model of transport of suspended particles · Upwind Leapfrog scheme · Partial filling of cells · Three-dimensional model · Convection-diffusion equation · Parallel algorithm

1 Introduction

Over the past decade, not only in Russia but throughout the world, there has been an increase in the number of adverse and extreme natural phenomena affecting coastal, marine, and river systems. The list includes the flood of the end of July 2013 in the Russian Far East and China, which was the worst in the last 115 years, and the flood in May–June 2013, which caused the inundation of significant areas of Central and Southern Europe with total damages of more than 10 billion euros; at the same time, floods were recorded in India,

The reported study was funded by the Russian Foundation for Basic Research (project No. 19-31-51017).

Afghanistan, Pakistan, and the United States (the flood in Colorado was the strongest in the last 10 years). In Russia, a catastrophic flood struck the city of Krymsk (Krasnodar Krai) in July 2012; the water level drastically rose in the Sea of Azov as a result of a storm in 2014 and dust storms in 2019 caused by the negative effect of tidal surges in the waters of the Sea of Azov and Taganrog Bay. The actual assessment of the impact of these phenomena on fish food supply is impossible without the use of the most modern and optimized mathematical models that allow predicting the distribution of plumes of suspended sediments in the aquatic environment and changes in the bottom topography due to the settling of suspended soil particles [1]. Based on numerous studies [2–4], Rosselkhoznadzor and FSBE TsUREN recommended the following threshold values of the level of particles for calculating the damage to fish stock: 50% losses at particle levels from 20 to 100 mg/l and 100% at particle levels above 100 mg/l. At particle levels from 0.25 to 20 mg/l, losses are estimated at 20%. In most cases, large organisms from loose soils remain viable when caught in the zone of deposition of suspended soil particles. At sediment levels of more than 10 mm, 100% of benthic organisms would die, while 50% of organisms perish on bottom areas covered by layers of sediments of 5 to 10 mm [5, 6].

These hydrophysical processes can be described by a complex system of initial boundary value problems for partial differential equations, including equations of hydrodynamics, transport of heat, salts, and suspended sediments. The obtained mathematical models of hydrophysics are spatially three-dimensional, nonstationary, and essentially nonlinear. Such classes of problems can be investigated using methods applied to the solution of the diffusion-convection equation. Another urgent task is the development of difference schemes for solving hydrodynamic problems in case of the prevalence of the convective operator over the diffusion one [7], something that is typical for the occurrence of such natural hazards as storm surges and the transport of pollutants in reservoirs.

In Sect. 2, we pose the problem of transport of suspended particles. In Sect. 3, we consider a discrete analog of the continuous suspension transport problem based on a linear combination of the Upwind and the Standard Leapfrog difference schemes that takes into account the cell filling functions. Section 4 describes the solution of the problem on a multiprocessor computing system. In Sect. 5, we provide the results yielded by the software package in the case of a model problem of hydrobiological processes occurring in dredging works. In the Conclusions, we summarize the main results of the study.

2   Model of Transport of Suspended Particles

To describe the transport of suspended particles, we use the diffusion-convection equation, which can be written as follows [8]:

$$\frac{\partial c_k}{\partial t} + u\frac{\partial c_k}{\partial x} + v\frac{\partial c_k}{\partial y} + (w - w_{s,k})\frac{\partial c_k}{\partial z}$$

$$= \frac{\partial}{\partial x}\left(D_h\frac{\partial c_k}{\partial x}\right) + \frac{\partial}{\partial y}\left(D_h\frac{\partial c_k}{\partial y}\right) + \frac{\partial}{\partial z}\left(D_v\frac{\partial c_k}{\partial z}\right) + F_k, \tag{1}$$

where c_k is the concentration of impurity of the k-th fraction [mg/l]; $V = \{u, v, w\}$ are the components of the velocity vector [m/s]; $w_{s,k}$ denotes the hydraulic size of the k-th fraction or fall velocity in the vertical direction [m/s]; H stands for the depth of the reservoir [m]; D_h and D_v denote the horizontal and vertical turbulent diffusion coefficients [m^2/s]; x, y are the coordinates in the horizontal direction [m], and z is the coordinate in the vertical direction [m]; t is the time variable [s], and F_k denotes the function that describes the intensity of pollutant sources of the k-th fraction [mg/(l · s)].

There is no flow on the free surface, that is,

$$(c_k)'_n = 0, \tag{2}$$

where n is the unit normal vector to the open boundary pointing toward the interior of the computational domain.

On the free surface Γ_s, the flow in the vertical direction is zero:

$$D_v (c_k)'_z + w_s c_k = 0. \tag{3}$$

Near the bottom surface Γ_b, we have

$$D_v (c_k)'_z = E - D + w_s c_k, \tag{4}$$

where E is the erosion flux [kg/(m^2 · s)], D is the intensity of sedimentation [kg/m^2·s], and c_k denotes the mass concentration of the k-th suspension fraction [kg/m^3].

Integrating Eq. (1) with conditions (2)–(4) along the vertical axis, we obtain a two-dimensional model:

$$h\frac{\partial c_k}{\partial t} + U\frac{\partial c_k}{\partial x} + V\frac{\partial c_k}{\partial y} = \frac{\partial}{\partial x}\left(D_h h\frac{\partial c_k}{\partial x}\right) + \frac{\partial}{\partial y}\left(D_h h\frac{\partial c_k}{\partial y}\right) - w_{s,k} c_k + F_{h,k}, \tag{5}$$

where $U = \int_{-h}^0 u\, dz$, $V = \int_{-h}^0 v\, dz$, $F_{h,k} = \int_{-h}^0 F_k\, dz$, and h is the depth of the reservoir.

Equation (5) in the two-dimensional model of transport of suspended particles is considered under the boundary condition

$$(c_k)'_n = 0. \tag{6}$$

3   Approximation of the Problem of Transport of Suspended Particles

Consider the approximation of the 2D and 3D models of transport of suspended particles on the example of the two-dimensional diffusion-convection equation [8]

$$c'_t + uc'_x + vc'_y = (\mu c'_x)'_x + (\mu c'_y)'_y \tag{7}$$

with boundary conditions

$$c'_n(x, y, t) = \alpha_n c + \beta_n, \tag{8}$$

where u and v denote the components of the velocity vector, and μ is the coefficient of turbulent exchange.

The computational domain is inscribed in a rectangle. A uniform grid is introduced for the numerical implementation of a discrete mathematical model of the problem (7)–(8):

$$w_h = \{t^n = n\tau, \; x_i = ih_x, \; y_j = jh_y; \; n = 0, \ldots, N_t,$$

$$i = 0, \ldots, N_x, \; j = 0, \ldots, N_y; \; N_t\tau = T, \; N_x h_x = l_x, \; N_y h_y = l_y\},$$

where τ is the time step, h_x and h_y are the space steps, N_t is the upper time bound, and N_x and N_y are the space bounds.

To approximate the homogeneous Eq. (7), we use the following space splitting schemes [9,10]:

$$\frac{c^{n+1/2} - c^n}{\tau} + u \, (c^n)'_x = \left(\mu (c^n)'_x\right)'_x, \tag{9}$$

$$\frac{c^{n+1} - c^{n+1/2}}{\tau} + v(c^{n+1/2})'_y = \left(\mu(c^{n+1/2})'_y\right)'_y.$$

Let us introduce the coefficients q_0, q_1, q_2, q_3, and q_4 to describe the volume of fluid (VOF) of the corresponding control areas located near the cell. The coefficient q_0 characterizes the filling area D_0, where $x \in (x_{i-1/2}, x_{i+1/2})$, $y \in (y_{j-1/2}, y_{j+1/2})$. Correspondingly, q_1 characterizes the filling area D_1, where $x \in (x_i, x_{i+1/2})$, $y \in (y_{j-1/2}, y_{j+1/2})$; q_2 characterizes the filling area D_2, where $x \in (x_{i-1/2}, x_i)$, $y \in (y_{j-1/2}, y_{j+1/2})$; q_3 characterizes the filling area D_3, where $x \in (x_{i-1/2}, x_{i+1/2})$, $y \in (y_j, y_{j+1/2})$, and finally, q_4 characterizes the filling area D_4, where $x \in (x_{i-1/2}, x_{i+1/2})$, $y \in (y_{j-1/2}, y_j)$.

The filled part of the regions D_m will be denoted by Ω_m, where $m = 0, \ldots, 4$. By this, the coefficients q_m can be computed from the following equations:

$$(q_m)_{i,j} = \frac{S_{\Omega_m}}{S_{D_m}}, \quad (q_0)_{i,j} = \frac{o_{i,j} + o_{i+1,j} + o_{i+1,j+1} + o_{i,j+1}}{4},$$

$$(q_1)_{i,j} = \frac{o_{i+1,j} + o_{i+1,j+1}}{2}, \quad (q_2)_{i,j} = \frac{o_{i,j} + o_{i,j+1}}{2},$$

$$(q_3)_{i,j} = \frac{o_{i+1,j+1} + o_{i,j+1}}{2}, \quad (q_4)_{i,j} = \frac{o_{i,j} + o_{i+1,j}}{2}.$$

Let us write the discrete forms of the convective operator uc'_x and the diffusion transfer operator $(\mu c'_x)'_x$ in the case of partial filling of cells [11]:

$$(q_0)_{i,j} \, uc'_x \simeq (q_1)_{i,j} \, u_{i+1/2,j} \frac{c_{i+1,j} - c_{i,j}}{2h_x} + (q_2)_{i,j} \, u_{i-1/2,j} \frac{c_{i,j} - c_{i-1,j}}{2h_x},$$

$$(q_0)_{i,j} \, (\mu c'_x)'_x \simeq (q_1)_{i,j} \, \mu_{i+1/2,j} \frac{c_{i+1,j} - c_{i,j}}{h_x^2} - (q_2)_{i,j} \, \mu_{i-1/2,j} \frac{c_{i,j} - c_{i-1,j}}{h_x^2}$$

$$- \left|(q_1)_{i,j} - (q_2)_{i,j}\right| \mu_{i,j} \frac{\alpha_x c_{i,j} + \beta_x}{h_x}.$$

To approximate the model expressed by Eq. (7), we use a scheme that is a linear combination of the Upwind and the Standard Leapfrog difference schemes and takes into account the VOF of cells [12,13]:

– the difference scheme for Eq. (9) describes the transfer in the Ox direction:

$$\frac{2q_{2,i,j}+q_{0,i,j}}{3}\frac{c_{i,j}^{n+1/2}-c_{i,j}^n}{\tau} + 5u_{i-1/2,j}q_{2,i,j}\frac{c_{i,j}^n-c_{i-1,j}^n}{3h_x}$$
$$+ u_{i+1/2,j}\min\left(q_{1,i,j},q_{2,i,j}\right)\frac{c_{i+1,j}^n-c_{i,j}^n}{3h_x} + \frac{2\Delta_x c_{i-1,j}^n q_{2,i,j}+\Delta_x c_{i,j}^n q_{0,i,j}}{3}$$

$$= 2\mu_{i+1/2,j}q_{1,i,j}\frac{c_{i+1,j}^n-c_{i,j}^n}{h_x^2} - 2\mu_{i-1/2,j}q_{2,i,j}\frac{c_{i,j}^n-c_{i-1,j}^n}{h_x^2}$$

$$- |q_{1,i,j}-q_{2,i,j}|\,\mu_{i,\,j}\frac{\alpha_x c_{i,j}^n+\beta_x}{h_x},\, u_{i,j}\geq 0;$$

$$\frac{2q_{1,i,j}+q_{0,i,j}}{3}\frac{c_{i,j}^{n+1/2}-c_{i,j}^n}{\tau} + 5u_{i+1/2,j}q_{1,i,j}\frac{c_{i+1,j}^n-c_{i,j}^n}{3h_x}$$

$$+ u_{i-1/2,j}\min\left(q_{1,i,j},q_{2,i,j}\right)\frac{c_{i,j}^n-c_{i-1,j}^n}{3h_x} + \frac{2\Delta_x c_{i+1,j}^n q_{1,i,j}+\Delta_x c_{i,j}^n q_{0,i,j}}{3}$$

$$= 2\mu_{i+1/2,j}q_{1,i,j}\frac{c_{i+1,j}^n-c_{i,j}^n}{h_x^2} - 2\mu_{i-1/2,j}q_{2,i,j}\frac{c_{i,j}^n-c_{i-1,j}^n}{h_x^2}$$

$$- |q_{1,i,j}-q_{2,i,j}|\,\mu_{i,\,j}\frac{\alpha_x c_{i,j}^n+\beta_x}{h_x},\, u_{i,j}< 0,$$

where $\Delta_x c_{i,j}^n = \dfrac{c_{i,j}^{n-1/2}-c_{i,j}^{n-1}}{\tau}$;

– the difference scheme for Eq. (9) describes the transfer in the Oy direction:

$$\frac{2q_{4,i,j}+q_{0,i,j}}{3}\frac{c_{i,j}^{n+1}-c_{i,j}^{n+1/2}}{\tau} + 5v_{i,j-1/2}q_{4,i,j}\frac{c_{i,j}^{n+1/2}-c_{i,j-1}^{n+1/2}}{3h_y}$$

$$+ v_{i,j+1/2}\min\left(q_{3,i,j},q_{4,i,j}\right)\frac{c_{i,j+1}^{n+1/2}-c_{i,j}^{n+1/2}}{3h_y} + \frac{2\Delta_y c_{i,j-1}^{n+1/2} q_{4,i,j}+\Delta_y c_{i,j}^{n+1/2} q_{0,i,j}}{3}$$

$$= 2\mu_{i,j+1/2}q_{3,i,j}\frac{c_{i,j+1}^{n+1/2}-c_{i,j}^{n+1/2}}{h_y^2} - 2\mu_{i,j-1/2}q_{4,i,j}\frac{c_{i,j}^{n+1/2}-c_{i,j-1}^{n+1/2}}{h_y^2}$$

$$- |q_{3,i,j}-q_{4,i,j}|\,\mu_{i,\,j}\frac{\alpha_y c_{i,j}^{n+1/2}+\beta_y}{h_y},\, v_{i,j}\geq 0;$$

$$\frac{2q_{3,i,j}+q_{0,i,j}}{3}\frac{c_{i,j}^{n+1}-c_{i,j}^{n+1/2}}{\tau} + 5v_{i,j+1/2}q_{3,i,j}\frac{c_{i,j+1}^{n+1/2}-c_{i,j}^{n+1/2}}{3h_y}$$

$$+ v_{i,j-1/2}\min\left(q_{3,i,j},q_{4,i,j}\right)\frac{c_{i,j}^{n+1/2}-c_{i,j-1}^{n+1/2}}{3h_y} + \frac{2\Delta_y c_{i,j+1}^{n+1/2} q_{3,i,j}+\Delta_y c_{i,j}^{n+1/2} q_{0,i,j}}{3}$$

$$= 2\mu_{i,j+1/2}q_{3,i,j}\frac{c_{i,j+1}^{n+1/2}-c_{i,j}^{n+1/2}}{h_y^2} - 2\mu_{i,j-1/2}q_{4,i,j}\frac{c_{i,j}^{n+1/2}-c_{i,j-1}^{n+1/2}}{h_y^2}$$

$$- |q_{3,i,j}-q_{4,i,j}|\,\mu_{i,\,j}\frac{\alpha_y c_{i,j}^{n+1/2}+\beta_y}{h_y},\, v_{i,j}< 0,$$

where $\Delta_y c_{i,j}^{n+1/2} = \dfrac{c_{i,j}^n-c_{i,j}^{n-1/2}}{\tau}$.

4   Parallel Algorithm for the Problem of Transport of Suspended Particles

In this study, we construct a parallel algorithm for solving the three-dimensional problem of transport of suspended particles (1)–(4) on a supercomputer system with distributed memory using MPI technology [14,15]. Figure 1 depicts the architecture of the "Sirius" multiprocessor computer system.

We compared the results of the parallel algorithm for several numbers of processors. Data on computational grids and software operating time are given in Table 1.

Table 1. Results of the algorithm using MPI technology, for several numbers of processors on different computational grids

Grid	1	2	4	8	12	16	20	24
$200 \times 200 \times 100$	1.3167	0.7747	0.3401	0.2053	0.1392	0.1352	0.1118	0.0974
$1000 \times 1000 \times 100$	55.303	30.031	16.640	6.890	4.601	4.421	3.268	2.900

To increase the efficiency of parallel computations, the domain was decomposed in two spatial directions. We split the domain into rectangles by dividing it into p_1 intervals in one direction and p_2 intervals in the other [16]. This decomposition method allows reducing the amount of data transmitted. If we use a single-direction decomposition, the number of transfers equals $2 \times p \times N_y \times N_z$, where p is the number of involved processors. In the case of two-direction decomposition, the number of transfers is $2 \times (p_1 \times N_y + p_2 \times N_x) \times N_z$, where N_x, N_y, and N_z are the numbers of computing nodes in the directions of the OX, OY, and OZ axes, respectively.

Below, the parallel algorithm is described:

1. Call the functions that return p and m, where p is the number of processes inside the communicator and m is the number of the current processor within the private group of the communicator.
2. Specify the values p_1 and p_2. Conditionally, p_1 and p_2 are the numbers of processors in the Ox and Oy directions, respectively.
3. Compute the values m_1 and m_2, where m_1 and m_2 are the processor numbers in each direction:

$$m_1 = m \mod p_1, \quad m_1 = \left\lfloor \frac{m}{p_1} \right\rfloor.$$

4. Compute the numbers N_{11} and N_{22} of initial elements and the sizes N_1 and N_2 of the computational domain fragment in the Ox and Oy directions:

$$N_{11} = \left\lfloor \frac{m_1 (N_x - 2)}{p_1} \right\rfloor, \quad N_1 = \left\lfloor \frac{(m_1 + 1)(N_x - 2)}{p_1} \right\rfloor - N_{11} + 2,$$

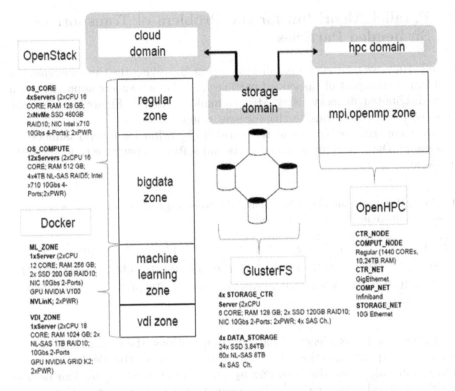

Fig. 1. The architecture of the cluster at "Sirius" Educational Center

$$N_{22} = \left\lfloor \frac{m_2 (N_y - 2)}{p_2} \right\rfloor, \quad N_2 = \left\lfloor \frac{(m_2 + 1)(N_y - 2)}{p_2} \right\rfloor - N_{22} + 2.$$

5. Decompose the computational domain.
6. Start the time loop.
7. Compute the array elements (this corresponds to a single-threaded algorithm).
8. Exchange data in the Ox direction.
   8.1 Data transmission/reception in the direction of decreasing processor number:
       – if $m_1 > 0$, then transmit elements with index $i = 1$ to the processor with number $p - 1$;
       – if $m_1 < p_1 - 1$, then receive elements with index $i = N_1 - 1$ from the processor with number $p + 1$.
   8.2 Data transmission/reception in the direction of increasing processor number:
       – if $m_1 < p_1 - 1$, then transmit elements with index $i = N_1 - 2$ to the processor with number $p + 1$;
       – if $m_1 > 0$, then receive elements with index $i = 0$ from the processor with number $p - 1$.

The amount of data exchange is equal to $(N_2 - 2) \times (N_z - 2)$.
9. Exchange data in the Oy direction (same as previous).
   9.1 Data transmission/reception in the direction of decreasing processor number:
   - if $m_2 > 0$, then transmit elements with index $j = 1$ to the processor with number $p - p_1$;
   - if $m_2 < p_2 - 1$, then receive elements with index $j = N_2 - 1$ from the processor with number $p + p_1$.
   9.2 Data transmission/reception in the direction of increasing processor number:
   - if $m_2 < p_2 - 1$, then transmit elements with index $j = N_2 - 2$ to the processor with number $p + p_1$;
   - if $m_2 > 0$, then receive elements with index $j = 0$ from the processor with number $p - p_1$.
   The amount of data exchange is equal to $(N_1 - 2) \times (N_z - 2)$.
10. End of the loop body.
11. Data output.

Table 2 contains the results yielded by the parallel algorithm for several numbers of processors and decompositions of the computational domain.

Table 2. Results of the parallel algorithm based on the decomposition of the computational domain in two spatial directions

p	p_1	p_2	$200 \times 200 \times 100$			$1000 \times 1000 \times 100$		
			Time	Acceleration	Efficiency	Time	Acceleration	Efficiency
16	16	1	0.1352	9.74	0.6757	4.421	12.51	0.7818
16	8	2	0.1232	10.69	0.6854	3.52	15.71	0.9821
16	4	4	0.1123	11.72	0.7881	3.499	15.8	0.9878
20	20	1	0.1118	11.78	0.5891	3.268	16.92	0.846
20	10	2	0.1104	11.93	0.5965	3.203	17.27	0.8633
20	5	4	0.09686	13.6	0.6798	3.153	17.54	0.877
24	24	1	0.09744	13.51	0.5631	2.9	19.07	0.7946
24	12	2	0.09134	14.42	0.6007	2.846	19.43	0.8096
24	8	3	0.08365	15.74	0.6559	2.831	19.53	0.8139
24	6	4	0.07407	17.78	0.7407	2.77	19.97	0.8319

In Fig. 2, we see the graphs of the acceleration versus the number of involved processors, for different sizes of the grid. The maximum number of processors is 24; the maximum size of the grid is $1000 \times 1000 \times 100$ computational nodes.

Additionally, Fig. 2 shows the graph of the linear acceleration, i.e., a model acceleration (100% efficiency). At the intersection points of the linear acceleration with the acceleration graph of the parallel algorithm, the computational

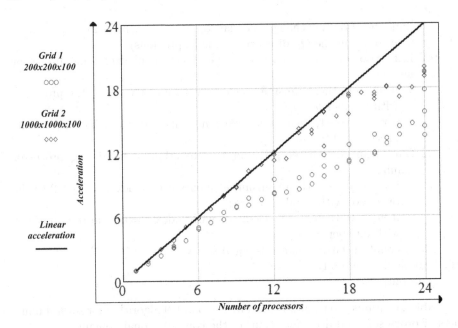

Fig. 2. Dependence of the acceleration on the number of processors

efficiency approaches 100%, and at some points exceeds this value, indicating that the developed parallel algorithm shows superlinear acceleration. Moreover, the figure shows that the efficiency of the algorithm is lower on small grids (up to $200 \times 200 \times 100$ computational nodes) than it is on large computational grids ($1000 \times 1000 \times 100$ computational nodes and more). Developed based on MPI technology, the parallel algorithm used for solving three-dimensional diffusion-convection problems shows high efficiency (above 75%) on large computational grids.

5   Results of Numerical Experiments with the Model of Transport of Suspended Particles

The software was tested in the study of hydrobiological processes that take place during dredging works. This is considered a model problem [1]. Figure 3 shows the concentration field of suspended particles in the cross-section of the computational domain determined by the plane passing through the discharge point and spanned by a vector directed vertically and a vector in the direction of the flow. The direction of the water flow is from left to right.

The transport of suspended particles was simulated on an area of 1 km by 720 m with a grid step $h = 10$ m in the horizontal directions. The depth of the reservoir was 10 m; the vertical grid step was 1 m. The source of suspended particles was located at a distance of 5.5 m above the bottom surface. The average flow velocity in the area contaminated with suspended matter was equal to 0.075 m/s.

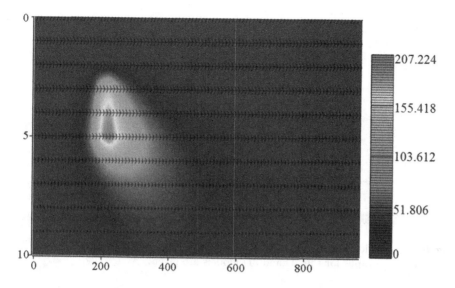

Fig. 3. Concentration of suspended particles

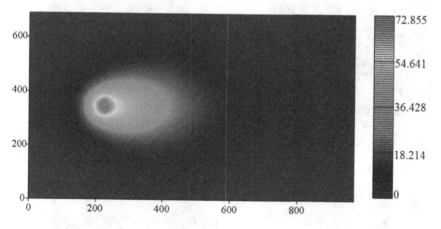

Fig. 4. Concentration of suspended particles averaged over the depth of the reservoir

For the sedimentation rate of the suspension, we had $w_s = 2.042$ mm/s. Thus, the sedimentation time of the suspension to the bottom was 2693 s (45 min approximately), and the suspension spread on average for 202 m along the current. Diffusion transfer contributes to the spreading of sediments. However, the spreading of sediments due to diffusion transfer would not exceed 200 m under any circumstances. We see from Fig. 3 that the suspension gets deposited at a distance of 100 to 300 m from the discharge point, which is consistent with the expected result. Figure 4 shows the concentration of suspended particles (g/l) averaged over the depth of the reservoir.

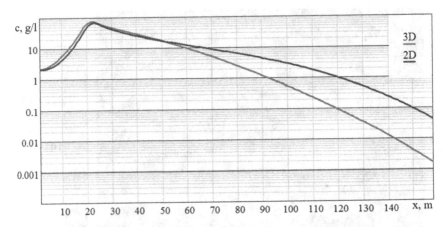

Fig. 5. Distribution of the concentrations of suspended particles 2 h after disposal. The corresponding graphs for the 2D and 3D models are given.

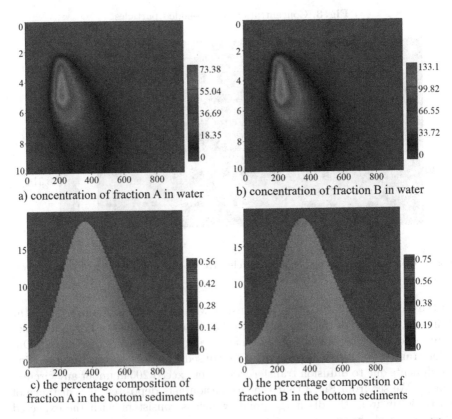

a) concentration of fraction A in water

b) concentration of fraction B in water

c) the percentage composition of fraction A in the bottom sediments

d) the percentage composition of fraction B in the bottom sediments

Fig. 6. Concentration of suspended particles in water and granulometric composition of the bottom

When using 2D models, the change in the concentration of suspended particles in the vertical direction is not taken into account. According to the 2D model, the suspension sets down much more slowly. According to the model, it takes much more time for the suspension concentration to drop down from N_1 to N_2 if N_2 is significantly less than N_1, provided that the step τ is rather small. We compared the results of the experimental computations for the 2D and 3D models of transport of suspended particles described above. A comparison of the distribution functions for the concentration of suspended particles under the 2D and 3D models is given in Fig. 5. The vertical axis corresponds to the concentration of suspended particles (a logarithmic scale is used). The horizontal axis passes through the dredging area and is directed along the current.

Figure 5 shows that the 2D model gives a higher concentration near the disposal area. At a distance of 50 m from the disposal area, both models yield identical results. At a distance of 120 m or more from the disposal area, the results of the 2D and 3D models differ by an order of magnitude. The results of computations based on the 3D model indicate a higher deposition rate compared to the 2D model.

Figure 6 shows the graphs of changes in the granulometric composition of the bottom at different initial concentrations of suspended particles. In the process of modeling the transport of suspended particles, we considered the sedimentation of two distinct fractions. The deposition rate of fraction A was 2.4 mm/s, and the percentage of fraction A in dusty particles was 36%. The deposition rate of fraction B was 1.775 mm/s, and the percentage of fraction B was 64%.

The horizontal axis in Fig. 6 passes through the dredging area and is directed along the flow. In Figs. 6a and 6b, the vertical axis indicates the depth of the reservoir (in meters) and is directed vertically downward. In Figs. 6c and 6d, the vertical axis represents the level of bottom sediments (in centimeters) and is directed vertically upward. Figures 6a and 6b show the concentrations of fractions A and B in the water, respectively. Furthermore, Figs. 6c and 6d show the percentage compositions of fractions A and B in the bottom sediments, respectively.

Figure 6 indicates that the heavier fraction A is deposited closer to the dredging zone and lies deeper in the sedimentary rocks than fraction B. The experimental results allow us to analyze the dynamics of changes in the geometry and granulometric composition of the bottom, the formation of structures and sediments, the transport of suspensions in the water, and the level of water pollution. The mathematical model and the software we have developed enable the prediction of sea ridges and land spits, their growth and transformation, changes in suspension concentration, the siltation of approach channels, and the drift of hydraulic structures.

6   Conclusions

The actual assessment of the impact of natural phenomena and human activities on the fish food base is impossible without resorting to the most modern and optimized mathematical models that allow predicting both the propagation of suspension plumes in the aquatic environment and changes in the bottom topography due to the precipitation of suspended soil particles. In this study, we used 2D and 3D models to describe the transport of suspended particles. The numerical implementation of the problem of transport of suspended particles is based on a scheme that is a linear combination of the Upwind and the Standard Leapfrog difference schemes with weight coefficients obtained from the condition of minimization of the approximation error. To describe the geometry of the computational domain, we relied on the filling function. In this paper, we presented a parallel algorithm for solving the three-dimensional problem of transport of suspended particles on a supercomputer system with distributed memory using MPI technology. The parallel implementation of the algorithm showed an efficiency of more than 75% on large computational grids ($1000 \times 1000 \times 100$ computational nodes and more). We carried out a comparison of the experimental results yielded by the 2D and 3D mathematical models of the problem of soil disposal. Computations were performed to simulate the process of propagation of a multicomponent suspension and changes in the geometry and granulometric composition of the bottom.

References

1. Kovtun, I.I., Protsenko, E.A., Sukhinov, A.I., Chistyakov, A.E.: Calculation of the impact on aquatic biological resources of dredging in the White Sea. Fundam. Appl. Hydrophys. **9**(2), 27–38 (2016). (in Russian)
2. Chernyavsky, A.V.: Transformation of bottom zoocenoses in the area of the Grigorovskaya landfill. Dredging and problems of protection of fish stocks and the environment of fishery reservoirs, pp. 208–210 (1984). (in Russian)
3. Susloparova, O.N.: Fisheries monitoring during dredging in the water area of the Oil Harbor. GosNIORKh Funds (2003). (in Russian)
4. Ivanova, V.V.: Experimental modeling of zoobenthos collapse during soil dumping. GosNIORKh Funds **85**, 107–113 (1988). (in Russian)
5. Adjustment of the "Project for the development of the sand deposit "Sestroretskoye" located in the Gulf of Finland of the Baltic Sea" in connection with the reconstruction of the open pit. LLC Eco-Express-Service (2012). (in Russian)
6. Morozov, A.E.: Bottom fauna of small rivers and the influence of suspended solids of drainage waters on it. Fish. Res. Water Bodies Urals (1979). (in Russian)
7. Sukhinov, A.I., Chistyakov, A.E., Protsenko, E.A.: Difference scheme for solving problems of hydrodynamics for large grid Peclet numbers. Comput. Res. Model. **11** (5), 833–848 (2019). https://doi.org/10.20537/2076-7633-2019-11-5-833-848
8. Samarskiy, A.A., Vabishchevich, P.N.: Numerical Methods for Solving Convection-Diffusion Problems. Mathematical Models and Editorial, URSS, Moscow (1999). (in Russian)
9. Belotserkovsky, O.M., Gushchin, V.A., Shchennikov, V.V.: Application of the splitting method to solving problems of the dynamics of a viscous incompressible fluid. Comput. Math. Math. Phys. **15**(1), 197–207 (1975). (in Russian)
10. Samarskiy, A.A., Nikolaev, E.S.: Methods for Solving Grid Equations. Nauka, Moscow (1978). (in Russian)

11. Sukhinov, A.I., Chistyakov, A.E., Protsenko, E.A., Sidoryakina, V.V., Protsenko, S.V.: Accounting method of filling cells for the solution of hydrodynamics problems with a complex geometry of the computational domain. Math. Models Comput. Simul. **12**(2), 232–245 (2020). https://doi.org/10.1134/S2070048220020155

12. Sukhinov, A.I., Chistyakov, A.E., Protsenko, E.A.: Upwind and standard Leapfrog difference schemes. Num. Methods Program. **20**(2), 170–181 (2019). https://doi.org/10.26089/NumMet.v20r216

13. Sukhinov, A.I., Chistyakov, A.E., Kuznetsova, I.Y., Protsenko, E.A.: Modelling of suspended particles motion in channel. J. Phys. Conf. Ser. **1479**(1), 012082 (2020). https://doi.org/10.1088/1742-6596/1479/1/012082

14. Voevodin, V.V., Voevodin, V.L.: Parallel Computing, p. 608, BHV, St. Petersburg (2010). (in Russian)

15. Chetverushkin, B.N., Yakobovskiy, M.V.: Numerical algorithms and architecture of HPC systems. Keldysh Inst. Preprint. **52**, 12 (2018). https://doi.org/10.20948/prepr-2018-52. (in Russian)

16. Sukhinov, A.I., Chistyakov, A.E., Alekseenko, E.V.: Numerical realization of three-dimensional model of hydrodynamics for shallow water basins on high-performance system. Math. Models Comput. Simul. **3**(5), 562–574 (2011)

Author Index

Printed in the United States
by Baker & Taylor Publisher Services